THE FLESH/SPIRIT CONFLICT IN GALATIANS

D1604134

Walter Bo Russell, III

University Press of America, Inc.
Lanham • New York • Oxford

University Press of America,® Inc.
4720 Boston Way
Lanham, Maryland 20706

12 Hid's Copse Rd.
Cummor Hill, Oxford OX2 9JJ

Library of Congress Cataloging-in-Publication Data

Russell, Walter Bo.
The flesh/spirit conflict in Galatians / Walter Bo Russell.
p. cm.

Includes bibliographical references and indexes.
l. Flesh and spirit antithesis (Pauline doctrine). 2. Bible. N.T.
Galatians--Criticism, interpretation, etc. 3. Bible. N.T. Galatians--
Theology. I. Title.
BS2545.F55R87 1997 227'.406--dc21 97-17070 CIP

ISBN 0-7618-0797-7 (cloth: alk. ppr.)
ISBN 0-7618-0798-5 (pbk: alk. ppr.)

⊖™ The paper used in this publication meets the minimum
requirements of American National Standard for information
Sciences—Permanence of Paper for Printed Library Materials,
ANSI Z39.48—1984

Dedicated with deepest gratitude

to my most loving, remarkably supportive, and richly

inspiring partner and wife,

Martha Ann Russell;

to our very patient, life-affirming, and joy-engendering

children,

Elizabeth Dawn Russell

and

Jonathan Bo Russell;

and to my very loving, always encouraging, and

unspeakably generous parents,

Ida Mabel Russell

and

Walter Bo Russell, Jr.

iii

Contents

List of Abbreviations

ANRW	*Aufstieg und Niedergang der romischen Welt.* Geschichte und Kultur Roms im Spiegel der neueren Forschung, II. Herausgegeben van Hildegard Temporini und Wolfgang Haase. Berlin und New York: Walter de Gruyter, 1984.
ASV	American Standard Version of the Bible.
BAGD	Bauer, Walter. *A Greek-English Lexicon of the New Testament and Other Early Christian Literature.* Translated and adapted by William F. Arndt and F. Wilbur Gingrich. 2nd ed. edited by Frederick Danker. Chicago: University of Chicago Press, 1979.
BDF	Blass, F. and A. Debrunner, *A Greek Grammar of the New Testament and Other Early Christian Literature.* Revised by A. Debrunner. Translated and edited by Robert W. Funk. Chicago: The University of Chicago Press, 1961.
Bib	*Biblica*
BJRL	*Bulletin of the John Rylands University Library of Manchester*
BSac	*Bibliotheca Sacra*
BTB	*Biblical Theology Bulletin*
BZ	*Biblische Zeitschrift*
CBQ	*Catholic Biblical Quarterly*
CTJ	*Calvin Theological Journal*
EstBib	*Estudios bíblicos*
ExpTim	*Expository Times*
HTR	*Harvard Theological Review*
HTS	Harvard Theological Studies
HUCA	*Hebrew Union College Annual*
IBS	*Irish Biblical Studies*
Int	*Interpretation*
ITQ	*Irish Theological Quarterly*
JAC	Jahrbuch für Antike und Christentum
JBL	*Journal of Biblical Literature*
JES	*Journal of Ecumenical Studies*
JETS	*Journal of the Evangelical Society*
JQR	*Jewish Quarterly Review*
JSNT	*Journal for the Study of the New Testament*
JSNTSup	Journal for the Study of the New Testament--Supplements
KJV	King James Version of the Bible
Lg	*Language*

LN	Louw, Johannes P., and Eugene A. Nida, eds. *Greek-English Lexicon of the New Testament Based on Semantic Domains*. 2 vols. New York: United Bible Societies, 1988.
LSJ	Liddell, Henry George, and Robert Scott. *A Greek-English Lexicon*. Revised and augmented by Henry Stuart Jones with Roderick McKenzie and with a supplement by E. A. Barber. 9th ed. Oxford: At the Clarendon Press, 1968.
LXX	The Septuagint
NASV	New American Standard Version of the Bible
NEB	New English Bible
Neot	*Neotestamentica*
NIV	New International Version of the Bible
NovT	*Novum Testamentum*
NovTSup	Novum Testamentum, Supplements
NTS	*New Testament Studies*
REB	Revised English Bible
RevExp	*Review and Expositor*
RevThom	*Revue thomiste*
RSPT	*Revue des sciences philosophiques et théologiques*
RSV	Revised Standard Version of the Bible
SBL	Society of Biblical Literature
SBLDS	SBL Dissertation Series
SBLSBS	SBL Sources for Biblical Study
SBT	Studies in Biblical Theology
SE	*Studia Evangelica*
SEÅ	*Svensk exegetisk årsbok*
SJT	*Scottish Journal of Theology*
SNTSMS	Society for New Testament Studies Monograph Series
ST	*Studia theologica*
SWJT	*Southwestern Journal of Theology*
TDNT	Kittel, Gerhard, and Gerhard Frederich, eds. *Theological Dictionary of the New Testament*, 9 vols. Translated and edited by Geoffrey W. Bromiley. Grand Rapids: William B. Eerdmans Publishing Company, 1964-1974.
TEV	Today's English Version of the Bible
TLZ	*Theologische Literaturzeitung*
TrinJ	*Trinity Journal*
TynBul	*Tyndale Bulletin*
TZ	*Theologische Zeitschrift*
WTJ	*Westminster Theological Journal*
ZNW	*Zeitschrift für Theologie und Kirche*

Preface

This book is a work of biblical theology. It sets forth a creative thesis that swims against the theological current of the last few generations. The flow of this current is this: Whenever Paul speaks of the flesh/Spirit struggle, he is referring to an *internal* struggle within Christians. *The thesis of this book* is that this understanding of a flesh/Spirit struggle within believers is a misreading of Galatians (and elsewhere) and results in a wrong theological anthropology. Rather, I set forth the premise that Paul uses the flesh/Spirit antithesis in Galatians (and elsewhere) in *a redemptive historical sense* to refer to eras or modes of existence in the history of God's people. In other words, rather than "flesh" and "Spirit" referring to internal entities within the Christian (i.e., old and new natures), they actually refer to *external* bodily modes of existence. Rather than flesh and Spirit being entities that are within Christians in these contexts, these terms actually refer to bodily states in the world that God's people were or are within. In Paul's usage of the flesh/Spirit conflict, flesh and Spirit represent successive eras in God's redemptive program. This is why Paul says in Romans 8:9 that Christians are not *in* the flesh, but are *in* the Spirit. However, in typical individualistic fashion, we in the West have moved all of the action, so to speak, to the interior of individual Christians. Rather than "flesh" referring to an external, historical (and theological) bodily state, we have transformed it into an internal *nature*. Not that we do not have natures as human beings. I believe that we do. However, I do not believe that Paul is referring to such entities in his use of the flesh/Spirit antithesis. Paul is not speaking of natures

My initial methodology is to seek to establish the redemptive historical perspective of Paul through a series of four perspectival studies. Chapters 1-4 view the Galatian conflict from historical, rhetorical, sociological, and thematic lenses, respectively. Chapters 5-6 are exegetical studies of Galatians 5:13-26 and 6:1-18, respectively. Chapter 7 is a summary of these various perspectives and a suggestive treatment of other flesh/Spirit passages (e.g., Romans 7-8).

* Flesh and Spirit refer to external entities

ix

This material is an updating and rewriting of my 1991 doctoral dissertation in Hermeneutics and Biblical Studies at Westminster Theological Seminary in Philadelphia, Pennsylvania. I wrote it under the gracious expertise of Professor Moisés Silva. To Dr. Silva for his unflagging commitment to excellence and for his patient tutelage and enormously helpful feedback I owe a debt I cannot repay. Thank you, Moisés, for your kindness. My hearty thanks also to Westminster Professor Vern Poythress for his innovative approaches to hermeneutics that are manifested in various places throughout this work, but especially in my multi-perspectival approach. Thank you, Vern. To Professors Richard Gaffin at Westminster and Stephen Westerholm at McMaster University, my second and third dissertation readers, I am grateful to you also for your contributions to my development.

The seemingly endless task of translating earlier manuscripts from one computer program to another and the tedious work of editing the resulting mess would have been even more nightmarish except for the sterling work of my research assistant, Lisa Choe. Thank you, Lisa, for your faithful and excellent work.

To my wife, Marty, and our children, Elizabeth and Jonathan, I pray that my absence over the years of rewriting this material will be worth your consistent sacrifice of not seeing me regularly clothed and in my right mind! To my parents, Bo and Mabel Russell, we finally made it, Mom and Dad! To my faithful and inspiring friend, J. P. Moreland, my endless thanks for your steadfast encouragement throughout this project. I would not have made it without you.

If this book results in any increased insight into Galatians and other parts of God's Word, then may God be glorified. If this book results in any of God's people being freed from sub-biblical views of the flesh/Spirit struggle, then may God be glorified. If this book results in a clearer understanding of the freedom and empowerment that are in Jesus Christ, then may God be glorified. Amen.

Acknowledgments

All biblical quotations are from the *New American Standard Bible* (La Habra, CA: The Lockman Foundation, 1960, 1962, 1963, 1968, 1971, 1972, 1973, 1975, 1977), unless otherwise indicated. All quotations from the Greek text of the New Testament are from *Novum Testamentum Graece*, 26th edition (E. Nestle and K. Aland, eds; Stuttgart: Deutsche Bibelstiftung, 1979).

Reprinted by permission of the publishers and the Loeb Classical Library is the material quoted from Aristotle, XXII: *The "Art" of Rhetoric*, LCL Vol. 193, translated by J. H. Freese, Cambridge, Mass.: Harvard University Press, 1926, and the material quoted from [Cicero I]: *Rhetorica ad Herennium*, LCL Vol. 403, translated by H. Caplan, Cambridge, Mass.: Harvard University Press, 1954.

The quoted material from John Barclay, *Obeying the Truth. A Study of Paul's Ethics in Galatians*, Studies of the New Testament and Its World (copyright © 1988) is used by permission of T & T Clark Publishers Ltd.

The material reprinted from Hans Dieter Betz, *Galatians: A Commentary on Paul's Letter to the Churches of Galatia*, Hermeneia Series (copyright © 1979, Fortress Press) is used by permission of Augsburg Fortress Press.

Quotations from Robert Jewett, *Paul's Anthropological Terms. A Study of Their Use in Conflict Settings*, Arbeiten zur Geschichte des antiken Judentums und des Urchristentums 10 (copyright ©1971) are used by permission of E. J. Brill.

The quoted material from George A. Kennedy, *New Testament Interpretation through Rhetorical Criticism* (copyright © 1984) is used by permission of The University of North Carolina Press.

The material quoted from Bruce J. Malina, *The New Testament World. Insights from Cultural Anthropology. Revised Edition* (copyright © 1993) is used by permission of Westminster/John Knox Press.

Chapter 1

The Flesh/Spirit Conflict in Theology, Lexicography, and History

I. The Central Thesis

This monograph is an attempt to question the long standing and pervasive view that σάρξ is a force within the life of the Christian that he or she must continually struggle against and overcome only by choosing to walk in the power of God's πνεῦμα. This internal dualism between the forces of σάρξ and πνεῦμα is viewed as both a central paradigm for the spiritual life and a major construct in approaching Paul's theology (e.g., Davies 1980, 17-35). It is the central thesis of this book that this internal dualism, while accurate in some respects, is nonetheless significantly flawed in viewing σάρξ and πνεῦμα as an internal polarity.

Apart from Romans 7, Galatians 5-6 is perhaps the most vivid proof text for this internal dualistic perspective. If Paul's use of σάρξ and πνεῦμα in these chapters can be shown to represent a different kind of duality, then we will be well on our way to understanding *his* sense of the σάρξ/πνεῦμα polarity. Placing Paul's use of σάρξ and πνεῦμα in Gal 5-6 within the context of his use of these terms in the rest of the epistle (especially in Gal 3-6) and within the context of the argument of Galatians should help to validate this different kind of duality. This new understanding of Paul's dualism can then be used as a lens to view Paul's use of the σάρξ/πνεῦμα antithesis in other passages that have been understood in terms of an internal clash between σάρξ and πνεῦμα. This book will be concerned only with the construction of this new lens within Galatians. Its application to other relevant passages like Romans 7-8 and Philippians 3 will be only suggestive. However, once this fresh view of Paul's use of σάρξ and πνεῦμα in Gal 5-6 is grasped, the ramifications for the interpretation of the corollary passages will be obvious and the ramifications for our view of the spiritual life and Paul's theology will be considerable and far-reaching.

My central thesis is that σάρξ and πνεῦμα do not represent an internal duality within the Christian, but represent an external contrast between two conflicting eras or modes of existence with corresponding mind-sets (φρονήσετε in Gal 5:10). Herman Ridderbos has championed this general perspective of σάρξ and πνεῦμα in his works on Pauline theology:[1]

Support of Russell's view

> Rather, "flesh" and "Spirit" represent two modes of existence, on the one hand that of the old aeon which is characterized and determined by the flesh, on the other that of the new creation which is of the Spirit of God. It is in this sense that the difference is also to be taken between the first Adam as "living soul," i.e., flesh, and the second as life-giving Spirit. The contrast is therefore of a *redemptive-historical nature:* it qualifies the world and the mode of existence before Christ as flesh, that is, as the creaturely in its weakness; on the other hand, the dispensation that has taken effect with Christ as that of the Spirit, i.e., of power, imperishableness and glory (1 Cor 15:42, 43, 50; Phil 3:21). It is within this *redemptive-historical contrast* of flesh and Spirit as the mode of existence of the old and new creation that Paul now views the life of Christ before and after his resurrection. (1975, 66; emphasis is mine)

Three aspects of this definition of σάρξ and πνεῦμα are particularly relevant in Gal 3-6. First, from Gal 3:3 onward when σάρξ and πνεῦμα are used in an antithetical manner (which excludes 4:13, 14), they become theological abbreviations for the two competing identities of the people of God in Galatia. The "flesh community" is a community identified and characterized by a person bodily in his or her frailty and transitoriness unaided by God's Spirit. This is a person on his own--still under sin's dominion over his body. This community is representative of a person *before* or *apart from* Jesus Christ's liberating death, burial, and resurrection. Therefore, such persons can think and feel the right thing to do, but are unable to do it fully. If

Definition of flesh community

Jewish, this community has encountered the greater accountability of the whole Mosaic Law (Gal 5:3), but also the tragic inability to obey it (Gal 6:13). This is a community now associated with the greater "flesh" community of all those who are apart from Christ (cf. Eph 2:3). By contrast, the "Spirit community" is a community identified and characterized by a person bodily aided and enabled by God's presence and also bodily liberated from sin's dominion. This is a person experiencing the full liberation of Jesus Christ's death and resurrection. These persons are experiencing the freedom that Jesus Christ set them free to experience (Gal 5:1).

Definition of Spirit community.

Secondly, these two competing identities of God's people represent two successive eras in God's program of redemptive history. Σάρξ and νόμος are a constant tandem in Galatians and underscore that "flesh" is identified with the era of the Mosaic Law (e.g., Gal. 5:13-14; 5:17-18; 5:19-21 and 23; 6:12-13). "Flesh" is descriptive of the era of slavery to the στοιχεῖα and submission to the guardians and managers, which is being ὑπὸ νόμον (4:1-5, 8-10). The Mosaic Law was needed during this childish, immature era of failure to "shut up all men under sin" (3:19-22) and to be a παιδαγωγός (3:23-25) until the fullness of time would come and God would send forth His Son (4:4-5). In its anachronistic manifestation in the Judaizer community, "flesh" now entails an unhealthy, inordinate emphasis on marks on the body (circumcision) and bodily conformity to the Law (Gal. 5:11-12; 6:12-13). In contrast, "Spirit" is descriptive of the era of the Messianic fullness of time (4:4) and the era of the universal fulfillment of the promised blessing of Abraham (3:8-9, 13-14). It is during the present era of the Spirit that the proclamation of Abrahamic blessing to the Gentiles is carried out in a decentralized, centrifugal, aggressive universal manner. This stands in contrast to the Judaizers' pattern of a centralized, centripetal layering of the Gentiles around restored ethnic Israel (e.g., 1:11-2:21; 3:26-29; 4:8-11; 4:21-31). "Flesh" represents this particularistic, ethnocentric gospel (which is a non-gospel--Gal 1:6-10), while "Spirit" represents the universal, multi-ethnic gospel (3:8-9, 13-14).

KEY STATEMENT

Lastly, σάρξ and πνεῦμα represent the Judaizer and Pauline communities, respectively. Each community is characterized by an *identity* (flesh or Spirit) and a *pattern of behavior* ("according to" the flesh or the Spirit). In Gal 5-6 we see these patterns of behavior manifested as the two communities are contrasted side-by-side. The "deeds of the flesh" and the "fruit of the Spirit" equal the two contrasting patterns of behavior. Paul's challenge in Gal 5:16, πνεύματι περιπατεῖτε, is a challenge to the Galatians to continue to live within the community of the Spirit (the true people of God) and to live according to the pattern of behavior he taught in the churches he started. To avoid "fulfilling the desires of the flesh" (5:16b) is to reject living according to the standards of the Judaizer/Mosaic Law-oriented community. Paul's challenge is a challenge to live according to the objective standards that Christ brought (6:2) and not to revert to the preparatory, now-inferior standards of the Mosaic Law and flesh era.[2] The choice that the Galatian Christians faced was not a choice between conflicting *internal* personal agencies or means: "walk *by* the Spirit" versus "walk *by* the flesh." Rather, their choice was between conflicting *external* rules/directions/standards: "walk *according to the rule of* the Spirit" versus "walk *according to the rule of* the flesh."

Makes sense

II. A Summary of this Study

Chapter One is an attempt to prove that the threat in Galatia was a particularly appealing one because it was from Judaizing Jewish Christians from Jerusalem and/or Judea. The "in house" nature of this threat explains the redemptive-historical cast to Paul's argumentation. In Chapter Two I seek to trace Paul's very consistent response to this Judaizing threat and to prove that Gal 5-6 is his third, and culminating refutation of their non-gospel. "What Paul is leading to in chapters 1-4 is the exhortation of chapters 5-6. That is the point of the letter" (Kennedy 1984, 146). Therefore, Gal 5-6 continue Paul's antithetical contrast between the true gospel and the Judaizers' non-gospel. In Chapter Three, I continue laying the foundation by underscoring even more the *corporate/group dimension* and the redemptive historical nature of the Judaizer threat through social analysis of some of the dynamics at work in Galatia. I hope to validate the external, community-nature of the flesh/Spirit contrast in Gal 3-6. My premise in even desiring such an analysis is that emphasis on the group aspect of Gal 5-6 will illumine the way that *the Galatians* viewed the world. Their central focus on group identity stands in stark contrast to our individualistic, pietistic interpretation of the dynamics of the Galatian conflict. Seeing flesh/Spirit as an internal duality tells us more about *our* view of the Galatian struggle, than about theirs.

Chapter Four is a thematic analysis of Paul's use of the σάρξ/πνεῦμα antithesis in Galatians and a tracing of his development of these contrasting elements within Galatians 3-6. This chapter adds the thematic perspectival analysis to the historical, rhetorical, and sociological perspectives in chapters 1-3. These four chapters form the foundation upon which the exegesis of Galatians 5-6 in Chapters Five and Six rests. This exegesis is then supplemented in the final chapter with a suggestive analysis of other Pauline passages that contain the full σάρξ/πνεῦμα antithesis or elements of it.

III. The Traditional Theological Understanding

The predominant understanding of σάρξ and πνεῦμα in Gal 5-6 is remarkably uniform and transcends most theological lines. Σάρξ or "flesh" is seen as an anthropological concept in these chapters that describes "man who has chosen to be left to himself, man's *cor incurvatum in se* (to use Luther's vivid phrase)" (Barrett 1985, 75). "Flesh" is defined as "the inclination or tendency within man that drives him to do evil" (Barrett 1985, 75). This is the aspect of man that is juxtaposed with God's Spirit so that Paul describes the Christian in Gal 5-6 "as a battlefield of the opposing forces of flesh and Spirit" (Betz 1979, 272). After a very helpful discussion of "flesh" (1951, Sec. 22-23), Bultmann later underscores this internal dualistic perspective of σάρξ and πνεῦμα when he discusses "Man under Faith" and his "Freedom from Sin and Walking in the Spirit" (1951, Sec. 38). The flesh/Spirit dualism manifests itself in the Christian as a constant choice:

> *The life of him who is released from the power of death* is no phenomenon of nature, either, but is the life of the striving, willing self which is always after something and is always faced with its various possibilities, but it is constantly faced with those two basic possibilities: to live "according to the flesh" or to live "according to the Spirit"--to and for one's self or to and for God or the Lord. (1951, 331; emphasis is his)

This choice between flesh-living or Spirit-living that the believer in Jesus Christ presumably faces is more clearly understood when the exact theological nature of σάρξ is delineated. Eduard Schweizer brilliantly achieves this delineation in his lengthy article on σάρξ in the *TDNT* (Friedrich 1971, 7:98-151). Of particular theological significance are four aspects of σάρξ noted by Schweizer (with only specific references to uses in Galatians used here):

> 1. σάρξ *as an object of trust* - This means that σάρξ takes on a negative aspect from the fact that it is the object which man can display and of which he can boast...What is sinful is not the σάρξ, but the confidence in it. Gl. 6:12f should probably be mentioned in this connection. (130)

2. Κατὰ σάρκα *as a life-orientation* - Finally γεννᾶν κατὰ σάρκα in Gl. 4:23,29...is a generation which takes place only with regard to human possibilities and not with regard to the promise. If this means that there are two διαθῆκαι for Paul..., this brings out a new aspect of Paul's view, namely, that the decision to orientate one's life to the σάρξ, or to the Lord and His promise and Spirit is obviously not just the single decision of a moment but a fundamental decision which affects the whole of life. (131)

3. σάρξ *as the subject of sin* - The σάρξ, then, is not a power which works in the same way as the πνεῦμα. The σάρξ never occurs as the subject of an action where it is not in the shadow of a statement about the work of the πνεῦμα, while the πνεῦμα on the other hand is often presented as an acting subject with or without σάρξ in the context. (132)

Schweizer goes on to discuss Paul's concept of sowing to the flesh in Gal 6:8 and says: "In antithetical parallelism to πνεῦμα, however, σάρξ approximates to the idea of a power which works on man and determines his destiny even beyond life on earth" (132). Regarding Gal 3:3 and 4:8-10, Schweizer adds:

Σάρξ is for Paul everything human and earthly, which includes legal righteousness...But since this entices man to put his trust in it, to find security and renown thereby, it takes on for Paul the character of a power which is opposed to the working of the Spirit. The sharpest formulation is in Gl. 5:13,17, where σάρξ is an independent force superior to man. Paul realises, of course, that this power which entices away from God and His Spirit is not just a power alien to man. It belongs to man himself. (133)

4. Σάρξ *as a vanquished entity* - According to R. 7:5; 8:8f; Gl. 5:24 the believer no longer lives in the σάρξ; he has crucified it.... The σάρξ of Gl. 5:24 is not, then, a part of man which he may put off or overcome. It is the man himself. Where σάρξ is understood in a full theological sense as in Gl. 5:24, it denotes the being of man which is determined, not by his physical substance, but by his relation to God....(134). The man ruled by the Spirit must no longer secure his life by the σάρξ, whether by wealth or by good works. But this means that the splitting of life into thousands of individual acts, which is typical of legalists and scrupulous penitents, is quite impossible. Life is determined as a totality by σάρξ or πνεῦμα...But the man who has come to faith in the Son of God is no longer in the σάρξ, for he believes, and he has thus ceased to build his life on the σάρξ, which is to sin. That Paul is very far from being a

Luther & Calvin set the tone for belief in the flesh @ sinful nature

perfectionist is due to his realization that man has to receive and to practise his faith afresh each day. (135)

This very carefully reasoned and skillfully crafted study of σάρξ is reflective of the same conclusions, though often less cautious and more exaggerated, that have been reached by a variety of scholars. For over four hundred years, since the commentaries on Galatians by Luther (1535) and Calvin (1548), the scholarly consensus has been essentially the same as that expressed by Schweizer. Luther's vivid comment on Gal 5:16 that "there be two contrary captains in you, the spirit and the flesh" ([1850] 1979, 330) is repeated in some fashion by almost every commentator since. For example, in commenting on Gal 5:13-26, commentators as diverse as Lightfoot ([1890] 1957, 208-14), Burton (1921, 291-325; 486-95), Bring (1961, 247-81), Schlier (1971, 279-312), Bonnard (1972, 108-17), Mussner (1974, 364-96), Betz (1979, 271-95), Bruce (1982, 239-58), Ebeling (1985, 247-61), Fung (1988, 243-78), Cole (1989, 202-23), Longenecker (1990, 235-67), Hansen (1994a, 162-82), and George (1994, 374-407) express the view that "the new life, too, is subject to a penetrating, internal dualism" between the σάρξ and the πνεῦμα (Ridderbos 1953, 204).[3] Less definitive in emphasizing this internal struggle is Matera 1992, 192-212 and Dunn 1993b, 284-318.

Recent technical monographs on Galatians by David J. Lull (1980, 113-28) and Charles H. Cosgrove (1988, 154-67) also repeat the perspective of internal dualism when dealing with Gal 5-6. The same can be said of the monograph on the terms σάρξ and πνεῦμα by E.D. Burton (1918, 191-8) and Alexander Sand (1967, 165-218). Following this type of internal dualism to a slightly lesser degree and adding the apocalyptic dimension which sees σάρξ and πνεῦμα as cosmic spheres and powers are the monographs on Galatians by Bernard H. Brinsmead (1982, 78-82, 163-85) and John Barclay (1988, 106-45, 178-215). Robert Jewett's fine work on Paul's anthropological terms also fits into this recently-emerging perspective (1971b). This apocalyptic view builds upon the earlier work on the σάρξ/πνεῦμα dualism by Egon Brandenburger (1968, 42-48) and the view of Ernst Käsemann (1971, 25-27). While this more cosmic perspective is a very welcome and helpful addition, it does not stray as far as one would imagine from the traditional perspective and leaves a certain vagueness in defining what σάρξ really is (e.g., Barclay 1988, 202-15). Therefore, in spite of this outpouring of scholarly interest in the σάρξ/πνεῦμα dualism and the recent emergence of a slightly different perspective, the traditional understanding of the σάρξ/πνεῦμα internal polarity within the Christian persists as the overwhelmingly dominant and pervasive view.

IV. The Traditional Lexicography

Logic would seem to dictate that the lexical dimension of the terms σάρξ and πνεῦμα be surveyed before the theological understanding is scanned. However, this book's reversal is by design. The lexicography of σάρξ in particular may be one of the classic cases, in this writer's opinion, where a received theology has heavily colored lexical work. This predisposed lexicography may also have distorted further the theological conclusions that flow out of the word-study approach to New Testament theology, now so soundly rejected by modern linguistics (e.g., Brown 1989, 129). The treatment of σάρξ in some of the standard Greek lexicons should validate that this concern may indeed be warranted.

There is really no controversy over the "non-ethical" uses of σάρξ in the New Testament and here the lexicons are basically in agreement (e.g., BAGD 1979, 743-44; LSJ 1968, 1585; LN 1988, 1:94, 102, 105-6, 112, 262; 2:220). Of the eighteen occurrences of σάρξ in Galatians,[4] half of the uses are typical of LXX uses that translate בָּשָׂר and שְׁאֵר in the following body-oriented senses with no ethical connotations (BAGD 1979, 743-44):

1. the material that covers the bones of a human or animal body
   Gal 6:13
2. the body itself, viewed as a substance - Gal 4:13, 14
3. a man of flesh and blood or a human being in contrast to God and other supernatural beings - Gal 1:16
4. human or mortal nature, earthly descent - Gal 4:23, 29[5]
5. corporeality, physical limitation(s), life here on earth - Gal 2:20
6. the external or outward side of life - Gal 6:12[6]

While the uses in Gal 4 and 6 have great theological and ethical significance in their contexts, there is no great difficulty so far with these six lexical senses. However, it is when the seventh sense of "ethical" uses is added that the theological beast seems to intrude into the lexical cave![7] With this intrusion the other nine occurrences of σάρξ in Galatians take on the intruder's nature. BAGD reflects this in its lexical listing:

7. In Paul's thought esp. , the *flesh* is the willing instrument of sin, and is subject to sin to such a degree that wherever flesh is, all forms of sin are likew, present, and no good thing can live in the σάρξ- Gal 3:3; 5:13, 16, 17, 17, 19, 24; 6:8. (1979, 744)

The difficulty with this lexical listing is that it does not give a definition for σάρξ in these passages. Rather, it is more of a description of the *theological function* of the σάρξ in lieu of a discussion of its lexical sense. In this case, theologizing may have replaced the work of lexicography. However, this need not be problematic with a term like σάρξ that appears to have a theological referent. It is only problematic when the theological referent is errant. That, of course, is this book's thesis.

The Greek lexicon very admirably arranged according to semantic domains by Louw and Nida (1988) highlights even more vividly the expanded sense that σάρξ is supposed to display in its ethical uses. In this work σάρξ is viewed as a part of six semantic domains (LN 1988, 2:220):

1. body, body parts, and body products
2. people
3. kinship terms
4. physiological processes and states
5. nature, class, example
6. psychological faculties

It is the sixth domain that corresponds to the ethical uses of σάρξ and that reflects the same theological anthropology described in the seventh listing in BAGD (1979, 744). These ethical uses of σάρξ are viewed by Louw and Nida as functioning within a sixteen-member "psychological faculty" domain which includes terms and their equivalents like:

ὁ ἔσω ἄνθρωπος ("the inner person") and ὁ ἐν τῷ κρυπτῷ ἄνθρωπος ("the hidden person"), καρδία ("heart, inner self, mind"), ψυχή ("the inner self, mind, thoughts, feelings, heart, being"), πνεῦμα ("spirit, spiritual, spiritual nature, inner being"), νοῦς, νόημα, διάνοια ("mind"), etc. (LN 1988, 1:320-25)

The occurrences of σάρξ in the New Testament that fall within this semantic domain, according to Louw and Nida, are equivalent to "human nature, human aspects, natural, human" (1988, 1:322). They define σάρξ in this semantic domain as:

the psychological aspect of human nature which contrasts with the spiritual nature; in other words, that aspect of human nature which is characterized by or reflects typical human reasoning and desires in contrast with aspects of human thought and behavior which relate to God and spiritual life...1 Cor 1.26, Gal 5.19, Gal 6.8. (1988, 1:322)

This equivalent of σάρξ is used in the United Bible Societies' translation (TEV) and creates a very heightened internal dualism in passages like Gal 5:17:

For what our *human nature* wants is opposed to what the Spirit wants, and what the Spirit wants is opposed to what our *human nature* wants. These two are enemies, and this means that you cannot do what you want to do. (Arichea and Nida 1976, 134; emphasis is mine)

This "human nature" translation raises some interesting theological questions when one gets to Gal 5:24 in the TEV: "And those who belong to Christ Jesus have put to death their *human nature* with all its passions and desires" (Arichea and Nida 1976, 141; emphasis is mine). Has the Christian lost something similar to his or her "heart," "mind," "inner person," or "inner self"? Has he or she lost an essential psychological aspect of "human nature" in order to gain a "spiritual nature"? Is this kind of dichotomizing of a person really what Paul had in mind in his uses of σάρξ in Gal 5-6 (and elsewhere)?

Also problematic is the translation of the NIV (1973, 1978) which asserts that the σάρξ in Gal 5:24 that has been crucified is "*the sinful nature*" (cf. the same translation in Gal 5:13, 16, 17, 19 and 6:8). If the Christian has lost his or her nature or capacity to sin, then how do we explain the fact that the Christian still sins in spite of a "sinful nature" that is supposed to be dead? The only escape from this kind of a theological quandary is to explain away the crucifixion of "the sinful nature" as not really being dead. In the process, of course, the theologian negates the very purpose for Paul's specific use of ἐσταύρωσαν in Gal 5:24: the reality of the death of the σάρξ for the Christian is intimately associated with the reality of the death of Jesus Christ. Both were really crucified! The lexical sense of σάρξ must not do injustice to this historical association that Paul's careful terminology brings to mind.

While this "*human nature/sinful nature*" meaning of σάρξ certainly fits nicely within the "psychological faculties" semantic domain, one must explain the extension from the first six *rather concrete, body-oriented senses* within the semantic range of σάρξ (as listed in BAGD, 743-44) to this seventh, *more abstract sense* that describes a nature or impulse. Although it is never specifically stated in BAGD's or Louw and Nida's listings, in Schweizer's treatment of σάρξ, or even in Burton's lengthy examination of σάρξ in Pauline passages (1918, 184-98), this extension in the meaning of σάρξ appears to be due to metonymy. Specifically, σάρξ appears to be a metonymy of source, or instrument, or perhaps container. In the Pauline passages where σάρξ has an ethical connotation, the traditional view appears to be that the evil nature or impulse within persons is focused upon by referring to the bodily tissues which gave source to it, or contain it, or are the evil nature's willing instrument.

While there are examples of extending the meaning of a Greek term so that it can be used of *both* the material and the immaterial dimensions of human beings (e.g., ψυχή) my thesis is that Paul does not, in fact, do this in his "ethical" uses of σάρξ. Rather, he continues a much closer semantic connection among the senses of σάρξ in his use of the term in Galatians (and elsewhere) than the semantic connection of the extended, immaterial sense. While the extension of the sense of σάρξ by metonymy is lexically possible and not uncommon in Koiné Greek, I will seek to prove that it is contextually unnecessary. This is not to say that Paul does not enrich the basic bodily sense of σάρξ in these ethical uses. However, this enrichment of *the continued bodily sense* will be shown to be of a redemptive historical nature, rather than of an extension-by-metonymy nature. If this is the case, then the seventh lexical sense for σάρξ listed by BAGD (1979, 744) and the sixth semantic domain of σάρξ listed in Louw and Nida (1988, 1:322) do not apply in the uses in Galatians and the term is not extended so significantly. In particular, the nine occurrences of σάρξ in Gal 3:3; 5:13, 16, 17, 17, 19, 24; 6:8, 8 and the two additional uses in Gal 4:23, 29 will be shown to be very body-oriented uses by Paul and to be immensely material, rather than extended, in reference. I will seek to prove that the theological and ethical connotations of these occurrences do not necessitate an extended sense of σάρξ that appears to have become the lexical standard (cf. Barclay 1962, 16-22).[8]

V. The Identity of Paul's Opponents

One last introductory issue needs to be confronted. If I am to succeed in overturning both a theological and lexical view of σάρξ that is pervasive and formidable, then crucial to this task is the identifying of Paul's opponents in Galatia. They are central to the argument of Galatians because they appear in every chapter (1:6-9; 2:4-5; 3:1; 4:17; 5:10, 12; 6:12-13). Their identity is also pivotal because it is these opponents that Paul describes in Gal 4:23 and 29 as "having been born according to the flesh" (κατὰ σάρκα γεγέννηται). If Schweizer is correct in his understanding that these opponents' life-orientation is to the σάρξ and not to the Lord, His promise, or His Spirit (TDNT, 7:131), then correctly identifying them will give us great insight into the nature of the σάρξ/πνεῦμα duality associated with them (e.g., in Gal 4:29). However, our initial identifying of these opponents must be a cursory one that will be validated more fully as our in-depth analysis of Galatians proceeds. Our focus on Gal 5-6 will prove to be especially helpful since these chapters are particularly problematic elements in the identifying process (Fletcher 1982, 1-4).

There are three major views of Paul's opponents in Galatia that encompass numerous minor views:

1. *The Traditional View* - they are "Judaizers" or those pressuring Gentiles to live as if they were Jews.
2. *The Two-Opponent View* - both Judaizers and libertinistic "pneumatics" plague Paul in Galatia.
3. *The Gnostic/Syncretistic Jewish Christians View* - there is *one* group of opponents which has both Judaistic and libertinistic traits found in some of the peripheral groups within Judaism and Asia Minor.

The Traditional View: Judaizers

Since the second century Marcionite Prologues to Galatians (preserved only in Latin translations), it has been inferred that Paul's opponents were over-zealous Jewish-Christians from Jerusalem who penetrated the churches of Galatia. They advocated the traditional Jewish proselyte model of attachment to ethnic Israel for the Gentile Christians. This identity of these false apostles was carefully confirmed by John Calvin ([1556] 1965, 4-7) and more casually assumed by Martin Luther ([1850] 1979, 2). Since Calvin's and Luther's day, the majority of Protestant scholars have identified Paul's opponents in some way with the Jewish Christians from the Jerusalem Church.

This identity was solidified by F. C. Baur of the Tübingen School who made these opponents a decisive interpretive key to all of Paul's writings. Baur's definitive reconstruction of the history of the early church does not so much pit Paul against the Jerusalem apostles, as is popularly understood, but rather against the party of Jewish Christians identified with James and the Jerusalem Church (Baur 1963, 49). These Judaizers had an Ebionite tendency and had not broken out of the limits of Judaism in their understanding of Christianity and the sufficiency of Christ's ministry (Baur 1875a, 1:113, 129-30). To Baur, the Epistle to the Galatians was a microcosm of the universal struggle between Pauline and Jewish Christianity. Therefore, while he never wrote a commentary on Galatians, his central and emphatic identity of Paul's opponents in Galatia became the almost unquestioned standard, even to those who opposed such a view:

> There are few problems in the realm of New Testament introduction in which the scholars of all eras are so unanimously and indisputably of *one* mind as here .
> The heretics in Galatia are Judaizers, that is, Christians who demand the observance of the Jewish law on a greater or lesser scale, but in any case including circumcision: thus they are Christians in whose opinion membership in the eschatological community of the Messiah who has appeared in Jesus depends upon membership in the national Celtic union, constituted through the rite of circumcision, of the ancient people of the covenant. This thesis is the presupposition of the exegesis of the Galatian epistle in the commentaries, not its conclusion; and it can be such a presupposition because no one would deny it. (Schmithals 1972, 13)

Of course, Schmithals goes on to deny the traditional identity of Paul's opponents, but the status of the "Judaizers'" identity up to his day was generally unquestioned. Ironically, since Schmithals, recent New Testament introductions may be guilty of assuming some form of *his* position (e.g., Koester 1982, 118-19).

Viewing Paul's Galatian opponents as Judaizers seems to be supported by strong internal evidence. Those "who distort the gospel" in the churches seem to have come in from the outside (1:7) and they "confuse the churches" (1:7; 5:10, 12). They certainly appear to be Christians since they are offering "another gospel" (1:7) and desire to avoid persecution from the Jewish community (6:12). Paul's focus on Jerusalem and Judea in Gal 1-2 and 4:21-31 seems to point to the opponents' origin from this area, although this is not held as firmly as other aspects of their identity. Their Jewish roots seem unassailable given their emphasis on circumcision (5:2; 6:12-13), observance of the Mosaic Law (3:2; 5:4) and certain festivals (4:10), and apparent interest in being "sons of Abraham" (3:6-29; 4:21-31). Given this straightforward reading of Galatians and the nice correlation with Acts 15, scholars continue to espouse this traditional view in standard New Testament introductions (e.g., Kümmel 1975, 298-301), technical monographs (e.g., Howard 1979, 1-19), recent commentaries on Galatians (e.g., Fung 1988, 3-9), and recent journal articles (e.g., Martyn 1985a; Barclay 1987).[9]

Worthy of mention and inclusion under this major view is the position argued by Johannes Munck (1959, 87-134). While he was strongly reacting to Baur's bifurcation of the early church into competing Pauline and Jewish segments, Munck nonetheless saw Paul's Galatian opponents as Judaizers. The uniqueness of his view is that he saw these Judaizers as *Gentile* Christians from within Galatia itself (1959, 87; cf. Wilson 1992 on the phenomenon of Gentile Judaizers). They had been circumcised only recently according to Gal 6:13 where Paul uses the present participle οἱ περιτεμνόμενοι to describe them (1959, 87-89). While Munck perceived himself to be on the opposite end of the spectrum from Baur with this particular view, his identifying of Paul's opponents does not lead to any substantial difference from that of Baur's in the interpretation of the epistle as a whole. The same can be said of the similar position of A. E. Harvey (1968, 319-32) who identifies Paul's opponents as "not Jews by birth, but Gentiles who have become Jewish proselytes only recently, or who are still contemplating doing so" (324). The uniqueness of Harvey's view is that he argues that these proselytes are pressuring their fellow Christians to avoid persecution from the synagogue by adopting *Jewish practices*, not Jewish theology. Harvey reasons that this is so because of the Jewish emphasis on strict adherence to Jewish practices, rather than to Jewish orthodoxy (327-29). Paul's attack is to show the theological consequences of embracing Jewish practices out of fear and expediency (Gal 6:12-13).

The Two-Opponent View: Judaizers and Antinomians

In reaction to Baur's dominant reconstruction of the early church, Wilhelm Lütgert (1919) opposed the one opponent/Judaizers' view by arguing for the additional resistance of a second group in Galatia. While conceding the existence of the Judaizers, Lütgert was convinced that an even more threatening group was the primary focus of Paul's attack in Galatians. Like Luther before him ([1850] 1979, 325-29), although seeing them more as an organized party, Lütgert identified this second group of Christians as the antinomians who "die Freiheit zum Antrieb für das Fleisch gebrauchen" (1919, 16). The common thread that holds Galatians together as Paul addresses this two-front battle is the subject of *the Law* (1919, 9). Paul's arguments with both the Judaizers and the antinomians involve the law and its relationship to the Christian life. Therefore, Lütgert argued, Paul vacillated between addressing these two groups as he wrote Galatians. For example, while Gal 3-4 is primarily concerned with the Judaizers, Paul's focus on them ends at Gal 5:6 and he begins to address the antinomians' abuses of the law in 5:7 (1919, 27-28). Therefore, the majority of Gal 5-6 is no longer seen as Paul's defensive limitation of the boundaries of freedom in light of possible Judaizers' criticism, but rather as a much more aggressive and overt attack on the antinomians' real abuses (1919, 14-19).

Lütgert's views were not broadly disseminated until James H. Ropes championed them in a small monograph in 1929 called *The Singular Problem of the Epistle to the Galatians*. Ropes made only very minor adjustments to Lütgert's thesis and sought to show how it manifested itself by briefly, but systematically, going through Galatians chapter by chapter. Interestingly enough, he perceived the break from the lengthy Judaizers' discussion of Gal 3-4 to end in 5:10, not in 5:6 as Lütgert had argued. Paul begins the practical section in 5:11 and Ropes notes:

> The transition to the next topic is an important one, sharper than any other transition in the epistle. Our theory requires the break to be made after verse 10, not after verse 12. (1929, 38)

As Douglas Fletcher has wryly noted, "For such a sharp division, it does not seem that it would be necessary to rely upon one's presuppositions to discern it" (1982, 42). Weaknesses like this kind of questionable audience theory have limited the wholesale acceptance of Lütgert's and Ropes' two-opponent view. Nevertheless, their emphasis on the presence of libertinistic "pneumatici" or "spiritual persons" (Ropes 1929, 10) helped to shape the next reaction to the traditional view.

The Gnostic/Syncretistic Jewish Christian View

Although the Gnostic identity of Paul's opponents in Galatia tends to be identified with Walter Schmithals, other scholars had previously written of the gnostic presence in Galatia (Brinsmead 1982, 10). However, it is Schmithals that has firmly tied Paul's ministry to the combating of some form of first century Gnosticism (1965, 103-17; 1972, 13-64; and 1983). Schmithals follows Lütgert's study in two crucial areas: the dating of Galatians after the Corinthian epistles and the identification of gnostics in both communities. Like Lütgert, Schmithals follows the methodology that "the picture of the Galatians heresy is to be filled out in details from the Corinthian epistles" (1972, 59 note 134). While building upon Lütgert's and Ropes' identity of libertinistic pneumatics in Galatia, Schmithals (and those who have followed him) significantly deviates from the former theory by positing a *single* battle front in Galatia. The questionable audience theory of the two-opponent view is rightly criticized and rejected as unsatisfactory (1972, 17). In its place is offered a single group of opponents who manifest both sets of characteristics previously attached to the Judaizers and antinomian pneumatics.

Rather than refuting the traditional view of Judaizers in Galatia, Schmithals' strategy is to develop a strong and coherent picture of Gnostics in Galatia and to demonstrate how this best explains the particulars of Galatians. To do this, however, involves some question begging on his part. For example, Gal 3-4 is seen as the heart of the argumentation against the Judaizers in the traditional view. Rather than contesting the particulars of the Judaizer interpretation of this section, however, Schmithals virtually ignores it and alleges that Paul did not really understand his Gnostic opponents or he would not have argued in this manner (1972, 18). Others who adhere to this Gnostic identity find that they too must assert that their knowledge of the Galatian opponents exceeds Paul's because in Gal 3-4 he argues about the law "in such a way as he might have done if his opponents had been Pharisaic Judaists, which they obviously were not" (e.g., Marxsen 1968, 53).[10] It is *possible* that a critic's knowledge can exceed an author's knowledge of *the subject matter*, but this is not to be confused with the critic thinking that his knowledge of the author's *meaning* is superior (Hirsch 1967, 19-23). Therefore, the value of this alleged superior knowledge by Schmithals is perhaps much more limited than he and his followers have assumed.

Before looking at the basic supports for this view of Paul's opponents, the closely related identity of syncretistic Jewish Christians should be discussed. This view has been argued for some time also, but it came into particular prominence through the writing of Frederic R. Crownfield (1945). He identified Paul's Galatian opponents as a group that was syncretizing Christianity and a mystical understanding of following Torah and Jewish legal practices (1945, 492-93). The "Judaizers" and "spirituals" were actually the same group. The leaders of this group were theorized to have been early converts to Christianity, and although not followers of the earthly Jesus, were nonetheless connected with Jerusalem. Crownfield conjectured that it was plausible that these opponents were adherents of Jewish mystery cults seeking spiritual illumination through legalism. As he built upon Lütgert's thesis to develop his view, one can see how Schmithals also built upon Crownfield's view of the opponents, specifying that they were *Gnostic* groups. Both writers tended to correlate the Colossian errorists with those of Galatia who combined some Jewish rites with laxity in morals (Crownfield 1945, 493; Schmithals 1972, 44-46). A similar view is held by Heinrich Schlier in his commentary on Galatians (1971). He embraces an identity for the opponents that explains their nomism coupled with their libertinistic tendencies as an early stage of Gnosticism demonstrating a sort of Jewish apocalypticism similar to that found at Qumran (1971, 21-24). This is not far from the view of Brinsmead who sees Paul's opponents as possessing an Essene theology and ethics that espoused a "nomistic enthusiasm" (1982, 164-78). Brinsmead's elaborate picture of the Galatian intruders has been devastatingly criticized by Aune (1984), Russell (1984), and Barclay (1987, 81-83).

Following this trajectory more fully in a similar direction is Dieter Georgi who sees the troublers of the Galatian churches as pneumatics using Christian elements as the ultimate completion of a Jewish syncretism previously enriched with Gentile motives (1965, 35). Against Schmithals who sees Paul's opponents as Jews who were never baptized (1972, 14), Georgi views these false brethren as a faction within the Jerusalem church pressing for the circumcision of Gentile Christians. This faction viewed the law as a source of speculative wisdom, not simply for the Jews, but as the norm for the universe. However, their goal was the attainment of pneumatic completion through individualistic and ascetic religious experiences (1965, 35). Klaus Wegenast holds a very similar view to Georgi and underscores the importance of circumcision and the law to these opponents (1962, 39). This represents a basic following of the general thesis of Crownfield *in this area* against Schmithals, while still working within the general Gnostic identity championed by the latter.

Both the Gnostic and syncretistic Jewish Christian identities are built upon the reasoning that Paul is primarily addressing the sarkic conduct of his opponents in Galatians and that this libertine lifestyle, not the legalistic theology, is the basic threat facing the Galatians (e.g., Schmithals 1972, 51-55). Following Lütgert, Schmithals focuses on the passages like Gal 4:9 and 5:1 that appear to point to this threat. However, of particular importance are:

Gal 5:3 - And I testify again to every man who receives circumcision, that he is under obligation to keep the whole Law.

Gal 5:13 - For you were called to freedom, brethren; only do not turn your freedom into an opportunity for the flesh, but through love serve one another.

Gal 5:16 - But I say, walk by the Spirit, and you will not carry out the desire of the flesh.

Gal 6:13 - For those who are circumcised do not even keep the Law themselves, but they desire to have you circumcised, that they may boast in your flesh.

In a similar fashion, Hans Dieter Betz asserts that the fundamental problem facing the churches of Galatia is the conflict of the Spirit and the flesh. He proposes that the churches were wrestling with how being ἐν πνεύματι conflicted with life's daily realities: "How can the πνευματικὸ coexist with 'trespasses' in his daily life?" (Betz 1974, 154). Paul's opponents were answering this question with the security that Torah offered. By accepting Torah and circumcision, the Galatians would then become partakers of the safety offered by the Sinai covenant (Betz 1973; 1974, 154-55). One can see with this reconstruction and emphasis that Gal 5-6 becomes the specific recommendation that Paul makes to the Galatians. The locating of the focal point of Galatians in Gal 3-4 associated with the traditional view of Judaizing opponents has now shifted to a focal point in Gal 5-6 in this third major view. Methodologically, the procedure is to seek to wrap the remainder of Galatians around a primary core of Gal 5-6. While Betz essentially subscribes to this third view (though not emphasizing the opponents' identity in his exposition), his masterful literary analysis of Galatians in his commentary locates the body of the epistle in Gal 3-4 (1979, 14-25).[11] This runs contrary to his belief that it is really Gal 5-6 that has real force for the Galatians' problems. The mere polemic against accepting circumcision and law in Gal 2:15-5:12 "does not do justice to the Galatian trouble" (Betz 1979, 273). However, the force of Betz' identity of the problem in Galatia is offset by the weight of his literary analysis, as Fletcher has noted (1982, 82-83). A similar problem is shared by H. Schlier in his commentary on Galatians. In essence, he accepts a conservative version of the Gnostic identity, but interprets Galatians as if Paul were addressing Judaizers (1971, 20-24).

Solving the Identity Crisis

The goal in identifying Paul's opponents in Galatia is to make sure that all of the particulars of the epistle are accounted for in the most meaningful and comprehensive way. In seeking to do this, John Barclay has delineated three major problems in this kind of "mirror-reading" (1987, 74-79):

> 1. Paul is not directly addressing the opponents in Galatians, but he is talking to the Galatians about the opponents.
> 2. Galatians is a fierce polemic and the intense rhetoric may tend to distort the opponents' actual positions.
> 3. We encounter the linguistic distortion of only hearing one partner in the conversation.

Barclay goes on to describe four dangerous pitfalls that occur in recent attempts to mirror-read Galatians (1987, 79-83):

> 1. The danger of *undue selectivity* (deciding which of Paul's statements are particularly revealing about the opponents' message).
> 2. The danger of *over-interpretation* (imagining every statement of Paul is a rebuttal of an equally vigorous opponents' counter-statement).
> 3. The danger of *mishandling polemics* (making more out of Paul's attacks than is warranted with polemical language).
> 4. The danger of *latching onto particular words and phrases* (using these brief bits of data as the flimsy pegs upon which the whole thesis should hang).

Keeping in mind the seven methodological criteria that Barclay suggests (1987, 84-86), I shall attempt to weigh the particulars of Galatians and to sift through the three major views.[12]

In agreement with the first and third views, it seems that the problems raised by Paul's opponents are of a unitary nature. Gordon's observation (1987, 33-34) is on point when he states:

> An examination of the variety of connecting terms and particles reveals that Galatians is, essentially, a single argument. We do not find in this epistle indicators of a shift in topic such as we find in First Corinthians. One does not have to agree with every dimension of Betz' argument to recognize the validity of his claim of unified rhetoric. At least by literary canons, Galatians is not a series of arguments about different matters but a series of sub-arguments about essentially one matter (which itself may, of course, have many ramifications).

In lieu of the in-depth rhetorical analysis in the next chapter that will seek to validate this perspective, two significant structural observations will have to suffice at this point. The first is that we encounter the phenomenon of *the bracketing* of the epistle to the Galatians with the prescript (1:1-5) and the postscript (6:11-18). E. W. Bullinger noticed the similarity between 1:1-5 and 6:17-18 and labeled it "complex correspondence of repeated alteration" (1968, 388). Betz calls it "the epistolary framework" and notes "that it appears almost as a kind of external bracket for the body of the letter" (1975, 355). Betz goes on to note the structural ramifications of this bracketing effect when he comments on the nature of the prescript (1:1-5):

> It is also interesting that at several points there are interrelations between the preface and the body of the letter. It is at these points that the theological tendencies and the purpose of the letter can be observed. (1979, 37)

Betz observes that the postscript (6:11-18) serves a similar purpose:

> It contains the interpretive clues to the understanding of Paul's major concerns in the letter as a whole and should be employed as the hermeneutical key to the intentions of the Apostle. (1979, 313)

Given the significance of these beginning and ending paragraphs for determining the purpose of Galatians and Paul's intentions, noting their three common topics should prove insightful.

First, the issue of *Paul's threatened apostolic authority* occurs in both passages. He takes a tour of Greek prepositions in describing his apostleship in 1:1: Παῦλος ἀπόστολος οὐκ ἀπ' ἀνθρώπων οὐδὲ δι' ἀνθρώπου ἀλλὰ διὰ Ἰησοῦ Χριστοῦ καὶ θεοῦ πατρός. Such a definitive description of his apostleship is unique among the salutations of the traditional thirteen-epistle Pauline corpus. Paul ends on an even more picturesque note of his authoritative identity in 6:17 where he flatly states that he bears in his body the στίγματα τοῦ Ἰησοῦ. He begins and ends Galatians with unique claims of identity with both the person and ministry of Jesus.

Second, *the Fatherhood of God* is emphasized in both the prescript and postscript of Galatians. Again, among the salutations of the Pauline corpus, this emphasis is unique in that θεοῦ πατρός (ἡμῶν) is mentioned three times. The norm in the salutation of eleven of the

epistles is that God's fatherhood is mentioned only one time. Second
Thessalonians has two occurrences (1:1, 2). But Galatians is *unique*
with its three-fold repetition within the five verses (1:1, 3, 4).
Apparently the underscoring of God's Fatherhood over the Galatian
ἀδελφοί (1:2) weighs heavily in Paul's thoughts as he begins this
particular epistle.

If the Galatians questioned Paul's apostolic status, and therefore his
gospel, then they probably questioned if Paul's gospel really did bring
them into the family of God and the community of His children. It
appears that Paul begins to provide reassurance of God's paternity
from the very beginning of this epistle. It is from θεοῦ πατρὸς ἡμῶν
καὶ κυρίου 'Ιησοῦ Χριστοῦ that "grace and peace" come in Paul's
typical salutation (1:3). In 6:16 it is the conditional blessing of "peace
and mercy" that are upon those who walk by the rule (τῷ κανόνι)
that Paul just explained in 6:14-15. It is also these who are
appositively called τὸν 'Ισραὴλ τοῦ θεοῦ (this will be discussed
more fully in Chapter 6). It is *these* people who deserve this term
denoting God's chosen people. He is *their* Father.

Third, *deliverance from the present evil age* (αἰῶνος) is tied to the
death of Jesus Christ and promised to His people in both the prescript
and postscript. In 1:4 Christ's giving of Himself was for the purpose
(ὅπως as a conjunction with the subjunctive) of delivering us from the
present aeon. In 6:14-15 Paul ties the deliverance from the κόσμος to
the cross of Christ and being a καινὴ κτίσις in contrast to being
circumcised as Paul's opponents asserted (6:12-13). Apparently, these
opponents offered an alternative means of deliverance from the tug of
the aeon or cosmos. That means was apparently connected to being
identified with Israel via circumcision. In contrast, the deliverance
Paul preaches identifies the Galatians primarily with the death of
Christ that created a new creation. As both J. Louis Martyn (1985b)
and Bernard H. Brinsmead (1982, 58-67) have observed, this
bracketing of the epistle with this apocalyptic language gives the
epistle an apocalyptic tone: "Thus the subject of his letter to the
Galatians is precisely an apocalypse, the apocalypse of Jesus Christ,
and specifically the apocalypse of his cross" (Martyn 1985b, 421).[13]

The point of this sketchy picture of prescript and postscript
parallelism is that Paul begins and ends his letter expressing concerns
about his threatened apostolic authority, the Fatherhood of God, and
the deliverance from this present age. If these really are the
theological tendencies and purpose of the epistle and reflect Paul's
major concerns in the letter as a whole, then the body of the letter in
between these brackets must give primary attention to the development

of these three points. This development, in turn, should reflect the major questions of the Galatians and should thereby give some indication of the identity of the opponents who raised these questions. If the first structural clue comes from the bracketing effect of the prescript and postscript that underscores the unitary nature of the problem in Galatia, then the second structural clue flows out of the first and bears great significance in helping to establish the identity of Paul's opponents. This second structural insight is simply that Gal 3-4 must be considered a significant and meaningful part of Paul's argument. These two chapters cannot be brushed aside as Schmithals does when he says Paul did not really understand his opponents' theology so that "it is indeed characteristic that this middle section of the Galatian epistle [3:1-5:12], in contrast to all other sections, contains hardly any direct references to the situation in Galatia" (1972, 41).

Betz realized that this section was the core of Paul's argument. Gal 3-4 was the *probatio* that followed the *propositio* of 2:15-21 and preceded the *exhortatio* of 5:1-6:10 (1979, 18-23). He had no other alternative in light of the structure of the epistle that emerged from his rhetorical analysis. Therefore, he was left to criticizing the persuasive value of rhetoric itself since "no kind of rational argument can be adequate with regard to the defense Paul must make" (1979, 25). Betz' solution is to see the epistle as functioning as a "magical letter" since Paul begins it with a curse and ends it with a conditional blessing (1979, 25). Since Paul allegedly "does not leave things to be decided by the reasonableness of the Galatians" (1979, 25), then the value of Gal 3-4 in his argumentation is greatly diminished in Betz' analysis. However, at best, this seems to be a very questionable view of Gal 3-4. Is it legitimate to appeal to the genre of a magic letter that is supposedly acting as some "supra-genre" at the *real* level of the persuasion of the Galatians? Indeed, is this legitimate when Betz himself admits that "no satisfactory investigation of the genre [of magical letter] exists" (1979, 25)? Is this not a similar response to Schmithals' where final appeal rests with an extra-textual entity to which there is no access?

Would not a simpler and less incredible conclusion be that Gal 3-4 *is* important in Paul's argumentation since it is the structural middle of his epistle? Even more importantly, it contains significant discussions of two of the three bracketing themes: the Fatherhood of God and deliverance from the present evil age. *The Fatherhood of God* permeates Gal 3-4 as the metaphoric umbrella of the section that covers the themes of sonship (3:15-29), heirship (4:1-7), and line of blessing (4:21-31). While the *deliverance theme* receives in-depth treatment in Gal 5-6, it is also a central part of Paul's argument in Gal 3-4 as he discusses possible perfection according to the flesh (σαρκὶ ἐπιτελεῖσθε in Gal 3:3). However, rather than deliverance, such a flesh-strategy will lead to the bondage of slavery in various forms (3:22-3; 4:1-11; 4:21-31). Without Gal 3-4 Paul's beginning and ending concerns with the themes of God's Fatherhood and deliverance from the present evil age would be developed very minimally. These chapters must be considered as primary data in the identification of Paul's opponents. If that is the case, then Robert Jewett's assertion (following H. J. Holtzmann's) is probably correct "that their mottoes were σπέρμα 'Αβραάμ (3:16) and 'Ιερουσαλήμ ἥτις ἐστιν μήτηρ ἡμῶν (4:26)" (Jewett 1971a, 200-201). Both mottoes represent opposition to Paul's viewpoint about the three bracketing themes of apostolic authority, God's Fatherhood, and present deliverance. Both mottoes are discussed by Paul in-depth in Gal 3-4.

Some who hold the Gnostic/Syncretistic Jewish Christian identity of Paul's opponents may be able to embrace all that I have concluded so far in terms of the three bracketing themes and the centrality of Gal 3-4 in Paul's argumentation. However, we must now part company. First, we part with those who hold the Gnostic identity because of the highly unlikely and extremely ill-fitting presence of Gnostics in Galatia (Wilson 1968; Jewett 1971a, 199-200).[14] Secondly, the more generic reason for separating from those who hold this third view is that I perceive the presence of antinomian or libertinistic elements in Paul's opponents to be fundamentally wrong-headed. If this is true, then both the two-opponent view of Lütgert and Ropes and the third view that flowed out of it can be rejected because they are founded upon the presupposition that the primary issue of Galatians is the antinomian or libertinistic threat.

In light of some widespread recent acceptance of the third view, how can I make such a brazen claim? I can make it because this Gnostic/Syncretistic Jewish Christian view is built upon the foundation of several verses that are all interpreted from the same faulty perspective. In particular, fundamental to this third view is the premise that these opponents of Paul did not want to keep all of the Law, but only that part of it that served their purposes: circumcision and sacred days. Hence, Paul had to remind them of the unity of the Mosaic Law and the obligation to the whole Law if one puts himself in submission to any part of it:

Gal 3:10 - For as many as are of the works of the Law are under a curse; for it is written, "CURSED IS EVERYONE WHO DOES NOT ABIDE BY ALL THINGS WRITTEN IN THE BOOK OF THE LAW, TO PERFORM THEM."

Gal 5:3 - And I testify again to every man who receives circumcision, that he is under obligation to keep the whole Law.

However, this is where the opponents apparently were caught in a serious conflict because they did not *want* to keep the law because of their basic antinomian and libertine desires:

Gal 5:13 - For you were called to freedom, brethren; only do not turn your freedom into an opportunity for the flesh, but through love serve one another.

Gal 6:13 - For those who are circumcised do not even keep the Law themselves, but they desire to have you circumcised, that they may boast in your flesh.

The evidence seems straightforward and irrefutable.   These opponents mixed nomistic theology with antinomistic lifestyles. But is this what Paul is really saying? I think not. Paul never says that his opponents lacked a *desire* for law obedience. In fact, he says just the opposite. Paul's opponents apparently held forth the ideal of a whole life under Torah's protection, such that the Galatians could be described as οἱ ὑπὸ νόμον θέλοντες εἶναι (4:21a). They were considering taking up the yoke (ζυγός) of the law, which Paul derisively describes as a ζυγῷ δουλείας in 5:1. "To take up a yoke" is a phrase for a life of submission in the New Testament.   In Matt 11:28-30 it refers to identification with and submission to Jesus.   In Acts 15:10 Peter refers to the identification with and submission to the Law as "a yoke which neither our fathers nor we have been able to bear." The term ζυγός itself is a neutral term and was also used throughout rabbinical literature as a symbol of obedience, not of oppression (Herford 1962, 70; Abrahams 1967, 4-14). When the yoke of Torah was referred to, it was seen as a gracious blessing compared to other possible yokes.   This well known quote from the Mishnah about the yoke of Torah from Pirqé 'Abot 3:5 is attributed to Rabbi Nehunia ben Haqqaneh, who was supposed to have been a young disciple of Rabbi Yohanan ben Zakkai (A.D. 1-80):

Whosoever accepts the yoke of the Law from him shall be removed the yoke of the kingdom and the yoke of mundane care, but he that casts off from him the yoke of the Law upon him shall be laid the yoke of the kingdom and the yoke of worldly care. (Translation from Blackman 1977, 4: 508)

While the final editorial form of this saying was probably completed about A.D. 250 (Neusner 1987, 71), traditional Jewish scholars have no difficulty accepting that the basic thrust of the original saying is at least as old as the first century (e.g., Abrahams 1967, 7 and Lerner 1987, 265-66). Therefore, Paul's reminder that the whole law is binding was probably not perceived as a negative statement within first century Judaism, and it certainly would not be perceived as a surprise to his opponents. But was it not necessary if these opponents do not even keep the Law (6:13)? Yes, it was necessary to make his point, but for different reasons than the advocates of the third view assume. Their assumption is that the reminders about the whole Law's binding nature were necessary because of the opponents' desire to disobey much of the Law (e.g., 5:13 and 6:13). However, Paul has already explained why the opponents do not even obey the Law. It is *not* from lack of desire to obey, but rather from an inherent inability to obey. Their failure to keep the Law is due to identifying with a community that is not aided by God's Spirit (e.g., 3:1-5). Therefore, it is unable to meet the demands of the Law.

In Gal 3:19-4:11 Paul has already attributed this inability to an earlier, preparatory, more immature period in God's redemptive program where enslavement to sin and failure were the norm (3:23; 4:3, 8-11). The opponents of Paul in Galatia were wanting to revert back in an anachronistic fashion to this period by their intense nomistic emphasis. With their commitment to Torah-observance comes the accompanying failure of the Law era: its shutting up under sin (3:22), its keeping in custody (3:23), its childish, slave-like state (4:1-3), and its enslavement to the elemental things of the world (4:8-10; cf. 4:3).[15] Those who prefer this kind of childish failure, evidenced by receiving circumcision (5:2), need to realize that they are subjecting themselves again to a yoke of slavery (5:1), are putting themselves under the obligation of the whole Law (5:3), and are severing themselves from Christ--the only One Who could set them free from the Law and failure (2:15-21; cf. Rom 8:1-4).

Therefore, the "opportunity for the flesh" in Gal 5:13 is not the turning of the freedom in Christ into license or libertinism, but it is the continued fleshly failure that characterized the Law era. Paul explains this further in 6:13 by stating that his opponents cannot keep the Law themselves, but they still want the Galatians to join them in this fleshly failure for the purpose (ἵνα) of "boasting in your σαρκί." The Law era and ἡ σάρξ go together as an inseparable twosome. This is expressed repeatedly by Paul in Galatians (e.g., 5:13 and 14; 5:17 and 18; 5:19-21 and 23; 6:12 and 13). The failure to tie νόμος and σάρξ together has needlessly bred this third view of Paul's opponents and has almost hopelessly muddied the waters about their identity. This failure has also greatly hindered a correct understanding of the σάρξ/πνεῦμα duality. An accurate, contextual understanding of the opponents should go a long way in helping to unravel the σάρξ/πνεῦμα issue.[16]

The Identity of the Galatian Opponents

We are now at a point to conclude who Paul's opponents in Galatia appear to be. The first or *Traditional View* seems correct: Paul's opponents were Jewish Christians who sought to "judaize" the Gentile Christians of Galatia.[17] In spite of over seventy years of scholarly attacks, this identity of Paul's opponents has not been effectively overturned. The Judaizers' identity best satisfies the "mirror-reading" criteria and limitations. John Barclay (1987, 86-90; 1988, 36-74) also reaches the conclusion that the troublers were probably Jewish Christians who questioned the adequacy of both Paul's apostolic credentials and the gospel he preached. They also apparently made circumcision the central issue among the Gentile Christians of Galatia because it was the classic symbol for one who was choosing to live life like a Jew (᾽Ιουδαϊκῶς ζῶς and ἰουδαΐζειν in Gal 2:14):

> In fact Paul's concern about "works of the law" (3:1-10) and his extended arguments to prove the temporary validity of the law (3:6-4:11), taken together with remarks like 4:21, make it highly probable that the opponents wanted the Galatians to observe the law as circumcised proselytes....(Barclay, 1987, 86)

Barclay goes on to conclude that:

> Taking the argument of the letter as a whole, there is sufficient evidence that the Galatians were informed of (and responded warmly to) the requirements of Torah-observance as the hallmark of the people of God. (1987, 87)

Such a conclusion and the lack of viable support for a Gnostic or libertine identity make the presence of such opponents in Galatia or the presence of a dual nomistic/libertinistic threat (e.g., Jewett 1971a, 209-12) totally unwarranted and unnecessary (Lategan 1992, 260-1). The struggles over ethics and law in Gal 5-6 can be explained much more naturally and holistically within the context of Galatians with a unified Judaizers' threat in the background. In fact, one of the by-products of this book will be the underscoring of this traditional identity even more strongly than before by tying Gal 5-6 much more closely and logically to Gal 3-4. My premise is that rather than stepping back and defensively clarifying and limiting the boundaries of Christian freedom in Gal 5-6, Paul is actually continuing his attack on the Judaizers in an overt and aggressive manner--only in the area of ethics and behavior now. This heightened sense of continuity underscores the identity of the opponents as Judaizers. Such continuity will also serve to undercut the predominant understanding of the σάρξ/πνεῦμα internal duality which arose in part due to a *failure* in understanding the proper linkage of Gal 3-4 and 5-6 in Paul's argument.

These conclusions do not mean that we have satisfied all of the questions about the Judaizers' origin and motivation. Because of the emphasis in Gal 1-2 and 4 on Jerusalem and Judea, it is not inconceivable to suspect some link to the Jerusalem church. Jewett (1971a, 204-8) asserts that Jewish Christians in Judea, stimulated by Zealot pressure in the forties and fifties, responded to this threat of persecution (Gal 6:12) and launched a nomistic campaign among the Gentile Christians in areas that included Galatia. As Barclay has pointed out (1987, 88), the weakness of this thesis is the very slender thread of Gal 6:12 from which it hangs. Fung more pointedly refutes it based on the sharply antithetical relationship between the Zealots and the Church at the outbreak of the Jewish War and based on the Zealots' lack of interest in bringing Gentile Christians to the "perfection" of Gal 3:3 (1988, 6-7).

Perhaps a more viable origin and motivation is that suggested by J. Louis Martyn that the Judaizing threat came from a Law-observant mission among the Gentiles by Jewish Christian "Teachers" (not "opponents"):

> In the main it is not they who are reacting to Paul's theology, but rather he who is reacting to theirs. To be sure, the Galatians heard Paul's gospel first and only later that of the Teachers. But the finely formed theology of the Teachers is best understood on the

hypothesis that the order of events in Galatia is for them atypical.
Elsewhere they will have worked in virgin fields, impelled not by a
desire to correct Paul, but by a passion to share with the entire world
the only gift they believed to have the power to liberate humankind
from the grip of evil, the Law of God's Messiah. In the full sense of
the expression, therefore, they represent a law-observant mission to
Gentiles, a mission inaugurated not many years after the death of
Jesus. (Martyn 1985a, 323)

While this thesis is attractive and lessens the malevolence of the
Judaizers' motives, it does not lessen the significance of their
theological error. Additionally, the thesis cannot really be validated
based on first century data, but is a reading from second century
Jewish Christian documents back into the first (Martyn 1985a, 310-
12). Therefore, it must remain in the category of an attractive
possibility. However, this thesis does highlight the fact that whatever
the specific motivation of these Jewish Christian opponents was, *they*
obviously viewed their cause as righteous and biblical. Their apparent
use of the Abraham and Sarah-Hagar narratives seems to point to such
a perspective as numerous writers have observed. (e.g., Barrett 1982;
King 1983, 361-69)

Given that the Judaizers felt that it was imperative that Gentiles be
saved in continuity with God's people Israel and in accordance with
the Law and customs of Moses via the proselyte model, the final issue
of their geographical origin is worthy of some focus. There is no
overwhelming consensus about their origin. Kirsopp Lake (1979, 215)
identified them as local *Jews* who were proselytizing the Gentile
Christians.   Joseph Tyson (1968, 252-54) correctly identifies the
opponents as Jewish Christians, but follows Lake's lead in arguing that
they were native to Galatia.   Johannes Munck's view of Judaizing
Gentile Christians also places the opponents' origin within Galatia
from within Paul's own ministry (1959, 87-100, 130-34).   The
difficulty with the Galatian origin, as many have observed (e.g.,
Martyn 1985a, 313), is that Paul seems to refer to the agitators as
coming into the churches of the area from the outside (e.g., 3:1-5; 4:8-
16; 5:7-8) and he underscores their "outsider" identity by referring to
them in third person pronouns, while he refers to the Galatians in the
second person (e.g., 4:17).

Based on the sketchy external and internal evidence, the best
choice of the origin of these mistaken Jewish Christians is Jerusalem
or possibly Judea.   Externally, two passages in Acts point to the
presence of these very strong Law-observant attitudes in the Jewish

Christians in Jerusalem/Judea. In Acts 21:17-26 Paul first arrives in Jerusalem on his collection visit after his third missionary journey. The next day he is informed by James and the Jerusalem elders of the animosity toward him among the local Jewish Christians because of his perceived threat to traditional Jewish Christianity:

> You see, brother, how many thousands there are among the Jews of those who have believed, and *they are all zealous for the law,* and they have been told about you, that you are teaching all the Jews who are among the Gentiles to forsake Moses, telling them not to circumcise their children nor to walk according to the customs. What, then, is to be done? They will certainly hear that you have come. (Acts 21:20b-22; emphasis is mine)

In light of the chronological work of Knox (1987, 68), Jewett (1979, foldout page), Luedemann (1984, 262-63), Hoehner (1989), and Riesner (1994), Paul's final visit to Jerusalem is dated between A.D. 54-57. This visit could have been as much as eight years after the Jerusalem Conference of Acts 15. Even if the elapsed time is half of that amount, it demonstrates the continuation of a powerful, Law-observant wing in the Jerusalem Church. It is apparently these same Jewish Christians who are ζηλωταὶ τοῦ νόμου and whom we see causing trouble a few years earlier in Antioch in Acts 15:1: "And some men came down from Judea and began teaching the brethren, 'Unless you are circumcised according to the custom of Moses, you cannot be saved.'"[18]

After Paul and Barnabas greatly dissented with these teachers (Acts 15:2), the Jerusalem Conference was convened to settle the issue. The discussion continued at the conference: "But certain ones of the sect of the Pharisees who had believed, stood up, saying, 'It is necessary to circumcise them, and to direct them to observe the Law of Moses'" (Acts 15:5). After the conference decided against such a notion, it recorded its decision and addressed it to the Gentiles in the churches of Antioch, Syria, and Cilicia (Acts 15:23) and purposely distanced from the troublers: "Since we have heard that some of our number to whom we gave no instruction have disturbed you with their words, unsettling your souls,..." (Acts 15:24). While admitting to being the origin of these Pharisaic Jewish Christians (τινὲς ἐξ ἡμῶν [ἐξελθόντες]), the Jerusalem Church disavowed any authorization of them or their teaching (οἷς οὐ διεστειλάμεθα). Considering that this external data sounds very much like the problems in Galatia, it is not unreasonable to conclude that the Acts 15 and 21 troublers and the Galatian troublers share a common origination and "they represent a

wider group of ritually strict Jewish Christians" (Ellis 1968, 391; see also Bruce 1985b, esp. 651-61; cf. Wedderburn 1993).
Internally, the epistle to the Galatians strongly supports such a correlation. Given Paul's recurring emphasis on Jerusalem/Judea in Gal 1-2 and 4, it is not difficult to conclude that the Pharisaic troublemakers from Jerusalem and Judea kept going past Antioch, Syria, and Cilicia into Galatia. This is why Paul persistently strikes at their home base and at those Jerusalem pillars (στῦλοι) to whom they fallaciously appeal for support of their position (cf. Acts 15:24). This may also explain why Paul recounts the confrontation in Antioch that was so embarrassing to Cephas and Barnabas (Gal 2:11-21). His point is that the Judaizers' view has *already* been rejected at one of their prior stops: the most prominent Gentile church, Antioch of Syria. That rejection was *public in scope* (ἔμπροσθεν πάντων--2:14), *apostolic in authority* (involving both Peter and Paul), and *apparently accepted as legitimate* (else Paul would not have appealed to it as being authoritative for the Galatian situation).

Only one last point needs to be made about these Jerusalem/Judea-based opponents. This involves the motive for their apparent claims against Paul. As Daniel H. King has observed in his fine analysis of the situation (1983, 349-61), these Pharisaic Judaizers made three main claims against Paul:

1. Paul was on their side but trimmed the demands of the gospel to please his hearers. (1:10)
2. He received his gospel from the same Jerusalem authorities who supported their mission. (1:18-2:9; and 1:11)
3. In Paul's work as a representative of the "pillars" (1:12, 15-19), he began a work which they had come to complete. (3:3) (351)

As King notes, these Jewish Christians from the sect of the Pharisees expressed a conception of revelation typical of Second Temple Judaism (1983, 352-54). Revelation flowed from the seat of authority (Jerusalem) where Rabbi Jesus had left his disciples (the Jerusalem apostles) to carry on the line of tradition. Paul was a *tanna,* another link in the line of tradition, who had broken the chain by not faithfully nor accurately passing on the tradition. Assuming that Paul was a pupil of the Jerusalem apostles, the Judaizers apparently accused him of failing in his duty to transmit the exact words of Jesus' tradition as it had been mediated to Paul by the apostles. Such "iterative incompetence" was viewed as one of the gravest offenses according to ancient rabbinical rules (e.g., m. 'Ed. 1:3; b. Sabb. 15a.; m. 'Abot 3:8

and 6:6). The Judaizers had to correct and fill in the breach in Paul's preaching of the Jesus tradition among the Galatians. It is to this attempt to correct and complete his gospel that Paul responds in Galatians. In light of these charges against him, Paul's purpose in Gal 1-2 is now quite understandable:

> Contra the insinuations of the agitators, he maintained that his gospel was not of human origin; Christ had communicated it to him in person. He was also careful to assure his readership the pillars of the church in Jerusalem had recognized its truth and his right to preach it in its present form. He denied the charge of tanna-oriented dependency, but also maintained consistency with Jerusalem on all important matters. (King 1983, 354)

Paul's reasoning in Gal 1:11-2:14 also reveals that in the fourteen to seventeen years following his conversion he spent time in Arabia and Damascus (1:17) and Syria and Cilicia (1:21). He had three contacts with *some* of the Jerusalem apostles for *brief* periods of time in Jerusalem (1:18-20 and 2:1-10) and Antioch (2:11-14). This contact was too infrequent and too brief for the tannaitic process of tedious repetition and memorization to occur. This obvious fact coupled with Jesus Christ's direct teaching of Paul (1:11-12) and the Jerusalem acceptance of Paul's gospel (1:22-24 and 2:7-10) powerfully refute the Judaizers' claims against him. All of the particulars of Gal 1-2 can most simply and coherently be explained in light of this reconstruction.[19]

VI. Conclusion

The identity of Paul's opponents in Galatia is a crucial issue in understanding Paul's use of σάρξ and πνεῦμα in Gal 5-6 because it provides the historical backdrop for understanding why he made these terms so central to the development of his argument. It is the integrating of this historical perspective with the lexical and theological understanding of σάρξ and πνεῦμα in Gal 3-6 that unlocks a more accurate view of the terms. The traditional internal dualistic view essentially assumes that Paul is using σάρξ and πνεῦμα in a metaphysical sense. In other words he is supposedly looking at persons *vertically* and observing two aspects or parts of persons. One can see how σάρξ and πνεῦμα can easily become "natures" or "capacities" within persons when this vertical perspective is assumed. A fundamental proposition of this paper is that this so-called vertical perspective is wrongly assumed in both the lexical and theological handling of σάρξ and πνεῦμα. Of course, this proposition will have to be validated in the following chapters. In place of this metaphysical or vertical view of σάρξ and πνεῦμα, I will set forth an historical or *horizontal* view of these terms. Since Paul's opponents are arguing for identification with the ongoing historical entity of Israel, then it seems reasonable to think that his refutation of such a view must be basically framed within similar historical and theological parameters. Such historical/theological argumentation has always been readily recognized in Gal 1-4. My premise is that this horizontal or historical perspective continues unabated even through Gal 5-6. The terms σάρξ and πνεῦμα in Gal 5-6 are immensely significant terms to Paul because they identify the competing historical manifestations of the true people of God. In Galatia they specifically serve as the identifying marks of the communities of the Judaizers and Paul. Further analysis of the argument of Galatians and Paul's use of these important terms in the following chapters will seek to validate these identities.

Notes

[1]As noted below (note 3), while Ridderbos' redemptive historical interpretation was the impetus for and the general framework of this study, he nevertheless seems to hold to some form of the internal duality view in Gal 5-6 (e.g., 1975, 254). While the interpretive perspective advocated in this book is a redemptive historical one, it is not to be conflated with an "apocalyptic" view of Paul, per se. On the abuses of this latter perspective, see Matlock 1996.

[2]The option facing the Galatians is *not* between the Judaizers' clearly-formulated objective standards of Torah versus the mystical, subjective standards of "walking by the Spirit," as many commentators have suggested. For example, Burton 1921, 298, says "Paul enjoins them to continue to govern their conduct by the inward impulse of the Spirit." Rather, the option is between two equally-objective standards. On the one hand is Israel's Law which apparently includes the attached Oral Law of these Pharisaic Judaizers (e.g., 5:2). On the other hand is the Law of Christ (Gal. 6:2) with its greater relational emphasis (e.g., 5:13-15, 22-26; 6:1-10).

[3]In fairness to Herman Ridderbos, it appears that he modified his view of σάρξ in later works ([1957] 1982 and 1975). "Flesh" is now seen

> not primarily [as] an existential notion, but [as] a redemptive-historical one. Flesh is the mode of existence of man and the world before the fullness of times appeared. Flesh is man and the world in the powers of

darkness (1982, 52).

It is Ridderbos' later perspective that has been the most influential source in shaping this book's thesis and it is this perspective that I will attempt to validate and enrich in Gal 5-6. However, in seeking to validate this redemptive historical perspective in Gal 5-6, I will be going beyond what appears to be Ridderbos' understanding of this specific passage (e.g., 1975, 254) and will be applying the redemptive historical perspective in an even more pervasive manner than he did. See also Matera 1992, 192-212 and Dunn 1993b, 284-318 for perspectives similar to mine. In particular, see Fee 1994a and 1994b who calls this redemptive historical perspective "eschatological."

[4]The *Computer-Kondordanz zum Novum Testamentum Graece* (Bachmann und Slaby 1985) and *Vollstandige Konkordanz zum griechischen Neuen Testament* (Aland 1980) both list eighteen occurrences of σάρξ in Galatians.

[5]Burton 1921, 492 sees this sense achieved by metonymy: "the basis or result of natural generation." Later on I will quibble with this particular sense.

[6]Burton 1921, 492 again notes that this is by metonymy: "the creature side, the corporeally conditioned aspect of life." Again I will beg to differ with this sense at a later point.

[7]While there is no complete agreement of which occurrences of σάρξ fit into this ethical category, Ladd is representative when he lists the following as the "ethical use of the term": Rom 6:19; 7:5, 18,25; 8:3, 4, 5, 6, 7, 8, 9, 12, 13; 1 Cor 5:5; 2 Cor 1:17; 11:18; Gal 3:3; 5:13, 16, 17, 19, 24; 6:8; Eph 2:3; Col 2:11, 13, 18, 23 (1974, 469, note 44). Compare the lists in Davies 1957, 163; Robinson 1926, 114; and Burton 1918, 186.

[8]Additionally, the works of Nida and Taber 1969, 16-17 and Kraft 1979, 264-69 speak to the range of dynamic English equivalents in translating σάρξ in the New Testament. Their surveying of approximately fifty Bible translators on this topic led to the consensus that "flesh" is an "unnatural and misleading" translation in passages like Rom 8:3 (which parallels the usages in Gal 5-6). These authors advocate translations of σάρξ in these passages with what they deem the more contextually consistent terms "lower nature" (NEB) or "human nature" (TEV). While I do not necessarily disagree with these scholars' arguments for dynamic equivalence in translating, I would argue that their preferred equivalents for σάρξ are more heavily influenced by *their theological context* than by the actual verbal or cultural context of the New Testament passages.

[9]On the paralleling of the accounts in Acts and Paul's letters, see Wenham 1993, 215-58.

[10]In fairness to Marxsen, it should be noted that he changed this view in the fourth edition of *Einleitung in das Neue Testament* (Gütersloh: Gerd Mohn, 1978) 56-71 to one similar to Betz'.

[11]This is also noted by Gaventa 1991, 148.

[12]Also helpful in giving an overview of several different methodological approaches in identifying Paul's opponents is Berger 1980.

[13]As Gaventa 1991 has noted, this also gives Galatians a Christocentrism within which Paul's remarks about the Mosaic Law should be interpreted.

[14]Both Wilson and Jewett point out that the very meager information about these late first century or early second century syncretists represents a later stage of development in Gnosticism. This should not be read back into the mid-first century. Also, the later Gnostic interest in circumcision was as a symbol of transcendence over the bodily sphere. This emphasis is not the least bit comparable to the Judaizers' emphasis on circumcision as an ethnic identifier essential for salvation. For a helpful background description of the province of Galatia, see Hansen 1994b, 377-95.

[15]See Bundrick 1991 for a defense of the "elemental teachings" interpretation. Preferably, see Wright 1994 and especially Arnold 1996 for a convincing defense of the "evil spirits' interpretation of τά στοιχεῖα τοῦ κόσμου in Gal 4:1-10. Cf. Rusam 1992.

[16]Accurately seeing the continuity in Paul's argument from Gal 1-4 to 5-6 in addressing the fleshliness of the Judaizers is G. Howard 1979, 11-17, B. H. Brinsmead 1982, 164-92, D. J. Lull 1980, 113-30, J. Barclay 1988, 106-77, and Fee 1994b, 420-5.

[17]For three recent treatments of the identity of Paul's opponents see Walter 1986, Suhl 1987, 3082-3088, and Lea 1994. For an earlier, but still helpful work, see Hawkins 1971.

[18]The Western text (D) of Acts 15:1-5 makes the Pharisaic identity even stronger with several extensive additions. See Metzger 1971, 426-28 and Epp 1966, 100-104.

[19]At the risk of stating the obvious, the epistemological and hermeneutical maxim of "simplicity" is worth emphasizing at this point. It is that the "simplest" hypothesis fitting the facts is the best hypothesis. This goes back to William of Ockham (1285-1349), author of "Ockham's Razor", which is widely paraphrased as "entities are not to be multiplied beyond necessity" (Bynum, Browne, Porter 1981, 386-87). While fully recognizing the complexities of persons and communities, the principle of *simplicity* can still be applied in a non-reductionist manner. In hypothesizing about the identity of Paul's opponents in Galatia, the traditional Judaizer identity is the simplest hypothesis that allows for the human complexities associated with the clash of cultures and traditions. There is no need to multiply other entities or identities.

Chapter 2

A Rhetorical Analysis of Galatians
and
the Flesh/Spirit Conflict

I. Introduction

To be properly understood, Paul's use of σάρξ and πνεῦμα in Gal 5-6 must be set within the context of the entire epistle of Galatians. Specifically, the role of Gal 5-6 within the argument or rhetoric of the epistle must be clearly determined. As the rhetorical role of Gal 5-6 emerges, an accurate identification of these chapters within the epistolary structure of Galatians should also emerge. This twofold determination is the purpose of this chapter.

While rhetorical criticism and epistolary criticism[1] are normally applied in separate processes, there is great need for the integration of these two hermeneutical tools within a single analysis. In responding to Bernard H. Brinsmead's analysis of Galatians (1982), David Aune has noted the necessity of such integration:

> The chief value of this book lies in the author's persuasive argument that the letter form (in view of the flexibility of its use) cannot be used as the hermeneutical key for understanding compositions like Galatians. One must, of necessity, turn to other genres taken into the letter form (such as those from oratory) in order to understand adequately NT letters (1984, 147).

As many have noted (e.g., Betz 1975), the apologetic nature and persuasive intent of Galatians seem to indicate that the epistle can legitimately be analyzed and described according to the canons of ancient rhetoric[2]. In fact, it is the first of the New Testament epistles to be submitted to such a hermeneutical process. Assuming for the moment that rhetorical analysis is appropriate for Galatians, one should expect that it will reveal the extent to which Paul wed oratorical or rhetorical genres with the epistolary genre in Galatians. It should thereby provide some additional hermeneutical keys for understanding the contextual setting of Gal 5-6. However, the anticipated difficulty of integrating rhetorical and epistolary analyses is having to answer, "Which *schema* is the dog and which is the tail and which wags which?"[3] For our purposes the rhetorical analysis will provide the primary *schema*.

II. A Description of Rhetorical Analysis

Rhetoric then may be defined as the faculty of discovering the possible means of persuasion in reference to any subject whatever (Aristotle 1926, 1.2.1/p. 15).

The task of the public speaker is to discuss capably those matters which law and custom have fixed for the uses of citizenship, and to secure as far as possible the agreement of his hearers ([Cicero] *Rhetorica ad Herennium* 1954, 1.2.1/p. 5)

Finally, those critics who hold that the aim of rhetoric is *to think and speak rightly*, were on the correct track (Quintilian 1920, 2.15.37/1:317)

These ancient descriptions of "rhetoric" by Aristotle, the author of *Rhetorica ad Herennium*, and Quintilian reveal that rhetoric was viewed essentially as the art of persuasive thinking and communicating. Quintilian's very helpful survey of the views of rhetoric within the handbooks of his day reveal that this persuasion was generally in the form of an oration (1920, 2.14-15/1:297-319).

Modern works on rhetoric recognize that while

classical rhetoric was not as monolithic in its rationale as some histories have led us to believe, the system of rhetoric that prevailed in the schools for the next 2000 years was remarkably uniform in its main orientation and in a good many of its accidental features (Corbett 1969, xii).

Because of this uniformity, modern scholars still define "rhetoric" as "the art of persuasive oratory" (Corbett 1969, xi; cf. Lyons 1994) or as "a communicator's *intentional* use of language and other symbols to *influence* or persuade selected receivers to act, believe, or feel the way the communicator desires in problematic situations" (Cathcart 1981, 2). "Rhetoric is that quality in discourse by which a speaker or writer seeks to accomplish his purposes" (Kennedy 1984, 3). Therefore, "rhetorical analysis" is the attempt "to understand *how* or *why* a message was *effective*" (Cathcart 1981, 4). This hermeneutical analysis

> takes the text as we have it, whether the work of a single author or the product of editing, and looks at it from the point of view of the author's or editor's intent, the unified results, and how it would be perceived by an audience of near contemporaries (Kennedy 1984, 4).

Given these basic descriptions of rhetoric and rhetorical analysis, the question of the Apostle Paul's exposure to rhetoric and rhetorical training is often raised. The issue is one of the appropriateness of using classical rhetorical canons to evaluate an epistle written by a Jewish Christian missionary. There are critics like Philip Kern (1994) who strongly deny that Paul wrote in conformity with the Greco-Roman rhetoric. However, E. A. Russell is typical of those critics who simply question the value of rhetorical analysis on one of Paul's epistles. He raises four significant objections to H. D. Betz' application of rhetorical analysis to Galatians (1984, 157-61):

> 1. The strange terminology of rhetorical analysis seems to obscure rather than illumine the text. In other words, at the pragmatic level it does not seem to be helpful to the reader.

> 2. Did Paul really sit down and dictate Galatians with the carefully shaped apologetic structure already in place? Does not the passionate, deeply concerned, fierce, uninhibited language of the epistle militate against Paul's preoccupation with the literary and rhetorical concerns?

> 3. Did Paul really make use of a Greek or Latin apologetic genre? Betz can offer no single instance of an apologetic genre with which to compare Galatians. Also, this genre ignores elements in the epistle that are not apologetic at all.

> 4. As Wayne Meeks had pointed out elsewhere, Betz (1973, 88-108) treats his *theory* of apologetic genre as if it were *accepted fact* in his

later arguments. If this theory fails, then much of his argumentation will have to be seriously qualified.

While agreeing with Russell's specific criticisms of Betz' use of the apologetic genre, I would nevertheless want to counter Russell's arguments against the general use of rhetorical analysis. A twofold response quickly comes to mind. First, given the broad, pervasive, and foundational nature of rhetorical training in the Mediterranean world, it is *extremely likely* that the Apostle Paul was trained rhetorically in Tarsus or Jerusalem.[4] Even if this is not the case, he may have "picked up his rhetorical skills during his career as an itinerant preacher and disputant, in debate and possibly by self-tuition" (Forbes 1986, 23). Both Forbes (1986, 22-24) and Brinsmead (1982, 45-46) launch passionate arguments that Paul's exposure was actually through a full education in formal Greek rhetoric. Such rhetoric had already penetrated the Jewish system of education as E. A. Judge has noted:

> The question of Paul's educational level is probably less clearcut than often thought, but the answer simpler. It has traditionally been posed in terms of Tarsus or Jerusalem, with the balance now tipped strongly in favour of the latter. But this choice may have set a false trail. To have been brought up in Tarsus need not have committed Paul to a full rhetorical education, let alone a philosophical one (both of which were a matter of tertiary training involving much time and money), while being in Jerusalem need not have excluded him from at least a general acquaintance with the Greek cultural tradition. Half of Gamaliel's pupils are said to have been trained in the wisdom of the Greeks (1972, 29).

Respected Jewish scholar David Daube has gone much further in admitting the influence of Greek rhetorical education upon early Rabbinical thought. Daube has argued that by 30 B.C., when Hillel set forth his seven main ideas and seven hermeneutical rules[5], both of these fundamental expressions of Judaism had already been derived from Hellenistic rhetoric (1949, 239-64). Daube's paralleling of these hermeneutical rules with amazingly similar rules from Greek rhetorical sources is particularly persuasive (1949, 251-60). Even as a rabbinical student Paul may have been exposed to Hellenistic rhetoric as a foundational element of his training.

In arguing for the legitimacy of the rhetorical analysis of Galatians, there is not just this first response of historical justification, but there is also a second response--that of philosophical justification as George A. Kennedy has argued:

Though rhetoric is colored by the traditions and conventions of the society in which it is applied, it is also a universal phenomenon which is conditioned by basic workings of the human mind and heart and by the nature of all human society. Aristotle's objective in writing his *Rhetoric* was not to describe Greek rhetoric, but to describe this universal facet of human communication (Kennedy 1984, 10).

If, in fact, the use of rhetoric and the analysis of such use is a universal and transcultural phenomenon, then Russell's criticism of such use is undercut. Two concessions must be made in concluding this, however. One is that the universal nature of rhetoric is greatly clouded when only the classical Greek and Latin rhetorical terms are used. If one persists in using this somewhat esoteric terminology (at least it is esoteric to those of us who have been deprived of a classical education!), then he should explain that this is just one cultural expression of universal patterns of thought. This admission avoids an over-dependence upon the historical justification of Paul's training in rhetoric, even though it is probably legitimate. A second concession is that the supposed "universal" nature of rhetoric may also somewhat cloud the issue. The limitation of the rhetorical phenomenon to Western culture and those cultures greatly influenced by Western culture may be a safer and less ethnocentric way to express the widespread appearance of rhetoric until its true universal aspect can be validated.[6] Even with this limitation, however, the influence of the Greek education system upon Jewish culture is well established (cf. Judge 1972, 30, note 60; cf. Fairweather 1994a, 22-38).

III. The Procedure of Rhetorical Analysis

We saw in the previous section that use of rhetorical analysis on Galatians is justified on the historical grounds of Paul's probable exposure to rhetorical training, even within the confines of a Jewish education, and also upon the philosophical grounds of the "universal" nature of rhetoric within Western-influenced cultures. By beginning to lay out some of the procedure of rhetorical analysis, we should be convinced even more of the validity of this enterprise as the rhetorical aspects of Galatians are briefly illumined. However, in using rhetorical categories as an analytical lens through which to view this epistle, we should stop short of assuming that Paul is consciously conforming his argument to the ancient rhetorical schema. Rather, it appears that Paul's use of rhetorical figures is less formal and more dynamic than commentators like Betz have proposed (see Classen 1991, 1993 and Fairweather 1994a, b).

David Greenwood has spoken clearly and concisely to the issue of the logical procedure of rhetorical analysis:

> The first concern of the rhetorical critic is to define the limits of the literary unit, his second is to recognize the structure of a composition and to discern the configuration of its component parts, noting the different rhetorical devices that it contains (1970, 418).

While showing good sensitivity to the circular process of any hermeneutical analysis, George A. Kennedy expands Greenwood's suggested procedure for rhetorical analysis to six different stages (1984, 33-38):

> 1. Determine the *rhetorical unit* to be studied, which corresponds to the pericope in form criticism.

> 2. Define the *rhetorical situation* of the unit. This roughly corresponds to the Sitz im Leben of form criticism.

> 3. In many rhetorical situations the speaker may face one overriding *rhetorical problem* that may be particularly visible at the beginning of the discourse.

> 4. Determine which of the three *species of rhetoric* the rhetorical unit fits--judicial, deliberative, or epideictic.

> 5. Consider the *arrangement of material* in the text in terms of its subdivisions, persuasive effect of the parts, their coordination, devices of style, etc.

> 6. *Review the process* of analysis by looking back over the entire unit and reviewing its success in addressing the rhetorical situation and what the implications may be for the speaker or audience.

This six-stage procedure will be the procedure employed in our analysis of Galatians.

IV. Stages 1-4 in the Rhetorical Analysis of Galatians: Determining the Rhetorical Unit, Situation, Problem, and Species

We can confidently assume that Galatians is the *rhetorical unit* to be analyzed. However, in doing this first stage of rhetorical analysis a brief word about the nature of this unit of text is needed. Paul addressed the Galatian epistles to the ἐκκλησίας (Gal 1:2) of Galatia. This almost certainly means that the epistle was designed to be read aloud in these assemblies.[7]   In this sense Galatians functions like a speech and thereby emphasizes linear presentation:

> the audience hears the words in progression without opportunity to review what has been said earlier, and an orally received text is characterized by a greater degree of repetition than is a text intended to be read privately (Kennedy 1984, 37).

Martyn (1991, 161) has also noted,

> Paul wrote Galatians in the confidence that *God* intended to cause a certain event *to occur* in the Galatian congregations when Paul's messenger read the letter aloud to them. Let me suggest, then, that the theology of Galatians is focused on that *aural event, as it was intended and actively anticipated by Paul,* an event closely related to what one may call the letter's argument, but not identical with it (emphasis is his).

While the rhetorical unit of Galatians has some of the features of an epistle, particularly in its prescript and postscript (cf. Brinsmead 1982, 57-67), the bulk of the epistle (1:6-6:10) has more of the features of a speech than an epistle. In fact, modern rhetoricians view Galatians and all or parts of other Pauline epistles from this oration-perspective and work within the framework of tracing the "argumentation," rather than from within the traditional perspective of literary theory (e.g., Wuellner 1977, 152-53).   In their analyses argumentation is viewed as the use of discourse "to influence the intensity of an audience's adherence to certain theses" (Perelman and Olbrechts-Tyteca 1969, 14).[8]   These features of argumentation within Galatians and its obvious public and oral nature make it a prime candidate for rhetorical analysis. The rhetorical situation of Galatians underscores this fact.

The second stage in rhetorical analysis is defining the *rhetorical situation* or essentially the Sitz im Leben that gave rise to the discourse. In his definitive article entitled "The Rhetorical Situations," Lloyd F. Bitzer formally defined such a situation as

> a complex of persons, events, objects and relations presenting an actual or potential exigence which can be completely or partially

removed if discourse, introduced into the situation, can so constrain human decision or action as to bring about the significant modification of the exigence (1968, 6).

Bitzer goes on to define any "exigence" as "an imperfection marked by urgency" (1968, 6). To be a *rhetorical* exigence it must be capable of being modified only by means of the discourse and not by other action other than that advocated in the discourse. Additionally, there is generally "at least one controlling exigence which functions as the organizing principle: it specifies the audience to be addressed and the change to be effected" (Bitzer 1968, 7).[9] Determining this controlling "imperfection marked by urgency" corresponds to the third stage of Kennedy's rhetorical analysis which is determining the *rhetorical problem*.

When applying these insights to the rhetorical unit of Galatians to determine the *rhetorical situation* that called forth this discourse and the *rhetorical problem* that functions as an organizing principle, the conclusions reached in the first chapter about the identity of Paul's opponents come to bear. Specifically, the rhetorical situation is the entry into Galatia of Jewish Christian "teachers," apparently from Jerusalem or Judea, who advocate the long-held Jewish model of Gentile attachment to ethnic Israel via becoming proselytes. In the words of Galatians these Gentiles are being "judaized" or taught that they must Ἰουδαϊκῶς ζῆν if they are to be considered a part of God's people (Gal 2:14). These teachers also must have overtly taught or at least inferred that Paul's apostolic credentials were inadequate and his gospel was a distortion of the tradition that had been handed down to him from the Jerusalem apostles. He was, therefore, an untrustworthy *tanna* who distorted and contradicted the "true gospel" represented by the Twelve and themselves (King 1983, 349-61). Therefore, they, the Judaizers, had come to supplement Paul's trimmed down gospel and to bring to completion the Galatians' salvation (Gal 3:3) (Barclay 1987, 86-90). Their appeal to the Jerusalem apostles was, of course, fallacious (Acts 15:24), but the Galatian Christians apparently did not know that yet.

The third stage of rhetorical analysis, determining the *rhetorical problem*, naturally flows out of the determination of the second stage. Specifically, the rhetorical problem of Galatians that functions as an organizing principle is twofold. Paul was responding to the two problems of *identity* and *behavior* or *ethics* created by his Judaizing opponents. This understanding means that the traditional view of the problem of Galatians as being primarily one of justification by faith versus justification by works (e.g., Luther [1850] 1979, xi-xviii) should be nuanced somewhat. While emphasizing justification by faith, Paul was addressing the broader issues of Gentile incorporation into the church and how the behavior or ethics of these Gentile converts was to be constrained. Others have previously nuanced the traditional understanding of the main problem in Galatians (e.g., Betz 1979, 2833 and Davies 1984, 172-88) While this nuancing is frequently overstated, it is necessary nevertheless.[10] A particularly helpful compromise is set forth by T David Gordon who proposes this expression of the problem in Galatia:

> One can now see that Paul's polemic at Galatia may best be understood as a polemic regarding identity symbols. Shall the people of God be identified by Torah or by Christ? Which symbol is appropriate for the present redemptive-historical circumstances? The polemic is not in the first place soteriological (that is, faith or works as instrument of justification) but eschatological (whether God has fulfilled the promises to Abraham by means of the Christ-event) and, by consequence, ecclesiological (whether the believing Gentiles are in fact full members of the covenant community) (Gordon 1987, 40).

John Barclay echoes this understanding of the problem and appropriately adds the second aspect of the rhetorical problem:

> The issues at stake in the Galatian crisis were *the identity* of these Galatian Christians and their *appropriate patterns of behaviour.* should they regularize and confirm their place among God's people by getting circumcised and becoming proselytes? And should they adopt the ritual and ethical norms of the Jewish people? Our investigation has demonstrated how attractive and reasonable the agitators' proposal in these matters appeared (Barclay 1988, 73; emphasis is his).

Succinctly stated, the *rhetorical problem* of Galatians caused by the *rhetorical situation* of the contrary Judaizing opponents' teaching is the newfound confusion among the Galatian churches about their *identity* (Should they adopt Jewish practices of circumcision and Torah observance to become a part of the true people of God?) and about their *pattern of behavior* (Should they take up the yoke of Torah to pattern and constrain their behavior?) (cf. Lategan 1992).[11] In response to this *rhetorical problem*, Paul responded with this very specific *rhetorical purpose* for the Epistle to the Galatians:

to persuade the Galatians to reject the Judaizers' non-gospel and to continue in the true gospel which he had preached to them because its universal nature alone was legitimately confirmed, while the Judaizers' non-gospel was rejected, it alone placed them in the true people of God through their faith in Christ, and it alone provided them true deliverance from sin's powers through their receiving of the Holy Spirit.

The question now becomes, "In responding to the overriding rhetorical problem of confused *identity* and *conflicting patterns of behavior/ethics* with this purpose, which of the three *species of rhetoric* does Paul exhibit in Galatians?" Aristotle described these species in his *"Art" of Rhetoric*:

> The *deliberative* kind is either hortatory or dissuasive; for both those who give advice in private and those who speak in the assembly invariably either exhort or dissuade. The *forensic* kind is either accusatory or defensive; for litigants must necessarily either accuse or defend. The *epideictic* kind has for its subject praise or blame.

> Further, to each of these a special time is appropriate: to the *deliberative* the future, for the speaker, whether he exhorts or dissuades, always advises about things to come; to the *forensic* the past, for it is always in reference to things done that one party accuses and the other defends; to the *epideictic* most appropriately the present, for it is the existing condition of things that all those who praise or blame have in view. It is not uncommon, however, for epideictic speakers to avail themselves of other times, of the past by way of recalling it, or of the future by way of anticipating it (1926, 1.3.3-4/p. 34-35; emphasis is mine).

In light of the persuasive purpose of Galatians and Paul's desire to exhort the Galatians to make a decision in the *immediate future* about their identity and pattern of behavior, the *deliberative* species seems to be the most appropriate of Aristotle's labels for Galatians.[12] Such a choice is not without its opponents, as the following brief survey of previous rhetorical analyses of Galatians will reveal.

V. A Brief Survey of Previous Rhetorical Analyses of Galatians

This brief survey will focus on two aspects of the analyses of others: first, the determination of Galatians' rhetorical problem and species (stages 3-4); and second, the rhetorical arrangement of the material within the epistle (stage 5). As we will see, these two aspects tend to stand or fall together to a large extent in rhetorical analysis. Pride-of-place for the first modern and still-definitive rhetorical analysis of Galatians goes to Hans Dieter Betz and his corpus of work on Galatians that has covered a period of about fourteen years (1974-1987).[13] His determination of the rhetorical problem and judicial rhetorical species has been followed with only minor deviations by Bernard H. Brinsmead (1982), Hans Hübner (1984), Joop Smit (1984, 1985a, 1985b, 1986), James D. Hester (1984, 1986; who changed to "epideitic" in a 1991 work), and Troy Martin (1995). These scholars view Galatians as "an apologetic letter", and therefore of the **judicial** or **forensic species** (e.g., Betz 1975, 354-55). In the ensuing courtroom setting, Paul is said to view the Galatians as the jury, the opponents as the accusers, and himself as the defendant (Betz 1975, 377).[14]

Betz views the rhetorical problem as primarily an ethical one:

> Thus in their midst "transgressions" have occurred and the claim to live "in the Spirit" (ἐν πνεύματι) came into conflict with the realities of daily life. From Paul's words we may conclude that the problem with which the Galatians felt they were confronted was this: how can the "pneumatic" (ὁ πνευματικός) live with "trespasses" in his daily life? (1979, 8).

Therefore, Paul must launch an apologia and defend himself against the accusations of the Judaizers that he preached a deficient gospel and that the Gentile Christians of Galatia need the additional help of circumcision and Torah to be delivered in their battles against the σάρξ (Betz 1979, 8-9). Brinsmead bases his whole identity of Paul's opponents as Christians associated with apocalyptic and sectarian Judaism (particularly Qumran) by reading Galatians as an apologetic and dialogical response to them (1982, 195-96). Both of these authors, plus Hester, appeal to the judicial or forensic species of rhetoric to provide the very specific five-part argumentative structure of Paul's defense.[15]

The *rhetorical arrangement of the material* within Galatians (stage 5 in our rhetorical analysis procedure) is essentially the same in these works with only small variations. Betz (1979, 16-23) suggests this arrangement:

1:1-5 Epistolary prescript
(with typical sequence of *superscriptio*, *adscriptio*, and *salutatio*)

1:6-11 *Exordium (or prooemium* or *principium)*
(= Introduction/Prologue that states the cause of the case or the main reason for writing; Betz sees 1:10-11 as the *transitus* or *transgressio* [smooth transition] into the following narrative section)

1:12-2:14 *Narratio*
(= persuasive "statement of the facts of the case"; generally given with as much clarity, brevity, and plausibility as possible)

2:15-21 *Propositio* or *Partitio*
(= outline summation of the legal content of the *Narratio* and also provides the smooth transition into the *Probatio*)[16]

3:1-4:31 *Probatio*
(= the proof, the most decisive and important part of the letter; composed of 6 arguments and a digression (3:19-25), according to Betz)

5:1-6:10 *Paraenesis* or *Exhortatio*
5:1-12 = a warning against acceptance of Jewish Torah;
5:13-24 = a warning against corruption by the "flesh";
5:25-6:10 = Recommendations in the form of *sententiae* with regard to ethical praxis

6:11-18 Epistolary Postscript
(also serves rhetorically as *Peroratio* or *Conclusio* which ends and concludes the apologetic speech, which is the body of the epistle)

Worthy of specific, but brief note among those who advocate the judicial species for Galatians is Troy Martin (1995). Martin uses stasis theory to revive an older hypothesis (but for different reasons) that Paul is actually addressing *two* threats in Galatians, not one. Martin asserts that in Gal 1:6-9, Paul accuses the Galatians of exchanging his gospel for a circumcision gospel and in Gal 4:8-11, he accuses the Galatians of apostatizing to paganism (440-1). Martin inverts the typical reading of Galatians that sees 1:6-9 as the principal stasis and 4:8-11 as a secondary one. Instead, he asserts that the Paul's principal accusation is that the Galatians are in danger of reverting to paganism in 4:8-11 and that the accusation about the Judaistic threat in 1:6-9 is a secondary refutation necessary in light of the defection of these gentiles to paganism (442-4).

From my perspective, it seems that Martin has misunderstood at a fundamental level Paul's ironic connection of his Judaistic opponents with paganism. It seems that *the Judaizers' premise* is that joining Israel via faith in Messiah Jesus plus submitting to circumcision and Torah *will deliver* the Galatians from the bondage of paganism and the sins of the flesh. By contrast, *Paul's premise* is that submitting to circumcision and Torah as Jewish proselytes will sever the Galatians from Messiah (Gal 5:1-4) and *will return them* to the fleshly realm of paganism, of which Judaism is now a part (4:8-11)! Of course, Paul's ironic point is that the means of deliverance is, in fact, actually the means of bondage! This is why Paul views the "deeds of the flesh" which his opponents manifest in 5:19-21 within the context of a classic pagan vice list (see the discussion of this passage in the following rhetorical analysis).

Therefore, there is no need to invert the traditional understanding of the stasis of Paul's rhetoric as Martin does. It seems that the majority understanding is more than capable of encompassing Paul's challenge in Gal 4:8-11. In fact, understanding the tragic irony in Paul's argumentation simply underscores that the Judaistic stasis is, in fact, the primary stasis of Galatians.

As one might expect, the above rhetorical analyses have not met with total acceptance. In particular, there has been a strong reaction from those primarily trained in rhetorical studies. Leading this group and providing a rather different rhetorical analysis of Galatians is George A. Kennedy (1984), followed by George Lyons (1985), Robert G. Hall (1987; 1991, 1996), B. Standaert (1985, 1986),[17] Francois Vouga (1988),[18] Joop Smit (who changed from judicial in a 1989 work), and Jegher-Bucher (1990). They have determined that the *rhetorical problem* and the *rhetorical species* is somewhat different than Betz has concluded. Regarding the *rhetorical problem*, Hall asserts:

> The major purpose of Galatians is not to defend some past action (judicial) or to praise some and to blame others (epideictic) but to persuade the Galatians to cleave to Paul and his gospel and to reject his opponents and their gospel (Gal 1:6-9, cf. 6:12-16) (Hall 1987, 279).

Kennedy had earlier reached the same conclusion about the *rhetorical problem* of Galatians:

> The letter looks to the immediate future, not to judgment of the past, and the question to be decided by the Galatians was not whether

Paul had been right in what he had said or done, but what they themselves were going to believe and to do. Since Betz wrongly identifies the question at issue, he is led wrongly to identify the stasis as qualitative (p 129). Insofar as stasis theory can be applied to deliberative rhetoric, the stasis is one of fact: *What gospel is true? What should the Galatians do?* (1984, 146-47; emphasis is mine).

While Betz had essentially defined the *rhetorical problem* as dealing with the struggle with the flesh (e.g., Betz 1974, 153-59), Kennedy and Hall have framed the problem so that it encompasses this ethical issue and includes the issue of "Which gospel is true, and consequently, which resulting identity is correct?" This more encompassing determination of the *rhetorical problem* seems correct and it does not lessen in the least the ethical concern that Betz has raised, as Hall rightfully observes:

> Since the debate requires the Galatians to decide between two antithetical modes of life and behavior and since the participants in the debate are not primarily concerned about Paul's past action but about what future action the Galatians will take, Galatians is most naturally classified as a deliberative work (1987, 279).

Kennedy argues strongly that the *rhetorical species* of Galatians is **deliberative** (1984, 144-47). Hall agrees and gives seven reasons why Galatians is deliberative, not forensic or judicial in species (1987, 278-82):

1. Gal 3:1-6:18 does not fit with the judicial species and the rightness or wrongness of a past action, but rather with a choice between Paul's gospel and his opponents' "gospel."

2. The choice facing the Galatians is obviously not in the past, but in the future. The judicial species focuses on the rightness or wrongness of a past action according to justice. Paul is seeking to exhort and dissuade the Galatians to or from some future action, claiming the action is expedient or harmful (e.g., Aristotle's *Rhetoric* 1.3.3-5). Where doubt exists (i.e., between two opinions), deliberation is necessitated.

3. Paul evidences aspects of what Quintilian described as "popular deliberative style" (3.8.58-60).

4. The narrative section of Galatians (1:10-2:14) is not a reminder of the facts central to the case surrounding the offense, but this narrative introduces relevant matters *external* to the case (Quintilian

3.8.10). A narration in a deliberative speech functions as a part of the proof taken.

5. The essence of Galatians and deliberative oratory is persuasion between choices. The Galatians have not decided definitely yet between Paul and the Judaizers (e.g., Gal 5:10; 6:17). Paul's appeal to the Galatians is that choosing his gospel (*the* gospel) is to their advantage. This is the main appeal of deliberative oratory.

6. Gal 5:1-6:10 is an exhortative section, but this does not fit well within the judicial species. It does fit well within the deliberative species (e.g., Quintilian 3.6.47).

7. Paul's defensive tone and defensive arguments in Gal 1-2 are best explained as ethical proof supporting his credibility that has been attacked, rather than as a statement of the facts of the case. Betz has misunderstood Paul's purpose for this narrative and has wrongly concluded that its inclusion in the epistle makes it a judicial species.

Kennedy's and Hall's arguments for categorizing Galatians as a deliberative *rhetorical species* rather than a judicial species seem more than adequate. Their conclusions reinforce the conclusions reached in the first four stages of rhetorical analysis in the previous section.[19]

Because this second cluster of rhetorical analyses has yielded what this writer believes to be a more accurate understanding of the basic issues Galatians addresses and the basic manner in which it addresses them, then the *arrangement of material* (stage five) in these analyses should prove more helpful also. This is exactly the case as the brief rhetorical outline of Kennedy (1984, 147-51) reflects:

1:1-5 Salutation

1:6-10 Proem
(= a general statement of the proposition of the letter)

1:11-5:1 Proof
(corresponds to the theological section in most of Paul's epistles and has two "headings" here)

  1:11-2:21 Narration and "Epicheiremene" (Heading #1)
    1:11-12   Restatement of the topic of the salutation
    1:13-2:14 Extended Narrative
    2:15-21   Epicheiremene (an argument with the parts fully stated; = conclusion to first heading)

3:1-5:1 Argument from Galatians' Experience (Heading #2)

5:2-6:10 Specific Ethical Commandments
(= the practical purpose of the letter)

6:11-18 Epilogue
(final attack and recapitulation of most important injunction)

Noted only in passing are the works of A. Pitta (1992) and James A. Hester (1991) which stand in the distinct minority of those who judge Galatians to be of the **epideictic** or **demonstrative** species. This view has gained few followers among Galatian commentators because of the apparent lack of praise/blame features that this species warrants.

Of greater significance are the epistolary and rhetorical analyses of Galatians by W. Harnisch (1987) and especially by G. Walter Hansen (1989, 21-93; 1994a, 23-24, 29-30) and Richard N. Longenecker (1990, c-cxix). Particularly, Hansen's and Longenecker's rhetorical analyses are of the highest quality. They follow in the footsteps of John L. White (1972) in his use of epistolary formulae, but especially follow in the steps of Nils A. Dahl and his rhetorical analysis of Galatians (1973). Hansen's/Longenecker's[20] (and Dahl's) analysis has two major distinctives: it sees Galatians as a "'real,' 'more private,' 'rebuke-request' letter" (1989, 27), and it views Galatians as composed of mixed rhetorical genre, **forensic rhetoric in 1:6-4:11** and **deliberative rhetoric in 4:12-6:10** (1989, 59-60). With this reading Hansen's analysis (1989, 53-54) is very similar to Betz' in Gal 1:6-4:11, but deviates significantly in 4:12-6:10:

1:1-5 Salutation

1:6-4:11 Rebuke section
  1:6-2:21 Rebuke for deserting the gospel
    1:6-10 Expression of rebuke
    1:11-12 Disclosure of central thesis
    1:13-2:21 Disclosure of Paul's autobiography

  3:1-4:11 Rebuke for foolishness about the gospel
    3:1-5 Expression of rebuke
    3:6-4:7 Disclosure of Scriptural teaching
    4:8-11 Expression of rebuke

4:12-6:10 Request section
  4:12-20 Personal appeal
    4:12 Request for imitation

4:13-19 Disclosure of autobiography
4:20 Wish for personal visit

4:21-31 Scriptural appeal
4:21-30 Appeal to the law
4:31 Conclusion from the law

5:1-12 Authoritative appeal
5:2 Decision
5:3-9 Disclosure of consequences
5:10 Confidence statement

5:13-6:10 Ethical appeal (paraenesis)[21]
5:13-15 Freedom in Christ expressed by serving one another
5:16-18 Freedom in Christ empowered by the Spirit, not law
5:19-21 Freedom in Christ is deliverance from the sinful
            nature
5:22-26 Freedom in Christ is complete moral transformation
            by the Spirit
6:1-10 Freedom in Christ fulfill the law of Christ

6:11-18 Autographic Subscription

Interestingly enough, while Hansen's labeling of Galatians as a rebuke-request type of epistle and his corresponding outlining of the structure of the epistle (1989, 53-54) are significantly different from my own choices in these two areas, we reach many of the same exegetical conclusions within the smaller units of the epistle. In particular, he underscores the continuity in Paul's argumentation from Gal 4:12-6:10 in a very forceful manner. Specifically, Hansen concurs that there is no libertinistic threat in Gal 5:13-6:10[22] and that the Hagar-Sarah application that Paul makes in 4:21-31 makes untenable such a turn in his argument:

> And in light of the freedom-slavery antithesis in the allegory, it would appear that the imperatives in 5:1 and 5:13 are aimed against the same threat to freedom in Christ: the threat of nomism which boasts in the flesh (1989, 152).

The strength of Hansen's analysis is that he consistently relies upon Paul's use of epistolary formulae to structure and interpret the individual units of the letter. This leads him to emphasize rightly Paul's tendency to cluster these formulae at transitional points in the epistle (1989, 27-54). The weakness of analysis is not at this analytical level, but at the synthetic level. Hansen's (and

Dahl's/Harnisch's/Longenecker's) choice of the rebuke-request type of letter seems somewhat artificial for a letter the length of Galatians. This is because all of the corresponding examples in the papyri (e.g., 1989, 34-42) are of much shorter epistles where such a genre is meaningful because it controls the entire epistle. However, to subsume all of Paul's argumentation in Gal 1:6-4:11 under the rubric of "rebuke" and all of his rhetoric in 4:12-6:10 under the corresponding rubric of "request" seems very forced and a meaningful descriptive genre becomes artificially prescriptive.

It would seem that broader categories for an epistle the length of Galatians would be more desirable, and workable (e.g., deliberative species). This is not to deny that a part of Galatians is of the "rebuke" genre and a part of the epistle is of the "request" genre. However, the operative word is *a part.*. Nevertheless, regardless of this one criticism, I would not want to diminish the fact that Hansen's (and Dahl's/Harnisch's/Longenecker's) work is a significant contribution to the epistolary and rhetorical analysis of Galatians.

While other works have been done that relate to the rhetorical analysis of Galatians,[23] the works I have surveyed are the major contributions to this point. Therefore, some concluding thoughts seem appropriate. The checkered history of rhetorically analyzing Galatians seems to demand one certain conclusion: the better part of wisdom is being sensitive to the rhetorical features of Galatians, yet not letting the rhetorical tail wag the exegetical dog! Dunn has noted this as he pondered the diverse corpus of rhetorical analyses of Galatians:

> Beyond that, however, attempts to label Galatians as a particular kind of letter or to determine its structure from conventional parallels are of questionable value. It is clear that Galatians does not accord closely with any ideal type, and there is a danger that analysis of the letter will be too much determined by fitting it on to a grid drawn from elsewhere rather than by the natural flow of the argument. More important, there is a danger that too much emphasis on rhetorical considerations may blur the extent to which the letter is driven by theological logic and passion (1993b, 20).

While largely agreeing with this assessment, I find that Matera is closer to the mark with his cautiously optimistic conclusions about the value of the rhetorical analysis of Galatians:

> In terms of rhetorical criticism, this letter is a sustained exercise in deliberative rhetoric; that is, Paul tries to persuade the Galatians not to accept the agitators' gospel of circumcision. To be sure, Paul employs other rhetorical strategies as well, Thus there are moments

when the Apostle rebukes the Galatians for having gone astray and appeals to them to change their present course of action. Moreover, there are sections in which Paul clearly defends the divine origin of his Torah-free gospel. But, taken as a whole, Galatians is primarily an example of deliberative rhetoric (1992, 11).

VI. Stages 5-6 in the Rhetorical Analysis of Galatians: Determining the Arrangement of Material and Reviewing the Process

The fifth stage in rhetorical analysis is obviously the longest and most difficult stage because it demands a painstaking analysis of the flow of the argumentation in the epistle. Again, the technical terminology of classical rhetoric will be kept to a minimum and briefly explained when it is used. Also, most of the explanatory information will be kept out of the analysis itself and will be confined to the endnotes.

> *The Rhetorical Purpose of Galatians*: to persuade the Galatians to reject the Judaizers' non-gospel and to continue in the true gospel which Paul had preached to them because...1) its universal nature alone was legitimately confirmed, while the Judaizers' non-gospel was rejected,...2) it alone placed them in the true people of God through their faith in Christ,...and...3) it alone provided them true deliverance from sin's powers through their receiving of the Holy Spirit.

1:1-5 PRESCRIPT/SALUTATION
While identifying himself (1:1a) and his co-senders (1:2a), naming the recipients (1:2b), and greeting the Galatian churches (1:3), Paul also introduces his three main points that will be proved successively in the three main sections of the epistle:[24]

1. (1:1) His apostleship is through Jesus Christ and God the Father (proved in the defense of his apostleship/gospel in 1:11-2:21)

2. (1:1,2,4) God is truly Father over them (emphasized by the three-fold repetition of θεοῦ πατρὸς [ἡμῶν], which is unique among the salutations of the traditional Pauline corpus)[25] (proved in the defense of their true identity in 3:1-4:31)

3. (1:4-5) The Lord Jesus Christ died substitutionally for them and that alone provided the eschatological deliverance of them from the present evil age (τοῦ αἰῶνος τοῦ ἐνεστῶτος πονηροῦ)

(proved in the defense of their true deliverance from sin's powers in 5:1-6:10)

*1:6-10 PROLOGUE OR PROEM OR EXORDIUM*²⁶

Paul states the two options (gospels) before the Galatians and the *general* proposition or *causa* of his letter (to be progressively specified in his following argumentation): "to persuade the Galatians to reject the Judaizers' non-gospel and to continue in the true gospel which he had preached to them." As Betz has observed (1975, 359-62), this general statement of Paul's intent has three parts:

1:6-7 Verse 6 is the ironic statement of the *causa* with a sense of θαυμασμός, or wonderment in verse 6a at their desertion (μετατίθεσθε), instead of a simple statement of fact,²⁷ so that "solemnly is our attention called to the whole subject-matter of the epistle" (Bullinger 1968, 923). This statement of the *causa* is then followed with an ἐπανόρθωσις or *correctio* in verse 7 where Paul retracts the status of "gospel" from these disturbers (οἱ ταράσσοντες), plus adds the charge against them of wanting to distort (μεταστπρέψαι) the gospel of Christ.²⁸ The key terms of this section are political terms (Betz 1975, 359), or better, are the terms of community and community loyalty. Paul's emotional appeal with these terms is to the unity of the community that the true gospel of Christ had previously created among them.

1:8-9 The gospel that they have already received is, in fact, the true gospel and Paul pronounces a curse upon anyone who preaches a contrary gospel in verse 8. He powerfully reiterates the curse in verse 9. The antithesis that Paul has now created between his opponents and himself is an antithesis between an apostle of Jesus Christ (1:1) and community disturbers and gospel-distorters (1:7) who are under divine curse.²⁹

1:10 Paul's hard words toward the Galatians (1:6-7a) and toward his opponents (1:7b-9) prove that he is not now (ἄρτι) seeking to please men, nor is he still (ἔτι) trying to please men.³⁰ Rather, he is now a bond servant of Christ and thus willing to displease men by preaching the gospel of Christ, which has obviously displeased his opponents.³¹

Paul expressed his *causa* or general purpose for the epistle in 1:6-10 to persuade the Galatians to reject the Judaizers' "non-gospel" and to continue in the true gospel which he had preached to them.

This purpose is now developed in a linear argument from 1:11-6:10 (until the *conclusio* of 6:11-18). In this lengthy linear argument, Paul will prove through three major arguments why his gospel is the true gospel and why the Judaizers have "no gospel."

1:11-6:10 PROOF, PROBATIO, OR CONFIRMATIO[32]

The Galatians should reject the Judaizers' non-gospel and continue in the true gospel which Paul had preached to them because...

   1) its universal nature alone was legitimately confirmed, while the nature of the Judaizers' non-gospel was rejected (*1:11-2:21*),

   2) it alone placed them in the true people of God through their faith in Christ (*3:1-4:31*), and

   3) it alone provided them true deliverance from sin's powers through their receiving of the Holy Spirit (*5:1-6:10*).

1:11-2:21 HEADING #1: An Historical Argument Proving the Superiority of Paul's Gospel via *Narratio* (Narrative)[33]

Paul preached the true gospel and the Judaizers a non-gospel because...1) his gospel's nature was divine, not κατὰ ἄνθρωπον,...and yet...2) his gospel's universal nature was repeatedly confirmed by the Jerusalem apostles because it did not contradict nor distort their understanding of the gospel's nature as the Judaizers' non-gospel did.

1:11-12 THESIS OF THE NARRATIVE[34]

In an echo of 1:1, Paul makes known that the universal nature of the gospel which he preached is not κατὰ ἄνθρωπον, nor is it received (παρέλαβον) from man nor taught (ἐδιδάχθην) by man, but it is through the revelation (ἀποκαλύψεως) of Jesus Christ. It appears that the basis of the Judaizers' authority is that they claim they received the tradition from and were taught by the Jerusalem apostles (cf. Acts 15:24); hence, the particular nature of their gospel is κατὰ ἄνθρωπον. The universal nature of Paul's gospel is divine, direct from Jesus Christ Himself. Paul now defends the universal nature of his gospel and dispenses with theirs in the two main points of his narrative.

1:13-17 POINT #1 IN THE NARRATIVE

Christ's direct revelation of the true gospel to Paul led to a radical change in both Paul's identity and his *pattern of behavior* (ἀναστροφήν) (1:13) apart from any consulting (προσανεθέμην) (1:16) with men. The universal nature of the true gospel changed Paul from Jewish zealot who persecuted the Church to Christian proclaimer of the gospel among the Gentiles apart from the Jerusalem apostles.[35]

1:18-2:21 POINT #2 IN THE NARRATIVE
That the universal nature of Paul's gospel is the true gospel was repeatedly confirmed by the Jerusalem apostles because it did not contradict nor distort their understanding of the gospel's nature.

1:18-24 CONFIRMATION #1   Three years after Paul's conversion, his 15-day visit to Jerusalem to see Cephas (and James) was too brief to be catechized by them (note his oath underscoring this fact in 1:20).[36] Yet afterward (1:21-24), the churches of Judea glorified God because of Paul's gospel proclamation in Syria and Cilicia, which they considered "preaching the faith" (εὐαγγελίζεται τὴν πίστιν) (1:23).[37]

2:1-10 CONFIRMATION #2   Then after 14 years, because of revelation, Paul again went to Jerusalem and this time presented his universal gospel to the Jerusalem apostles in private, and again his gospel was confirmed as the true gospel

2:1-3   The non-circumcising nature of Paul's gospel was confirmed by the apostles when the Greek Titus was not compelled to be circumcised (See Donaldson 1994).

2:4-5   At this time, "the truth of the gospel"--i.e., its non-circumcising nature for Gentiles--was defended by Paul and the Jerusalem apostles[38] against ψευδαδέλφους who advocated the bondage of "Judaizing" Gentile Christians (Walker 1992).

2:6-10   Again, the Jerusalem apostles contributed nothing to Paul (οὐδέν προσανέθεντο) (2:6) in terms of teaching him, but on the contrary (ἀλλὰ τουναντίον) (2:7), confirmed that they and he had been entrusted with the *same gospel* (2:7-8) and *apostleship* (2:9), but to different groups (Jews and Gentiles).[39]

2:11-21 CONFIRMATION #3   Later, the Judaistic behavior in Antioch of Cephas and certain men from Jerusalem contradicted and distorted "the truth of the gospel" (2:14) which they had previously confirmed.[40]

2:11-14 CONFIRMATION THROUGH REBUKE   Paul's public rebuke (ἔμπροσθεν πάντων) of this Judaistic behavior was because it was not consistent with (οὐκ ὀρθοποδοῦσιν) "the truth of the gospel" which eliminated the Judaizing of Gentiles (cf. 2:3-5).[41]

2:15-21[42] ***THE THEOLOGY BEHIND THE REBUKE***   "The truth of the gospel" also has specific application to Jewish Christians who still attempt to live Torah-observant lives (e.g., Cephas,[43] Barnabas[44], and the rest in 2:11-14). "The truth of the gospel" (2:5,14) has eliminated the barrier that Torah-observance created between Jewish and Gentile Christians because:

1.) *(2:15-16)* Neither Jew nor Gentile is justified by Torah-observance, but only through faith in Christ.[45]

2.) *(2:17-18)*[46] Being justified through faith in Christ apart from Torah-observance does not make Jewish Christians like non-observant Gentile "sinners" because nobody can be judged as a "transgressor" ($\pi\alpha\rho\alpha\beta\acute{\alpha}\tau\eta\nu$) of Torah if he is not required to obey it. (Cf. Rom 4:15 for this principle).

3.) *(2:19-20)* Jewish Christians died to Torah and live to God because of their co-crucifixion with Christ, which applies His substitutionary death to them to free them from the bodily constraints of Torah upon them.

4.) *(2:21)* If Jewish Christians nullify ($\acute{\alpha}\theta\epsilon\tau\hat{\omega}$) the universal nature of the gospel ($\tau\grave{\eta}\nu$ $\chi\acute{\alpha}\rho\iota\nu$ $\tauο\hat{\upsilon}$ $\theta\epsilon\sigma\hat{\upsilon}$)[47] by emphasizing Torah-observance, then Christ died needlessly.

3:1-4:31 HEADING #2: **An Experiential Argument Proving the Superiority of Their Sonship-through-Faith via Scripture Fulfillment**[48]

The Galatians should reject the Judaizers' non-gospel and continue in the true gospel which Paul had preached to them because it alone placed them in the true people of God through their faith in Christ.

3:1-5 1st External Proof:[49] ***The Evidence of their own Experience of the Holy Spirit and Miracles***

The undeniable physical evidence of the reception of the Holy Spirit by the Galatians clearly validates that they are already the true sons of Abraham who have received the blessing of the Spirit through faith, not through Torah-observance. Paul interrogates them *(interrogatio)*[50] about the evidence of which they are personal witnesses.

3:6-14 2nd External Proof: The Evidence of an Enthymematic Argument [51]

3:6-7 Premise: Just as (καθώς) Abraham believed and was reckoned righteous, then (ἄρα) those who are of faith are sons of Abraham.

3:8-14 Supporting Proof from Scripture:

3:8-9 God's justifying of the Gentiles through faith was foreseen in Scripture (Gen 12:3).

3:10-12 God's justifying of the Gentiles through faith is not replaced by the works of Law because the Law can bring a curse (Deut 27:26) and operates on a *quid pro quo* basis (Lev 18:5), while God justifies through faith (Hab 2:4).[52]

3:13-14 God's justifying of the Gentiles through faith is accomplished in Christ Jesus Who redeemed Jews from the curse of the Law (Deut 21:23) so that Abraham's blessing (the promised Holy Spirit) might come to the Gentiles through faith.[53]

3:15-29 3rd External Proof: The Evidence of Another Enthymematic Argument

3:15-16 Premise: The universal promissory aspects of the Abrahamic Covenant could not be set aside nor conditionally modified after it was ratified and these aspects are fulfilled in Abraham's singular seed, Christ. [54]

3:17-29 Supporting Proof from Scripture:

3:17-18 The Mosaic Law is an added covenant 430 years after the Abrahamic Covenant (Ex 12:40) and its addition does not nullify God's previous granting of inheritance based on promise.

3:19-25 A Digression:[55] Because of transgressions (παρα-βάσεων) and until Christ the seed should come, the Mosaic Law was added (προσετέθη) for the temporary purposes of shutting up (συνέκλεισεν) all under sin and becoming a tutor (παιδαγωγός) to lead the Jews to faith in Christ.

3:26-29 Faith in Christ is now all that is needed to enter into the full-privileged covenantal relationship of a son of God and Abraham's offspring.

4:1-11 4th External Proof: The Evidence of their Experience of the Holy Spirit Again

4:1-7 The Galatians' experience of the Spirit of God's Son crying "Αββα ὁ πατήρ" in their hearts proves that they have been adopted as God's son in τὸ πλήρωμα τοῦ χρόνου and have left behind the previous childish, slavish era of the Law.

4:8-11 To give up their status as God's full-privileged sons and to turn back again to the pagan status as slaves under bondage to the weak and poor στοιχεῖα and to Torah-observance causes Paul to fear for them.[56]

4:12-20 5th External Proof: The Evidence of their Previous Acceptance of Paul [57] and their Resulting Happiness[58]

4:12 *The Appeal for Continued Imitation of Paul:*[59] Paul pleads with them to identify again with his non-Judaistic behavior as he did with them because there is no alienation between them.

4:13-16 *The Galatians' Reversal*: They initially identified with Paul in spite of his bodily condition and received him with great hospitality (ἐδέξασθέ) as Christ Jesus Himself, but their present entertaining of the Judaizers' theology makes Paul now seem like their enemy and continued friendship unlikely.

4:17-20 *The Galatians' Need for Discernment*: The Judaizers seek the Galatians for their own personal benefit, not because of true friendships while Paul is deeply concerned for them as if he were *again* a mother in labor with them.[60]

4:21-31 6th External Proof:[61] The Ironic Reversal of a Judaizers' Proof-text to Prove in a Climactic Manner the Galatians' True Abrahamic Sonship[62]

4:21-23 The Mosaic Law speaks to those who want to be ὑπὸ νόμον about the slave-son Ishmael born κατὰ σάρκα to the slave woman Hagar and the free son Isaac born δι᾽ ἐπαγγελίας (or κατὰ πνεῦμα in 4:29) to the free woman Sarah.

4:24-27 These two women can allegorically represent the Hagar-covenant associated with the present Jerusalem and children in slavery to the Mosaic Covenant (i.e., Judaizers) and the Sarah-covenant associated with the heavenly Jerusalem and children in freedom (of the New Covenant) (i.e., the Galatian Gentile Christians).[63]

4:28-31 Those Ishmaelites who are born κατὰ σάρκα (Judaizers) are still persecuting the Isaacites who are born κατὰ πνεῦμα (Gentile Christians) and, therefore, should be cast out from the people of God.[64]

5:1-6:10[65] HEADING #3: A Causal Argument[66] Proving the Superiority of Their Present Deliverance in Christ via Community Comparisons[67]
The Galatians should reject the Judaizers' non-gospel and continue in the true gospel which Paul had preached to them because it alone provided them true deliverance from sin's powers through their receiving of the Holy Spirit.[68]

5:1-12 Paul Exhorts and Warns about the antithetical consequences of their identity choice for their continued deliverance from sin's powers.[69]

5:1 *The Opening Exhortation*: The antithetical identity choice they face is between continuing in the freedom of Christ or submitting again to the yoke of slavery (the Mosaic Law).[70]

5:2-6[71] *The Warning about Choosing the Judaizers' Identity:* Paul solemnly warns them that the deliverance from sin's powers that Christ offers to His community "will be of no benefit" (οὐδὲν ὠφελήσει) if they become part of the Judaizers' community (with its identifying mark of circumcision) and sever themselves from Christ and from His grace that is at work within His community by "faith working through love."[72]

5:7-12 *The Antithetical Impact of the Judaizers and Paul upon the Galatians* (The Contrasting Ethos of Paul and the Judaizers):[73] The Judaizers are actually hindering the continued obedience of the truth by the Galatians, while Paul is being persecuted for preaching the Judaizing-free truth to them.

5:7-9 *(The Anti-Models)* The Judaizers have hindered their "running" and their hearing of God's voice with their leaven-like persuasion, which is not from God.

5:10-11 *(The Consistent Model)* Paul, by contrast, has confidence in their choice and in the Judaizers' judgment and that the

Galatians will choose to follow him, even though he is still being persecuted for the Judaizing-free gospel he preaches.

5:12 (A Ridiculing Curse) Paul wishes that the Judaizers would even emasculate themselves!

5:13-26[74] **The Fundamental Manifestation of Deliverance from Sin's Powers** in the Community of God's people is not competitive striving with one another, but rather the serving of one another through love.[75]

5:13-15 The Initial Expression of the Antithetical Choices: The manifestation of freedom from the constraints of the Mosaic Law within the community of God's people should not be used as an opportunity (ἀφορμήν) for continued fleshly failure, which is vitriolic and self-consuming, but rather as an opportunity through love to serve one another, which is the summation principle of the whole Mosaic Law.[76]

5:16-24 The Antithetical Manifestations of the Two Choices: Those who insist on living according to the past standard of fleshly behavior within the community under the Mosaic Law will share in the sins of a community composed of those who will not inherit the kingdom of God; but those who identify with the community of the Spirit will be enabled by God's Spirit to manifest the fruit of loving unity apart from the daily constraints of the Mosaic Law.

5:16-18 The standards of the Holy Spirit and the community of the Spirit are diametrically opposed to the fulfilling of fleshly behavior that takes place within the community of the flesh which is ὑπὸ νόμον, so that those who possess the Spirit, but live within the flesh community will not be able to do what they wish.

5:19-21 The community of the flesh manifests the relationally destructive effects of fleshly behavior which confirm that this community is not composed of the true sons of Abraham who will inherit the kingdom of God.

5:22-24 In contrast, the community of the Spirit manifests the relationally edifying effects of spiritual behavior which are not legally prohibited and which evidence that those in the community of the Spirit have seen their σάρξ and its manifestations crucified.

5:25-26 The Closing Expression of the Antithetical Choices: Being a part of the community of the Spirit means that one should choose to live according to the rule or standard of the Spirit and not according to the competitive striving that characterizes the community of the flesh.[77]

6:1-10 Some Specific Manifestations of the Deliverance from Sin's Powers which fulfill the relational goal of the Law within the community of the Spirit are seen in the gracious restoration of sinning members and in the generous financial sharing with appropriate persons within the community.

> **6:1-5** The reality that even some Christians will be caught in παραπτώματι is to be dealt with by those in the community of the Spirit (ὑμεῖς οἱ πνευματικοί) in a spirit of gentleness and humility as restoration is sought in mutual concern and burden-bearing, not in arrogant competition.[78]

> **6:6-10** Also, the community of the Spirit should manifest generous financial sharing, especially with its teachers and other believers, because this is sowing to the Spirit and contrasts with sowing to the flesh, which emphasizes circumcision and Torah-observance and ends in corruption.[79]

6:11-18 POSTSCRIPT, EPILOGUE OR CONCLUSIO[80]

In an appended personal conclusion written in his own hand, Paul recapitulates[81] the Judaizers' man-pleasing, fleshly motives and his cross-oriented motives and reiterates the rule (τῷ κανόνι τούτῳ) of the καινὴ κτίσις which negates the necessity of circumcision. Additionally, before pronouncing his final benediction (6:18), Paul recapitulates his apostolic authority by pointing out how the στίγματα τοῦ Ἰησοῦ on his body should negate any further trouble from the Judaizers (6:17).

IV. Stage 6 in Rhetorical Analysis: Reviewing the Process

We are now at a point where we can look back over the entire rhetorical unit of Galatians and try to recapture the picture of the whole. The main points in our lengthy rhetorical analysis are:

1:1-5	**Epistolary Prescript/Salutation**
1:6-10	**Prologue/Proem/Exordium**

(General proposition/*causa* of letter = to persuade the Galatians to reject the Judaizers' non-gospel and to continue in the true gospel which Paul had preached to them)

1:11-6:10   Proof/*Probatio*/*Confirmatio*
(the *causa* expressed in 3 proofs)

1:11-2:21 Heading #1: An Historical Argument proving the superiority of Paul's gospel via Narrative or *Narratio*
(The universal nature of Paul's gospel alone was legitimately confirmed, while the nature of the Judaizers' non-gospel was rejected.)

1:11-12 Thesis of the Narrative (the nature of the gospel)

1:13-17 Point. #1 in the Narrative (it radically changed Paul)

1:18-2:21 Point #2 in the Narrative (it was repeatedly confirmed by the Jerusalem Church)

   1:18-24 1st visit, confirmed 3 years after Paul's conversion

   2:1-10 2nd visit, confirmed 14 years later in Jerusalem

   2:11-21 3rd visit, confirmed in Antioch confrontation with Cephas over Judaistic behavior

3:1-4:31 Heading #2: An Experiential Argument proving the superiority of their sonship-through-faith via Scripture fulfillment (in 6 External Proofs)[82]
(Paul's gospel alone placed them in the true people of God through their faith in Christ.)

   3:1-5 1st External Proof: The evidence of their own experience of the Holy Spirit and miracles

   3:6-14 2nd External Proof: The evidence of an enthymematic argument (faith of Abraham/sons of Abraham)

   3:15-29 3rd External Proof: The evidence of another

enthymematic argument (Particularistic Mosaic Covenant does not invalidate universal Abrahamic Covenant)

4:1-11 4th External Proof: The evidence of their experience of the Holy Spirit again (crying Abba in their hearts)

4:12-20 5th External Proof: The evidence of their previous acceptance of Paul and their resulting happiness

4:21-31 6th External Proof: The ironic reversal of a Judaizers' proof-text to prove in a climactic manner the Galatians' true Abrahamic sonship

5:1-6:10 Heading #3: A Causal Argument proving the superiority of their present deliverance in Christ via community observation
(Paul's gospel alone provided them true deliverance from sin's powers through their receiving of the Holy Spirit.)

5:1-12 Paul warns and exhorts about the **antithetical consequences** of their identity choice for their continued deliverance from sin's powers.

5:13-26 The **fundamental manifestation** of deliverance from sin's powers in the community of God's people is loving service, not competitive striving.

6:1-10 Some **specific manifestations** of the deliverance from sin's powers should be relational restoration and financial generosity.

6:11-18   **Postscript/Epilogue/***Conclusio*

Looking at this brief recapitulation of the argument of Galatians causes one to marvel at the genius and continuity of Paul's rhetoric. The question then becomes, "Was his rhetoric successful in helping him to achieve his rhetorical purpose for Galatians?" We have suggested the following rhetorical purpose of Galatians:

to persuade the Galatians to reject the Judaizers' non-gospel and to continue in the true gospel which Paul had preached to them because... 1) its universal nature alone was legitimately confirmed, while the Judaizers' non-gospel was rejected, . . 2) it alone placed them in the true people of God through their faith in Christ,...and...3) it alone provided them true deliverance from sin's powers through their receiving of the Holy Spirit.

If, in fact, this is a reasonable facsimile of the rhetorical purpose of Galatians, then it also seems reasonable to conclude that Paul successfully achieved this purpose. The combination of his powerful logical arguments, his authoritative use of Scripture, and his passionate appeal to his relationship with the Galatians seems more than adequate to persuade the Galatians to continue in his, the true gospel.

VII. Conclusion

An epistolary analysis of Galatians is a frustrating endeavor because it is an exercise in discovering the absence of normal Pauline epistolary features.[83]   While Galatians begins and ends with an identifiable prescript and postscript, it is the material in between that is problematic! First, the absence of a thanksgiving section must be explained. Secondly, without a thanksgiving section ending in an eschatological climax, the beginning of the body of the epistle is not as definitive as one would like (e.g., Roberts 1986a, 1986b; White 1984, 1744). Thirdly, there are no clear travel plans (only 4:20?) or a definitive beginning of a paraenesis section (Merk 1969). Is Galatians an epistle? Yes, of course it is. But the absence of these typical epistolary features reveals the limitations of using an epistolary analysis only. Additionally, the *presence* of rhetorical features throughout the epistle underscores the value of using rhetorical analysis to understand both the form and function of this epistle within the Galatian churches.[84] In the heat of the moment and in the face of an extreme need for immediate persuasion, Paul seems to have integrated very naturally rhetorical elements with epistolary form. An intimate knowledge of both rhetoric and epistle-writing would make this a natural response.

What has this lengthy attempt at establishing the context of Gal 5-6 accomplished? Ideally, it has achieved three things. First, tracing Paul's argument/rhetoric should have demonstrated the continuity in his argument from Gal 3-4 through Gal 5-6. This continuity should remove the chasm between Gal 4 and 5.[85] Secondly, by noting the continuity in argumentation, we should have been given a new and more accurate set of glasses for seeing how Paul used σάρξ and πνεῦμα in Gal 5-6. That is, we should now be able to see these terms in the light of the antithetical, argumentative fashion in which Paul used them. This should lead to a third insight. We should now have a glimmer of the continuity of the meaning of σάρξ and πνεῦμα in Gal 3-6 as external entities (i.e., community identities), not as internal dualities. This last insight is obviously the most difficult one to accept. Therefore, the next chapter will attempt to validate this meaning through an analysis of the social dynamics at work in the Galatian churches. The following chapters will be successive thematic and exegetical studies of σάρξ and πνεῦμα in Gal 3-6, with special emphasis on 5:13-6:18. Hopefully, these three chapters will underscore the sense of σάρξ and πνεῦμα as external entities.

Notes

[1] See Robbins and Patton 1980 for the history and development of modern rhetorical criticism in Biblical Studies up through 1979. See also Classen 1991, 1993; Cornelius 1994; Lyons 1994; and Vorster 1995 for similar surveys. Wuellner 1987 sets forth a stimulating overview of the two competing versions of rhetorical criticism and of the direction rhetorical criticism is taking in Biblical Studies. The rhetorical analysis in this chapter seems to be closer to the version preferred by Wuellner "in which rhetorical criticism is identical with practical criticism" (453). The specific model followed will be George A. Kennedy's classical model of rhetorical criticism (1984). For a fruitful analysis of Galatians using discourse analysis, see Parunak 1992 and Boers 1994.

[2] For a bibliography of ancient rhetorical theory, rhetoric in the Greco-Roman world and its modern legacy, and the rhetoric of the New Testament see Watson 1988a and Porter 1993. For a helpful introduction to rhetoric and the New Testament, see Walton 1996 and Mack 1990 (with a special section on Galatians on pages 66-73). Advocating the use of ancient and modern rhetorical theory is Classen 1991, 1993.

[3] The hermeneutical question here is really one of *form* versus *function*. Rhetorical analysis emphasizes the latter and the pragmatic dimension of texts, while epistolary analysis focuses on the literary form of the text. In terms of rhetorical traits and epistolary traits in Galatians, the former are both more obvious and numerous. Therefore, the following analysis will enter through what appears to be the easier door and will seek to shed light on the epistolary form as a byproduct. This will hopefully be more fruitful than

seeking to understand Paul's argument by first emphasizing the epistolary form of Galatians. A review of some of the major commentaries on Galatians should reveal how little insight this approach has yielded and how little structural consensus has been achieved. See Lategan 1988, 411-16 for helpful comments on these methodological considerations in the study of Galatians. On the theoretical justification for application of ancient and modern rhetorical categories to Paul's epistles with appropriate methodological cautions, see Porter 1993, Classen 1993, and Reed 1993. For a broader "interactional model," see Vorster 1990.

[4]See Betz 1986, 16-21 for a brief, but well-documented survey of the 1800-year history of the study of Paul's use of rhetoric. Betz notes that the question of Paul's study of rhetoric was debated as early as Clement of Alexandria and Augustine. Consult Fairweather 1994a for a helpful survey of Chrysostom's (ca. AD 350-407) "rhetorical analysis" of Galatians. Apart from the likelihood that Paul was well-trained in rhetoric, his use of rhetoric was quite possibly anticipated because of the rhetorical *expectations* of his readers. These expectations, if valid, may have necessitated Paul's use of at least some rhetoric. He would have little choice, in a very real sense, due to his readers' anticipation that he should use rhetoric. These kinds of cultural conventions and expectations are on the side of rhetorical argumentation. However, in lieu of further evidence, such expectations can only be deemed likely, not definitive, at this point. Admittedly, the use of rhetoric is more obvious in epistles like 1 Corinthians (especially 1 Cor 1-3). See also Classen 1991, 1993, 1995 and Fairweather 1994a,b for balanced conclusions and cautions in this area.

[5]Scholars like Jacob Neusner (1978) strongly question the traditional Jewish view that attributes these ideas and rules to Hillel.

[6]See Wuellner 1987, 449 footnotes 4 and 5 for some attempts in this direction.

[7]Indeed, Paul's letters seem to be intended to be read aloud, like formal lectures and literary epistles. Not that this renders them any less spontaneous, nor on the other hand does their undoubted rabbinic dialect (Turner 1976, 8.3).

Various authors have argued that Paul's letters were meant to be read orally to their first recipients. See Allo 1934, Funk 1966, 245; Hartman 1986, 139; and Hester 1986, 387-92. Additionally, Stowers 1986, 51-57 shows how close epistolary theory and ancient rhetoric are by demonstrating how the basic classification of types of epistles was borrowed from the three types of rhetoric. Even though this had limitations, it provided the fundamental structure for epistolary typology. See especially Malherbe 1988, 2-11 and White 1986, 189-93 for helpful discussions of the relationship of epistolary theory and rhetoric. Additionally, see Ong 1982, Achtemeier 1990, Botha 1992, 1993, Dewey 1995, Robbins 1995, and Loubser 1995 for strong advocacy of the oral nature of the New Testament in light of the oral environments of the first century.

[8]Again, see Watson 1988a, 470-72 and Porter 1993 for a bibliography on the Pauline epistles that have been rhetorically analyzed so far.

[9]For some of the varying responses to Bitzer's article, see Hester 1986, 391, note 16. For an understanding of the rhetorical situation as a perspectivally-constructed literary-rhetorical figure, see Stamps 1993.

[10]Whiteley 1973, 619 echoes this conclusion:

> That is, I believe St. Paul in Galatians was concerned primarily not with sin as such but with the Jew/Gentile tension in the Christian Church, which is simply one case of the inter-group tensions which now fill the headlines. Since this particular tension, the tension between Jews and Gentiles within the Christian Church, soon became a dead issue, the epistle was redeployed and made to apply to the problem of sin, one of the topics which can never be wholly out of season.

For a recent example of an argument against justification by faith being the central core of Paul's theology, see Wanamaker 1983. For a list of nine scholars who share this opinion and eight who still defend the traditional view, see Fung 1980, 246.

[11]See Dunn 1990, 1993c for an explication of the theology of Galatians as Paul's sustained attempt to deal with the "covenantal nomism" of his Judaistic opponents.

[12]Aristotle further describes the deliberative species in *"Art" of Rhetoric* 1.4.1-3 and underscores its applicability to Galatians when he writes:

> We must first ascertain about what kind of good or bad things the deliberative orator advises, since he cannot do so about everything, but only about things which may possibly happen or not. Everything which of necessity either is or will be, or which cannot possibly be or come to pass, is outside the scope of deliberation...But it is clear that advice is limited to those subjects about which we take counsel; and such are all those which can naturally be referred to ourselves and the first cause of whose origination is in our own power;...(1926, 39).

Paul seems to be persuading the Galatians to originate a decision about what their identity as the people of God will be and about what their pattern of behavior/ethics will be. Methodologically, one must not let the choice of a species of rhetoric dictate the analysis of an epistle, especially in light of eclectic usage of rhetorical features (Classen 1991, 1993). Also, one must understand the rhetorical *dispositio*, as Aletti 1992 has argued.

[13]See the "Works Cited" for the full listing of Betz' works on Galatians. In the 1987 German edition of his 1979 English commentary in the Hermeneia

Series, Betz briefly discusses the various reactions to his approach and essentially reiterates his original views (pp. 1-4).

[14]But, see Martin 1995, 460, who notes: "Although it belongs to forensic rhetoric, Galatians is a letter and not a speech designed for the courtroom. It is a pre-trial letter written to an offending party to summon that party back to the original agreement."

[15]Some ancient rhetoricians had as few as four and as many as six parts by subdividing the basic elements of a forensic speech Quintilian splits the difference and lists five parts *prooemium, narratio, probatio, refutatio,* and *peroratio* (1920, 3.9.1/1:515).

[16]Hester does not specifically deal with Gal 2:15 and following, but, "in general....finds this [Betz'] outline of the letter very satisfying, and it seems to me to hold up well under scrutiny" (1984, 224).

[17]In his very brief rhetorical analysis of Galatians (1985), Standaert identifies Galatians as *deliberative* in species (36-37) and sees the following main sections in the epistle (34-35):

1:1-5	Epistolary introduction
1:6-12	Announcement of the theme (vv. 11-12 = first *propositio*)
1:13-2:21	*Narratio* (with a concluding *peroratio* in 2:15-21)
3:1-4:31	*Refutatio* (framed by a double recourse on Abraham in 3:6-14 and 4:21-31)
5:1-6:10	*Probatio-Exhortatio*
6:11-18	Epistolary epilogue

The uniqueness of Standaert's analysis is labeling Gal 3-4 as the *refutatio* of the opponents' position. (cf. Brinsmead 1982, 52-54, who labels Gal 3:1-4:31 the *Probatio* and 5:1-6:10 the *Refutatio*!). While this label highlights a significant aspect of this section, it does not do total justice to Paul's argumentation, as the following analysis should demonstrate. Nevertheless, Standaert's work is helpful in underscoring the identification of Galatians as the deliberative species and in establishing the epistle's main seams.

[18]Vouga briefly argues for the deliberate species' identification, finding parallels in Demosthenes' ΠΕΡΙ ΤΗΣ ΕΙΡΗΝΗΣ.

[19]Bolstering the deliberative species identification, Hall 1996 also asserts that Paul appropriates an argumentative form prevalent in several Jewish apocalypses. Such argumentation is "apocalyptic" in that Paul claims inspiration, reveals God's judgment which distinguishes the righteous from the wicked, calls readers to join the righteous, and shows how joining with the community of the righteous entails specific modes of behavior. Central to Paul's argumentation is an apocalyptic (or better, "redemptive historical") understanding of God's actions in history.

[20]Because of Hansen's prior analysis (1989), references to this perspective will be to his work. Richard Longenecker served as his doctoral dissertation mentor, so the two analyses are remarkably similar.

[21]This section is filled in from the outline in Hansen 1994a, 30.

[22]Unlike Longenecker who sees such a threat (1990, 235-7).

[23]For example, see the brief semiotic analyses of Gal 1-2 in Panier 1986a, 1986b.

[24]Cook 1992 rightly asserts that this prescript functions in a programmatic manner in the absence of a thanksgiving section in introducing all of the main themes of the epistle. While the overall form of this section is clearly that of the salutation or prescript of an epistle and not that of a formal exordium (the introduction to a speech), it nonetheless has additional features normally found in an exordium (or proem/principium), as Hall 1987, 282-83 has observed. These features are the unusual additions of Paul's declaration of apostolic identity in 1:1 and his declaration of Christ's deliverance in 1:4. In this sense the salutation evidences at a micro level what is true at the macro level of Galatians: Paul has profoundly integrated epistolary and rhetorical features into one smooth-flowing entity (cf. L. Cranford 1994). One key element of this integration is Paul's rhetorical use of antithesis from the very first phrase of the epistle. "Antithesis occurs when the style is built upon contraries,..." (*Rhetorica ad Herennium* 1954, 4.15.21/p. 283). Antithetical argumentation pervades every section of Galatians. See Lategan 1991 for a grammatical validation of the use of anthithesis. Vorster 1992 calls this "dissociation."

[25]See Chapter 1, Section V for a fuller discussion of the theme of God's paternity over the Galatians. Also, this kind of subtlety may be an example of *insinuatio* or the "subtle approach" that ancient rhetoricians developed as a technique of introducing a difficult rhetorical problem. We see this in *Rhetorica ad Herennium*::

> Now I must explain the Subtle Approach. There are three occasions on which we cannot use the Direct Opening, and these we must consider carefully: (1) when our cause is discreditable, that is, when the subject itself alienates the hearer from us; (2) *when the hearer has apparently been won over by the previous speakers of the opposition*; (3) or when the hearer has become wearied by listening to the previous speakers (1954, 1.6.9/p. 17; emphasis is mine).

However, in Galatians this subtlety is found in an expanded salutation, not in an exordium. Nevertheless, in the oral setting of the Galatian churches, the salutation functions somewhat like an exordium functions in a speech Paul was apparently aware of this and introduced Galatians' major themes in subtle fashion from the very beginning of the epistle. He does the same thing in the expanded salutation in Rom 1:1-7. After introducing his hearers to his main themes with this salutatory subtlety in Galatians, Paul is then free to state his proposition in the next section (1:6-10) in very stark and direct language. Such skillful and sensitive communication would not be lost on the expert listeners of an oral culture! For a defense of this kind of emphasis on orality, see Ong 1982. Also underscoring the importance of oral communication due to the previously overstated literacy level in the Roman Empire is Harris 1989, 175-284.

[26]As many have noted (e.g., Roberts 1986b, 198), in the place of the customary thanksgiving section at this point in his epistles, Paul instead has this very direct, confrontive official introduction. It has the characteristics of and functions like the rhetorical exordium or prologue of a speech Aristotle observed that

> The exordium (προοίμιόν) is the beginning of a speech, as the prologue in poetry and the prelude in flute-playing; for all these are beginnings, and as it were a paving the way for what follows. So then the most essential and special function of the exordium is to make clear what is the end or purpose of the speech; wherefore it should not be employed, if the subject is quite clear or unimportant (1926, 3.14.1,6/pp. 427 and 431).

See also the discussion of the exordium in Quintilian (1921, 4.1/2:7-49) and *Rhetorica ad Herennium* 1.4:6-7 (1954, 13-15). There is presently a movement of sorts away from labeling Paul's introductory sections as "thanksgivings," preferring terms like "prooemium" or "exordium" (e.g., Arzt 1994). Ably defending the traditional understanding of Paul's epistolary "thanksgiving" is Reed 1996.

[27]Aristotle observed about the content of an exordium that

> Hearers pay most attention to things that are important, that concern their own interests, that are *astonishing*, that are agreeable; wherefore one should put the idea into their heads that the speech deals with such subjects (1926, 3.14.7/p. 433; emphasis is mine).

According to Stowers 1986, 22, the ironic rebuke is another convention used in place of a thanksgiving in the papyrus letters. This "signals the mood and purpose of the letter" (22) and also introduces blaming letters (139). Cronjé 1986 notes that this is just one of many rhetorical techniques that Paul uses in Galatians to create "defamiliarization" and more powerfully influence his recipients. Additionally, Paul's amazement makes their wavering relationally personal and sets up Paul's relational discussion in Gal 4:12-20 (see Kraftchick 1985, 220). Hansen 1989, 33-44 sees this as an "astonishment-rebuke" formula that is a major indicator of both the type of epistle and of the structure of the letter. Confirming this non-ironic emphasis in Paul's use of θαυμάζω to express genuine perplexity at the Galatians' defection are the fine works by Roberts 1991, 1992.

[28]Paul is using the Direct Approach in this exordium which many times included boosting the speaker's own *ethos* or credibility with his hearers and attacking the credibility of his opponents (e.g., *Rhetorica ad Herennium* 1954, 1.5./pp. 15-17). On Paul's use of εὐαγγέλιον and εὐαγγελίζομαι in Galatians, see Hughes 1994 and Wright 1994.

[29]Aristotle underscored the significance of this kind of language in deliberative exordia:

> Deliberative oratory borrows its exordia from forensic, but naturally they are very uncommon in it. For in fact the hearers are acquainted with the subject, so that the case needs no exordium, except for the orator's own sake, or on account of his adversaries, or if the hearers attach too much or too little importance to the question according to his idea. Wherefore he must *excite* or remove *prejudice*, and *magnify* or minimize the *importance of the subject*. Such are the reasons for exordia;...(1926, 3.14.12/p. 437; emphasis is mine).

Of course, Paul had theological reasons for pronouncing this curse that go beyond the techniques of oratory. Vorster 1992 calls this "dissociation."
[30]Betz has observed about verse 10 that

> The two rhetorical questions and the assertion in v.10 put a clear end to the *exordium*. They deny that Paul is a rhetorical "flatterer", "persuading" (ἀνθρώπους πείθω) or "pleasing" men (ἀνθώπους ἀρέσκειν), or a magician, trying to "persuade God" (πείθω τὸν θεόν) (1975, 362).

While Betz' observation is generally accurate, it nonetheless misses the main thrust of Paul's words, which is to contrast himself with Judaistic behavior. Verse 10 has this twofold temporal contrast: 1) *Now* there are those who are seeking to please men (e.g., Peter in 2:11-14 and the Judaizers in 6:12-13) and 2) *Previously* Paul himself was trying to please men with Judaistic behavior (e.g., 1:13-14). Paul's ethical appeal in v.10 has a narrower focus than Betz has allowed. See also Gräbe 1992. On rhetorical questions in Galatians, see Cronjé 1992.
[31]There is really no consensus among those who have rhetorically analyzed Galatians about whether verse 10 is connected with the preceding or the following verses. For example, Betz connects it with verse 11 and calls both of them *transitus* or *transgressio* (after Quintilian 4.1.76-79) because they end the exordium and provide the smooth transition in the *narratio* (1975, 361-62). Hester disagrees with this grouping and connects verse 10 to 1:6-9 as part of the exordium because he calls 1:11-12 a *stasis* which serves as the thesis for the *narratio* in 1:15-2:10 (1984, 225-29; see also Gräbe 1992 and Pelser, du Toit, Kruger, Lemmer, and Roberts 1992). Hall follows Hester in seeing 1:11-12 as the thesis for the narration section, but he adds verse 10

to this thesis because it relates to the theme of Paul seeking divine not human approval in the narration of 1:10-2:21 (1987, 285).

The best suggestion seems to be Kennedy's which sees verse 10 as the explanatory conclusion (γάρ) of the exordium:

> Verse 10 is very interesting in that Paul here shows how rhetorically conscious he is by calling attention to the fact that his proem does not seek favor with the audience. The verse is a written aside which contributes to his ethos by its candor (1984, 148).

Theologically, Kennedy's suggestion makes the most sense also in that Paul is beginning what will be a recurring contrast in Galatians between the true pattern of behavior in following Christ (which risks the rejection of men) and the man-pleasing pattern of behavior (which fears the rejection of men and seeks status among them) e.g., 1:13-14; 2:6, 11-14; 3:3-4; 4:15-20, 28-29; 5:10-12; 6:3-5, 12-16. The man-pleasing pattern is truly accursed (e.g., 5:21 and 6 8).

[32]This is the most decisive section of a speech because it gives proof or reasons why the hearers should accept the speaker's proposition. It is the proof section that ancient rhetoricians gave much of their attention to in their handbooks. This is especially true of the role of proof in the judicial or forensic species of rhetoric (e.g., *Rhetorical ad Herennium* 1954, 1.10.18-25/pp. 33-49; Quintilian 1921, Book 5/ 2:153-369). Paul, however, is now presenting his evidence as to why the Galatians should reject the non-gospel of the Judaizers and continue in the true gospel which he had preached to them within the *deliberative* species of rhetoric. Proof was a necessary part of this species, also (e.g., Aristotle 1926,3.17.4/p. 453; *Rhetorica ad Herennium* 3.4.8-9/pp. 169-73).

Because of the length of the proof section in Galatians, only the major contours of Paul's argument will be traced.

[33]This argument seems to anticipate the question forming in the minds of the Galatians: "Which *gospel* has been confirmed by the Jerusalem apostles and Jerusalem Church?" Normally in the forensic species of rhetoric, the purpose of *narratio* was to recount in brief fashion "the statement of facts" (διήγησις) (e.g., Quintilian 1921, 4.2.40/2:73). Although it was rare, Quintilian also allowed for *narratio* to be used in deliberative speeches:

> As regards the *statement of facts*, this is never required in speeches on private subjects, at least as regards the subject on which an opinion has to be given, because everyone is acquainted with the question at issue. Statements as to *external matters* which are relevant to the discussion may however frequently be introduced (1920, 3.8.10-11/1:485; emphasis is mine).

Quintilian later explains in a discussion of forensic rhetoric that external matters are those facts that have a bearing on the case, but are not the specific facts of the case itself (1921, 4.2.11-12/2:55). They do, however, contribute to the understanding of the speaker. In light of this, Kennedy has remarked: "This well describes the narrative in Galatians, the function of which is to establish Paul's ethos and thus to support his claim of the truth of his gospel" (1984, 145). See du Toit 1992 for a convincing explanation of this strategy in terms of "alienation" and "re-identification." See also Vos 1994 for a defense of Gal 1-2 as "didactic genre" which defends Paul's gospel and instructs as to its nature. As Gaventa 1991 and Martyn 1991 have noted, Paul's starting point in his argument is not his opponents' theology, but *his* Christocentric and universal gospel!

[34]Most commentators agree that Gal 1:11-2:21 is about *the origin* of Paul's gospel and his *independence* as an apostle. This is only partially true, however. Through the rhetorical analyses of Smit 1985a and Lategan 1988, the theological and rhetorical purpose of this autobiographical section of Galatians is also seen to be the *nature* or *quality* of Paul's gospel that originated with Christ and was preached independently from the Jerusalem apostles. This is seen from Paul's opening statement in Gal 1:11 that his gospel is not κατὰ ἄνθρωπον. This is not so much a statement about its origin (which occurs in 1:12), as it is a statement about his gospel's quality or nature. In essence, Paul is saying that his gospel is κατὰ θεόν (cf. Gal 1:1 and Rom 1:1). Specifically, Paul focuses on the *universal nature or quality* of the gospel in Gal 1:13-2:21. This universal nature of the gospel is characterized in this section as ἡ ἀλήθεια τοῦ εὐαγγελίου (2:5, 14). It is a gospel that is nonparticularistic and non-ethnocentric. This true gospel is opposed by the Judaizers' gospel which is particularistic and ethnocentric (e.g., 2:3-5), and thus, κατὰ ἄνθρωπον. This false gospel is therefore also contrary to τὴν χάριν τοῦ θεοῦ (Gal 1:15; 2:21). See especially Lategan 1988, 416-26, Koptak 1990, Kertelge 1992, and Verseput 1993 for helpful analyses of this section. There is a sense in which this thesis for the narrative section is also a thesis for the whole proof section (1:11-6:10). See also Bruce 1975, 21-25, Winger 1994, Brehm 1994, and Hughes 1994.

[35]Paul is accomplishing several things simultaneously in this section of the narrative that make powerful contributions to his ethos or credibility with the Galatians. One is *his modeling* of his changed *identity* and *pattern of behavior*, since these are the two issues perplexing the Galatians. Paul proves that he had the identity with Judaism and that his pattern of behavior as a persecutor of the Church and as a zealot for Jewish traditions gave him status within that community beyond many of his peers. In other words he *had already had* what the Judaizers are promising the Galatians! Paralleling Phil 3:1-11, Paul readily gave up this status for the privilege of having Christ revealed within him (Gal 1:16a). The second boost to his credibility is that his status within Israel was probably markedly greater than that of any of the Judaizers. Yet, he had readily given up that status to preach Christ among the Gentiles (Gal 1:16b). The nature of the gospel *demands* these changes in

identity and pattern of behavior, contrary to the Judaizers' charge! For a rousing defense of the paradigmatic purpose in Paul's autobiographical remarks in Gal 1-2 see Lyons 1985, 123-76 and Gaventa 1986. See Hansen 1994c for a defense of the view that Paul was presenting himself as a paradigm of the apocalypse of Jesus Christ's coming. For Paul's visit to Arabia (Gal 1:17), see Murphy-O'Connor 1993. Advocating that Paul was following the Phinehas/Elijah zealous prophet model is Wright 1996.

[36]See Sampley 1977 for further legal and rhetorical significance in this oath. Cf. Ulrichs 1990.

[37]With the recounting of this incident, the unity in understanding of the nature of the gospel message between Paul and the Jewish Christian churches of Judea is established. For a comparison of Paul's Jerusalem visits in Galatians and Acts, see Morgado 1994.

[38]For a wide range of views on the Jerusalem apostles as "pillars," see Aus 1979, Barrett 1953, Hay 1969, and Fung 1982. Regarding Paul's visit, see McLean 1991 and Schmidt 1992.

[39]In Gal 2:9 when Paul speaks of τὴν χάριν which had been given him, this is his favorite term for Christ's calling of him and appointing of him as apostle to the Gentiles (e.g., Gal 1:15-16; Rom 1:5; 15:15-16; Eph 3:1-13; Phil 1:3-7; 1 Cor 3:10; 15:10-11). This term becomes a sort of theological abbreviation for the doctrine of the universal nature of the gospel (cf. Betz 1979, 27-28). See the insightful note on this term in Robinson 1979, 221-26.

[40]While this part of the narrative is very embarrassing for Cephas and Barnabas, it still serves an edifying function for the Galatians. Aristotle observed this function of narrative in deliberative rhetoric:

> In deliberative oratory narrative is very rare, because no one can narrate things to come; but if there is narrative, it will be of things past, in order that, being reminded of them, the hearers may take better counsel about the future (1926, 3.16.11/p.451).

[41]While Paul states in Gal 2:11 that Cephas "stood condemned" (κατεγνωσμένος ἦν), the majority of scholars persists in asserting that Cephas was unmoved by Paul's rebuke, such that this event in Antioch became the watershed experience that led to a break between Jewish Christianity and Paul's Gentile mission (e.g., Catchpole 1976-77; Dunn 1982, 1983a, and Taylor 1992). Effectively refuting such a thinly-supported thesis are Houlden 1983 and Cohn-Sherbok 1983. See also Barclay 1988, 76-83, Jegher-Bucher 1990, Böttger 1991, and Esler 1995. Setting this conflict within the context of the communal love feast is Jewett 1994..

[42]Betz (1975, 367-68) and those who have followed him label this section the *Propositio* which is supposed to be a summation of the *Narratio* and an easy transition to the Proof section which follows. The following analysis will show that it does provide a very significant transition into the next section (3:1-4:31). However, it is not a summation of the legal content of 1:11-2:14, but rather a specific application of "the truth of the gospel" (2:5,14) to Jewish Christians. Further, Kennedy argues that "the main objection to calling it a

proposition as Betz does (pp. 113-14), is that it is argumentative, and it may indeed be derived as some have believed from an earlier speech" (1984, 148-49). See also Parunak 1992 for a helpful discourse analysis of Gal 2:15-21.

[43]See Pesch 1979, 302-8, Ehrman 1990, and Allison 1992.

[44]See Bauckham 1979.

[45]See Dunn 1983b, 103-18 for an excellent discussion of these verses; "*Covenant* works had become too closely identified as *Jewish* observances, *covenant* righteousness as *national* righteousness" (114).

[46]As he does in Rom 7:1-7a, Paul also does in Gal 2:15-17 where he begins the discussion of Jewish Christians' relationship to Torah in the first person plural and thereby emphasizes his solidarity with this, his group. However, in both Rom 7:7b-25 and Gal 2:18-21 Paul soon shifts to the first person singular. As Betz has observed, "rhetorically there is no difficulty with this form" (1979, 121) because of Paul's ongoing modeling within Galatians as the prototypical example of how Jewish Christians should be responding to the true gospel and its free offer to the Gentiles (e.g., 1:13-16a). It is unthinkable that this first person singular would signal Paul's uniquely individual response to the Torah-free gospel because such an emphasis would immediately undercut the very point he was making about his solidarity with Jewish Christians! Therefore, Paul's first person singular language in Gal 2:18-21 will be treated as a rhetorical and stylistic change that lowers the threat level to the Jewish Christians and holds Paul up as the model while still directly addressing the application of the truth of the gospel to them. See especially Kümmel 1973 for a defense of this stylistic usage. For a definitive exegesis of Gal 2:15-18, see Winninge 1995, 246-50.

[47]See note 38 for an explanation of Paul's use of χάρις in connection with the Gentile inclusion. Note this previous usage in Gal 1:15-16 and 2:9. This is another example of Paul's theological shorthand. On Paul's argumentation in Gal 2:18-21, see also Lambrecht 1991.

[48]This argument will overturn the central Judaizers' claim by causing the Galatians to view their experience in the light of Scripture The specific twofold question Paul addresses is "What is the *identifying mark* that God promised to the sons of Abraham (circumcision or the Holy Spirit) and *by what means* is that identifying mark to be received (by taking up the yoke of Torah or by believing in Jesus Christ)?" See especially Hong 1994 and M. Cranford 1994.

Paul will develop this argument in Gal 3:1-4:31 with six very diverse proofs (see Garland 1994). Quintilian strongly advocated the such diversity in argumentation:

> Are we to have nothing but premises and conclusions from consequents and incompatibles? Must not the orator breathe life into the argument and develop it? Must not he vary and diversify it by a thousand figures, and do all this in such a way that it seems to come into being as the very child of nature, not to reveal an artificial

manufacture and a suspect art not at every moment to show traces of an instructor's hand?   What orator ever spoke thus? (1921, 5.14.32/2:367).

[49]An "external proof" is a proof that exists outside the author's creation of it. "Internal Proofs" (artistic proofs) are invented by the author. As Kennedy has noted, there are three common kinds of external proofs in the New Testament: quotations from Scripture, the evidence of miracles, and the naming of witnesses (1984, 14). Paul uses all three forms of external proof in Gal 3:1-4:31. Notice he uses the evidence of miracles and the Galatians' own witness of these in this first argument (esp. 3:5).

[50] In regard to interrogation, its employment is especially opportune, when the opponent has already stated the opposite, so that the addition of a question makes the result an absurdity;...Again, interrogation should be employed when one of the two propositions is evident, and it is obvious that the opponent will admit the other if you ask him. But the interrogator, having obtained the second premise by putting a question, should not make an additional question of what is evident, but should state the conclusion...Thirdly, when it is intended to show that the opponent either contradicts himself or puts forward a paradox (Aristotle 1926, 3.18.1-4/pp 463-65).

Paul brilliantly executes the rhetorical use of *interrogatio* in Gal 3:1-5. See also Lemmer 1992.

[51]An "enthymeme" is a deductive proof in the form of a statement with a supporting reason and is a truncated syllogism of sorts. Aristotle called the enthymeme "a kind of syllogism, and deduced from few premises, often from fewer than the regular syllogism;" (1926, 1.2.13/p. 25). See Corbett 1971, 72-79 for a full discussion of the enthymeme.

[52]See Watson 1986, 63-72, Wright 1991 (Ch. 7), and Dunn 1993a for a helpful discussion of the real issue within this passage and the broader context of Gal 3-4: the antithetical conceptions of what is the distinguishing mark and core of God's people. See also Stanley 1990 and Vos 1992 on Gal 3:10-14.

[53]See Caneday 1989, Braswell 1991, and Pyne 1995 for helpful discussions of this bestowal. See Kruger 1992 for an elaboration of the relationship between Law and promise in Gal 3 and Pelser 1992 for the same on faith and works.

[54]See Wright 1991 (Ch. 8) for a helpful exposition of Gal 3:15-20.

[55]Betz 1979, 20 and 163 identifies this section as an extremely concise *digressio* and notes that "it does not add a new argument to the defense, but prevents a wrong conclusion the readers might reach on the basis of the preceding" (163). Given this strategic function in Paul's argumentation, one should not conclude that a digression by Paul is a wandering off into irrelevant material.   Digressions were noted elements in classical rhetoric (e.g., Quintilian 1921, 4.3.15-17/2:129-31). See Wuellner 1979 for a discussion of

Paul's rhetorical use of digressions in 1 Corinthians. See Wallace 1990 for how this digression gives insight into Paul's view of the Mosaic Law. Cf. Borchert 1994 and Tolmie 1992.

[56]On the persuasive impact of Paul's rhetorical question in 4:9-10, see Cronjé 1992. See Wright 1994, 233 for the tie of Israel to paganism via the στοιχεῖα.

[57]While one might conclude that this is a rambling and personal digression within a very tightly-reasoned section (3:1-4:31), such a conclusion would miss the powerful argumentative force of an appeal to an existing friendship and the experience of past hospitality in Mediterranean cultures. Paul's proof draws on both of these highly exalted values within the culture of his day. Betz notes the rhetorical value of this section when he observes that

> A personal appeal to friendship is entirely in conformity with Hellenistic style, which calls for change between heavy and light sections and which would require an emotional and personal approach to offset the impression of mere abstraction. The argumentative force lies in the topic itself, the marks of "true" and "false" friendship (1979, 221).

Hansen 1989, 44-50 regards 4:12 as a request formula (Γίνεσθε ὧ ἐγώ) within the personal appeal section (4:12-20) that initiates the long request section of the epistle (4:12-6:10). The context of Paul's original ministry was probably one of persecution (Goddard and Cummins 1993).

[58]Paul's rhetorical question in 4:15a: "Where then is that sense of μακαρισμὸς ὑμῶν (your happiness or blessedness)?" reflects the most basic appeal of the deliberative species of rhetoric. This is an appeal to what is most beneficial to the hearers:

> The end of the deliberative speaker is the expedient or harmful; for he who exhorts recommends a course of action as better, and he who dissuades advises against it as worse; all other considerations, such as justice and injustice, honour and disgrace, are included as accessory in reference to this (Aristotle 1926, 1.3.5/p. 35).

> Since in causes of this kind [deliberative speeches] the end is Advantage, and Advantage is divided into the consideration of Security and the consideration of Honour, if we can prove that both ends will be served, we shall promise to make this twofold proof in our discourse (*Rhetorica ad Herennium* 1954, 3.4.8/pp. 169-71).

Paul has already dealt with the advantage of *security* in inheritance by promise (e.g., Gal 3:6-14). He has also dealt with the advantage of *honor* in his explication of the Galatians' present status within the people of God as υἱοὶ θεοῦ not δοῦλοι in 3:26-4:11. Therefore, this appeal to their advantage is just another facet of the advantage of *honor* that they will have if they continue in the true gospel that Paul preached. This facet of honor deals with their corporate concern for their *reputation* and their *loyalty*. See Malina 1993, 28-62 for a discussion of how pivotal the "honor-shame" values were in the first century Mediterranean world.

[59]See Lyons 1985, 164-68 for a helpful discussion and defense of the *imitatio Pauli* nature of Gal 4:12-20.

[60]All throughout 4:12-20 Paul is using antithetical argumentation, and this section is no exception. On the maternity of Paul, see Gaventa 1990. On the exclusion metaphor of 4:17, see Smith 1996.

[61]This is both the climactic and most memorable of the six proofs of 3:1-4:31, as the rhetorical handbooks suggested:

> In the Proof and Refutation of arguments it is appropriate to adopt an Arrangement of the following sort: 1) the strongest arguments should be placed at the beginning and at the end of the pleading; 2) those of medium force, and those that are neither useless to the discourse nor essential to the proof, which are weak if presented separately and individually, but become strong and plausible when conjoined with the others, should be placed in the middle. For immediately after the facts have been stated the hearer waits to see whether the cause can by some means be proved, and that is why we ought straightway to present some strong argument. 3) And as for the rest, since what has been said last is easily committed to memory, it is useful, when ceasing to speak, to leave some very strong argument fresh in the hearer's mind. This arrangement of topics in speaking, like the arraying of soldiers in battle, can readily bring victory (*Rhetorica ad Herennium* 1954, 3.10.18/p. 189).

Paul's first proof in 3:1-5 which appealed to the Galatians' experience of the Holy Spirit by faith and this final proof in 4:21-31 seem to fit the rhetorical qualifications of the strongest proofs, as the following analysis should reveal.

[62]Many commentators contend that Paul has already fired his powder and now, as an afterthought, reiterates his argument about the seed of Abraham (e.g., Schlier 1971, 216 and Burton 1921, 251). However, such a perspective again shows cultural insensitivity to the weightiness of this kind of argumentation in Paul's day. It also shows insensitivity to the rhetorical coup that Paul achieves by reversing what appears to he a proof-text in the Judaizers' argumentation (contra Perriman 1993). In a definitive article entitled "The Allegory of Abraham, Sarah, and Hagar in the Argument of Galatians," C.K. Barrett (1982, 154-70) has argued that almost all of the Old Testament passages that Paul uses in Gal 3-4 are Judaizer proof-texts that he is responding to by putting them in the proper redemptive historical framework. This seems particularly true of the Sarah-Hagar story in Gen 16 and 21, which Paul would have no normal reason to use in his ministry.

However, the Judaizers' use of these narratives would underscore their central point: Gentiles are "Ishmaelites" and are not inheriting sons of Abraham and can only enter into the Abrahamic promise by attaching themselves to the Israelite sons of promise--the "Isaacites"--by the approved means of circumcision. This may have been the pinnacle of Judaistic argumentation, and may explain why Paul saves this proof as his climactic one. See Bouwman 1987 for an up-to-date bibliography on the Sarah-Hagar pericope. See also Hansen 1989, 141-50, Malan 1992, Jobes 1993, Perriman 1993, and Longenecker 1994 for diverse rhetorical analyses of 4:21-31..

[63]Paul creates historical correspondences by the use of these historical narratives. His connection of the Genesis narratives to the present Galatian situation is described by him as ἅτινά ἐστιν ἀλληγορούμενα in 4:24a. However, this methodology may be more of a mixture of what we presently call "typology" and "allegory" (Betz 1979, 238-40), with typology being the predominant method. Such historical correspondences were very appropriate and effective types of proof within the Jewish hermeneutics of his day (Ellis 1981, 51-54 and Steinhauser 1989). See Hansen 1989, 201-15 for an up-to-date discussion of the debate over this passage. Hansen's conclusion seems most judicious:

> Our examination of Paul's hermeneutical approach to the Hagar-Sarah story confirms the position that his basic typological interpretation is supplemented by an allegorical treatment in order to relate the people in the story to the specific issues in the Galatian church, and so to counteract the troublemakers' use of the same text (1989, 214-15).

[64]Again, this climactic proof of Paul's does not rest on his allegorizing, but on the first proof that he established in this heading (3:1-4:31). In that proof (3:1-5), Paul appealed to the Galatians' own witness of their possession of the Holy Spirit by faith in Christ alone and therefore their supernatural birth via God's Spirit (3:3, 5). By returning to the same issue of the possession of the Spirit in 4:21-31, Paul is effectively bracketing the whole argument of 3:1-4:31 with his most powerful evidence the Galatians' prior reception of the Spirit Who is the promised Abrahamic universal blessing (3:8-9, 14). The *interrogatio* method in both proofs also underscores the bracketing sense. The point of this sixth proof in 4:21-31 is that the "Isaacites" are characterized by a supernatural birth by God's Spirit, while the "Ishmaelites" are simply characterized by a birth according to human bodies unaided by God's Spirit. Given this simple means of identifying the sons of Abraham who will inherit (cf. Jub 16:15-19), then the Galatian Christians ironically qualify according to a strict reading of the Genesis narratives. *They* are the Isaacites because of their Isaac-like birth (κατὰ πνεῦμα), while the Judaizers are actually the Ishmaelites because of their Ishmael-like birth (κατὰ σάρκα)! Paul has taken what appears to be a prime piece of Judaistic argumentation and turned it on its head.

[65]This section will be dealt with in a somewhat cursory fashion now in light of the in-depth exegesis of it in Chapters 5-6. However, the presence of paraenetic material in this section warrants a comment. The limitations of epistolary analysis of Galatians manifest themselves very quickly when scholars seek to find the beginning of a purely paraenetic or exhortative section of the letter. As Merk 1969 has noted, six different beginnings for the moral exhortation section of Galatians have been championed (4:12; 4:21; 5:1; 5:2; 5:7; 5:13), and he prefers 5:13 (104). If Paul had used some of his more obvious stylistic transitions for the beginning of paraenetic section (e.g., Rom 12:1; 1 Thess 4:1), our task would be easy. But these transitions are more the exception than the rule. Additionally, past commentators have sought to separate this so-called paraenetic material too sharply from the theological argumentation of Gal 3-4. The following analysis should bear out Frank Matera's insightful comments about this section:

> Gal 5:1-6:17 forms the culmination of Paul's argument to the Galatians, the point he has intended to make from the beginning of the letter: the Galatians must not submit to circumcision. Thus, although these chapters contain a great deal of moral exhortation, they should not be viewed exclusively as paraenesis. They are the climax of Paul's deliberative argument aimed at persuading the Galatians not to be circumcised (1988, 79-80).

The choice of beginning this section at 5:1 rather than 5:13 (or elsewhere) is not so much based on a change to paraenetic language (which really begins in 5:13), but on a change in subjects. Gal 3:1-4:31 clearly deals with the topic of the Galatians' *identity* as sons of Abraham. Gal 5:1 builds very closely off of the "free man" conclusion of 4:31, but Paul then immediately transitions from this conclusion into the topic of *experiencing or using that freedom.* In 5:1 he summarizes the *identity* discussion of Gal 1-4, and then introduces the new topic of "How a child of God lives out this free identity" (cf. Duvall 1994a, 30-31 and Fairweather 1994b). Greater emphasis on the whole flow of Paul's rhetoric in Galatians reveals more readily this seam in his argument. Walter Hansen agrees with this assessment and asserts:

> Our analysis of the structure of Galatians suggests that the long debate regarding just where the paraenetic section of Galatians begins must now be concluded in favor of 5:13 as marking that beginning (1989, 50-51; see also 150-54).

[66]A "causal argument" is an argument that says "If A is the cause, then B should be its effect or manifestation." Many times it is argued backwards from the effect to the cause. This is the case here.

[67]The question Paul is answering in 5:1-6:10 is "Which community pattern of behavior manifests true freedom from sin's powers?" This issue of freedom from the power of transgressions was apparently the primary felt need to

which the Judaizers appealed (Betz 1974, 153-55). Of course, their answer was to take up the yoke of Torah and the mark of circumcision so that you can be included within the safety of God's covenant community--ethnic Israel. Paul's answer to this burning issue in 5:1-6:10 is found in a comparison of the behavior patterns of these two competing identities of the people of God. While the content of this section is ethical and exhortative in nature, its function is *argumentative* and not purely exhortative within Paul's epistle. First, he continues his antithetical or contrasting argumentation between the Judaizers' and himself. Of course, he argues for the superiority of his position over theirs. Secondly, he is now proving the superiority of his true gospel over their non-gospel in the third area. The first area concerned their antithetical natures (κατὰ ἄνθρωπον) versus κατὰ θεόν) and the confirmation by Jerusalem of his gospel (1:11-2:21). The second area involved the conflicting "gospels'" abilities to impart true Abrahamic sonship (3:1-4:31). Now in the third major area, Paul is proving the superiority of his gospel within *the ethical realm*. His gospel provides the only adequate and appropriate constraint for their behavior: the Holy Spirit (versus the constraint of circumcision and Torah-observance). There is nothing new about Paul's exhortation to choose between these choices. What is new in 5:1-6:10 is the realm of choice--the ethical or behavioral. Therefore, this paraenetic material serves a vital, perhaps climactic function, within the whole rhetoric of Galatians. See Kraftchick 1985, 3-61 and Barclay 1988, 1-35 for recent surveys of the role of Gal 5-6 within the whole epistle. See Duvall 1994a for a defense that Gal 5:1 transitions from the "identity" discussion of Galatians 1-4 to the "performance" or behavior section of Gal 5-6.

[68]The moral exhortation found in this argument is considered one of two kinds of deliberative rhetoric by Quintilian 1920, 3.4.9/1:393. The other kind of deliberative oratory is dissuasion. These same two are echoed by Aristotle 1926, 1.3.3/p. 33 and *Rhetorica ad Herennium* 1.2.2/p. 5. Letters of exhortation and advice are also a common type of epistle in the Mediterranean world. Galatians evidences many of the typical characteristics of letters of this type (Stowers 1986, 91152). See also the epistolary handbook of *Pseudo Demetrius* and his comments on types of epistles in Malherbe 1988, 31-41.

[69]Paul uses the term ἐλευθερία ("freedom") three times in Galatians (2:4; 5:1, 13). Each time it is used to express the opposite condition of slavery to the Mosaic Law. While Paul does not use the term ἐλευθερία in Gal 4:1-7 to describe slavery's opposite, it is obvious that such a term would be appropriate to describe the condition of sonship and heirship into which the Christian has entered (4:5-7). God sent forth His Son that He might redeem (ἐξαγοράση) those under Law *unto freedom* (4:4-5). This is significant in the discussion beginning in Gal 5:1 because "freedom" in this context in 5:1 and 5:13 is specifically freedom from the daily constraints of the Mosaic Law. Christ has delivered the believer from the bondage of the στοιχεῖα that existed during the era of the Mosaic Law (4:3, 9). Therefore, to return to Torah-observance is to be enslaved to these στοιχεῖα again (4:8-10). Conversely, standing firm

in ἐλευθερία is experiencing the continuing deliverance by Christ from sin's powers in one's life. Paul's point in Gal 5:1-6:10 is that the indwelling Holy Spirit, not Torah-observance, is the only adequate and appropriate constraint that Christ has provided to carry out His continuing deliverance. Therefore, "freedom" in Gal 5-6 is freedom from sin's powers via Christ's deliverance. See Loubser 1994 for a development of the slavery/freedom contrast.

[70]Paul's consistent message in this area is that Christ has delivered the Galatians from "this present evil αἰῶος (1:4) and from the bondage under the στοιχεῖα τοῦ κόσμου during the era of the Mosaic Law (4:3, 8-11). Therefore, it is absolutely amazing to him (1:6) that they would be so foolish (3:1) to do this fearful reverting (4:11) to the anachronistic and inferior mode of childish slavery that existed *before* the fullness of the time of the Son (4:1-7). The specific "yoke of slavery" (ζυγῷ δουλείας) of 5:1 is the Mosaic Law in the sense that it was the guardian and manager during the period of slavery to the στοιχεῖα (4:1-7).

[71]See Kraftchick 1985, 233-39 for a helpful explication of the rhetorical features of irony, amplification, *contentio*, and especially of pathos appeal in Gal 5:1-6.

[72]The issue here is not maintaining the eternal deliverance from sin's penalty (i.e., justification by faith), but going on to maturity in Christ (ἐπιτελεῖσθε in 3:3) and continuing to experience Christ's earthly deliverance from sin's *powers*. This is only achieved πνεύματι ἐκ πίστεως, "by the Spirit by faith" (5:5). In Rom 7:6 Paul affirms that this serving in "newness of the Spirit" is possible because we have been severed (κατηργύθημεν) from the Law. Ironically in Gal 5:4 Paul says that seeking to be justified by Law will lead to being severed (κατηργύθητε) from Christ! Both instances speak of releasing the Christian from the authority and benefit of another as they live the Christian life. In other words this is an existential, not an eternal deliverance that is only achieved when God's people...1) are appropriately arrayed around Christ (5:4a), 2) are operating on the principle of God's grace (5:4b), and 3) are emphasizing "faith working through love" (5:6b). As Paul will sketch out in 5:13-15, these three ingredients can not be present within the Judaizers' community which emphasizes circumcision and Torah observance. Further discussion of this will occur in Chapter 5.

[73]Again, see Kraftchick 1985, 240-47 for a more in depth rhetorical analysis of 5:7-12, especially in terms of the pathos and ethos content within this section. For Gal 5:11, see Baarda 1992.

[74]Betz 1975, 376-77 and those who follow his basic structuring of Galatians divide Gal 5:1-6:10 into three sections, each begun by a restatement of the "indicative" of salvation: 5:1-12; 5:13-24; and 5:25-6:10. This is an appealing structure, but not altogether convincing, especially in using εἰ ζῶμεν πνεύματι in 5:25 as the third indicative statement. A more accurate description of these three "indicatives of salvation" is that each of them is half of an antithesis contrasting the appropriate response to freedom from the Mosaic Law's daily constraints with the inappropriate Judaizers' response.

One must then see how these antitheses are being used in Paul's argument. The latter two antitheses in 5:13-15 and 5:25-26 seem to function as brackets for 5:13-26 because they deal with the same topic of community unity/coherence versus community jealousy/competitive strife. Additionally, 5:25 is related to 5:24 by asyndeton (no particle) and this makes for a forceful connection. Also, Paul's use of the vocative Ἀδελφοί in 6:1 is typical of usage in the beginning of a new section of the argument (e.g., Gal 1:11; 3:15; 4:12; and 5:13). See Wessels 1992 for a defense of Gal 5:13-6:10 being integrally connected to the rest of Galatians.

[75]We saw the causal argument of 5:1-6:10 manifested in 5:1-12 in comparing the antithetical effects or impacts that the two groups were having on the Galatians. The Galatians were being persuaded by Paul to question the cause behind the Judaizers if it resulted in that kind of effect (5:7-9). Now in 5:13-26 Paul continues his causal argument by again arguing from the effects backward to the cause that produced them. Now he is inviting the comparison of the two communities--the Judaizers and his--in the area of community unity and coherence. If, in fact, Christ is delivering them from sin's powers, then that deliverance should manifest itself in a unified and loving community of believers. This is the only appropriate community manifestation for those born κατὰ πνεῦμα. Speaking about the phenomena of human transformation in a causal argument, Patrick Sherry observed that

> It is assumed that certain phenomena in the world are *effects* brought about by the spirit of God, and that such effects resemble their cause. St. Paul speaks of men being changed by degrees into the likeness of God by the Spirit (2 Cor 3:18), and Aquinas maintains that human perfections like goodness and wisdom are caused by, and participate in, their divine exemplars (*S.T.* la.13.5, 6, 10; 14.6). To parody Scripture, by *their* fruits you shall know *Him* (1984, 35).

Conversely, those born κατὰ σάρκα will approach community as an opportunity for the σάρξ (5:13) and will manifest community phenomena or effects that are readily observable as a fulfilling of the desire of the σάρξ (5:16).

Therefore, structurally, Paul *brackets* the listing of these two antithetical *effects* or manifestations of community life in Gal 5:16-24 with the corresponding antithetical *causes* of those effects in 5:13-15 and 5:25-26. He is persuading the Galatians that the people of God who are born κατὰ πνεῦμα should manifest a life in community that is directly traceable to God's Spirit. An objective comparison of the community lives of the two groups will clearly reveal both the standards and causes of such a life.

[76]These verses introduce the theme of this section (5:13-26). Paul is showing the contrary ends of the two gospels that the Galatians have heard. The "gospel" preached by the community of the flesh ends up in providing

more opportunity for fleshly expression. The end of this kind of Judaizing emphasis is mutually destructive relationships. Ironically, the end of the true gospel and its manifestation is the fulfillment of the basic purpose of the whole Mosaic Law: loving edification of your neighbor. In other words the Law's fulfillment ultimately can be distilled into *relational terms*! Therefore, in another manifestation of the causal argument of this whole section (5:1-6:10), Paul is arguing that observing the *effects* of community relationships and unity should reveal the *true cause* of those effects. This is why mutual destruction is powerfully tied to σάρξ and mutual edification to πνεῦμα. Observing the community *effects* reveals the root community *cause*.

[77]In addition to the rhetorical devices of *contrarium* (which I have called antithetical expressions) and *repetitio* (of flesh and Spirit) in 5:13-26, Kraftchick 1985, 248 has observed the use of *synonymia* in this section. Paul describes the Christian life in relationship to the Holy Spirit with the terms περιπατεῖτε (5:16), ἄγεσθε (5:18), ζῶμεν (5:25), and στοιχῶμεν (5:26). Duncan 1934, 178 paraphrases Gal 5:25 to bring out the *corporate* nature of Christians' relationship with the Holy Spirit that στοιχῶμεν seems to indicate "If our individual lives are lived 'by the Spirit,' let us allow the Spirit to marshal us in our corporate relationships."

[78]The thesis of Strelan 1975 that Gal 6:1-5 (along with Gal 6:6-10) is about the bearing of a common financial burden is very appealing, but not totally convincing. As Barclay 1988, 131-32 and Young 1977 have noted, the phrase "bear burdens" (τὰ βάρη βαστάζετε) usually has a more general reference to the many physical and spiritual burdens of everyday life. This less restricted sense seems to fit more smoothly into the general relational picture that Paul has been sketching.

[79]Hurtado 1979 makes a strong case that this financial sharing is specifically Paul's appeal for the Jerusalem collection and therefore it relates to Gal 2:10. However, this appeal is most allusive and oblique if that is what Paul is doing! Apart from my chronological problem with this later collection's conflict with my early dating of Galatians (A.D. 49), I have two problems with tying Gal 6:6-10 to the Jerusalem collection for the Jerusalem Church under the motive of a temple offering of some sort as if the Galatians were new proselytes. Secondly, it might be that Gal 6:6-10 is also an antidote for *a Judaistic collection*. The Galatians financial "sowing" should be with their local teachers and the household of faith, than a very subtle appeal for his Jerusalem collection for the poor (which I think is still future), Paul may be correcting the inappropriate Judaistic collection that may have been levied out of a wrong subsuming of the Gentile churches of Galatia under the Jerusalem Church (cf. Bruce 1985b, 651-61). While all of this is speculative, it does seem to treat Paul's language in Gal 6:6-10 in a more straightforward manner than Hurtado's thesis.

[80]Aristotle describes the ideal content and function of an epilogue:

The epilogue is composed of four parts [1] to dispose the hearer favourable towards oneself and unfavourably towards the adversary; [2] to amplify and depreciate; [3] to excite the emotions of the hearer; [4] to recapitulate. For after you have proved that you are truthful and that the adversary is false, the natural order of things is to praise ourselves, blame him, and put the finishing touches. In the exordium we should state the subject, in order that the question to be decided many not escape notice, but in the epilogue we should give a summary statement of the proofs (Aristotle 1926, 3.19.l/p. 467; numbering is mine).

Paul includes all four of these elements with great passion in his epilogue, which has both the epistolary and rhetorical elements of a conclusion. See Weima 1995 for Paul's letter closings in general and Weima 1993 for Gal 6:11-18.

[81]Betz 1979, 23 notes that 6:12-17 is technically the *peroratio* or brief conclusion containing the *indignatio* of 6:12-13 and the *conquestio* of 6:17. This *peroratio/recapitulatio* is bracketed by Paul's handwritten authentication in 6:11 and the final benediction in 6:18. See also Hansen 1989, 51-52, 65-66, and 69-70.

[82]As noted above, an "external proof" is a proof that exists outside the author's creation of it. An "internal or artistic proof" is a proof invented by the author.

[83]However, Hansen 1989, 21-54 seeks to demonstrate that there are a number of customary epistolary formulae that indicate the epistolary structure of Galatians (especially pp. 30-31). However, in signaling the actual epistolary structure, these formulae are not as definitive nor as conclusive as Hansen seems to believe, as evidenced by the significant degree of disagreement about the structure of the epistle, even by those who recognize the epistolary formulae!

[84]Hansen 1989, 79-93 lists the presence of at least 15 different rhetorical arguments that Paul uses in Galatians.

[85]Also seeing this continuity is Feuillet 1982, who outlines the argument of Galatians according to salvation history and sees Gal 4:21-6:10 as a continuation of Paul's argument, not as a closing paraenesis only.

Chapter 3

The Social Dynamics of the Flesh/Spirit Conflict[1]

I. The Basic Dynamics of the Galatians' Crisis

Why would a first century Mediterranean person living in Galatia who was a relatively new Christian be vulnerable to the Judaizers' non-gospel? Traditionally, Western scholars have viewed their vulnerability within the parameters of an abstract search for "truth." The sense is that the Judaizers came along and made a more logical and believable appeal to the "truth" and thereby won over the searching Galatians. In this view the inherent weakness of the Christian's "flesh" for self-justification enters in, as Martin Luther so brilliantly expressed in his 1535 lectures on Galatians:

> But such is human weakness and misery that in the terrors of conscience and in the danger of death we look at nothing except our own works, our worthiness, and the Law...Thus human reason cannot refrain from looking at active righteousness, that is, its own righteousness; nor can it shift its gaze to passive, that is, Christian righteousness, but it simply rests in the active righteousness. So deeply is this evil rooted in us, and so completely have we acquired this unhappy habit! Taking advantage of the weakness of our nature, Satan increases and aggravates these thoughts in us (Luther 1963, 5).

Almost 450 years later, Gerhard Ebeling adds a moral or ethical dimension to the Galatians' search for "truth," yet still summarizes the Galatians' vulnerability in basically ideological terms:

The inner reason why the Galatians deserted Paul, it seems to me, cannot be derived primarily from the question of how Scripture is to be understood. The real reason for their instability must be connected with the liberating effect of the Spirit they had experienced when they first became Christians....On the other hand, the Judaizers can hardly have precipitated a crisis not already in the making. Thus it is reasonable to suppose that the Galatians had been dizzied by their enthusiastic freedom, so that the transports of their religious experience left them finally without religious anchor. The Judaizing message rushed in to fill this vacuum (Ebeling 1985, 54).

Were the Galatians really vulnerable *primarily* at the ideological level? In fact, did they even have a separate category called "Religion" like Westerners have to go along with their basic categories of "Kinship," "Politics," and "Economics"? Bruce Malina, along with other cultural anthropologists, answer this question with a resounding "No!".

In other words, all "religion" in the first century Mediterranean world was embedded in either kinship or polity. There was no freestanding social institution recognized as "religion," no discernible separation of church and state or church and family, even if one wished to make such a separation (Malina 1986a, 95).

Anthropologist Murray Wax underscores this conclusion:

Now we know that in most non-Western societies the natives do not distinguish religion as we do; indeed field workers have found it difficult to delineate a religion that is distinct from culture. While anthropologists are more sophisticated [now], we still tend to be ethnocentric in our discussion of religion, and we too easily impute to others the characteristics of Western religious practices (Wax 1984, 16-17).

Malina then goes on to describe how a change in theology (e.g., from Paul's gospel to the Judaizers' non-gospel) would take place in a society where "religion" is imbedded in the other major institutions:

In other words, any change in theology would not have derived from the demands of logical, "scientific," consistency or the demands of some philosophical system. Rather theological change derived from valued objects, events or behaviors that contributed to some person's or group's honor, social standing, influence and reputation. Concern for some abstraction such as "truth," was of little value unless it were convertible to some more socially significant symbol (Malina 1986a, 98).

It is therefore very likely that the Galatians were not vulnerable primarily at an ideological level, but were vulnerable to the Judaizers' non-gospel because it was expressed in socially significant group terms. In other words the Judaizers apparently were able to make an appealing case for a more meaningful group identity for the Galatian Christians that would place them in closer continuity with God's historic people, Israel. How else can one explain why so many adult males would even consider submitting to the trauma of adult circumcision? Additionally, the Judaizers must have promised that Torah-observance was God's great gift of grace to His people that would rightly constrain their behavior. Without the Mosaic Torah, how would God's people know what the acceptable group patterns of behavior were? Such socially significant group terms, of course, had a theological hook in them, but the Galatians apparently were willing to consider swallowing this hook given the very culturally-meaningful Judaizer bait.

However, Western scholars have generally not viewed the Galatian crisis in such culturally-sensitive terms, but may be guilty of imputing their religious practices and concerns to them. Krister Stendahl has argued in his much-discussed article "The Apostle Paul and the Introspective Conscience of the West" (1976, 78-96) that this Western insensitivity can be traced all the way back to Augustine, "the first modern man." The Medieval Church supposedly institutionalized Augustine's introspective, individualistic view of Paul. The Reformers allegedly modified without dislodging the basic perspective, as the above quote of Luther seems to illustrate. Stendahl critiques this reinterpretation of Paul and especially Paul's opposition to imposing the Mosaic Law upon the Gentiles:

> In the common interpretation of Western Christianity, the matter looks very different. One could even say that Paul's argument has been reversed into saying the opposite of his original intention....So drastic is the reinterpretation once the original framework of "Jews and Gentiles" is lost, and the Western problems of conscience become its unchallenged and self-evident substitute (1976, 86-87).

According to Stendahl, at root is a Western ethnocentrism that filters out Paul's emphasis on groups of people and their identities within salvation history (i.e., Jews and Gentiles).[2] In the place of Paul's attempt to clarify how these groups are to relate now that Jesus

Christ has come is substituted an individual concern for the removal of guilt through justification by faith in Christ. In other words, in place of a corporate redemptive historical concern is substituted an individual, existential concern. Stendahl points to how this has distorted our understanding of first century texts like Galatians:

> And yet, if our analysis is on the whole correct, it points to a major question in the history of mankind. We should venture to suggest that the West for centuries has wrongly surmised that the biblical writers were grappling with problems which no doubt are ours, but which never entered their consciousness (1976, 94-95).

While Stendahl's rather sweeping critique of lens-distortion is probably overstated, it does highlight the legitimate need for more of a balanced treatment of these issues. The following analysis of some of the social dynamics of the conflict in Galatia is offered to underscore the corporate sense of σάρξ and πνεῦμα in Gal 3-6 and thereby to provide balance to the individual emphasis. Hermeneutically speaking, this is an attempt to transcend our own horizon and to seek to understand the Galatians' horizon.[3]

II. The Dyadic Personality and the Sociological Thinking of the Galatians

A "dyadic personality" is a non-individualistic self-awareness that is characteristic of first-century Mediterranean peoples who do not share our Western views of an individual identity. Bruce Malina sketches the basic contours of how dyadic people like the Galatians would view their identity:

> A dyadic personality is one who simply needs another continually in order to know who he or she really is....Such a person internalizes and makes his own what others say, do, and think about him because he believes it is necessary, for being human, to live out the expectations of others. That person would conceive of himself as always interrelated to other persons while occupying a distinct social position both horizontally (with others sharing the same status, moving from center to periphery) and vertically (with others above and below in social rank). Such persons need to test this interrelatedness, with the focus of attention away from ego, on the demands and expectations of others who can grant or withhold reputation. Pivotal values for such persons would be honor and shame, not guilt (Malina 1993, 67).

There are four major aspects of people with a dyadic identity that we see evidenced in Galatians.[4] The first trait is that of "embeddedness" or distinction because of existence within a certain group. Clifford Geertz contrasts this sense of a person with the Western sense:

> The Western conception of a person as a bounded, unique, more or less integrated motivational and cognitive universe, a dynamic centre of awareness, emotion, judgment, and action organized into a distinctive whole and set contrastively both against other such wholes and against its social and natural background, is, however incorrigible it may seem to us, a rather peculiar idea within the context of the world's cultures (Geertz 1976, 225).

However, a sense of embeddedness moves the focal point of identity from the individual to his or her group:

> To such a social pattern, a concept of selfhood which marks public identity contextually and relativistically, but yet does so in terms--tribal, territorial, linguistic, religious, familial--which grow out of the more private and settled arenas of life and have a deep and permanent resonance there, would seem particularly appropriate. Indeed, the social pattern would seem virtually to create this concept of selfhood (Geertz 1976, 234).

Malina paraphrases this sense of group identity and applies it to the Mediterranean peoples of the New Testament: "our first-century person would perceive himself as a distinctive whole *set in relation* to other such wholes and *set within* a given social and natural background" (1993, 68).

This sense of "embeddedness" is central to the Galatians conflict between the gospel according to Paul and the non-gospel according to the Judaizers. The issue is not primarily one of how *individuals* can be justified by faith, although, of course, this is encompassed by the real issue. Rather, the issue in Galatia is how *groups of people* (Gentiles) are to be included in God's people. At stake is "the truth of the gospel" (Gal 2:5, 14), which, in this context, is specifically the inclusion of Gentiles who exercise faith in Jesus Christ *without* any prescribed Judaistic attachments (2:1-4; 2:11-21).[5] Paul defines this "gospel" in this group language in Gal 3:8-9, 13-14 in terms of the application of the Abrahamic blessing to all τὰ ἔθνη. While the gospel obviously addresses and demands responses from individuals, it nonetheless views these individuals as embedded within groups of people within salvation history.[6]

This leads to a second aspect of group-oriented people. Because of their sense of embeddedness, dyadic peoples tend to see *the groups* in which persons are embedded as unique and individualistic, not the individual representatives of the groups. Individuals are not the unpredictable factor in the equation. Instead, their behavior is rather fixed and unchanging because it is specified and defined by the unique and distinct *group* in which they are embedded. This may be one overlooked interpretive factor that could help explain Paul's lapsing from the first person *plural* (Gal 2:15-17) into the first person *singular* (2:18-21) right in the middle of the description of the desired perspective and behavior of his group, the Jewish Christians. Paul's perspective was probably typical of anyone in his dyadic-thinking culture. He was simply describing the appropriate and expected behavior of Jewish Christians in light of "the truth of the gospel" (2:5, 14). This was a unique and distinct group of Christians and therefore they had a unique and distinct set of behaviors. Paul's first person singular language on behalf of this group or as a representative of this group was totally understandable within such a cultural setting. His perspective was not described in order to be deviant from his group-- an unacceptable move! Rather, his singular perspective in Gal 2:18-21 was given as the appropriate and representative paradigm for his group. The "we" sense of Gal 2:15-17 continues through the "I" language of Gal 2:18-21 because of the sense of embeddedness and group, not individual, uniqueness.[7]

This emphasis on the uniqueness of groups, not individuals, leads to a closely related and third aspect of dyadic personalities. This trait is the aspect of "sociological thinking" or group stereotyping. In Gal 2:18-21 Paul could refer to his group (the Jewish Christians) by referring to himself because dyadic peoples make sense of other people's behavior by looking at the group that person is embedded within and seeing what *the group's* values and standards are. In other words an individual embodies only the values of his or her identity group in a stereotypical (and uninteresting) manner. In fact, Paul has already done this in Galatians in 1:6 (Did all the Galatians desert?) and in the immediate context of 2:13-15. In particular in 2:15, Paul applies sociological thinking or group stereotyping to the Gentiles who are collectively considered "sinners." Paul does this elsewhere with the Cretans (Titus 1:12) and with Jews and Greeks (e.g., 1 Cor 1:22-24). Such group-oriented thinking is common throughout the New Testament. One of the most vivid examples is Nathanael's "Can anything good come out of Nazareth?" in John 1:46. In this kind of a culture, understanding of some person is based on his or her embeddedness in family, village or city, or ethnic group. The individual is symptomatic and representative of his or her group:

> Thus to get to know one member of the group is to get to know the whole group. While many in our society do in fact make judgments of this sort, a culture that does not go beyond general "sociological" criteria would lack individualism in our sense of the word. And, it seems, the first-century Mediterranean world reveals such a culture (Malina 1993, 70).

A fourth trait of dyadic personalities is that the responsibility for morality and deviance is not borne solely by the individual, but is also shared by the whole group in which the individual is embedded. Because of this dynamic, the sin of some can cause the whole group to be stigmatized (e.g., Greeks and Jews in Rom 1:18-3:8). Paul seems to be stigmatizing all of the Galatians in 3:1 because of the wavering of some of them. Also, the sin of some within the group taints the whole group according to the leaven principle (1 Cor 5:6 and especially Gal 5:9). The only appropriate response is for *the whole group* to mourn as a public protestation of the presence of this evil and to purify itself (1 Cor 5:2; 2 Cor 12:21; Gal 4:30). While the individuals within the churches have clear responsibility to avoid evil and obey the moral norms, the focus of moral descriptions in the New Testament is *primarily* upon the group.[8] Righteousness is never expressed in terms of the individual Christian in abstraction or isolation, but rather in terms of his or her embeddedness within the local congregation:

> Such descriptions are written from the viewpoint of the supraindividual, objective horizon of the social body. Examples of such descriptions are the various sin lists (e.g., Mark 7:21-22 and parallels); lists of vices and virtues (e.g., Gal. 5:16-24); and household codes (e.g., Eph. 5:21-6:9; Col. 3:18-4:1; 1 Tim. 2:8-3:15). The main problem is to keep the family, the village, and the nation sound, corporately and socially. In Christian communities, the main problem was to keep the Christian group, the individual church, in harmony and unity, in sound state (e.g., 1 Cor 12; Rom 12:3-21). The individual as such, our dyadic personality, is expendable...(Malina 1993, 71).

While Gal 5:19-23 is widely recognized as a catalog of vices and virtues (e.g., Betz 1979, 281-83), there has been a general failure to tie these relational traits to the respective opposing communities in Galatia. However, the rhetorical analysis of Galatians in the previous chapter gave contextual evidence that this is, in fact, the only meaningful way to understand the ἔργα τῆς σαρκός and the καρπὸς τοῦ πνεύματος. Rather than holding up these vices and virtues in abstraction, Paul seems to be pointing to their embodiment in the Judaizer and Pauline communities. The bracketing of the vices and virtues list with antithetical descriptions of the general relational patterns of these opposing communities in Gal 5:13-15 and 5:25-26 underscores this embodiment. Paul is contrasting in stereotypical terms how members within these two communities relate to one another.[9] Again, "such descriptions are written from the viewpoint of the supra-individual, objective horizon of the social body" (Malina 1993, 71). However, it has become increasingly difficult for Western scholars, and especially American interpreters, to see and interpret these ethical passages from a group-orientation.[10]

III. The Central Values of Honor and Shame

J. G. Peristiany, writing in *Honour and Shame: The Values of Mediterranean Society*, has explained the pivotal role that these two values play in societies like the Galatians':

> All societies have rules of conduct, indeed the terms 'society' and 'social regulations' are coterminous. All societies sanction their rules of conduct, rewarding those who conform and punishing those who disobey. Honour and shame are social evaluations and thus participate of the nature of social sanctions, the more monolithic the jury, the more trenchant the judgement. Honour and shame are two poles of an evaluation. They are the reflection of the social personality in the mirror of social ideals. What is particular to these evaluations is that they use as standard of measurement the type of personality considered as representative and exemplary of a certain society. Whoever is measured by its standards and is not found wanting may, without falling from grace, break a number of rules considered minor in relation to those of honour. Honour is at the apex of the pyramid of temporal social values and it conditions their hierarchical order. Cutting across all other social classifications it divides social beings into two fundamental categories, those endowed with honour and those deprived of it (Peristiany 1966, 9-10).

Specifically, "honor" can be defined as

> the value of a person in his own eyes, but also in the eyes of his society. It is his estimation of his own worth, his *claim* to pride, but it is also the acknowledgement of that claim, his excellence recognized by society, his *right* to pride....Honour, therefore, provides a nexus between the ideals of a society and their

reproduction in the individual through his aspiration to personify them. As such, it implies not merely an habitual preference for a given mode of conduct, but the entitlement to a certain treatment in return. The right to pride is the right to status....and status is established through the recognition of a certain social identity (Pitt-Rivers 1966, 21-22).

"Shame" is the flip-side of honor and is

a positive symbol, meaning sensitivity for one's own reputation, sensitivity to the opinion of others. To have shame in this sense is an eminently positive value. Any human being worthy of the title "human," any human group worthy of belonging to the family of man, needs to have shame, to be sensitive to its honor rating, to be perceptive to the opinion of others (Malina 1993, 50-1).

To be "shameless" is to be without an honorable reputation and therefore to be outside the boundaries of the acceptable moral norms. Only a "fool" shows courtesy to a shameless person since it is foolish to respect social boundaries with a person who acknowledges no social boundaries.

The pivotal Mediterranean values of honor and shame play a significant role throughout Paul's argument in Galatians.[11] But this is not unusual because "the Mediterranean peoples...are constantly called upon to use the concepts of honour and shame in order to assess their own conduct and that of their fellows" (Peristiany 1966, 10). Essentially Paul's argument from this perspective can be summarized as follows:

1. Paul's gospel brought the Galatians *honor* as equals within the people of God (e.g., Gal 3:25-29).

2. The Judaizers' non-gospel will make the Galatians *dishonored and ashamed* because it will make them inferiors within the Judaizers' community since they will boast in the Galatians' *circumcision*, not in their *inclusion* (e.g., Gal 4:17-18; 6:12-13).

3. Additionally, the status that the Judaizers advocate within God's economy is the less-honorable one of a child or slave still under the guardianship of the Mosaic Law (Gal 3:19-4:7). Therefore, to revert to such status is to dishonor the work of Christ (4:4-5) and to dishonor the present expression of God's people (4:8-11).

4. Also, the Galatians risk publicly affronting Jesus Christ *again* if they really do desert the gospel (1:6-10; 3:1, 3; 5:1-12). They would

be "foolish" by showing respect for the shameless Judaizers who again publicly affront the crucified Christ (3:1, 3).

The heart of Paul's honor/shame appeal is rooted in the difference between ascribed honor and acquired honor.[12]   *Ascribed honor* is honor "passively" gained by bestowal at birth (e.g., upon Paul in Phil 3:5) or by bestowal from a notable person of power (e.g., upon the crucified Jesus in Phil 2:6-11). *Acquired honor* is honor "actively" gained by excelling over others in social interaction (e.g., Paul in Gal 1:13-14).

Paul's basic argument is that the Galatians have *already* been *ascribed* incredible honor by God based on their spiritual birth into His family as sons (4:1-7) and based on God's bestowal of the Abrahamic blessing of the Holy Spirit upon them (3:6-29). God their Father willed that they be delivered from this present evil age (1:3-4). They are now υἱοὶ θεοῦ through faith in Christ Jesus without any distinction in their ascribed honor because of their oneness in Christ (3:25-29). The honor ascribed the Galatians is symboled in Paul and in the gospel he preached. The honor Paul was *ascribed* by God (1:11-12, 15-17) is far more significant than any honor he could have *acquired* in Judaism (1:13-14). The honor ascribed him by God is also attached to the gospel he preached because of its divine nature (1:11-12) and its universal scope (1:15-17). Of course, the powerful point Paul is making to the Galatians in this passage (1:11-17) is that he greatly excelled in the agonistic contest for *acquired* honor being advocated by the Judaizers (1:13-14), but such honor unspeakably pales in comparison to the *ascribed* honor bestowed upon him (and thereby the Galatians) by Jesus Christ and the Father (1:11-12, 15-17). This ascribed honor of Paul and particularly of his gospel was recognized by the Jerusalem Apostles, which validated its reality within the community of God's people (Gal 1:18-2:21).[13]

Additionally, this ascribed honor is the legitimate basis for the Galatians' claim to honor before God, i.e., the basis for their "boasting" (καυχάομαι). This is contrary to Rudolf Bultmann (TDNT, 3:648-50) who may have culturally misunderstood the role of boasting or claiming honor within an honor/shame society when he called it *the* greatest human sin: self-glorying pride before God.[14] Actually, it is not sinful to boast or claim honor in and of itself. Paul allows for this in Gal 6:4: "But let each one examine his own work, and then he will have reason for boasting (τὸ καύχημα ἕξει) in regard to himself alone, and not in regard to another."

The problem in Galatia paralleled the problem in Corinth: boasting in the flesh or in human characteristics apart from the work of Christ (e.g., 1 Cor 1:26-31). In Galatia this manifested itself in the Judaizers claiming *acquired* honor inappropriately based on their success in getting the Galatians circumcised: "For those who are circumcised do not even keep the Law themselves, but they desire to have you circumcised, *that they may boast in your flesh* (ἵνα ἐν τῇ ὑμετέρᾳ σαρκὶ καυχήσωνται)" (Gal 6:13). Paul's correction is the same one that he applied in Corinth: "Let him who boasts, boast in the Lord" (1 Cor 1:31b [Jer 9:24]). In Galatians this means boasting only in the *ascribed* honor bestowed in Jesus Christ: "But may it never be that I should boast, except in the cross of our Lord Jesus Christ, through which the world has been crucified to me, and I to the world" (Gal 6:14). Such a basis for boasting or claiming honor is legitimate (cf. Rom 5:1-2). The Judaizers' basis, like that of the Jews with whom they want to be associated, is illegitimate (cf. Rom 2:17-29 for a blistering attack on the Jewish boast).[15]

The honor/shame perspective also sheds light upon Paul's conflict with Cephas and Barnabas in Gal 2:11-14. Paul's challenge to Cephas would not have been received by Cephas had he not perceived Paul to be an equal, for it would be dishonorable otherwise. However, Paul's account of his rebuking of Cephas in Antioch is not presented as Paul's acquisition of honor at Cephas' and Barnabas' expense. Such competitive struggles for honor are contrary to the nature of life in the Spirit (Gal 5:25-26). Rather, at risk is the unity of the Christian *societas* created previously in Jerusalem (Gal 2:1-10) (Sampley 1977, 161-66). Additionally, the honor of the universal, non-particularistic gospel was at stake in Antioch. When certain men from James and the Jerusalem Church said that eating with Gentile Christians was dishonorable, Cephas, Barnabas, and the rest of the Jewish Christians in Antioch complied. Paul's public rebuke of Peter showed that the universal, non-Judaistic nature of the gospel did not make eating with Gentiles shameful. In fact, "the truth of the gospel" (2:5, 14) was dishonored when the Jewish Christians withdrew from the Gentile believers. Additionally, as a Jewish Christian, Paul was dishonored by these actions of his fellow Jewish Christians. The point Paul makes in Gal 2:14-21 is that all Christians have *ascribed honor* through justification by faith in Christ. They do not need to get *acquired honor* through Judaistic practices, because to do so would be to contradict the dynamics of the new society in Christ with the old dynamics of Judaism. Although he does not tell of Cephas' response to his challenge on behalf of the truth of the gospel, Paul's rebuke of Peter must have been successful and accepted by Peter and the other Jewish Christians. If it had been unsuccessful (as Dunn 1982, 1983a asserts), then Paul and the non-Judaistic gospel would have been dishonored. Such an outcome would have then made it both unthinkable and counter-productive to chronicle the confrontation for the Galatians.[16] Paul's rhetorical argument from Gal 1:11-2:21 is consistent throughout every passage of this section: the universal, non-Judaistic nature of the gospel he preached was repeatedly confirmed in numerous ways by the Jerusalem apostles and the Judean believers. The gospel Paul had preached brings honor to the Galatians, while the Judaizers' non-gospel dishonors them.

IV. The Significance of God's Fatherhood over the Galatians

Persons who draw their primary identity from their group or community also normally have a very strong identification with the leader or head of the community. If this is a kinship group, then the head is normally the father or head of the clan. Paul goes to great lengths in Galatians to demonstrate that these believers have a (fictive) kinship relationship with God as their Father through the work of Christ (e.g., Gal 1:15; 3:6-9; 13-14; 3:26-4:8; 4:21-31).

As the Galatians' Heavenly Father, God is therefore responsible for protecting and providing for the general well-being and honor of the Galatians--His children (Malina 1993, 125-6). In return, the Galatians as children are responsible to be loyal to God as their Father. Given these well known basic roles,[17] Paul may be making a strong and fundamental appeal to the Galatians' relationship with God as their Father from the very beginning of the epistle. In Gal 1:1-5 Paul uniquely stresses God as Father three times and asserts that *He* willed the Galatians' deliverance from the present evil age through the Lord Jesus Christ's substitutionary death (1:3-4). In 6:14 Paul restates this deliverance in terms of the crucifixion of the κόσμος to him through Christ's cross. Such a gift is obviously something only God could do because of His monopolization of heavenly power (cf. Eph 2:1-10). It is *God* Who initiated this Father/child relationship and "who called you by the grace of Christ" (1:6). Therefore, it totally amazes Paul that the Galatians are so quickly (οὕτως ταχέως) showing their disloyalty by deserting (μετατίθεσθε) this Father Who called them into their gracious relationship (1:6).[18] In one sense the whole theme of Galatians is this amazingly rapid and uncalled-for defection of the Galatians as children from their Father God and the Lord Jesus Christ.

Paul underscores that God has given the Galatians two gifts when they believed in Jesus Christ that they could never hope to attain apart from *His* gracious initiation: deliverance from this present evil age (1:4; 6:14) and the promised Abrahamic blessing--the indwelling Holy Spirit (3:2-5, 7-9, 13-14). In light of such protection and provision through Jesus Christ's death on the cross, their defection is unthinkable. However, their possible defection to the gospel of the Judaizers is also a *further* humiliation to Jesus Christ, whose initial humiliation on the cross was already publicly portrayed to the Galatians (3:1). If the Head of their family had already suffered public humiliation through the crucifixion of His Son for their benefit, then to be disloyal to Him would be to be bewitched (ἐβάσκανεν) by Satan or his demonized representatives (3:1).[19] Further, to have suffered already on behalf of their Father and then to defect is also to risk making *their* suffering vain (Gal 3:4).

However, the worst result of the Galatians' defection to the Judaizers' gospel, and therefore to their community, would be that they would then live as if their deliverance from this present evil age had not occurred and they would therefore become enslaved again to τὰ στοιχεῖα τοῦ κόσμου (4:3, 8-11). Also, to receive circumcision would be to enter the Judaizer community and therefore to be under a different father. This, of course, would then isolate them from *experiencing corporately* their real Father's protection in the work of Christ (5:2). Such a defection to the Judaizer community would effectively sever (καταργέω) them from *experiencing corporately* the gracious benefits of Christ's work, such that they would fall from the protection of χάρις to the vulnerability of νόμος (5:3-4). They would trade corporate life "by the Spirit" (πνεύματι) (5:5) for corporate life according to the Law (5:3-4) while they wait for final eschatological righteousness (5:5).[20] Therefore, the Galatians' loss deals with the *present, earthly* benefits of their salvation in Christ, not with the future, eternal aspects. Paul's focus is on their present running of the race and their continued obeying of the truth (5:7). The immediate context is a challenge to the Galatian Christians to live a life of freedom versus a life of slavery (5:1). As strange as it sounds to Western ears, Paul therefore seems to be saying that the Christian life has *a corporate essence or nature* such that it cannot be lived within an alien community.

The father/child perspective helps to illumine this corporate essence by sensitizing us to the fundamental response demanded of children to their father: ongoing loyalty and public honor. As a model for them to emulate, Paul has maintained *his* loyalty to God and His gospel since his call by God (1:11-12). His loyalty continued in spite of persecution from fellow Jews because he did not preach circumcision among the Gentiles (5:11).   In fact, his loyalty to the Father who chose him is now evidenced in the στίγματα τοῦ 'Ιησοῦ on his body (6:17), not by the marks of circumcision.[21] The traditional benefits of God's children (peace and mercy) await the Galatians if they will also choose to continue to be loyal to the God Who called them and to walk by τῷ κανόνι which Paul preached (6:14-16). This, of course, means to live within the community of the Spirit, i.e., within the churches created by the gospel Paul preached.

V. The Competing Views of Kinship with God in Galatia

The Judaizers had apparently advocated a very attractive alternative for the identity of the people of God to the Galatians. We cannot know definitively if they directly attacked Paul or if they simply sought to add to the identity of the people of God that he had already established in Galatia. Given the Galatians' immense respect for Paul (Gal 4:12-20), the latter choice seems preferable.   However, the following comparison of the Judaizers' and Paul's community identities and structures reveals that the Judaizers' alternative for the identity of the people of God in no way builds upon Paul's identity.[22] In fact, their community identity fundamentally contradicts and negates Paul's identity of God's people at every significant point.[23]

A. JUDAIZERS[24]	B. PAUL
Advocated a *Contractive Commitment* based on "Homogeneous Ethnic Pseudo Kinship"	Advocated an *Expansive Commitment* based on "Pluralistic Non-Ethnic Pseudo Kinship"

A. **Judaizers:** Essentially they defined kinship *ethnically* as being "in Abraham" or becoming sons of Abraham. This is because the blood descendants of Abraham are the chosen ones of God in Pharisaic theology (e.g., Pss. Sol. 9:9; 18:3-5; cf. Matt 3:7-9).   Therefore, Gentiles had to approximate being born Jewish when they converted to Judaism or to Judaistic Christianity through ritual birth (e.g., circumcision).[25]   In Galatia this apparently involved becoming a proselyte to "Messianic" Judaism by being circumcised, taking up Torah, and being baptized (Gal 5:1-3; 6:12-13; 4:21; 3:27-29).[26] This kind of commitment is *contractive* in the sense that it is "exclusive" of normal Gentile ethnic identity and is an overt narrowing of ethnic Gentile identity boundaries to that of Jewish identity.[27] This *kinship* is "pseudo" or "fictive" in that it approximates blood kinship and functions in lieu of true Jewish racial kinship for the Gentile proselytes. If the general attitude of the Jewish rabbis was reflected by the Judaizers, then they would regard these Gentile proselytes equal in status *in the essentials* to born Israelites regarding duties and rights (Schürer 1986, 3.1:175-76). However, there were at least three significant gaps in this "equality" that reveal that proselytes did not, in fact, have full social equality (Schürer 1986, 175-76):[28]

> 1.) They could never call the Israelite ancestors--e.g., Abraham-their father: ".... and when he is in the Synagogue, he says 'O God of *your* ancestors'..." (m. Bik. 1:4; Blackman 1977, 1:469; emphasis is mine).
>
> 2.) They were ranked much lower than natural-born Israelites within the theocracy of Israel:
>
> A priest takes precedence over a Levite, a Levite over an Israelite, an Israelite over a bastard, (and) a bastard over a Gibeonite descendant, (and) a descendant of a Gibeonite over a proselyte, and a proselyte over a freed slave (m. Hor. 3:8; Blackman 1977, 4:574).[29]
>
> 3.) Apparently the temptation to taunt a descendant from proselytes with the deeds of his forefathers (m. B.M. 4:10) reveals that proselytes still did not enjoy the full trust accorded to born Jews and that they were considered more prone to err in halakhic matters by some rabbis (m. Nid. 7:3) (See also Seltzer 1988, 47-53).

Additionally, there seems to be a *theocratic dimension* to the Judaizers' view of kinship (and politics) that flows out of their sense of Messianic Theocracy and kingdom concerns (cf. Gal 5:21; 1:3-5; 6:15-16). This would explain some of their emphasis on the original twelve apostles (Gal 1:11-2:21) and the need to subjugate the new, largely-Gentile churches to apostolic rulership as promised by Jesus (Matt 19:23-30; Lk 22:24-30). Since Jesus promised this apostolic rulership over the twelve tribes of Israel (Matt 19:28; Lk 22:30), then the Judaizers may have reasoned that the Gentile believers must be racially, politically, and economically knitted together with restored ethnic Israel (Christian Jews).

This theocratic dimension may be most obvious in the Judaizers' geographical emphasis on Jerusalem and Judea, to which Paul seems to be responding at times in Galatians (e.g., 1:17-2:10; 4:24-27). Perhaps, Judaistic Christians from the Jerusalem Church took it upon themselves to layer the Gentile Christians of Antioch (Gal 2:11-13) and later Galatia around the theocratic core of the Twelve in Jerusalem (cf. Acts 15:23-24).   The precedent may have been set by the Jerusalem Pharisees who had taken it upon themselves to mediate their conception of the religious/cultural expression of Judaism to the villagers in the Palestinian countryside and to the world beyond (Malina 1993, 92-94). The Palestinian core of the Church, which was initially centered in Jerusalem, had been shaped by this Pharisaic mindset, which may have been stricter and more particularistic than that of the diaspora Jews (Schürer 1986, 159-60; cf. Hahn 1965, 18-25).[30] It is not the least bit unlikely that the more rigorous of the Pharisaic/Judaistic Christians within this core might perpetuate this model.   Within the anthropological model of the pre-industrial city within a peasant society,[31] they would be considered as "urban non-elites" (like the Jerusalem Pharisees) and would be the next class below the highest class of "urban elites" (e.g., Herodians and Sadducees) (Malina 1993, 92-93).   However, within the Church the apostolic "pillars" replaced the Herodian and Sadducean urban elites as the main shapers of the cultural tradition. But, the same urban non-elites (Pharisaic sect) still considered themselves to be the main mediators of the Christian culture of the apostolic στῦλοι to the outlying areas. They thereby perpetuated the same urban elite societal structure they had learned within Judaism.   However, as Paul passionately argues in Galatians, this dynamic from the old society of Judaism would not work within the new society of the Church.

B. Paul: Paul and the rest of the New Testament writers taught that kinship with God was *non-ethnically* defined by being "in Christ" through faith, not being in Abraham through blood (e.g., Gal 3:7-9, 26-28).[32] In addition, Paul launches a lengthy argument in Gal 3:6-29 also seeking to establish that now Christ is the one and only σπέρματι of Abraham through whom Abrahamic sonship is given.[33]   Paul's argument culminates with this promise: "And if you belong to Christ, then you are Abraham's offspring (σπέρμα), heirs according to promise" (Gal 3:29). Brendan Byrne has explained what Paul means with this terminology in his work on Paul's use of "sons of God" and "seed of Abraham" (1979, 141-90). Specifically, Byrne has noted that Paul does not just use the term υἱοθεσία (in Gal 4:5) to refer to the adoptive process in secular Hellenistic Greek. Rather,

> In Paul's usage υἱοθεσία represents the privilege of Israel, called according to the Scripture to be God's son (Rom 9:4). One acquires this privilege, not through a process of 'adoption'--a

juridical process alien to the Jewish tradition--but through aggregation 'in Christ' to the people of God (Israel), chosen, 'foreordained to glory' and 'called' into being (the traditional terminology) in the eschatological era (1979, 215).

In commenting on Paul's conclusions in Gal 3:29 and 4:7 that the sons of God are His heirs, Byrne also concludes: "As in the Jewish tradition, 'sons of God' designates the eschatological Israel destined to receive the inheritance promised to Abraham 'and to his seed'" (1979, 190; cf. Scott 1992 and Burke 1995).

In applying to the Gentile believers in Christ the Old Testament term "sons of God" (e.g., Gal 3:26) that was previously used corporately of God's redeemed people Israel (e.g., Ex 4:22; Hos 11:1), Paul is clearly arguing for a *pluralistic. non-ethnic* sense of (fictive) kinship for the Gentiles. While the Judaizers' view of kinship was exclusive and narrowing in nature, Paul's view of kinship with God through Christ is overtly inclusive and expansive. It is also *pluralistic*, not homogeneous, in its ethnic emphasis (Gal 3:28).[34]

Also, the geographical dimension of Paul's conception of the people of God directly conflicts with the Judaizers' apparent geographical centralizing of outlying Gentile churches around Jerusalem. In contrast, Paul gives very brief glimpses of the *decentralizing* spread of the gospel away from Jerusalem (e.g., Gal 1:21; 2:7-9).[35] While Paul's conception of decentralization is of minor concern in Galatians, it is more obvious in some of his other epistles (e.g., Rom 15:14-33). This has led Paul Bowers to observe that for Paul

> ...mission had a distinctly spatial dimension, that it implied a sense of vocation deliberately to extend the gospel land by land, so that eventually he could survey his achievement in geographical terms, could pronounce his assignment through a certain range of territories complete, and could announce intentions to travel within the same vocation to new lands further on in the same direction (Rom 15:17-24). For Paul, that is, mission was apparently in part a geographical accomplishment (1980, 317).

Bowers goes on to note how this planned spatial dimension of Paul's missionary work was unique among all first century religious movements, but especially contrasting with Jewish "missionaries":

> The first century also marked the high point of Jewish proselytism....While Paul's mission sustained, historically and conceptually, noteworthy connections with this movement, his efforts and intentions were in certain respects markedly distinct.

For while the influx of proselytes was supported from within Judaism by an eagerness to facilitate admission, by an extensive propaganda and apologetic literature, and by a largely favourable attitude on the part of the religious leaders, it must be defined, so far as the evidence goes, as a movement essentially of ingathering rather than outreach, *an expansion in which the lines of movement were primarily centripetal rather than centrifugal* (1980, 320; emphasis is mine).

This centripetal focus was ultimately centered in Jerusalem.[36] During the era of the Second Temple, in addition to circumcision and a purificatory baptism, an offering to the Sanctuary in Jerusalem was the third demand placed upon proselytes for full acceptance into the Jewish community (cf. Sifre on Num 15:14; m. Ker. 2:1; b. Ker. 9a; b. Yebam. 46a).[37] This geographically linked all diaspora proselytes to Jerusalem, and particularly to the Temple in Jerusalem. This linkage to the Temple was not a casual one, however, but was underscored by theological necessity: "R. Eliezer ben Jacob says, The atonement of a proselyte (גר) is still incomplete until the blood (of his *offering*) has been sprinkled for him (against the Altar base)" (m. Ker. 2:1.7-9; Blackman 1977, 5:394).

One can easily see that if the Judaizers from Jerusalem and Judea sincerely, but wrongly, believed that these new Gentile believers in Galatia needed to be attached to ethnic Israel in addition to being in Christ, then they were honor-bound to implement the proselyte model of Gentile attachment which they had learned in Palestine. Unfortunately, this model was probably far more particularistic than the proselyte model of the diaspora Jews and could rightly be described as the national religion of Israel simply "Messianized" and internationalized: "So long as the outlook of the religion was purely terrestrial and national, naturalization in the Jewish people was the only way by which an alien could hope to share its glorious future" (Moore [1927] 1971, 231).

It is against such a contractive, homogeneous ethnic concept of kinship that the Apostle Paul counters with the universalistic concept of kinship that is expansive, pluralistic, and non-ethnic at its core: "For you are all sons of God through faith in Christ Jesus" (Gal 3:26). As Paul boldly declared in Gal 3:28, such an emphasis accords both full kinship *and full social equality* to Gentiles within the people of God that the Judaizers' proselyte model could never offer.

VI. The Contrasting Emphases on Purity in Galatia[38]

A. JUDAIZERS

Defined "Purity" in terms of *Group Commitment.* "Dirt" is *external* and outside of the self and the group; becomes a problem when it intrudes and mixes with the group; presence of dirt/impurity tests group integrity or wholeness.

B. PAUL

Defined "Purity" in terms of *Group Reputation.* "Dirt" is *internal* and is also behavior that is rated negatively by outsiders or not up to their standards; becomes a problem of impressing outsiders and thus maintaining group boundaries; presence of dirt/ impurity tests group solidarity or unity.

A. Judaizers: Jacob Neusner has observed that "purity is an essential element in the interpretation of Israel's total religious system" (1973, 28). Michael Newton noted that the separatists of Qumran had a very high emphasis on purity, especially as a part of the entrance requirements into the community of the elect (1985, 10-51). This was true of all the sects of Judaism during the Second Temple era and their respective attitudes toward the Temple tended to distinguish them from one another (Smith 1960, 352). However, the common denominator was each sect's emphasis on purification as a part of entrance into their community. Those Jewish Christians who followed Paul into Galatia and advocated the proselyte model with the area Christians give evidence of holding the Pharisaic view of entrance purification.[39] This can be seen in their way of dealing with the anomaly of Gentile believers. If their reasoning followed that of the Pharisees of Palestine, it moved along this line:

1. Israel is the elect of God and is the pure seed (e.g., Pss. Sol. 7:8-10; 9:8-11; 11:7; 14:5; 17:4; 18:1-5).

2. However, some Gentiles have believed in Yahweh and in Jesus the Messiah (e.g., in Galatia).

3. But Gentiles, as a group, are rejected by God because they are by nature lawless and are profane, impure, and defiled (e.g., Pss. Sol. 2:2, 19-25; 7:1-3; 8:23; 17:13-15).

4. Therefore, Gentiles must be *purified* to be a part of elect Israel (cf. Acts 15:1,5).

This emphasis on the lack of purification on the part of the Gentile Christians in Antioch is what Paul chronicled in Gal 2:11-14 as a wrong precedent set by Cephas, Barnabas, and other Jewish Christians due to pressure from part of the Jerusalem Church (2:12). This is, of course, the heart of the Galatian controversy. The normal, profane condition of the Gentiles must be righted by aggregation to the *true* people of God, restored ethnic Israel. Therefore, the Gentiles must submit to the ζυγός of the Law (Gal 4:21; 5:1). They must follow the rightful "ceremonial leaders" (the Judaizers, not Paul) and finish going through the marginal condition that leads to aggregation by finalizing their purification, i. e. being circumcised (Gal 5:2-6). Circumcision is the pivotal issue that Paul has been building toward in the epistle. The final major section of the epistle (5:1-6:17) is bracketed in 5:1-12 and 6:11-17 with intense persuasion regarding not submitting to circumcision. As Matera 1988, 79-80 has observed, "Gal 5:1-6:17 forms the culmination of Paul's argument to the Galatians, the point he has intended to make from the beginning of the letter: the Galatians must not submit to circumcision. "

In addition to bringing the issue of purity into the realm of entrance requirements into the people of God, the Judaizers also made purity *the main focus* of the people of God. They created an *inward focus* by emphasizing "group commitment purity," which is commitment to the group's rules in order to maintain the corporate group's purity. As Neusner has noted (1971, 3:304-5; 1979, 67-96), the emphasis on maintaining the purity of table fellowship is at the very heart of first century Pharisaic theology. Gal 2:11-14 reveals the continuation of this theology applied to Gentile Christians by Jewish Christians. This then leads to the *main concern* of the group: maintaining the group purity and avoiding impure mixture within the group by avoiding impure outsiders (e.g., Gal 2:12) and by promoting the ongoing means of group purity. Both the defensive and offensive aspects of maintaining purity are achieved and the closed group boundaries are maintained through emphasizing the means of purity, which is the obedience of the true community to Torah (Gal 3:1-5; 4:8-11; 21; 5:1-6). In Galatia, this may have included the teaching similar to apocalyptically-minded Jews and the sect of Qumran that tied the festal calendar to deliverance from τὰ στοιχεῖα τοῦ κόσμου (Gal 4:3, 8-11) (Mussner 1974, 298-302). Living in accordance with the festal calendar of Judaism would allegedly provide relief from these celestial powers (Betz 1979, 204-5; cf. Williams 1988, 714-15 for the interpretive options of τὰ στοιχεῖα). This view of impurity and the means of avoiding and sanctifying it leads to a *group thrust* upon "transformative kinship." Outsiders need to be transformed and conformed to the group's core standards in order to gain entrance into the group. In fact, that is what comprises entrance into the group. The Judaizers eagerly sought the Galatians (4:17) to transform them for entrance into elect Israel via circumcision (6:12-13). Purifying transformation preceded entrance into the people of God in the model that the Judaizers advocated in Galatia.

B: Paul: What was the anomaly of Gentile belief in the Judaizers' view of purity was no anomaly at all for Paul because his concern was not how Israel approached a holy God, but how a holy God has approached Israel and the Gentiles in the work of Christ (Gal 3:10-14). While we will see that the purity of the people of God is an issue for Paul, it is striking to notice that purity is not an issue when Paul speaks of the entrance requirements into this group. This is because the Christian's impurity has been dealt with definitively by God. Paul makes this point by bracketing the epistle with these definitive statements about the Galatians' and his purity in 1:4 and 6:14. His emphasis, of course, is on what God has done in Christ to give His people an "ascribed purity" (versus "acquired purity"), if you will.

Even more enlightening is Paul's discussion of the Judaizing emphasis on purity as an entrance requirement into the people of God in Gal 2:11-21. While Paul begins the discussion with their concern for purity (2:11-14), he quickly moves into the discussion of *righteousness*. This is indicative of Paul's difference with all the sects of Judaism. While they speak of entrance into the people of God in terms of *both* righteousness and purity, Paul speaks of entrance *only* in terms of righteousness with little emphasis on purity. While the sects of Judaism continue to speak of *both* righteousness and purity in order to maintain your status within the covenant community, Paul again has a *single* focus:

> Paul's use of righteous terminology appears, for the most part, in connection with the believer's entrance into the community. The requirements for entry are couched in terms of righteousness. Once one is in, and a member of the Church, one enjoys the gift of the Spirit. Paul then switches to purity terminology in order to lay the framework for the behaviour pattern of believers (Newton 1985, 116).

Paul's concern for the purity of the people of God is also different from that of the Judaizers'. While they had an inward focus on group commitment purity, Paul had more of an *outward focus* on "group reputation purity." This is not to the exclusion of some inward focus, yet, in wheel terminology, could be characterized as more of a focus on the rim of the wheel than on the hub. This is due to the leveling in Christ of those historical distinctions related to purity like ethnicity, social status, and sexual identity (Gal 3:28) that had created an inner hierarchy within Judaism. "Purity lines now consisted only of a distinction between inside and outside, in-group and out-group" (Malina 1993, 177). A life of impurity (τὰ ἔργα τῆς σαρκός) is simply indicative of those who shall not inherit the kingdom of God (Gal 5:19-21), not of an inner hierarchy within God's people. This is because those who belong to Christ Jesus have definitively dealt with the σάρξ (Gal 5:24). Nevertheless, there will be Christians caught in trespasses and the community of the Spirit is to restore such ones in gentleness and humility in order to preserve the Church's reputation as a caring, mutually-supportive community (Gal 6:1-5). Such a reputation will be enhanced as the Christians do good to τοὺς οἰκείους τῆς πίστεως and also to all persons (6:10). Like Jesus before them, if the Christians will de-emphasize *the social purpose* of some of the purity rules like circumcision (Gal 6:15), then the original purpose of facilitating, not restricting, access to God will be realized and peace and mercy will be upon them (Gal 6:16).

While the inward focus of the Judaizers posed the threat of isolationism and ethnocentrism, Paul's outward focus posed the threat of dilution of Christian distinctives and looking like outsiders. Because Paul addressed this threat in part in Gal 5:13-6:10, it appears likely that the Judaizers appealed to it in Galatia. By examining this passage in this light, it reveals Paul's *main concern* regarding purity. While the Judaizers' main concern was avoiding outsiders and maintaining closed boundaries through observance of Torah, Paul's main concern was the delineating of internal standards and group boundaries in such a way that outsiders would socially accept the Church as a voluntary (fictive) kinship group (Malina 1986a, 101; see also Leary 1993). Contrasting with the Judaizers' *group thrust* of "transformative kinship," Paul set forth the Church's group thrust of "aggressive kinship." The sense of both the main concern and group thrust that Paul advocated is that the Church should be relationally appealing to those outside it and aggressively seeking to get those same outsiders to become a part of it, i.e., to be "in Christ." The delineating of the boundaries of the people of God in this manner in Gal 5:13-6:10 is set up in Gal 5:1-12 with Paul's anti-circumcision persuasion. In particular, Gal 5:5-6 lays out the contrasts:

> For we by the Spirit by faith are waiting for the hope of righteousness. For in Christ Jesus (it is) neither circumcision nor

uncircumcision that matters, but (it is) faith working through love (my translation).

Paul has replaced the objective standards of Torah with the objective standards of the Spirit, or τὸν νόμον τοῦ χριστοῦ (Gal 6:2). As one would expect from the prophecies concerning the New Covenant in Jer 31:31-34 and Ezek 36:24-32, God's Law under this covenant would be more relationally intensive, internalized, love-oriented, and Spirit-centered. It is this exact New Covenant texture that Paul captures in Gal 5:5-6 and 5:13-6:10. The old purity rules that came to have the social purpose of constricting and diminishing access to God have been replaced by a "softer" boundary with outsiders that opens up a fuller access to God for them (e.g., Gal 2:15-21). By avoiding the old purity rites that dealt with the σάρξ (Gal 3:3; 5:13), the Galatian Christians can fulfill the relational emphasis of the New Covenant Law (5:13-15). They can live out their identity as the καινὴ κτίσις (6:15-16).[40]

VII. Conclusion: The Galatian Social Dynamics and Paul's Use of SARX and PNEUMA in Gal 5-6

Two basic conclusions can be drawn from this lengthy analysis of the social dynamics of the Galatian controversy. The first is a general hermeneutical and methodological one. If the preceding social analysis has underscored anything, it should have underscored the fact that σάρξ and πνεῦμα have not always been interpreted adequately within their particular and contingent historical and social setting. J. C. Beker has made this point about Pauline theology in general (1980, 11-36; 1988; 1989), and it is especially relevant for this aspect of Paul's thought. Overall, σάρξ and πνεῦμα have specifically not been adequately recognized in their contextual corporate sense in Galatians 5-6 because of Western interpreters' concerns with individual, metaphysical (vertical) issues. As a result we have missed Paul's corporate, redemptive-historical (horizontal) concerns. In a different context, Beker has called this the clash of "an Hellenistic cosmology, which thinks only in spatial-vertical categories rather than in the temporal-historical categories of apocalyptic thought" (1989, 359). Paul's apocalyptic view of the Church's redemption clearly brackets the epistle in Gal 1:4 and 6:14 and encloses several extensive redemptive historical discussions relating to the identity of the people of God (e.g., Gal 3:15-4:7) (cf. Martyn 1985b). This book's central thesis is that

Gal 5:13-6:10 is one of those redemptive-historical discussions where Paul is again addressing the issue of group identity.

Additionally, as Francis Watson has observed, Paul's controversy with Judaism caused him to burst forth in profuse *antithetical language* of a redemptive-historical nature. There are at least ten examples of these antitheses in Galatians which serve to contrast the competing communities (Watson 1986, 46-47):

Galatians' Passage	**JUDAIZERS**	**PAUL**
2:16	works of the Law	faith in Christ
2:21	Law	Christ
3:10, 13-14	curse	blessing
3:15-18, 21	Law	promise
4:1-7	slavery	sonship
4:22-5:1	slavery	freedom[41]
5:2	circumcision	Christ
5:11; 6:12-13	circumcision	cross
5:4	Law	grace
3:3; 4:29	flesh	Spirit

Given Paul's general widespread use of these redemptive-historical contrasts in Galatians and his specific application of the flesh/Spirit antithesis to the Judaizers' and his communities in 3:3 and 4:29, it is not unreasonable to assume that he is using σάρξ and πνεῦμα in the same antithetical manner in Gal 5:13-6:10. In fact, it is far less reasonable to assume a *different* antithesis from that in Gal 3:3 and 4:29.

The second conclusion relates to the specific lens that the preceding social analysis provides for viewing Paul's argumentation in Galatians. Both the Judaizers and Paul expressed their viewpoints in socially significant group terms in Galatia because of the embedded nature of "religion" in kinship, politics, and economics. Paul brings the five aspects of these group terms that we have analyzed to a climactic peak in Gal 5-6 when he contrasts the Judaizers' and his communities through the flesh/Spirit antithesis:

1. Regarding their Dyadic Personality and Sociological Thinking

In Gal 5:13-6:10 Paul draws back the curtains and reveals the interpersonal characteristics of the communities of the flesh and of the Spirit. Within which community would the Galatians want to live given this stark contrast?

2. Regarding their Honor and Shame

Given the Judaizers' apparent perception of limited good--particularly in the realm of honor--they must competitively strive for acquired honor within their communities (Malina 1993, 94-103).

> The Pharisees, by establishing a superordinate prestige system, challenged authority based on wealth and birth. Their power claims had to do with membership in a group which involved special skills in interpretation and particular kinds of piety. Thus was introduced a *highly competitive system* which provided the possibility of social mobility and necessarily posed a threat to the established powers (Isenberg 1975, 42; emphasis is mine).

Paul reveals how shameful the flesh community is (5:13) because they bite and devour one another (5:15). Apparently, they also may be the ones who wrongfully boast and challenge and envy one another (5:26). Additionally, they may be guilty of not bearing one another's burdens, but rather having an inflated view of themselves (6:1-5).

3. Regarding God's Fatherhood over them

Paul has already said that joining the community of the flesh will corporately sever them from Christ and His benefits (5:2-4). He then adds that the community that manifests the deeds of the flesh is not a community under the fatherhood of God because it will not inherit His kingdom (5:19-21; 6:8).

4. Regarding their Kinship with God

The Galatians can be assured that they will sow to the Spirit and reap eternal life (6:8) because they have crucified the flesh when they believed in Christ (5:24). They also have full social equality in God's family because they are a new creation and circumcision or uncircumcision does not matter anymore (6:15-16).

5. Regarding their Purity

Ironically, the Judaizers' inward focus on maintaining purity does not enable them to escape the impurity that comes from disregarding Torah's central tenet of loving your neighbor (5:13-15). By focusing on Torah to constrain their desires (5:16-18), they defile themselves with the deeds of the flesh (5:19-21) and insure the impurity of corruption (6:8). In contrast, the Spirit community has victory over the flesh (5:16-18), produces pure behavior (5:22-23), and reaps eternal life (6:8).

We interpreters can be greatly aided in reading Galatians if we gain a better understanding of the social dynamics of the conflict in Galatia. If our perspective is primarily an individualistic one, then such an understanding illumines the great disparity between our world view and the Galatians' dyadic world view. Understanding the

Galatians' central concern for group identity then forces us to seek to approach the text as they would. Such an approach suggests a corporate lens for viewing Paul's use of σάρξ and πνεῦμα in Gal 5-6. If this is true, then the thematic and exegetical studies of the next three chapters should validate this conclusion.

Notes

[1]The phrase "social dynamics" is not used to describe what will be a full-orbed sociological analysis of the Galatian crisis, since this is the domain of trained sociologists, not exegetes. Therefore, the following analysis is more akin to what sociologists condescendingly call "social description" or "social history" (Richter 1984, 77-81; Scroggs 1980, 167-71; Best 1983, 185). However, it is really more than that since it actually draws more heavily from the work of cultural anthropologists, than from that of sociologists. Unfortunately, a term that cultural anthropologists condescendingly use to refer to this kind of description was not readily available!   On the methodological orientation of social science interpretation of the New Testament, see Craffert 1991, 1992, 1995.   For an orientation to reading Paul's letters from this perspective, see Neyrey 1990, 11-20.

[2]Ferdinand C. Baur was really the first scholar since the Reformation to counter this ethnocentrism in viewing Pauline theology.   His views in *The Church History of the First Three Centuries* (1875b ET, 1:47) countered what has come to be called "the Lutheran view of Paul," yet they were not adequately weighted among scholars until Krister Stendahl's writings.   See Watson 1986, 1-22 for a brief history of the overturning of the traditional Reformation view of Paul.   Also, see Luedemann 1989, 132 for a helpful survey of the research on the role of Jewish Christianity in understanding the early church.

[3]This use of "horizon" flows out of the usage of this term within the New Hermeneutic, and especially from Thiselton 1980 and his explication of continental hermeneutics.   For an attempt to understand the Romans' horizon in Paul's Epistle to the Romans, see Russell 1988.   The common hermeneutical task in interpreting a written text and in interpreting a culture, both via the hermeneutical circle, is noted by anthropologist Clifford Geertz 1976, 235-37.

[4]These four traits are taken from Malina 1993, 67-72 and I am heavily dependent upon his analysis for the anthropological content of this section. Additionally, see Neyrey 1988, 75-91.

[5]Charles Kraft has incisively noted that

> The Judaizing Christians were insistent that Hebrew culture prescribed the only proper forms for human response to God.   To them there was no coming to Christ without being circumcised and converting to Hebrew culture (Kraft 1979, 341).

[6]The corporate nature of justification (in particular) has been championed for a generation by Stendahl 1976, 78-96; Barth 1968; and Dahl 1977, 95-120. Cousar 1989, 17 advocates the same perspective for Galatians and adds that the corporate nature of justification "must not be neglected in any reading of the letter." This group aspect is certainly not in lieu of individual responsibility and personal response, but rather it is in addition to it. However, in seeking to remedy the historical imbalance toward the individualistic side, advocates like Stendahl have overstated the corporate dimension. For a critique of Stendahl's view, in particular, see Espy 1985. See Ziesler 1991 and Dunn 1992 for the status of justification by faith within "the New Perspective on Paul."

[7]The brief discussion of Gal 2:15-21 by Erich Stauffer in his article on ἐγώ in *TDNT* 2:257-58 points in this same interpretive direction.

[8]The corporate emphasis of both the Old and New Testaments should not be minimized as *only* a sociological trait of Middle Eastern or Mediterranean peoples. Rather, the corporate emphasis is *also* a theological trait, in that it is built into the ontology of the people of God (e.g., Eph 4:1-16).

[9]Malherbe observes of lists of virtues and vices that "as a supplement to precepts, they illustrated virtue and vice *concretely* and thus were useful in instruction..." (1986, 138; emphasis is mine). The most concrete illustration would be one embodied in a specific community of people with a recognizable way of life.

[10]Five American sociologists have researched the growth of individualism in American society and its effect upon commitment to group endeavors. They have recorded their findings in the best-selling book *Habits of the Heart*. Among their many revealing findings is the following one:

> Perhaps the crucial change in American life has been that we have moved from the social life of the nineteenth century--in which economic and social relationships were visible and, however imperfectly, morally interpreted as parts of a larger common life--to a society vastly more interrelated and integrated economically, technically, and functionally. Yet this is a society in which the individual can only rarely and with difficulty understand himself and his activities as interrelated in morally meaningful ways with those of other, different Americans. Instead of directing cultural and individual energies toward relating the self to its larger context, the culture of manager and therapist urges a strenuous effort to make of our particular segment of life a small world of its own (Bellah et al. 1985, 50).

[11]See the works of Halvor Moxnes 1980, 1988a, 1988b for a very stimulating and insightful application of the honor/shame perspective to Paul's argument in Romans. Much of Paul's argument in Romans from the honor/shame viewpoint is paralleled in Galatians. See Sills 1968, "Honor" for an overview of an honor-based culture and Domeris 1993 for its application in the New Testament.

114   *The Flesh/Spirit Conflict in Galatians*

[12]See Malina 1993, 33-37 for a very helpful discussion of these aspects. Note the critique and balance of Malina's model in Domeris 1993.

[13]See especially Winninge 1995, 213-332 for an illuminating discussion of Paul's theology of "status" based on "transfer" which modified certain elements of his Pharisaic background.

[14]See Dodd 1953, 67-82 and Barrett 1986, 363-8 for other New Testament scholars who share a similar perspective by overemphasizing the psychological and theological aspects respectively of Paul's use of καυχάομαι.

[15]See Moxnes 1988a, 68-71 for the development of boasting in Romans.

[16]Watson 1986, 56 is typical of many scholars who conclude "if Paul had won the argument, he would surely have said so." Watson goes on to assert the following about the confrontation between Peter and Paul in Antioch in Gal 2:11-21:

> This event therefore represented a disaster for Paul: his work in Antioch, based on the premise of the law-free gospel for the Gentiles, had been destroyed at a stroke. It is not surprising that as he recalls what had happened, he gives vent to his anger in sarcastic references to the leaders of the Jerusalem church (1986, 56).

Such reasoning is very Western and very psychological in its orientation. It tacitly assumes that Paul gives in Gal 2:11-21 the emotional or psychological reasons for the anger he described in 2:1-10. However, this kind of thinking is totally foreign and uninteresting to persons in a first century Mediterranean culture! Of their non-psychological reasoning, Malina asserts that

> Again, this is due to the fact that they knew or cared little about psychological development, psychological motivations, and introspective analyses...it is because such abilities are culturally unimportant; there are no cultural cues of perception highlighting this feature (1993, 71-2).

Avoiding a competitive, total humiliation of Peter seems a more culturally-sensitive and contextually-relevant reason why Paul would not record Peter's response to his rebuke. Additionally, *the defeat*, not the victory, of the Judaizers in Antioch is the foundation upon which Paul is supporting his argument (contra Taylor 1992). His point is that the Judaizers' edifice of a Jerusalem-centered "building" of God' s people built upon those in Jerusalem οἱ δοκοῦντες στῦλοι was not enlarged in Antioch! Why, therefore, should the Galatians choose to be added to this fallacious structure? See Wenham 1994, 1996 for additional support.

[17]The responsibility and authority of fathers over children was broadly recognized in the ancient world. This can be seen in Israel's legislation regarding parents' authority (e.g., Gen 18:19; Lev 18:21; 20:2-5; Deut 6:7), in the Church's adoption of these basic guidelines (e.g., Eph 6:4; Col 3:21), and in the Roman Empire's laws regarding *patria potestas*. Conversely, the

responsibilities of children are also clearly seen in both the Old and New Testaments (e.g., Ex 20:12; 21:15; Deut 21:18-21; Prov 6:20; 23:22; Eph 6:1-3; Col 3:20).

[18]Μετατίθημι is used elsewhere in the middle voice in Greek literature to describe someone who has changed opinions, Roman parties, or philosophical schools (*TDNT*, 8:161-62). In Diog. Laert. 7.166, Dionysius of Heracleia "deserted" the Stoics for the Epicureans (Moulton and Milligan 1930, 404-5). In 2 Macc 7:24 Antiochus is recorded as tempting the seventh and youngest son of a woman to turn from the Law of the fathers (μεταθέμενον ἀπὸ τῶν πατρίων νόμων), rather than to be tortured. At the heart of each of these usages is the giving up of membership in one community for membership in another.

[19]See Neyrey 1988 for a culturally-sensitive development of this perspective in Gal 3:1.

[20]See Fung 1988, 224-28 for the possible interpretations of ἐλπίδα δικαιοσύνης ἀπεκδεχόμεθα in Gal 5:5b.

[21]Pobee 1985, 94-96 argues that the στίγματα had a long history within the context of slavery, but even more importantly for Galatians, within the context of cultic and religious tattooing. In contrast to the scars of circumcision which allegedly show that the Jews are the possession of God and under his protection, Paul has the scars of his persecutions. These have branded him as belonging to Jesus and being his apostle. See also Baasland 1984 for an insightful discussion of Paul's defense of his suffering as a righteous Christian, not as a cursed man under the Law.

[22]This is not to ignore that Paul and the Judaizers share the same basic model of community according to the "Grid and Group Model" developed by Mary T. Douglas 1973, 77-92. In her model both the Judaizers' community and the Pauline churches would be "strong group/low grid." This means both sets of communities would have high pressure to conform to the strong group identity which has clear boundaries. This is combined with a low degree of correspondence between the group members' experiences and societal patterns of perception and evaluation. These patterns of the world outside of the group are largely incomprehensible and unpredictable. See Malina 1986b, 13-27 for a helpful explanation of Douglas' model and pages 131-38 for an application to Paul and his social norms.

[23]As the analysis of the following two sections should reveal, it is impossible to conceive of the Judaizers' and Paul's conceptions of community as sharing the same basic core, as Francis Watson assumes. The most basic of Watson's fundamental building blocks is that Paul made a transition from his mission only to Jews to a mission to the Gentiles when the Jews did not respond to his preaching (1986, 23-38). According to sociological analysis, this meant the transformation of a reform movement into a sect that then needed an ideology legitimizing its separation from society (38-48). This sociological application to Paul is rooted in a fundamental misunderstanding of the nature of the Pauline communities and of several key Pauline passages, including Gal 5:11a: "But I, brethren, if I still preach circumcision, why am I

still persecuted?" (30-31). This passage will be explained in Chapter 5. However, for now, it will be instructive to see if Watson's labels are validated in the next two sections: the Judaizers are a reform-movement with a hopeful attitude toward society and the Pauline churches are a sect with a hostile and undifferentiated view of society (38-40). For a more promising framework for viewing first century Judaism and the Pauline churches, see Craffert 1993. Cf. Nickelsburg 1993.

[24]The structure and substance of the main points in the following comparison is from the exceptionally helpful and insightful work of Bruce Malina 1986a, 100-101.

[25]Of the status of the Gentile convert, Bamberger says:

> This unique status is due, first, to the fact that the convert was born a Gentile. From the standpoint of Jewish law, he therefore had no paternity. For the same reason, a converted woman is not legally presumed to have been virtuous prior to her conversion. Both these provisions reflect the Rabbinical attitude toward the *heathen*, not toward the convert. They undoubtedly arose from the feeling-- largely based on realities, as we know from the literature of the Hellenistic and Roman world--that pagan standards of morality were very low in the centuries immediately before and after the beginning of the present era. However, the provisions were enforced automatically and technically, without regard to individual circumstances; so that no slight was implied in any particular case (Bamberger [1939] 1968, 141).

[26]Wayne A. Meeks notes that

> The Jewish-Christian reformers who followed Paul into Galatia probably understood the boundaries of God's people in a traditional Jewish way. The messianic age could bring more vigorous proselytism of Gentiles, but they must then become part of messianic Israel, with the same halakic tests of faithfulness to the covenanting God and thus the same means of social identity and social boundaries as the Jewish communities had established through such long experience in the Greco-Roman cities (1982, 273-74).

[27]For a criticism of this Jewish particularism see Hengel 1974,1:307, 313. For a Jewish defense, see Goldenberg 1988.

[28]On the status of proselytes in general, see Bamberger [1939] 1968, 60-146. He argues against some points of discrimination against Gentile proselytes (65-67), but agrees with Schürer on other points of discrimination (143-44). Also, see Braude 1940 for a very similar perspective.

[29]"The categories derive from proximity to the Temple (and its holy place)--priest, Levite, layman--along with two qualities: being a member of the Israelite community by birth or ritual birth, and the capacity to transmit one's status within the Israelite community" (Malina 1993, 162). See

Jeremias 1969, 270-74 for fuller purity lists, some conflated, and for a discussion of their role in Judaism.

[30]Since Martin Hengel's work (1974), most scholars no longer maintain a sharp cultural distinction between Palestinian and Diaspora Jews. However, this does not negate the possibility that some differences did exist in their attitudes toward Gentile inclusion. Luke highlights some of these differences in his treatment of the contrasting responses of Palestinian and Hellenistic Jewish Christians to Gentile incorporation in the church in Acts 1-15.

[31]See Sjoberg 1960, 108-44; Potter, Diaz, Foster 1967, 15-34; and Wolf 1966, 1-17, 60-95.

[32]See MacDonald 1988, 31-84 for a discussion of Pauline community building and institutionalization. See particularly pp. 32-45 for a description of these communities as "conversionist sects" and the boundaries and tensions that resulted. For similar treatments see Meeks 1983, 84-110 and Scroggs 1975.

[33]Daube 1956, 438-44 argues that Paul follows ample Rabbinic precedent in his hermeneutics in Gal 3:16 when he takes the term σπέρματί σου with its normal generic singular sense as a proper, specific singular (referring to Christ). See Williams 1988 for an explanation of how Paul could take what appears to be a *land* promise given to Abraham and his seed (Gen 15:18) and relate it to Christ and to the giving of the promised Holy Spirit to the Gentiles.

[34]See Sanders 1983, 171-79 for a discussion of Paul's view of the Church as "a third race" or as "recreated humanity." Cf. Moxnes 1989, 99-103.

[35]Offsetting the accusation that Paul now had *no concern* for the church in Jerusalem and Judea is his eager commitment to give to the poor Christians in that area. Therefore, Paul's decentralizing movement among the Gentiles (e.g., Gal 2:7-9) is balanced, not with a centralized ecclesiastical view of Jerusalem, but with a centralized concern for the well-being of Jerusalem (Gal 2:10). Paul's well-documented efforts to collect money for the Judean saints among the Gentiles further attest to his concern (e.g., 2 Cor 8-9). While not central in his strategy of spreading the gospel, Jerusalem is nonetheless central in his strategy of uniting the body of Christ on an international basis. Additionally, Jerusalem plays a role in Paul's eschatology (Rom 11:25-27). For a balanced discussion of Paul's view of Jerusalem and the land of Israel see Davies 1974, 164-220.

[36]See Wead 1978 for a defense of the legitimacy of the early centripetal mission philosophy of the church. He argues that such a philosophy fulfills the pure prophetic ideal of a Jerusalem-centered centripetal mission predicted in passages like Isa 2:2-4/Mic 4:1-3; Isa 45:2-25; 60; 66:10-21. However, according to Acts 1:6-8, it appears that Jesus set aside the centripetal model. See also Bowers 1991. For a very helpful analysis of Paul's mission philosophy, see O'Brien 1993, 1995.

[37]See Bamberger [1939] 1968 31-59 and Braude 1940, 74-78 for a discussion of these three initiation rites. See Schiffman 1985, 19-39 for a defense of the formulation of these requirements *before* A.D. 70 and Cohen 1983, 41 for the argument that this procedure was only standardized *after* the

fall of the Second Temple and was uncontrolled, spontaneous, and personal before that event. The pre-A.D. 70 formulation is generally accepted. Matt 23:15 and Hillel's statement about bringing all mankind to Torah in m. 'Abot 1:12 testify to the existence of Pharisaic proselytism early in the first century A.D. For Jewish surveys of this activity, see Cohon 1987, 324-28; Rosenbloom 1978, 33-64; and Hoenig 1965, 33-66. For a thorough review of recent works on proselytism, see Fredriksen 1991 and especially Paget 1996.

[38]Again, I am drawing from the following main points from Malina 1986a, 100-101. See also Neyrey 1988, 77-80, Douglas 1966, 114-39, and Sills 1968, "Pollution".

[39]On Pharisaic baptism see Abrahams [1917] 1967, 36-46.

[40]Such a conclusion negates the findings of Watson (1986, 23-48) and his thesis that Paul transformed the reform movement of the Judaizers into the sect of Pauline Christianity. This is a fundamental distorting of the data and a wrong sociological application.

[41]See Loubser 1994 for a development of the slavery-freedom contrast as a persuasive device in Galatians.

Chapter 4

A Thematic Analysis of the Flesh/Spirit Conflict in Galatians

This chapter's goal is to seek to validate Paul's continuity in his use of the σάρξ/πνεῦμα antithesis in Galatians and especially to connect his use of the antithesis in Gal 3-4 with his use in Gal 5-6. This thematic study should further set the stage for the exegesis of Gal 5:13-6:18 in the next two chapters. This is because an accurate understanding of the meaning of σάρξ and πνεῦμα in Gal 5-6 involves dealing with these terms in the broader context of their antithesis in Gal 3-6. Particularly, Paul's use of the σάρξ/πνεῦμα antithesis in Gal 3-4 gives the hearers/readers of Galatians a well-formed sense of the meaning of both terms by the time they reach Gal 5. If there is a persistent flaw in most exegetical treatments of Gal 5-6, it is the failure to establish this broader context of the σάρξ/πνεῦμα antithesis and to show how this context aids in understanding the turn in Paul's argument in Gal 5:13.

I. The Foreshadowing of the Antithesis: Gal 2:15-21

The term πνεῦμα does not occur in Galatians until 3:2. but Paul has already used σάρξ three times by this point. The first occurrence in 1:16 (σαρκί καί αἵματι) is not theologically significant to our discussion.[1] However, the next two uses both occur in 2:15-21 and give some insight into Paul's intense use of σάρξ. In 2:16b Paul concludes that by works of Law οὐ δικαιωθήσεται πᾶσα σάρξ. In this context σάρξ is used by Paul in place of ζῶν in what appears to be a deliberately reworded citation from Ps 143:2 in the LXX (Jewett 1971b, 97). Paul's use of σάρξ with δικαιωθήσεται in 2:16b parallels his usage of ἄνθρωπος with δικαιοῦτα in 2:16a and indicates that σάρξ in 2:16b has the sense of "a man of flesh and blood" (BAGD 1979, 743, #3). However, the substitution of the term σάρξ for ζῶν may have some linguistic and theological significance because of the substitution.[2] Robert Jewett argues that

> It seems even more plausible, however, to suggest that Paul substituted σάρξ for ζῶν because he wished to counter the Judaizers' claim that circumcised *flesh* was acceptable as righteous by God. This hypothesis has the advantage of relating closely and concretely to the historical situation. Furthermore, that the reworded quotation was directed against Judaizers and not against σάρξ itself, understood in a Hellenistic sense as the root of evil, is clear from Paul's second--and unparalleled--change in the wording, the addition of ἐξ ἔργων νόμου. Paul's aim is not to argue that σάρξ cannot be justified by any means at all. It can be justified when it depends solely on Christ; but if it depends upon its own fulfillment of the law, it is lost. Thus, as Paul goes on to say in Gal 2:20, the life he lived ἐν σαρκί was lived ἐν πίστει. Life in the flesh can be accepted as righteous by God as long as its sole boast is in Christ (Jewett 1971b, 98).

Concerning the LXX's association of σάρξ with circumcision in God's covenant with Israel, Jewett has also argued that

> The LXX speaks often of the σάρξ as that which is circumcised (Gen 17:11, 13, 14, 24, 25; Gen 34:34; Lev 12:3; Jud 14:10; Jer 9:26; Ezek 44:9). In two cases, as E. Schweizer has pointed out, the LXX adds chips to a circumcision context where the Hebrew text does not demand it. Elsewhere the LXX speaks of circumcision as the "covenant in your flesh" (Sir 44:20; cf. Gen 17:13). It was this sense that the Judaizers boasted of circumcision, for it was to them in the words of the promise in Gen 17:13 "my covenant in your flesh" (Jewett 1971b, 96).

Jewett's point is well taken and Paul's chiastic use of ζῶ with the next use of σάρξ in 2:20b seems to underscore this interpretation: ὃ δὲ νῦν ζῶ ἐν σαρκί, ἐν πίστει ζῶ τῇ τοῦ υἱοῦ τοῦ θεοῦ. To live ἐν σαρκί/ἐν πίστει is *not* a culpable state in this context, but rather it is held up by Paul as the model for *Jewish Christians* to emulate (see the discussion of Gal 2:15-21 in Chapter 2). *They* are the ones related to

Abraham bodily, yet they still need to be trusting in Christ as the sole basis of their confidence before God. In this context Paul seems to use ἐν σαρκί in the broader sense of "corporeality, physical limitations, life on earth" (BAGD 1979, 744, #5). It does not appear that he has enriched σάρξ with any redemptive historical significance yet. However, this is not to say that Paul's use of σάρξ in Gal 2:15-21 does not have the subtle significance that Jewett suggested.

Therefore, Gal 2:15-21 and these two occurrences of σάρξ create a subtle foreshadowing of the σάρξ/πνεῦμα antithesis which begins in 3:1-5. The specific topic that is expounded in 2:15-21 is the Jewish Christians wrong application of the Mosaic Law to Gentile Christians as a standard, and perhaps even means, of Christian living. Paul's rebuffing of this view is based on its compromising of τὴν ἀλήθειαν τοῦ εὐαγγελίου (2:5, 14). Specifically, Paul focuses on one aspect of the gospel that has invalidated the Judaizing of Gentiles: Christ's substitutionary death by crucifixion (2:19-21). It is this death that Paul has already referred to as delivering us "out of this present evil age" (1:4). As Ladd has observed, this view of Christ's death is overtly eschatological:

> The first and most explicit reference to Paul's eschatological outlook is found in the first lines of the epistle: "Christ gave himself for our sins to deliver us from the present evil age" (Gal 1:4). Here is a clear reference to the eschatological perspective that underlies Paul's theological thought. We do not need here to recite the passages where the two-age idea occurs in Paul, although it is a theme that has been singularly neglected by evangelical scholars. This verse tells us that the present age is evil (see 2 Cor 4:4). However, the work of Christ suffices to *deliver* men from the evil powers of this present age; and this can be accomplished only by the inbreaking of the powers of the future age. The death of Christ, as well as the gift of the Spirit, is an eschatological event (Ladd 1975, 213).

Schlier echoes a similar perspective:

> Since Jesus Christ gave himself to blot out our sins, he created the situation that we, in anticipation of the future aeon, are freed from the present aeon. The death of Jesus Christ, in the sacrifice that bears our sins, causes the future aeon to break in upon us (Schlier 1971, 34; my translation).

In addition to beginning Galatians with this eschatological or apocalyptic view of Christ's death, Paul culminates his letter by referring to this same death as the means "through which the world has been crucified to me, and I to the world" (6:14). In the καινὴ κτίσις that Christ's crucifixion has created, He has negated the now-old distinction between circumcision and uncircumcision (6:15). Paul anticipates this starkly-stated conclusion in 6:14-15 about the effects of Christ's crucifixion with his statement about Christ's death in 2:21b: εἰ γὰρ διὰ νόμου δικαιοσύνη, ἄρα χριστὸς δωρεὰν ἀπέθανεν. Of Paul's obvious apocalyptic reasoning about Christ's death in 1:4, 2:19-21, and 6:14-15, J. Louis Martyn has noted:

> He is saying rather, that the letter is about the death of one world, and the advent of another. With regard to the former, the death of the cosmos, perhaps Paul is telling the Galatians that one knows the old world to have died, because one knows that its fundamental structures are gone, that those fundamental structures of the cosmos *were* certain identifiable pairs of opposites, and that, given the situation among their congregations in Galatia, the pair of opposites whose departure calls for emphasis is that of circumcision and uncircumcision (1985b, 414).

Paul's statements in Gal 6:14-15 offer the final clarification of this world-changing perspective. However, the apocalyptic viewpoint has already been well established by Paul's statements in 1:4 and 2:19-21. To avoid living as if Christ died needlessly (δωρεάν), the Galatians must not seek to establish righteousness διὰ νόμου (2:21). Such an application of the Mosaic Law to Gentile Christians is "aeon-anachronistic" in light of Christ's crucifixion .

II. The Establishing of the Sarx/Pneuma Antithesis: Gal 3:1-5

It is therefore no incidental reference that Paul makes to Christ's crucifixion in Gal 3:1 when he accuses the foolish Galatians of being bewitched to a different understanding of the crucifixion from that which he publicly portrayed to them (οἷς κατ' ὀφθαλμοὺς Ἰησοῦς Χριστὸς προεγράφη ἐσταυρωμένος).[3] As Gal 2:15-21 set forth, the significance of Christ's crucifixion to the Judaizer threat is that it is an apocalyptic boundary marker that provides a new set of separators establishing the righteousness or purity of the people of God:

> Yet the world of Paul the Pharisee is structured by his faith in Jesus who died on the cross. Jesus himself exemplifies the structure of the covenant of Abraham, viz., "faith in God." His death, moreover, marks the exact boundary line between the former covenant of Law and the new covenant of faith and grace (3:13-

14)....The precision about one's relationship to God that was formerly given Paul the Pharisee by torah now comes from Jesus (Neyrey 1988, 79) .

Therefore, if the Galatians are bewitched about Christ crucified, then it follows that they will likewise be malevolently misled about the proper boundary markers and the appropriate standard or rule for the people of God. This new section of the epistle (3:1-4:31), in fact. continues this discussion of the new boundary that the crucifixion has brought. In every mention of the cross or death of Jesus in this section and in the rest of the epistle, it signifies the new boundary of the people of God in contrast to the old conception of God's people (e.g., 1:4; 2:20-21; 3:1 [cf. 3:2], 3:13-14; 5:11; 6:12; and 6:14). As Neyrey has noted, "the boundary, moreover, is endlessly presented in a series of redundant dualisms which replicate and reinforce the basic distinction between Christians and Jews according to Paul" (1988, 82). These dualisms have been noted by both Neyrey (1988) and Martyn (1985b):

Covenant with Abraham	Covenant with Moses
characterized by promise/faith	characterized by law/doing
Belonging through Sarah and Isaac	Belonging through Hagar
	and Ishmael
Blessing	Curse
Grace	Sin
Freedom	Slavery
Free gift of Spirit	Earned merit through deeds
Spirit	Flesh
Home: Jerusalem above	Home: Mt. Sinai below

From this set of dualisms, one can readily see that the σάρξ/πνεῦμα antithesis is but one of several such antitheses in Gal 3-6. All of them are rooted in the same historical contrast between the era of Israel and the newly arrived, apocalyptically oriented era of Jesus Christ, begun at his crucifixion.

This is made clearer in Gal 3:1-5 where Paul combines two sets of these antitheses or dualisms, and thereby gives insight into the meaning of the σάρξ/πνεῦμα antithesis.[4] Paul does this by a chiastic-type structure in 3:2-3:

Did you receive the Spirit ἐξ ἔργων νόμου or ἐξ ἀκοῆς πίστεως;

Having begun πνεύματι now are you now being perfected[5] σαρκί;

In discussing the beginning of the Christian life via the Spirit and the ongoing nurture of that life, Paul is contrasting two opposing tandems: ἐξ ἔργων νόμου/σαρκί versus ἐξ ἀκοῆς πίστεως/πνεύματι. The νόμος/σάρξ tandem is a common one in Galatians (5:13-14, 17-18, 19-23; 6:12-13) and the πίστις/πνεῦμα tandem appears elsewhere also (3:13-14; 5:5). Based on Paul's previous direct connection of σάρξ with ἔργων νόμου in Gal 2:16b and the logical connection between them in 2:20b-21, we can infer that the connection between νόμος, and σάρξ is a very close one and may appear to make more overt Paul's previously subtle references to circumcision. In these tandems ἐξ with ἔργων νόμου and ἀκοῆς πίστεως means "by reason of, as a result of, because of" and gives the presupposition for something (BAGD 1979, 235). Paul is ironically asking the Galatians if they received the Spirit by the presupposition of doing works prescribed in Torah or by the presupposition of hearing with faith.[6]

The datives σαρκί and πνεύματι in 3:3 are generally understood as *datives of instrument* ("by the flesh") or *agency* ("by or through the Spirit").[7] This understanding is reflected in many of the standard English translations (e.g., ASV, NASV, NIV, RSV, NEB, REB, TEV, and KJV in 3:3b and 5:5) and sets up a parallelism of sorts between Gal 3:2 and 3:3, exemplified by the NASV:

> This is the only thing I want to find out from you:
>   did you receive the Spirit *by* [reason of] the works of the Law,
>   or *by* [reason of] hearing with faith?
> Are you so foolish? Having begun *by* [means of] the Spirit,
>   are you now being perfected *by* [means of] the flesh?

The contrasts are from two different temporal perspectives. Gal 3:2 views the eschatological event of the receiving of the Holy Spirit from its *inception*. Gal 3:3 views the *culmination* of the life that is to be lived according to the eschatological means of the Spirit (although "means" is not usually used to refer to a person). The primary contrast is one between the means that characterized or identified God's people in two different historical eras. The Judaizers are advocating the continued identifications of Old Covenant Israel. Paul is advocating the eschatological identification begun with Jesus Christ's death and the imparting of the Spirit.[8] In other words in contrasting σάρξ and πνεῦμα, Paul is reasoning along a horizontal or historical plane. He is not only contrasting internal instrumentalities in Gal 3:3, but also external identifications. These external identifications of the two competing communities in Galatia will be enriched as Paul continues to use the σάρξ/πνεῦμα antithesis in a strategic manner within his argumentation.

III. Additional Occurrences of Pneumati

Gal 5:5 is the next use of πνεύματι. This verse is a positive statement about the expectant hope of righteousness that the Christian has in contrast to the tragic exclusion that following the Judaizers will cause in 5:2-4. Paul's warning about this exclusion culminates in 5:4 and sets up the positive contrast of "inclusion" that they can experience *with him* in 5:5: (4) κατηργήθητε ἀπὸ Χριστοῦ, οἵτινες ἐν νόμῳ δικαιοῦσθε, τῆς χάριτος ἐξεπέσατε. (5) ἡμεῖς γὰρ πνεύματι ἐκ πίστεως ἐλπίδα δικαιοσύνης ἀπεκδεχόμεθα.

In these verses we have the same face-off regarding justification between νόμος and πίστις that occurred in Gal 3:2, 5. The Judaizers advocated justification by means of Torah observance (ἐν νόμῳ) in 5:1-4, while Paul asserts in 5:5 that "we" (in the emphatic position) await the eschatological hope of justification by reason of faith (ἐκ πίστεως).[9]

Within this argument it is again reasonable to conclude that Paul uses πνεύματι to express the instrument or agent of this justification: "by or through the Spirit" (e.g., Burton 1921, 278).[10] However, again the emphasis of the context is not just on the instrumentality or agency of the Spirit, but upon the identification that the Spirit represents. This is due to the role that Paul assigns to πνεύματι within his antithetical argumentation in 5:1-6. The issue in 5:1-12 is the ongoing freedom of the Galatians (5:1), probably from the power of sin. This is because Paul reiterates the freedom declaration of 5:1 in 5:13 (after the attacks on the Judaizers in 5:2-12) and specifies that the "freedom" the Galatians have been given is a freedom from the bondage of sin and the σάρξ. This is not a new theme in the epistle, but simply picks up previous references to this specific freedom in 1:4, 4:1-11, 31. Apparently both of the competing communities promised this freedom. Therefore, Paul begins in 5:1-6 to contrast their abilities to deliver the desired freedom from sin's bondage. Broadly speaking, Paul contrasts his gospel and the Judaizers' non-gospel in the following areas in Gal 5:1-6:

	Paul	Judaizers
relationship to Christ	in Christ (5:5)	of no benefit (5:1) severed from Christ (5:4)

means of justification	by faith (5:5) (ἐκ πίστεως)	by Law (5:4) (ἐν νόμῳ)
principle at work	grace (5:4)	non-grace (5:4)
the resulting distinctions	faith working through love (5:6b), which is no fleshly distinctions in this context[11]	circumcision versus non-circumcision (5:6a)
the community identifiers	by the Spirit (5:5) (πνεύματι)	by circumcision and the whole Law (5:3)

The clash of "gospels" is also expressed in the clash of authoritative marks of identification of the two competing communities. The Judaizers demand submission to circumcision (5:1-2), which entails an obligation to keep the whole Law (5:3). By contrast to this submitting to the total yoke (standards) of the Law in 5:1-4, Paul sets forth a life "by the Spirit" in 5:5. The contrast is between two objectively identifying marks, not an objective identifier (circumcision/Torah) versus a subjective identifier (the Spirit). This is because the objective nature of the identifying work of the Spirit has already been established in 3:5 with the working of miracles among the Galatians at the time of the provision of the Spirit.

Additionally, both sets of identifying marks bring corresponding standards for believers who are "ethically engaged" (in Cosgrove's words) as they anticipate the eschatological judgment. The Galatians face the choice of which community identification and corresponding way of life they are going to embrace during this period of "waiting." In 5:6a Paul seems to assume that choosing to live according to Torah with its circumcision and uncircumcision distinction is ethically worthless (τι ἰσχύει). The contrasting set of standards results in faith working through love (5:6b) and it is this set of standards that Paul labels in 5:5 as life *by the Spirit* (πνεύματι). This community's rule/standard is a set of standards as objective as Torah is (e.g., 5:22-6:10), even though it may not be as exhaustive a set of standards. Paul is now at a point in his argument where he must make this truth clear and where he must effectively counteract the clear way of life that Torah must have represented.

The next occurrence of πνεύματι is in Gal 5:16. However, this exhortation, πνεύματι περιπατεῖτε, will be more understandable if the clear use of πνεύματι in 5:18 is dealt with first. These two uses of πνεύματι stand or fall together:

(16) Λέγω δέ, πνεύματι περιπατεῖτε καὶ ἐπιθυμίαν σαρκὸς οὐ μὴ τελέσητε.

(17) ἡ σὰρξ ἐπιθυμεῖ κατὰ τοῦ πνεύματος, τὸ δὲ πνεῦμα
κατὰ τῆς σαρκός, ταῦτα γὰρ ἀλλήλοις ἀντίκειται, ἵνα μὴ
ἃ ἐὰν θέλητε ταῦτα ποιῆτε.
(18) εἰ δὲ πνεύματι ἄγεσθε, οὐκ ἐστὲ ὑπὸ νόμον.

Paul's statement about the Law in 5:18 has been particularly
troublesome to commentators because it appears to involve a sudden
shift from the alleged *internal* σάρξ/πνεῦμα conflict of 5:16-17 to the
πνεῦμα/νόμος antithesis of 5:18. Additionally, another problem arises
with the traditional view of σάρξ/πνεῦμα as an *internal conflict* of
competing instrumentalities within the Christian. This problem is that
again commentators pit the subjective leading of the Spirit against the
objective demands of Torah. Betz' (1979, 281) comment is typical
when he says, "If they are driven by the Spirit, they do not need to be
under the Torah." However, this reasoning is unnecessarily existential
and convoluted. There are two major weaknesses with it:

1.) Πνεύματι ἄγεσθε in 5:18 is not a regular existential choice that
the believer makes (contra Fung 1988, 251-52), but rather it is
another of Paul's descriptions of a Christian. Gal 5:18 is a statement
of an "indicative of salvation" (Betz 1979, 281). Paul uses the same
terminology in an equally definitive statement of what a Christian is
in Rom 8:14: ὅσοι γὰρ πνεύματι θεοῦ ἄγονται, οὗτοι υἱοὶ θεοῦ
εἰσιν.

2.) Therefore, to be πνεύματι ἄγεσθε is to have the status of a New
Covenant believer expressed in terms of the eschatological gift of
the Spirit (cf. Gal 3:2, 5). This status makes unnecessary the need
to conform to the status of Old Covenant believers and be ὑπὸ
νόμον. However, the issue in Gal 5:16-18 is not about status as a
believer per se, but rather the issue is about what constrains the
behavior of the Christian (5:17b). Therefore, the contrast in 5:18 is
between the new standards inaugurated by Christ's death and the
sending of the Holy Spirit versus the old standards of Torah. In
other words, the contrast is between *being led according to the rule
of the Spirit*" versus "being led according to the rule of Torah."
Paul's contrast is between comparable entities, both of which have
been expressed in objective, verifiable forms.

This means that there is really no sudden shift in emphasis from
the σάρξ/πνεῦμα duality in 5:16-17 to the πνεῦμα/νόμος antithesis in
5:18. This is true because πνεύματι has the same meaning in both
verses! Paul's exhortation in 5:16 is to walk *according to the rule of
the Spirit* not to walk "by the instrumentality/agency of the Spirit."[12]
If the Christians will walk according to the rule of the Spirit, then they

will avoid both parts of the flesh/Law tandem.   In 5:16-17 they will avoid fulfilling the ἐπιθυμίαν σαρκὸς--the behavior that occurred during the preparatory, now-inferior era of Law before the indwelling work of the Spirit began (4:1-7). Christ's deliverance from the powers of this evil age had not occurred yet (1:4), and the result was bodily bondage to the στοιχεῖα τοῦ κόσμου (4:3, 8-11). But since σάρξ and νόμος go together, in 5:18 Paul states that walking according to the rule of the Spirit (πνεύματι) also invalidates the rule of the Law over them. But what does it mean "to walk according to the rule of the Spirit"? Within the context of the epistle, to walk according to the rule of the Spirit is simply to continue to follow the gospel that Paul preached and the teaching that he had previously given the Galatians. This is in contrast to walking according to the rule of the (circumcised) flesh or according to Torah, as the Judaizers were advocating. In other words, Paul's use of πνεύματι in these contexts suggests a basic relationship with the Holy Spirit expressed in the realm of ethics, as Kendell Easley has noted:

> Seven times Paul uses the anarthrous form *pneumati* in reference to general truth of Christian experience. These passages do not deal with specifics, such as "love" or "gifts of the Spirit," but rather with *overarching patterns for Christian living* that the Spirit produces (Easley 1984, 308; emphasis is mine).

This general, non-technical use of πνεύματι is also seen in Paul's last use in Gal 5:25: Ἐι ζῶμεν πνεύματι, πνεύματι καὶ στοιχῶμεν. Again, πνεύματι can easily be conceived of as functioning as a dative of agency.   However, the immediate context again suggests that understanding πνεύματι as a dative of rule or direction makes more sense of the grammatical combinations.[13]   In Gal 5:24 Paul affirms that those who belong to Christ Jesus have crucified τὴν σάρκα with its passions and lusts. Therefore, this makes life according to the old rule of the σάρξ unthinkable because of the eschatological change wrought by Christ's crucifixion. On the heels of mentioning Christ's death again, Paul once more immediately appeals to the same pattern involving the Holy Spirit that he used in Gal 3:3: the source of the Christian life (εἰ ζῶμεν πνεύματι) and the completion of the Christian life (πνεύματι καὶ στοιχῶμεν).[14]

Verse 25 is structured chiastically around πνεύματι, but the emphasis seems to fall on the last word, στοιχῶμεν (Betz 1979, 293). This would be expected since 5:25-26 functions as the closing bracket to the contrasting patterns of relationships between the Pauline and Judaistic communities that were begun in 5:13-15 (see discussion of

Gal 5:13-26 in Chap. 2). Paul is summarizing in verses 25-26 these relational patterns. In 5:25 he summarizes the relational pattern of the communities he started: being in step or agreement according to the rule of the Spirit. In 5:26 he summarizes the pattern of relationships that the Judaizers' fleshly communities manifest: being boastful, making one another angry, and envying one another (i.e., being in agreement according to the rule of the flesh--Gal 5:19-21). The Galatians must choose between these two patterns or standards of behavior. Ironically, the Judaizers' pattern does not fulfill the most basic demand of the Mosaic Law (5:14-15), and one would therefore expect their standards *not* to be in agreement with the rule of the Spirit.

Additionally, Gerhard Delling has argued that while Paul's use of στοιχέω in Gal 5:25 parallels 5:16, it is more than a synonym for περιπατέω meaning "to walk." Delling argues that στοιχέω has the added sense of "to be in agreement with" or "to be in step with" (*TDNT*, 7:667-69; cf. Louw & Nida 1988, 41:12). This gives the term more of an association with the rule or standards of a community of like-minded people. In fact, this is the exact usage of στοιχέω in its other four New Testament uses in Acts 21:24, Rom 4:12, Phil 3:16, and Gal 6:16. The last three of these uses seem to create "datives of rule or direction" in their grammatical combinations. Arguably, all of these are related to the Judaistic controversy.

Of particular importance for our purposes is Paul's use in Gal 6:16a, where he summarizes his lengthy argumentation about the competing standards or rules of the two communities in overt language: καὶ ὅσοι τῷ κανόνι τούτῳ στοιχήσουσιν, εἰρήνη ἐπ᾽ αὐτοὺς καὶ ἐπὶ τὸν Ἰσραὴλ τοῦ θεοῦ. Here the dative τῷ κανόνι τούτῳ ("this rule") functions as a summarizing term for the principle of the καινὴ κτίσις in the previous verse. This "new creation" is the eschatological community created by Christ's crucifixion (6:14) that has destroyed the circumcision/non-circumcision distinction (6:15). Therefore, the Galatians are to "live in agreement with this rule" τῷ κανόνι τούτῳ στοιχήσουσιν). Is not this "rule" the same rule as the "rule or direction of the Spirit" in 5:25, 5:18, and 5:16? Have not these appeals to the Spirit through his use of πνεύματι been Paul's appeals to this "rule"?

Therefore, while it cannot be proved definitively, it seems more than reasonable contextually to conclude that Paul's use of πνεύματι in the verbal combinations of Gal 5:16, 18, and 25b creates what we can best describe as "datives of rule or direction." Such a sense would parallel Paul's σάρξ/πνεῦμα antithesis in Rom 8:4-8 where he

contrasts those who walk "according to the flesh" *(κατὰ σάρκα)* with
those who walk "according to the Spirit" *(κατὰ πνεῦμα)*, where "κατὰ
πνεῦμα designates the standard of ethical normality, both as to being
and striving (Rom 8:5)" (Vos [1921] 1980, 111).[15]
In the Galatian context, Paul is appealing to the objective standards
or rule of conduct that he had shared with them previously, be they
called τὸν νόμον τοῦ Χριστοῦ (6:2) or whatever. Certainly the
instrumentality or agency of the Spirit is encompassed in such an
appeal. However, the persuasive contrast that Paul makes at crucial
junctures in his tightly-argued epistle between *the Mosaic Law/flesh*
versus *faith in Christ/Spirit*, is only as powerful as it is legitimate. Its
legitimacy is rooted in its contrasting of comparable entities. These
entities are ultimately expressed in the objective, verifiable standards
of the two competing communities and the objective, verifiable
patterns of behavior that result within each community.

IV. The Enriching of the Sarx/Pneuma Antithesis in Gal 3-6

Gal 3:1-5 establishes the basic σάρξ/πνεῦμα antithesis. Jewett sees
this passage as the first step in the three-stage development of the
σάρξ category in Galatians:

> At first, however, Paul used flesh and spirit in a way which was not
> fully dialectical. The contrast between flesh and spirit which was
> only implicit in Gal 2:16 and 6:12ff. becomes explicit for the first
> time in 3:3...Here Paul brings the terms into an undefined contrast
> but not yet into dialectic with one another. One gains from Gal 3:3
> no impression that the flesh might be an active realm which
> independently opposes the spirit (Jewett 1971b, 112).

In particular, Gal 3:3 lays out the choice before the Galatians in
σάρξ/πνεῦμα terminology: "Are you so foolish? Having begun by the
Spirit, are you now being perfected by the flesh?" As the previous
section sought to prove, the choice between completing the Christian
life "by the Spirit" or "by the (circumcised) flesh" ultimately becomes
the choice between walking according to two objective sets of
community standards and patterns of behavior. These two sets of
community rules and standards are historically successive. The first
one is the rule or direction of the σάρξ, which is in tandem with the
νόμος of Moses, and thereby identified with the nation of Israel. The
second community rule of the πνεῦμα is in tandem with πίστις in
Jesus Christ, who has brought his own νόμος (6:2) . If this is an

accurate representation of the basic σάρξ/πνεῦμα antithesis, then one would expect it to be enriched in the sections of Galatians that follow 3:1-5. The following brief thematic sketch is an attempt to validate that this enrichment does, in fact, occur.

Σάρξ does not occur again until Gal 4:23, 29, excluding the uses in 4:13, 14 which refers to Paul's "bodily illness."[16] However, the πνεῦμα side of the antithesis gets enriched in Gal 3:6-4:11 in two sections: 3:6-14 and 4:1-7. The thrust of both sections is that the new condition of the eschatological giving of the Holy Spirit to God's people has changed things dramatically. It has created a new historical era with a corresponding new rule or set of standards for God's people that supersedes the previous historical era's rule and standards, i.e., the Mosaic Law. Therefore, to make this same point from two different perspectives, Paul follows each of the sections about the giving of the Holy Spirit with a discussion of the superseding of the Mosaic Law and the new boundaries for God's people that result. The structure of Gal 3:6-4:11 reveals this repetition:

> 3:6-14 *The Giving of the Spirit:* The true sons of Abraham are those who are ἐκ πίστεως and they share in the universal, eschatological blessing promised through Abraham: the indwelling Holy Spirit.

> 3:15-29 *The Superseding of the Law:* These universal promissory aspects of the Abrahamic Covenant could not be set aside nor conditionally modified by the giving of the Mosaic Law since the Law was only preparatory and temporary until Christ would come and singularly fulfill God's covenant with Abraham of universal blessing.

> 4:1-7 *The Giving of the Spirit:* The Galatians' experience of the Spirit of God's Son crying "Αββα, ὁ πατήρ" in their hearts proves that they have been adopted as God's sons in the present eschatological era ("the fullness of the time")[17] and have left behind the previous childish and slavish era of the Law.

> 4:8-11 *The Superseding of the Law:* However, to give up their status as God's full-privileged sons and to turn back to the status of slaves under bondage to the weak and poor στοιχεῖα and to Torah-observance causes Paul to fear for them.

This interchange between πνεῦμα and νόμος again reveals the correspondence that Paul recognized within the tandem of σάρξ and νόμος. His initial stating of the antithesis in Gal 3:1-5 was between σάρξ and πνεῦμα. However, his development of this antithesis was in terms of νόμος and πνεῦμα in Gal 3:6-4:11. Therefore, it should not be surprising that one would encounter the interchanging of σάρξ and νόμος in passages like 5:16-18 or in the application of 4:21-31. According to Jewett, Gal 4:21-31 is the second step in the development of the technical "flesh" category in Galatians, building on the first step of Gal 3:1-5. In this second stage, flesh and spirit are brought into full dialectic:

> He correlates flesh with the old aeon, the law, slavery, the present Jerusalem and the agitating Judaizers, while opposing flesh with spirit, which in turn was correlated with the new aeon, the promise given to Abraham, freedom, and the church (Jewett 1971b, 113).

While it is somewhat questionable (and unprovable) that Paul was developing the σάρξ/πνεῦμα antithesis in his thinking as he wrote Galatians, it is not questionable that he was developing the antithesis in the argument of Galatians. The pivotal role that the σάρξ/πνεῦμα antithesis plays from Gal 4:21 onward testifies to that development and it is Paul's "allegorizing" (4:24) of the Sarah/Hagar narratives in 4:21-31 that establishes this centrality. Of particular importance are Paul's descriptions of the birth of Hagar's son Ishmael in Gal 4:23 as κατὰ σάρκα γεγέννηται and in 4:29 as κατὰ σάρκα γεννηθείς. The latter reference is contrasted with Isaac's birth, which is referred to as κατὰ πνεῦμα. This use of κατά establishes the norm, similarity, or homogeneity in the sense of "according to, in accordance with, in conformity with, or corresponding to" (BAGD 1979, 407).

Paul's sense seems to be that the Judaizers' father is not the chosen seed Isaac, as they had probably proudly proclaimed, but ironically, their father is the rejected seed Ishmael. How can Paul reverse their apparent proof-text (Barrett 1982) and prove that they are Ishmaelites and not Isaacites in God's sight? His argument rests on the standard of their birth. The Judaizers prided themselves in their "fleshly" birth from Abraham. Therefore, Paul turns their own claim back on them and shows that being born κατὰ σάρκα makes one an Ishmaelite! They can claim only a birth according to a body unaided by God's Spirit. Pressing Paul's applicational language about the two Jerusalems in 4:25-26, the Judaizers can claim only a birth from below, not from above. The words of Jesus in John 3:6 to one holding a view similar to the Judaizers' are strikingly parallel: τὸ γεγεννημένον ἐκ τῆς σαρκὸς σάρξ ἐστιν, καὶ τὸ γεγεννημένον ἐκ τοῦ πνεύματος πνεῦμα ἐστιν.

The upshot of Paul's argumentation is that the Judaizers can offer only a birth-of-sorts that is according to the era of the Law (4:24-25), and is therefore "according to the flesh." It is according to the standard of bodies unaided by God's Spirit, and thereby lacking both the presence of the supernatural and the stamp of God's sonship (cf. 4:1-7).[18] Those relying on birth κατὰ σάρκα from Abraham are the rejected seed. Only those born κατὰ πνεῦμα can enter into the inheritance of Abraham (3:7-9, 13-14, 29). However, the inheritance of those born κατὰ πνεῦμα will not be without persecution from those born κατὰ σάρκα (4:29; cf. 3:4; 5:11; and 6:12). Therefore, the same principle that was necessary in the patriarchal era of Abraham is also necessary in this present era: those whose births are according to two conflicting standards cannot coexist in the same family. Those born κατὰ πνεῦμα must cast out (ἔκβαλε) those born κατὰ σάρκα (4:30).

Noting Paul's rationale is very crucial at this point. The summarizing conjunction διό links Paul's left-handed call for the excommunication of the Judaizers in Gal 4:30 to his conclusion in 4:31 about the Galatians' identity as children of *freedom*. Living out this freedom will be his concern throughout all of Gal 5 (cf. 5:1 and 5:13). Therefore, the need to separate from those who advocate a different set of entrance standards into the family of God is linked to the preservation of freedom in Christ. This is because those *born* κατὰ σάρκα also advocate living κατὰ σάρκα. They advocate the perfection of the Christian life (σαρκί in 3:3) according to the prior and dominant standard of their birth (κατὰ σάρκα in 4:23, 29). The same standards of the (circumcised) σάρξ and the νόμος of Moses are applied to both the entrance into and the daily norms of the Christian life. Therefore, if the Galatians are to maintain their freedom in Christ, they must not allow any opportunity for the continued proclamation of the standards κατὰ σάρκα (5:13) and they must reject walking according to the ongoing rule or direction of the σάρξ (5:16). The rule of the πνεῦμα is in direct conflict with the rule of the σάρξ (5:17). But the good news is that the Galatians are not under the rule of the σάρξ; that is, they are not ὑπὸ νόμον (5:18). This intense discussion about maintaining their freedom in Christ by choosing to live πνεύματι versus living σαρκί is the third and climactic step in the development of the σάρξ/πνεῦμα antithesis in Galatians, according to Jewett (1971b, 114). It is to this discussion beginning in Gal 5:13 that we now turn.

V. The Alleged Transformation of the SARX/PNEUMA Antithesis in Galatians 5-6

Robert Jewett summarizes well Paul's view of σάρξ at the end of an extended discussion of the σάρξ/πνεῦμα antithesis in Gal 3-4:

> Anthropologically this implies that man's dilemma is *not the conflict between his own fleshly desire and the spirit.* Man's alternative is between trusting in that which his own flesh can accomplish and in trusting in Christ. What emerges here is that *flesh is not a part of man but rather the sum total of his virtues and possibilities.* Those who boast in their flesh are for Paul not primarily the weaklings or the libertinists but the religious Jews. It is religious man who rests on his own virtuous obedience and thus enters into conflict with the spirit. For the spirit is that eschatological action of God which grants man sonship as a gift. To depend upon one's own accomplishments is to oppose the proffered gift of sonship through the spirit and thus to live according to the flesh (Jewett 1971b, 100-101; emphasis is mine).

Specifically, Jewett recognizes that the origin of Paul's use of σάρξ in Galatians and the opposition between flesh and Spirit rest not in a Hellenistic or Gnostic dualism between the material and pneumatic worlds, "but rather in Paul's apocalyptically oriented polemic in a specific historical situation where in his view there was a danger of replacing the boast in the cross with a boast in the circumcised flesh" (Jewett, 1971b, 100).

After building such a context-dependent sense of σάρξ, one would expect that Jewett would continue to advocate the same sense in Gal 5:13 and following. But this is only partially true. Relating Gal 4:21-31 to Gal 5:13-6:17, he asserts that

> Thus Paul can say that all who presently belonged to this sphere were slaves just as Hagar was. Σάρξ is both personal and extrapersonal in its scope. The same may be said for σάρξ in Gal 5:13ff. On the one hand man's concrete bodily flesh constitutes the source of sensual desires, and on the other hand it acts independent of man to oppose the spirit. And yet despite these formal similarities, there seems to be considerable disparity between the situation of trusting in circumcised flesh which is dealt with in Gal 4:21ff. and the situation of sensual libertinism which is dealt with in Gal 5:13ff (Jewett 1971b, 103).

While Jewett certainly minimizes this disparity more than most, he nevertheless must admit that Paul seems to broaden the sense of σάρξ from the virtues and possibilities of circumcised bodies to "Paul's term for everything aside from God in which one places his final trust"

(Jewett 1971b, 103). Only with such an expanded sense of σάρξ can Jewett harmonize his view of Paul's uses:

> The key to flesh as it relates both to law and lawlessness is its implied promise of that which it cannot possibly provide. This is the deeper significance of the warning about sowing and reaping which is placed so enigmatically at the end of this discussion (Gal 6:7-8)...The circumcised flesh lures the nomist to place his final confidence in it; in this case man depends upon the obedience to the law which his own flesh can perform. In like manner the realm of flesh lures the anti-nomist to seek life through enjoyment of dependence upon itself (Jewett 1971b, 104-5).

Jewett valiantly tries to validate this broadened sense of σάρξ in Gal 5:13-6:17 through some creative theologizing. However, all of his theologizing cuts against the grain of continuity in a term's meaning, apart from a radical shift in context, topics, or audiences. In essence, Jewett (and most commentators) assume a major shift in *topics* in Gal 5:13-6:17 when he assumes that Paul shifts to a discussion of libertinistic from Judaizing problems. The first two chapters of this book sought to prove that no such shift occurs. If such a shift in topics had occurred, a comparable shift in the sense of σάρξ would not be unreasonable. However, in the absence of this major shift in topics (or contexts or audiences), then continuity in the sense of σάρξ would be expected.[19]

Additionally, when considering the meaning of σάρξ in Gal 5-6, the semantical rule of "maximal redundancy" may apply in this case also. This is a heuristic principle used to decide the meaning of *hapax legomena* or other words deemed mysterious in their context. This rule of thumb states that "the best meaning is the least meaning" (Joos 1972, 257).[20] This "least meaning" is defined by Joos so as "to make it contribute least to *the total message derivable from the passage where it is at home*, rather than, e.g., defining it according to some presumed etymology or semantic history" (1972, 257). Joos advocates that the best guess of the meaning of a word is "that one which maximizes the redundancy of word and environment together" (257). He goes on to note that "the popular blunder is to assume that an odd word must have some odd sense, the odder the better" (263). However, this approach ignores the remarkably redundant nature of language and communication and the *maximally redundant* approach to understanding that we normally use in decoding messages (263). If we can appropriate the general principle of this semantical reasoning about mysterious words and apply it to Paul's use of σάρξ in Gal 5-6,

then the "least meaning" of σάρξ, would be the *same sense* that Paul
uses in Gal 3-4: "bodily existence in its weakness and transitoriness
under the authority of Judaistic constraints and in contrast to the
working of God's Spirit" (e.g., Gal 3:3).
    However, this kind of semantic continuity is generally not
recognized in dealing with σάρξ in Gal 5:13 and following. The
extended replication of Jewett's views was given as an example of the
widespread acceptance among scholars of a shift in the meaning of
σάρξ from Gal 4 to Gal 5. Burton is also typical of this change in
perspective at Gal 5:13:

> The word σάρξ, previously in this epistle a purely physical term, is
> used here and throughout this chapter (see vv. 16, 17, 20, 24) in a
> definitely ethical sense, "that element of man's nature which is
> opposed to goodness, and makes for evil," in which it appears also
> in Rom, chap. 8;....Of any physical association with this ethical
> sense of the term there is no trace in this passage (Burton 1921,
> 292).

In a largely uniform manner, most recent commentaries on
Galatians agree with this perspective of Paul's use of σάρξ in Gal 5:13-
6:17 (e.g. Schlier 1971, 241-44; Bonnard 1972, 108; Betz 1979, 272-
74; Bruce 1982, 239-41; Fung 1988, 244-45; Longenecker 1990, 238-
48; and George 1994, 378-89). Some powerful force must be at work
if most scholars ignore the more probable continuity in Paul's
terminology. Both the general redundancy of Paul's language is
ignored *and* the rhetorical redundancy of the σάρξ/πνεῦμα antithesis
in Gal 3-6 is ignored. Amazingly, negating this redundancy about the
meaning of σάρξ neuters not only Paul's argument in Gal 5-6, but it
also seems to have hopelessly confused us about the exact nature of the
σάρξ/πνεῦμα antithesis in Gal 5-6 .
    Again, one must wonder if an assumed anthropology of an internal
duality between σάρξ and πνεῦμα is what causes this significant
semantic shift. If this is true, then the theological horse is before the
semantic cart and our exegesis of Gal 5:13-6:17 has been unduly
affected by this theological presupposition. While our theological
presuppositions are an inescapable part of our preunderstanding, they
still must be subject to interface with exegesis as one element in the
exegetical process, and thereby open to modification if that exegesis
proves these presuppositions to be errant (H. W. Johnson 1988). To
achieve this modification, however, interpreters must escape the
hermeneutical circle in which they may be entrapped by their

interpretive hypothesis of the passage. E. D. Hirsch has expressed this well:

> Thus, the distressing unwillingness of many interpreters to relinquish their sense of certainty is the result not of native close-mindedness but of imprisonment in a hermeneutical circle. Literary and biblical interpreters are not by nature more willful and un-self-critical than other men. On the contrary, they very often listen patiently to contrary opinions, and after careful consideration, they often decide that the contrary hypotheses "do not correspond to the text." And of course they are right. The meanings they reject could not possibly arise except on the basis of a quite alien conception of the text. It is very difficult to dislodge or relinquish one's own genre idea, since that idea seems so totally adequate to the text. After all, since the text is largely constituted by the hypothesis, how could the hypothesis fail to seem inevitable and certain? (Hirsch 1967, 166).

VI. Conclusion

This book's fundamental premise is that interpreters have indeed had a wrong interpretive hypothesis about Paul's use of σάρξ and πνεῦμα in Gal 5:13-6:18. *Chapter One* attempted to address the historical dimension of this wrong hypothesis by demonstrating the unitary nature of the Galatian threat and of Paul's refutation of it. In particular, Paul was shown to be addressing the *Judaizers'* inability to keep the Law in Gal 5:13-6:17 because of their identifying with a community unaided by God's Spirit (3:1-5) and their attempting anachronistically to revert to the preparatory, more immature era of Torah (3:19-4:11). This era was characterized by enslavement to sin and the failure that accompanied such a childish and slave-like state (3:23; 4:3, 8-11). Paul's exhortations in Gal 5:13-6:17 are best and most simply explained by seeing his continued addressing of the Judaizers' threat.

The rhetorical analysis of *Chapter Two* sought to underscore this understanding of the historical situation in Galatia by tracing Paul's tightly-reasoned argument. Specifically, it was demonstrated that there was no chasm between Gal 4 and 5, but that there was quite normal continuity in Paul's argument from Gal 3-4 through Gal 5-6. Paul continued the same antithetical, argumentative use of σάρξ and πνεῦμα in Gal 3-6. Gal 5-6 was shown to be the third and climactic argument in the extended Proof section (1:11-6:10). While Gal 5:13-6:10 is filled with more exhortative language, it was shown to be a continuation of Paul's deliberative argument that moves into the ethical realm. Therefore, Gal 5-6 are climactic in function within the argument of the epistle (see Matera 1988, Barclay 1988, and Kraftchick 1985).

Chapter Three sought to highlight the corporate or group nature of Paul's and the Galatians' view of the world through analysis of the social dynamics of the Galatian conflict. Specifically, the primary issue of the conflict was seen to be "Which of these two gospels provides the true identity and behavior for the people of God?" This insight added further proof to the historical and rhetorical dimensions that σάρξ and πνεῦμα are external entities that represent community identities within the Galatian conflict. In other words, in Gal 5:13 Paul is not abruptly turning to view the conflict anthropologically or "vertically" (metaphysically) by discussing the internal conflict within the Christian between σάρξ and πνεῦμα. Rather, he is continuing to use these significant terms in the corporate sense that he carefully developed in Gal 3-4. That is to say, he is continuing to use the terms "horizontally" or historically to represent two competing and successive eras in God's redemptive program. This is the exact sense for these two terms (in similar passages) that Herman Ridderbos has long advocated ([1957] 1982, 52 and 1975, 64-68) as he built upon the perceptive insights of Geerhardus Vos ([1912] 1980, 91-125 and [1930] 1979).

Therefore, as we conclude this chapter's thematic study of the σάρξ/πνεῦμα antithesis in Gal 3-6, it is with the continuing awareness that Paul does *not* change the sense in which he uses σάρξ in Gal 5-6 from the sense in which he used it in Gal 3-4. As we turn to the exegesis of Gal 5:13-6:18 in the next two chapters, it is in light of this lengthy argumentation about his consistent sense of σάρξ and πνεῦμα in Gal 3-6. From this point onward this sense will be assumed and the exegesis that follows will seek to validate the reasonableness of this choice.

Notes

[1]However, Stacey notes the general theological significance of σάρξ καὶ αἷμα in Paul's usage:

> In 1 Cor 15:50, this phrase is used for humanity in its transience and mortality. In Gal 1:16, it is used for humanity with the stress on the inadequacy of human knowledge. Both imply limitation, but not the same limitation (1956, 157).

[2]Paul's parallel usage of this same reworded Psalms' passage in Rom 3:20 underscores Paul's use of this terminology in a context where Jewish

Christians may misunderstand the theological significance of their Jewishness and the place of Torah (e.g., Rom 3:9-20).

[3]The idea of portraying something before their eyes is taken from the rhetorical tradition, as noted by Betz 1979, 131.

[4]The combining of the σάρξ/πνεῦμα antithesis with the νόμος/πίστις antithesis brings the issue of σάρξ and πνεῦμα into the focal point of the epistle as Burton observes:

> The two contrasted phrases ἐξ ἔργων νόμου and ἐξ ἀκοῆς πίστεως express the leading antithesis of the whole epistle, and by this question [of 3:2] Paul brings the issue between the two contrasted principles of religious life to the test of experience (1921, 147).

See also Campbell 1992 for the relationship of πίστις to νόμος in Paul.

[5]There is no consensus about the exact sense of ἐπιτελεῖσθε in 3:3. The main issue involves the choice between the sense of "to end" versus "to bring to completion or perfection." The latter choice is rooted in a broader understanding of the Judaizers' claim to bring maturity or completion to the Galatians by placing them under Torah's perfecting constraints (see Ch. 1). This does place the onus on the believer to do the works of the Law and thereby to be perfected according to the standards of Torah. If this is an accurate view of the controversy, then Paul's use of σαρκὶ ἐπιτελεῖσθε in 3:3 is an ironic one. See further Schlier 1971, 123-24 and Fung 1988, 133-34.

[6]The contrasting of "works of Law" and "hearing with faith" via parallel uses of ἐκ should not be theologically problematic in Gal 3:2 because Paul has already established the contrast in a definitive manner in Gal 2:16. There he asserts that no one is justified ἐξ ἔργων νόμου, but only διὰ πίστεως. Gal 3:2 must be read in light of this definitive statement of the role of faith in salvation.

[7]The general consensus is that πνεύματι is a dative of instrument or agency in Gal 3:3; 5:5, 16, 18, 25 (e.g., Turner 1963, 240; Easley 1984, 301). I will offer an alternative suggestion below for the identification of the datives in Gal 5:16, 18, and 25. Of the limitations of the whole process of arguing from grammatical forms and of the danger of over-identifying by this means, see Poythress 1984, 364-66 and Silva 1990b.

[8]See Howell 1993a,b and Fee 1994b, 803-26 for a discussion of the eschatological dualism at the core of Paul's theology.

[9]Charles Cosgrove has insightfully commented on this waiting:

> The statement "We wait in (or by) the Spirit" describes believers as *ethically engaged* (cf. "walking by the Spirit," 5:25) in expectation that their labors will find fulfillment and vindication in the future kingdom. The verb "wait" (ἀπεκδέχεσθαι) points to the eschatological judgment (cf. 1 Cor 1:7; Phil 3:20; Heb 9:28; Rom 8:19, 23, 25). *As in Romans 8:25, this "waiting" means obedient living for the future and not merely "expectation" by itself* (1988,

153; emphasis is mine).

[10]Similarly, see Hamilton 1957, 34 who sees a combination of an instrumental dative and a dative of respect: "Out of regard to this present working of the Spirit (πνεύματι), a faith arises which produces (ἐκ πίστεως) an expectation concerning the future." Close to Hamilton is Vos [1912] 1980, 111 who says that πνεύματι is the objective ground (versus the subjective ground of ἐκ πίστεως) on which the confident expectation is based: "In the Spirit, not in the σάρξ, in faith, not in ἔργα νόμου, has the Christian assurance that the full eschatological righteousness will become his (cf. also Titus 3:7)."

[11]The unloving distinction among Christians based on circumcision or non-circumcision is again contrasted with the loving service of one another by Paul in Gal 5:13-15.

[12]Lightfoot [1890] 1957, 209 also sees πνεύματι as a dative of rule or direction in Gal 5:16 and 5:25. An additional use of πνεύματι in 2 Cor 12:18 underscores Paul's understanding of this term in this more objective sense of rule or direction when combined with περιπατέω, rather than in a subjective or instrumental sense. The fact that this usage of πνεῦμα does not refer to the Holy Spirit does not affect its value as a parallel:

> I urged Titus to go, and sent the brother with him. Titus did not take advantage of you, did he? *Did we not walk according to the same spirit?* (οὐ τῷ αὐτῷ πνεύματι περιεπατήσαμεν;) *Did we not [walk] according to the same examples?* (οὐ τοῖς αὐτοῖς ἴχνεσιν) (cf. Rom 4:12 for this last sentence).

Rather than arguing from the identification of the dative, the real thrust of πνεύματι is gained from its combination with the verbs περιπατεῖτε in 5:16, ἄγεσθε in 5:18, and also στοιχῶμεν 5:25. It is these grammatical combinations that convey the idea of rule or direction for living. In these kinds of constructions, the label "dative of rule or direction" simply becomes a helpful, though ad hoc, type of dative. It is not found as a typical category for the dative in the standard grammars.

[13]Lightfoot [1890] 1957, 214 concurs and states that "the dative with στοιχεῖν, περιπατεῖν, etc., marks the *line* or *direction*." Again the sense of the dative is derived by its combination with these verbs which signify an ethical thrust.

[14]Fung 1988, 275 says it concisely: "The two expressions deal, respectively, with the Spirit as the source and sustaining power of believers' spiritual life and the Spirit as the regulative principle of believers' conduct."

[15]Ridderbos 1975, 223 ties Rom 8:4-9 and Gal 5:16-25 together in a similar fashion: "The requirement of the law can only be fulfilled in those who walk not after the flesh, but after the Spirit, i.e., in accordance with his operation and intention (Rom 8:4ff.; cf. Gal 5:16, 25). "

[16]If σάρξ has any theological significance in Gal 4:13-14, it might be that it is additional evidence of the irrelevance of *bodily* conditions, as modeled by

the frailty of Paul in his first preaching of the gospel to them. The Galatians did not emphasize bodily conditions *then*, nor should they *now*.

[17]Geerhardus Vos [1912] 1980, 93, states:
The sending forth of Christ marks to him [Paul] the πλήρωμα τοῦ χρόνου (Gal 4:4), a phrase which certainly means more than that the time was ripe for the introduction of Christ into the world: the fullness of the time means the end of that aeon and the commencement of another world period.

[18]One must appreciate a fundamental concept of Jewish thought to grasp the thrust of what must have been the Judaizers' argument and is now Paul's: the beginning of something establishes the norm for what follows. Bernard Lategan has insightfully grasped this nuance in Galatians:

According to Jewish thinking, the natural order of things plays an important role. This is especially true of the first in any chronological or hierarchical sequence. The importance of the first-born, the first fruits, and similar examples testify to this assumption and is underlined by the surprise caused by any reversal of this order....The basic assumption is that the first should be dominant and decisive for what follows--in other words, a combination of priority and dominance (1989, 178).

[19]At the root of this discussion is the degree of shift in topics that occurs in Gal 5:13. I would want to minimize the amount of shift that occurs by arguing that Paul has been building *very gradually and slowly* to his exposition of the relational workings of the communities of the Spirit and the flesh that begins in 5:13. What he means by his use of "having begun by the Spirit" in Gal 3:3 is very carefully enriched and expanded in Gal 3-4. His use of "waiting by the Spirit" in Gal 5:5 continues this expansion and points even more toward what life according to the Spirit means ethically. Therefore, Paul's exposition of what life according to the Spirit looks like in contrast to life according to the flesh in Gal 5:13-6:10 is the logical and anticipated end of his previous discussion of the Spirit.

[20]I am indebted to Silva 1983, 153-56 for this source and the application of Joos' principle to cases of polysemy (multiple meanings). Cf. also Hill 1970, 254-56.

Chapter 5

The Flesh/Spirit Conflict
in Galatians 5:13-26

The preceding historical, rhetorical, sociological, and thematic analyses can now be coalesced into a systematic explanation of this focal passage. These previous studies should give a helpful contextual backdrop for this task. Again, my goal is to validate that the σάρξ/πνεῦμα antithesis describes an external contrast of the rule or direction of the Judaizer and Pauline communities, respectively, not an internal duality within the Christian.

I. Galatians 5:13-15 and 5:25-26

These two passages will be dealt with together because of their function as brackets in Paul's argument. They bracket the antithetical sets of behavior of the σάρξ and the πνεῦμα that are described in 5:16-24. The first bracket in 5:13-15 is preceded by the epistle's first overt warning about the danger of submitting to circumcision in 5:1-12. While Paul has been building to this warning throughout the entire epistle, this is the clearest confrontation yet. Paul ends Galatians with an equally ringing warning in 6:11-17, so this topic is obviously very much in his thinking in Gal 5-6.[1] Clearly in this context also, circumcision is the official symbol of taking up the yoke of Torah (Gal 5:2-3). It is the most obvious act that ties the body as σάρξ to νόμος Therefore, when Paul follows his warning about submitting to circumcision in 5:1-12 with an exhortation about the σάρξ, it is most natural to read it as an exhortation about Judaistic behavior.

The structure of Gal 5:1-6:10 underscores this understanding of σάρξ in Gal 5:13 also.   This section is an argument proving the superiority of the Galatians' present deliverance in Christ over what the Judaizers could offer by contrasting the relational dynamics within the two communities.   Gordon Fee (1994, 205) has noted very powerfully this community emphasis in 5:13-6:10:

> A final very important observation needs to be made.   Quite in contrast to how this material is read by most of us and is presented in many of the commentaries[15]–the concern from beginning to end is with *Christian life in community, not with the interior life of the individual Christian.*   Apart from 5:17c, which is usually completely decontextualized and thus misread (see below), there is not a hint that Paul is here dealing with a "tension" between flesh and Spirit that rages within the human breast–in which the flesh most often appears as the stronger opponent.   To the contrary, the issue from the beginning (vv. 13-15) and throughout (vv. 19-21, 26; 6:1-4, 7, 10) has to do with Spirit life within the believing community.   The individual is not thereby brushed aside; after all, one both enters and lives within the Christian community at the individual level, which is where the individual believer fits into the argument (emphasis is his).

Paul's point in 5:1-6:10 is that his gospel alone provided them true deliverance from sin's powers through their receiving of the Holy Spirit:

> 5:1-12 Paul warns and exhorts about the antithetical consequences of identity choice for their continued deliverance from sin's powers.

> 5:13-26 The fundamental manifestation of deliverance from sin's powers in the community of God's people is loving service, not competitive striving.

> 5:13-15 (Front bracket) *The Initial Expression of the Antithetical Choices*: Manifestation of freedom from the constraints of the Mosaic Law within the community of God' s people should not be used as an opportunity (ἀφορμήν) for continued fleshly failure, which is vitriolic and self-consuming, but rather as an opportunity through love to serve one another, which is the summation principle of the whole Mosaic Law.

> 5:16-24 *The Antithetical Manifestations of the Two Choices*:
> Those who insist on living according to the past standards of fleshly behavior within the community under the Mosaic Law will share in the sins of a community composed of those who will not

inherit the kingdom of God; but those who identify with the community of the Spirit will be enabled by God's Spirit to manifest the fruit of loving unity apart from the daily constraints of the Mosaic Law.

5:25-26 (Back Bracket) *The Closing Expression of the Antithetical Choices*: Being a part of the community of the Spirit means that one should choose to live according to the rule or standard of the Spirit and not according to the competitive striving that characterizes the community of the flesh.

6:1-10 Some specific manifestations of the deliverance from sin's powers which fulfill the relational goal of the Law within the community of the Spirit are seen in the gracious restoration of sinning members and in the generous financial sharing with appropriate persons within the community.

Paul's argument takes a strong relational turn in Gal 5:6 which continues through 6:16. In this discussion the relational standard that Paul holds up is "faith working through love" (5:6b). This standard is introduced as a strong contrast (ἀλλά) to making distinctions in Christ according to circumcision or uncircumcision (5:6a). This contrast signals that the following relational discussion harnesses the *antithetical contrasts* between Paul's community and the Judaizers' seen in 3:1-5:5. Specifically, the antithesis discussed in 5:1-5 of the freedom of Paul's gospel versus the bondage of the Judaizers' non-gospel is continued in the relational discussion of 5:6-6:16.

In this light the relationship of 5:7 to 5:6 is instructive. In 5:7 Paul commends the Galatians for "running well" in the past (ἐτρέχετε καλῶς). In its immediate context, this commendation must be for their past relational health, which is exercising "faith working through love" (5:6b). However, Paul goes on to say that the Judaizers were hindering them from obeying [τῇ] ἀληθείᾳ. "The truth" is tied earlier in the epistle to the Judaizing-free gospel with the phrase ἡ ἀλήθεια τοῦ εὐαγγελίου (2:5, 14). The Galatians were presently being hindered from obeying the Law-free gospel by considering adopting the Judaizers' circumcision/uncircumcision distinctions. Therefore, they were being hindered from continuing to have "faith working through love" (5:6b). The point of Paul's discussion is a tying of the Judaizers' *mindset* (5:10) to a *destructive relational pattern* which is antithetical to freedom (5:1), love (5:6b), and the truth (of the gospel) (5:7).

In 5:13a Paul ties these three threads together in an explanatory fashion (γάρ) by reiterating *the Galatians'* call to freedom of 5:1a.

The ὑμεῖς is emphatic in 5:13a and heightens the contrast between the disturbers of 5:12 and the Galatians. However, he also uses the additive, yet specifying use of μόνον to qualify further their freedom relationally:[2] ὑμεῖς γάρ ἐπ ἐλευθερίᾳ ἐκλήθητε, ἀδελφοί μόνον μὴ τὴν ἐλευθερίαν εἰς ἀφορμὴν τῇ σαρκί, ἀλλὰ διὰ τῆς ἀγάπης δουλεύετε ἀλλήλοις. Gal 5:13b-c gives the *purpose* for their freedom in negative, then positive terms. Negatively, Paul says "Do not use (μή plus an understood imperatival verb)[3] the freedom for (εἰς) an opportunity for τῇ σαρκί." Positively, and contrastingly (ἀλλά), they have the freedom from sin's powers so they can serve one another through "the love" (διὰ τῆς ἀγάπης).[4] Both the negative and positive statements of the purpose are really more forceful and more overtly relational restatements of the same two aspects, first set in antithesis in 5:6:

5:6a	For in Christ Jesus neither circumcision or uncircumcision means anything,...
5:13b	you do not have your freedom for an opportunity for the flesh, . . .
5:6b	but faith working through love.
5:13c	but through the love serve one another.

Paul circumscribes the focus of "love" in this context as the treatment of others apart from the distinctions based on circumcision and uncircumcision. Therefore, the use of σαρκί in 5:13b is a continued use of the body term with the continued ethical cast of the Judaizers' emphasis on circumcised tissues. This is the same sense of σάρξ begun in Gal 3:3 after being foreshadowed in 2:15-21. This is the same sense of σάρξ so carefully developed by Paul in Gal 4:21-31. Therefore, the occasion or opportunity (ἀφορμήν) for τῇ σαρκί in 5:13b is an occasion to emphasize *circumcised* flesh or bodily tissues. This is the same sense of σάρξ in 6:12a: "Those who desire you to make a good showing ἐν σαρκί try to compel you to be circumcised."

However, in noting Paul's emphasis on the Judaizers' sense of σάρξ in 5:13, he is also beginning to place their present anachronistic emphasis on circumcised σάρξ within the broader context of the σάρξ-life of paganism. In other words, this is an ironic twist to the Judaizers' premise that circumcision of the σάρξ *will deliver* the Galatian Christians from the identity and behavior of paganism. Paul's point is quite the contrary! Using their freedom in Christ as an opportunity for the flesh *will connect* the Galatians with the community of all unbelievers (including Israel) which lives only in the flesh, i.e., in bodies not indwelt by God's Spirit. Therefore, Paul is setting up a powerful connection between the Judaizers/Israel and paganism that he will make more explicit shortly. In fact, Paul's point in Gal 5:19-21 in enumerating the classic vice list of the pagans is that those who identify with the flesh and manifest its behavior are not inheritors of the kingdom of God. In this sense, whether one emphasizes circumcised or uncircumcised flesh-life matters not. It is all indicative of life apart from God's Spirit. This is the same point that Paul makes in Eph 2:3: "Among them we [Jews] too all formerly lived in the lusts of our flesh, indulging the desires of the flesh and of the mind, and were by nature children of wrath, *even as the rest [Gentiles]*" (emphasis is mine).

Inextricably linked to this emphasis on bodily tissue via circumcision is the way of life where bodily deeds are constrained by Torah. "The reason was that among the Jews of that time, circumcision was understood to portray the removal of passions, desires, and evil inclinations" (Borgen 1988, 127). The Judaizers' non-gospel includes this total package (5:2-3). However, this life of circumcision and Torah-observance is not a proper use of Christian freedom. For the Galatians to think that they have their freedom for such an occasion is fallacious. To have freedom εἰς ἀφορμὴν τῇ σαρκί is to attempt to be perfected by the Judaizers' bodily emphases (3:3) by emphasizing birth into God's family κατὰ σαρκά (4:23, 29), which is wanting to be under Torah (4:21; 5:1).[5]

But why should Paul need to repeat in 5:13 the overt freedom statement of 5:1 and the overt love statement of 5:6? This repetition seems necessary because Paul is launching into the antithetical contrast of the internal dynamics of the Judaizers' and his communities in Galatia in 5:13-6:10. His restatement of the freedom of the Galatians' calling in 5:13a, his reiteration of the inappropriateness of circumcision-oriented living in 5:13b, and the repeat of the lifestyle of loving service in 5:13c all introduce Paul's climactic point: his communities, not the Judaizers, manifest true freedom from the στοιχεῖα[6] and are able to engender the relational ideal of neighbor-love that truly fulfills the Mosaic Law.[7] While the Judaizers' communities bite and devour one another (5:15) and are boastful and challenging and envying one another (5:26), the Pauline communities are seeking to serve one another in love (5:13c) and to walk according to the Spirit (5:25). While the Judaizers' communities manifest the deeds of the flesh and give evidence that they will not inherit God's kingdom (5:19-21), the Pauline communities manifest the fruit of the Spirit and the true fulfillment of the Mosaic Law (5:22-23). This relational fulfillment of neighbor-love (5:14) is seen in the handling of the difficult issues of believers' sinning (6:1-5) and the sharing of material resources within and without the community (6:6-10). In both of these areas, the churches Paul planted are to manifest the behavior appropriate for the new creation that is living according to the standard of the Spirit, rather than according to the standard of the flesh (6:12-16). Both Pretorius 1992 and Fee 1994 concur that this focus on *love in community* is the main thrust of the paraenesis of Gal 5:13-6:10.

In Gal 5:14 Paul relates the Mosaic Law as a whole or entire unit (ὁ πᾶς νόμος) in an explanatory way (via γάρ again) to both τῆς ἀγάπης of 5:13c and τῇ σαρκί of 5:13b. Paul's use of Lev 19:18 in Gal 5:14 as a summarizing relational statement of the Law (ἀγαπήσεις τὸν πλησίον σου ὡς σεαυτόν) connects very obviously with his love statement in 5:13c. However, the νόμος/σάρξ tandem also plays a significant role in Paul's use in 5:13-26 (e.g., 5:13-14, 17-18, 19-23). The connection between the whole Law which "has been *fulfilled* in one word"[8] and τῇ σαρκί in 5:13b is an ironic connection. Its irony rests in the Judaizers' attempt to persuade the Galatians to fulfill the Mosaic Law through emphasis on the (circumcised) σάρξ. However, inherent in this emphasis is the central distinction between those who are circumcised and uncircumcised in Christ (5:6a). This may have led the Judaizers to redefine who their neighbor was by using their freedom as an occasion for fleshly distinctions and thereby greatly restricting those who qualified as their "neighbors in Christ.[9] If this is the case, then Jesus' words about neighborliness to the lawyer in Lk 10:25-37 are germane: such fleshly distinctions and concerns lead to casuistic lovelessness and negate the Law's central tenet of neighbor-love. Nevertheless, if the Galatians should choose to follow the Judaizers in their emphasis on τῇ σαρκί in order to fulfill the Mosaic Law, the tragic irony is that they will risk negating its central tenet about human relationships!

It is important to note that Paul is not advocating a love antinomianism in Gal 5:13-14 any more than he is advocating a Spirit antinomianism in 5:16-18. Rather, he is contrasting the Judaizers' Torah-centered nomism with a Christ-centered nomism of love, which he apparently already had taught them. Therefore, he can appeal to and enhance τὸν νόμον τοῦ Χριστοῦ (6:2) and a previously-given set of standards about the Kingdom of God (e.g., 5:21b). The Pauline churches were given a κανών (Gal 6:16) and a τύπος (Phil 3:17) to follow. Therefore, Paul can confidently assert in Gal 5:14 that the Christ-centered law he had taught fulfilled Torah. This Christ-centered law is fulfilled in Christians when they walk κατὰ πνεῦμα:

"He condemned sin ἐν τῇ σαρκί in order that the requirement of the Law might be fulfilled in us, who do not walk κατὰ σάρκα, but κατὰ πνεῦμα" (Rom 8:3c-4).

By contrast in 5:15 (δέ), the risk that the Galatians run if they enter into the Judaizers' communities and attach themselves to Israel is that they may annihilate themselves through an animalistic type of biting and devouring of one another. As Betz has noted, "comparisons of bad conduct with the behavior of wild animals were commonplace in the diatribe literature" (1979, 276-77). Is Paul describing the Galatians' rivalries and behavior, as some advocate (e.g., Schmithals 1972, 43-46; Duncan 1934, 164-65), or is he merely speaking in hypothetical and hyperbolic language (e.g., Betz 1979, 277)? If these are the only two options, then the latter one seems preferable. However, while Paul may be using some hyperbolic language, it seems unlikely within the terse antithetical argumentation that he has been using that he would choose to describe a hypothetical situation. Therefore, a third option is preferred: Paul is describing concrete instances of the relationships *within the Judaizers' communities* (also Fee 1994, 205). They have created intensely competitive communities (Isenberg 1975, 42) where distinctions based on the σάρξ breed rivalries and animosities.

In Gal 4:17 Paul noted that their exclusive mentality first shut out the Galatians (ἀλλὰ ἐκκλεῖσαι ὑμᾶς θέλουσιν) for the purpose that the Galatians would be motivated to seek them (ἵνα αὐτοὺς ζηλοῦτε). This kind of group exclusion to group-oriented people engenders deep and powerful emotions. It is not the least bit unreasonable to see how such a highly competitive core and such an exclusive mentality have great potential for "animalistic" interpersonal behavior. The most likely option for the description of Gal 5:15 seems to rest with the Judaizing group against whom Paul is competing. While his language is obviously somewhat hyperbolic, it must have had some correspondence in observable fact with which the Galatians could relate (cf. Pretorius 1992, 454-58)..

While Gal 5:13-15 functions as the initial bracket of the whole section of 5:13-26, Gal 5:25-26 functions as the closing bracket. While the front bracket sets forth the initial expression of the antithetical relational choices between the two competing communities in Galatia, this back bracket reiterates the same choices. While Gal 5:13-15 appeals to the Galatians to continue as they had begun in freedom, in 5:25-26 Paul appeals to them to continue as they had begun in living out corporately the life according to the rule or direction of the Spirit: εἰ ζῶμεν πνεύματι, πνεύματι καὶ στοιχῶμεν. μὴ γινώμεθα κενόδοξοι, ἀλλήλους προκαλούμενοι, ἀλλήλοις φθονοῦντες.

The contrast between the Pauline and Judaizer communities in these two verses centers on the life of relational unity that the Spirit brings forth versus the life of competitive strife that communities devoid of God's Spirit manifest. Paul again refers to the beginning of life in Christ as life beginning according to the direction of the Spirit (εἰ ζῶμεν πνεύματι) (cf. 3:2-3). This beginning has shaping priority and dominance over the whole life that follows. Hence, the Galatians should seek to walk in agreement with or in step according to the same rule or direction of the Spirit (see the discussion of πνεύματι and στοιχῶμεν in section III of Chapter Four). This is similar to the appeal in Eph 4:1-3 *to preserve* the bond of the Spirit (τὴν ἑνότητα τοῦ πνεύματος). The Spirit desires to produce His fruit among the Galatian churches (Gal 5:22-23) and this crop is one that brings strong relational unity. However, the Galatians will never experience the fullness of the Spirit's relational fruit and the walking in agreement with His standard if they enter the Judaizers' communities. This is because of the Judaizers' competitive core that seems to produce division and unhealthy individualism in the form of boasting, challenging one another, and envying one another (Gal 5:26). Again, Paul must have been appealing to characteristics of the Judaizers' communities that the Galatians had been able to observe, at least in part. The hierarchical sense of distinctions (5:6a; 6:12-13, 15) and the fleshly means of being perfected within the Judaizers' communities (3:2-3) must have fueled the relational dynamics described in Gal 5:26.

II. Galatians 5:16-18

Within the bracketing passages of Gal 5:13-15 and 5:25-26, which summarize the antithetical relational dynamics of the Pauline and Judaistic communities, Gal 5:16-24 functions as Paul's fuller delineation of the internal dynamics of the two groups. As one would expect with Paul's rhetorical approach begun in Gal 3:1, these two competing communities are delineated in an antithetical manner. In fact, within Gal 5:16-24 we reach the climax of the antithesis of the community of the Spirit with the community of the flesh.

The logical linkage of 5:16-24 to 5:13-15 is one of *means* to the desired *end*. In Gal 5:13-15 Paul expressed the desired *end* of the Galatians' freedom in Christ: loving service of one another, not making fleshly distinctions or biting and devouring one another. It is in Gal 5:16-24 that Paul now explains the *means* of achieving this desired relational end. Grammatically, the linkage is with Λέγω δέ in 5:16 ("But I say"), which is probably used in an adversative sense for continuing a discussion, and especially for emphasizing an aspect of the previous argumentation (cf. Gal 1:9; 3:17; 5:2; and especially 4:1). The adversative sense sets the contrast with the undesired relational end described in 5:15. Rather than this animalistic annihilating of one another, Paul offers the sure means to avoid completing this kind of fleshly behavior. While in 5:13 he described this behavior as "an opportunity for the flesh" (ἀφορμὴν τῇ σαρκί), in 5:16 he describes it in a parallel fashion as "the desire of the flesh" (ἐπιθυμίαν σαρκός). Walking according to the rule of the Spirit (πνεύματι περιπατεῖτε) is the gracious and sure means of not fulfilling (or ὁυ μὴ τελέσητε) the desire associated with the σάρξ way of life.

If the ἐπιθυμίαν σαρκός of 5:16 is truly parallel to the ἀφορμὴν τῇ σαρκί of 5:13, and it appears to be in context, then Paul's strategy is to connect the opportunity for circumcised σάρξ with the desire of the uncircumcised σάρξ (paganism), which results in τὰ ἔργα τῆς σαρκός in its behavioral manifestations (5:19-21). Paul's antidote is, therefore, to walk according to the rule of the Spirit so that the Judaizers' passion for the circumcision of the σάρξ will not be fulfilled in pagan living according to the σάρξ.

Gal 5:17 explains this clash of the desire of the σάρξ and the desire of the πνεῦμα and verse 18 gives the resolution to the conflict: "But if you are led according to the rule of the Spirit, you are not ὑπὸ νόμον." The antithesis of πνεῦμα and νόμος in 5:18 must surely parallel the antithesis of πνεῦμα and σάρξ in 5:16-17 or else Paul's resolution to the conflict of verses 16-17 is meaningless. If this is the case, then the ἐπιθυμίαν σαρκός of 5:16 is also the desire to place people ὑπὸ νόμον. To this threat Paul espouses the same antidote in first the active, and then the passive voices: walk according to the rule of the Spirit (5:16) and be led according to the rule of the Spirit (5:18).

The imperative περιπατεῖτε in 5:16 is a very common and extremely important term in both Jewish and Greek ancient ethics, as Betz 1979, 277 has noted in this insightful passage:

> The term expresses the view that human life is essentially a "way of life." *A human being must and always does choose between ways of life as they are presented in history and culture.* For ancient man, ways of life are more than "styles of life": they are not only different in their outward appearance, but their different appearance is the result of different underlying and determining factors. These factors influence human behavior by providing the "way" in which human beings "walk." *Therefore, the way of life of human beings*

determines the quality of their life. More than merely a matter of
outward style, the way of life provides continuity, guidance, and
assistance for the task of coping with the daily struggle against evil
(emphasis is mine).

Betz' insights help inform us how the Galatians would have related
to Paul's command to "walk according to the rule or direction of the
Spirit." Given the clear πνεῦμα/σάρξ antithesis of 5:16-18, the
Galatians would see that their choice was between two "ways of life,"
or, as we have been translating the dative πνεύματι, between two
"rules or directions" in life. Apparently both of the communities had
promised the Galatians that life σαρκί and life πνεύματι would
provide the necessary continuity, guidance, and assistance for coping
with the daily struggle with evil that Betz described. In Gal 5:16-24
Paul rips back the ethical curtain to convince the Galatians that
walking σαρκί (or ὑπὸ νόμον) will not result in the kind of behavior
that they desire in Christ (5:17) and is tantamount to walking in the
way of those outside the kingdom of God (5:21b).

Perhaps a further word about understanding πνεύματι as a dative
of rule or direction in 5:16 (and also in 5:18 and 5:25) is appropriate
at this point. John Eadie ([1884] 1977, 407) and J. B. Lightfoot
([1890] 1957, 209) are in the minority of commentators who agree
with this book's perspective that πνεύματι is a dative of rule or
direction (Lightfoot) or a dative of norm indicating rule or manner
(Eadie). Specifically attacking this view is Elinor Rogers (1989, 170)
who says that

> πνεύματι does not mean here in [v.] 16b "by the rule or norm of the
> Spirit"...simply because στοιχέω "walk" in 5:25b and 6:16a implies
> certain information, dictates, rules or principles, and such a rule is
> explicit in 6:15a-b. With περιπατέω "walk" that idea probably
> would have been expressed as κατὰ πνεῦμα "according to the
> Spirit."

Rogers advocates understanding πνεύματι as a dative of
instrument or agency ("walk by the Spirit") (170). While this view is
very appealing and widely held, it has two difficulties. First, is the
obvious parallelism of the antitheses in Gal 5:16 and 5:18 and the
associating of σάρξ in v.16 with νόμος in v.18. As Rogers herself
admits, πνεύματι περιπατεῖτε in 5:16 and πνεύματι ἄγεσθε in 5:18
are a "sandwich structure" (1989, 169). However, Rogers' view of the
ethical uses of σάρξ as "your naturally evil selves" (170) tends to
lessen the impact of Paul's parallelism and negates the effect of the

sandwich structure by making the issue internal and individualistic rather than external and corporate.

Secondly, the sense of στοιχέω in 5:25b and 6:16a is not to be understood as arguing *against* a similar sense for πνεύματι in 5:16 and 5:18, but rather as arguing *for* a similar sense of a dative of rule or norm because of the widely recognized parallelism and virtual synonymity between these verses (e.g., Delling in *TDNT*, 7:667-69; Duvall 1994b, 23, 29-30). Even more importantly within this parallelism is the fact that the categorizing of the dative πνεύματι flows out of its attachment to the specific verbs περιπατεῖτε, ἄγεσθε, and στοιχῶμεν in Gal 5:16, 18, and 25, respectively. These *verbs of rule or direction* give the dative its ad hoc categorization as a dative of rule or direction.[10] The fact that Paul simply uses the dative πνεύματι instead of κατὰ πνεῦμα (as in Gal 4:29) could be explained as a stylistic alternative, or even better, as an overt attempt to show how life "according to the rule or direction of the Spirit" is inextricably linked to the life "begun by the Spirit" (ἐναρξάμενοι πνεύματι in Gal 3:3). The continuity in the use of πνεύματι would help to establish this linkage.

Within the argument of Galatians, the command to πνεύματι περιπατεῖτε in Gal 5:16 and the unpacking of this command in 5:17-24 is really the rhetorical and emotional pinnacle of all of Paul's persuasion using the σάρξ/πνεῦμα antithesis. In a sense, the following two sections are a "cool down" of sorts because they are a very specific application of this general way of life (in 6:1-10) and the conclusion to the entire epistle (in 6:11-18). But Paul is also reaching a theological climax in his description of the work of the Spirit in this section. In 5:16-24 we now see more clearly how walking according to the rule or direction of the Spirit is the divine means of deliverance from σάρξ.

Earlier Paul asserted that the Spirit is the One who mediates within the Christian the apocalyptic fullness of time that Jesus Christ has brought (Gal 4:4-6). Therefore (ὥστε), the Christian is no longer a slave to the στοιχεῖα τοῦ κόσμου, but rather a υἱός and κληρονόμος (4:7). Paul's point in Gal 5:13-6:10 is now to showcase relationally what this πνεῦμα-centered deliverance looks like when contrasted to the σάρξ-centered promises of the Judaizers. Their "deliverance" is still aeon-bound to the preparatory and inferior age of the Mosaic Law (3:19-4:3). Therefore, the best they can promise the Galatians is more child-like bondage under the στοιχεῖα τοῦ κόσμου (4:3). Ironically, since the Judaizers are the Ishmaelites, they will not live out the Abrahamic blessing κατὰ πνεῦμα, but only the Spirit-born Isaacites will (4:21-31).

In light of these promises of inheritance which are intimately connected to the work of the Spirit, Paul's promise to the Galatians in 5:16 is that if they will but walk according to the rule of the Spirit, there is absolutely no way (οὐ μή) that they will carry out (τελέσητε) the Judaistic emphasis (ἐπιθυμίαν σαρκός).[11]   He reiterates this promise from the nomistic side of the σάρξ/νόμος tandem in 5:18 when he bluntly states that if the Galatians are being led (ἄγεσθε = present passive indicative) according to the rule of the Spirit, then they are not in the state of being ὑπὸ νόμον (cf. 3:23; 4:4, 5, 21). But what about Paul's hard-to-understand statements about the fleshly opposition in 5:17?

A brief survey of some of the major views of the exact nature of the σάρξ/πνεῦμα opposition in Gal 5:17 will provide some historical backdrop to our exegetical conclusions.[12] The *first* view is that of Hellenistic dualism that sees σάρξ as a term for the physical part of man (not the entire man) and, while the σάρξ is not sinful itself, it is the abode of sin (Pfleiderer 1891, 48).   Therefore, because man physically is made of flesh, the sinful power that dwells in his material substance enslaves him.   Materiality itself becomes the source of evil in this view and its conflict is with the immaterial element in man (see Pfleiderer 1891, 47-67 for a full discussion).

A *second* view growing out of the material/immaterial dualistic view is the view of ethical dualism.   George B. Stevens has championed this view in his work on pauline theology (1897, 139-50). In particular, in opposing the view that Paul was influenced by Hellenistic thought regarding the evil of materiality, Stevens set forth the view that σάρξ and πνεῦμα represent the higher and lower principles within man:

> Σάρξ thus becomes a term to express the power of those natural sinful desires and impulses in unregenerate men. In such the flesh predominates, and not the spirit....σάρξ is seen to be a general term to denote unrenewed human nature...(1897, 145-46).

A *third* view that Rudolf Bultmann (1951, 233-38) set forth views σάρξ as Paul's term to denote the realm of man's earthly-natural existence or the merely human, earthly-transitory realm. Man's nature is not determined by his substance or possessed qualities, but "by the sphere within which he moves, the sphere which marks out the horizon or the possibilities of what he does and experiences" (1951, 235). Therefore, life in the sphere of the flesh only is a spurious life and is "proleptically denied" by the Christian who is now "in the Spirit" (1951, 236) .

A *fourth* view is that of W. D. Davies who advocates that Paul's view of the flesh and spirit conflict had its roots in the Old Testament, but even more so in the rabbinic doctrine of the two inclinations of the evil impulse (*yeser hara'*) and of the good impulse (*yeser hatob*) (1980, 17-35). This is most evident in Rom 7, according to Davies (1980, 24-27).[13] Some have advocated that σάρξ represents the evil impulse in Gal 5:16-17 and that Paul's opponents were advocating Torah as the only appropriate antidote to this impulse (Martyn 1985b; Markus 1986). Additionally, Kuhn 1957, 94-113 found similar parallels between Paul's view of the σάρξ and the view of Qumran, although Davies tempered the nature of these parallels (1957, 157-82).

A *fifth* view, and surely the predominant one at present, is the view of σάρξ in its ethical uses as referring

> neither to man's physical materiality nor to a lower element in man, but to man as a whole, seen in his fallenness, opposed to God. This usage is a natural development of the Old Testament use of *basar*, which is man viewed in his frailty and weakness before God. When applied to the ethical realm, it becomes man in his ethical weakness, i.e., sinfulness before God. *Sarx* represents not a part of man but man as a whole--unregenerate, fallen, sinful man (Ladd 1974, 472).

While this description of σάρξ is agreeable as far as it goes, those who hold this view generally carry the description even further and move from the realm of σάρξ as viewing man as a whole to the realm of σάρξ as viewing a *capacity* of man: "The flesh that makes for evil is not the body or matter as such, but an inherited impulse to evil. This force is not compulsory, but can be resisted by the power of the spirit" (Burton 1918, 197). Therefore, the ethical sense of σάρξ

> is that element in man's nature which is opposed to goodness, that in him which makes for evil; sometimes thought of as an element of himself, sometimes objectified as a force distinct from him, this latter usage being, however, rather rhetorical (Burton 1918, 186).

Echoing this view, Whiteley says of σάρξ that "sometimes also the word is used to mean 'the lower ethical level,' as in Gal 5:24" (1966, 39). Ladd concurs with this definition and shows how he has extended the sense of σάρξ beyond his "man as a whole" view noted above:

> While Paul makes a sharp and absolute contrast between being "in the flesh" (unregenerate) and being "in the spirit" (regenerate), there remains in the believer a struggle between the flesh and spirit. *If "flesh" means unregenerate human nature, the believer still*

possesses this nature even though he has received the Spirit. Even in the Christian the flesh struggles against the Spirit so that he cannot be the (perfect) man that he would wish to be (Gal 5:17) (Ladd 1974, 473; emphasis is mine).

The above survey reveals that there has been a bewildering set of views of the σάρξ/πνεῦμα conflict in recent decades ranging from an earlier Hellenistic view of a duality between materiality and immateriality to the presently dominant duality-of-natures view. Rather than respond individually to each view, I will add to the bewildering array of views by proposing a sixth view of the conflict, especially as it is set forth in Gal 5:17.

Any understanding of the σάρξ/πνεῦμα conflict in Galatians must adequately weigh that the terminology grew out of the polemics of the Judaizing controversy. If a blanket criticism could be leveled at the five views above, it would be that *this very specific polemical context is not weighted nearly enough* in Galatians, nor perhaps also in Romans 7-8 and Philippians 3.[14] In Galatians, σάρξ is a term probably drawn directly from the lips of the Judaizers when they boasted of God's eternal covenant with Abraham and his heirs in Gen 17:13b (LXX): καὶ ἔσται ἡ διαθήκη μου ἐπὶ τῆς σαρκὸς ὑμῶν εἰς διαθήκην αἰώνιον.[15] However, in the context of Galatians, Paul carefully enriches the basic Old Testament sense of σάρξ as "human bodily existence seen in its weakness, frailty, and transitoriness." Paul does this by adding the New Covenant distinctive of bodily existence: being indwelt by God's πνεῦμα. By contrast, a person as σάρξ within the Judaistic framework is a person under the Mosaic Law before the fullness of times when God's Spirit was given to Messiah and God's people (Gal 4:1-7).

Therefore, persons as σάρξ refers to persons *before* Christ, or now that he has come, persons *apart from* Christ. This means within Galatians that σάρξ is a body conformed to Judaistic practices and constrained by Torah. In opposition to σάρξ is πνεῦμα, which is the Holy Spirit and the practices and constraints that He represents when Paul uses the term πνεύματι.

Applying this understanding of σάρξ and πνεῦμα to the conflict described in Gal 5:17 sheds light on the exact nature of how they "set their desire against" one another (ἐπιθυμεῖ κατά) and stand in opposition (ἀντίκειται) to one another. The opposition of σάρξ and πνεῦμα is at least threefold. *First*, they are opposed in scope or ethnic inclusion. After the changes wrought by Jesus Christ's crucifixion (Gal 6:12-16), boasting in the racial distinction of their σάρξ is an inappropriate boast for the Judaizers (6:13-14). On this side of the cross, σάρξ now represents a wrongly exclusive era in redemptive history that is diametrically opposed to a universally inclusive era through faith in Jesus Christ (3:6-8; 13-14). The Judaizers were perpetuating this wrong-headed exclusiveness in contradistinction to "the truth of the gospel" (2:5, 14) with its absence of Judaistic practices (2:1-21).

Secondly, σάρξ and πνεῦμα now oppose each other temporally. Σάρξ represents an earlier, preparatory, now-inferior era of redemptive history because of its linkage to Torah (3:19-4:11). To advocate living κατὰ σαρκά as the Judaizers were doing (e.g., 4:23, 29) is to advocate an anachronistic set of standards and the anachronism of living according to the rule of the σάρξ versus living according to the rule of the πνεῦμα. Such an anachronistic rule negates the apocalyptical effects of Christ's crucifixion (1:4; 2:19-21; 3:1; 6:12-16). His crucifixion negated σάρξ (6:15) *and* its power over Christians (5:24).

Lastly, and probably closest to Paul's reasoning in Gal 5:17c, is not just the *temporal* and *ethnic* opposition of σάρξ and πνεῦμα, but also the *ethical opposition.* This opposition exists because of the negating effects of the Judaizers' non-gospel on Christ's crucifixion. Since they advocate righteousness διὰ νόμου, then they effectively advocate that Christ's death was needless (δωρεάν) (2:21). Therefore, they boast in circumcision (6:13) rather than in the cross of Christ (6:14). The *ethical effects* of the effective negation of the benefits of Christ's death is living as if one were still a part of this present evil age (1:4; cf. 5:2-4).

Even more importantly, the Judaizers essentially lived as if the σάρξ had not been crucified with Christ (5:24). This meant living according to the rule or direction of the σάρξ, not the πνεῦμα. Choosing not to walk according to the rule of the πνεῦμα, therefore removed *the only means* of not fulfilling the desire of the σάρξ (5:16). Therefore, *ethically,* the Judaizers were living a life in opposition to the Spirit and in conformity with the flesh. While *individually* the Judaizers were apparently Christians, *corporately* they identified with and lived attached to the *Jewish community.* Therefore, they embraced the fleshly set of behaviors that flowed out of this community of the σάρξ (5:19-21). Therefore, while *individually* they may have wished to do certain things, they could not (5:17c). This is the result of possessing the Spirit, but not walking according to the Spirit (5:16)! Therefore, they would fulfill the desire of the flesh. As a result (ἵνα in the consecutive sense), they could not do those things that they would wish or please to do. That is, those who follow the Judaizers' way of life will still wish/desire (θέλητε) to do the right things (e.g., loving service of others). However, they will be unable to do so because of not walking according to the Spirit's rule or direction.[16] Certainly encompassed in the Spirit's way of life is *the enablement* to live this new life according to the promises of the New Covenant (Jer 31:31-34; Ezek 36:26-27). Therefore, the dative constructions with πνεύματι, while understood as datives of rule or direction and emphasizing the objective standards of the Spirit, encompass the sense of the personal agency of the Holy Spirit, since He is the divine means of mediating New Covenant life (cf. 2 Cor 3:5-6). This is why Paul can immediately contrast the debilitating failure of Christians within the Judaizers' communities in Gal 5:17c with the personal terminology of 5:18a: εἰ δὲ πνεύματι ἄγεσθε. As many commentators have noted (e.g., Schlier 1971, 250; Bonnard 1972, 112), "to be led πνεύματι" is simply another way of saying "to walk πνεύματι." Note that the contrast between 5:17c and 5:18 is one of the failure of Judaistic living according to the σάρξ (5:17c) versus the freedom of Christian living according the πνεῦμα in reference to the Mosaic Law (5:18). Those Galatian Christians who choose to be led according to the rule of the Spirit are not under the rule of Torah and its accompanying fleshly failure. How else can the contrast of 5:18 with 5:17c be understood?

Fee concurs with this emphasis in his summarizing comments on Gal 5:16-18:

> At issue, therefore, is not some internal tension in the life of the individual believer,[24] but the sufficiency of the Spirit for life without Torah—a sufficiency that enables them to live so as not to *revert* to their former life as pagans (i.e., in the flesh, as vv. 19-21 make clear) (emphasis is his; 1994, 207).

To recap the logical flow of Gal 5:16-18 and to summarize the lengthy discussion of it, the following main points can be reiterated:

> 1.   σάρξ = bodily existence in frailty and weakness apart from God's indwelling Spirit, particularly in the circumcised state under Torah, when referring to Judaizers. Σάρξ specifically represents the redemptive historical era of the Mosaic Law when used in this manner. The irony in this usage of σάρξ is that Paul includes the Judaizers with all (including pagans!) who live apart from God's Spirit.

> 2.   πνεῦμα = the Holy Spirit and represents living in the freedom that Christ's crucifixion brought, which ended the mode of existence called σάρξ for God's people (cf. Gal 5:24; Rom 7:5-6; 8:9).

3.   Gal 5:16 = the command to walk according to the rule or direction of the Holy Spirit to avoid carrying out the desire of the σάρξ, which, in context, is the desire to be circumcised and to be under Torah. Choosing the way of life according to the Spirit would prevent the Galatians from carrying out the submission to circumcision (the desire of the σάρξ), which could lead to the deeds of the σάρξ (in 5:19-21).

4.   Gal 5:17 = an explanation (γάρ) of the final phrase of 5:16 ("and you will not carry out the desire of the flesh"). Therefore, the perspective is from *within the perspective of the sarx*. This means v. 17 explains the dynamic at work on Christians who become a part of the Judaizers' communities and attach themselves to Israel. These Christians will experience *ethically and interpersonally* what Paul warned them about in Gal 5:1-4. They will live out the now-inferior conditions of life under the Law (Gal 4:1-3, 8-11) because of the opposition of the Judaistic way of life to the Spirit-led way of life.

5.   Gal 5:18 = the contrast (δέ) to life within the σάρξ community. This contrast is being led according to the rule of the πνεῦμα. This means being within the Pauline communities and not being under Torah in the Judaizers' communities.[17]

III. Galatians 5:19-24

While Gal 5:13-15 and 5:25-26 act as brackets to the central section of 5:16-24, verses 16-18 function as the main statement of Paul's antithetical contrast of his and the Judaizers' communities. After the two elements of the antithesis (each representing a community) are clearly identified in 5:16-18, the resulting "ways of life" that flow out of each element/community are then set forth in antithesis in 5:19-21 (the σάρξ way of life) and 5:22-23 (the πνεῦμα way of life). Gal 5:24 then functions as the definitive historical and theological conclusion of the antithesis: σάρξ as an entity and its resulting way of life is no longer appropriate for those who belong to Christ Jesus.

For the first century person, choosing a way of life brought a corresponding set of behaviors with it (see this discussion in Sec. III of Chapter 3). Therefore, first century authors could appeal to the family or group identity of persons in order to inform or reinforce the behavior appropriate for the way of life that corresponded to that identity. These appeals occur quite overtly in other of the Pauline epistles (e.g., Rom 6:1-11; 1 Cor 6; Eph 4:1-3). The entire passage of Gal 5:13-26 fits this type of appeal. The uniqueness of this ethical exhortation, however, is that it is antithetically structured throughout

as Paul contrasts the way of life of the Pauline/πνεῦμα communities
with that of the Judaizer/σάρξ communities.

The crucial exegetical question when confronting the deeds of the
flesh in Gal 5:19-21 is the identity of those who do these deeds. To
say that the Judaizers are in view is to beg the question somewhat.
The stance of this book has been that the Judaizers were *Christian*
Jews from the Jerusalem/Judea area (see Chapter 1). If Paul is
referring only to the Judaizers in Gal 5:19-21, then he is implicitly
saying that *Christians* are capable of doing the deeds of the flesh. The
exegetical difficulty with this is that Paul culminates his description of
the behavior of the community of the flesh in 5:21b with the ringing
statement "that those who practice such things will not inherit (οὐ
κληρονομήσουσιν) the kingdom of God."[18] This statement also occurs
in almost identical form in 1 Cor 6:9-10 and Eph 5:5. Both of the
broader contexts of these passages (1 Cor 6:1-11 and Eph 5:3-14)
clearly describe the conduct of non-Christians or pagans *in contrast to
Christians* (cf. Rom 8:1-11). Therefore, one must conclude that Paul's
straightforward statement in 5:21b means what it appears to say: the
description of those who do the deeds of the flesh in 5:19-21 is a
description of pagans or non-Christians.

The simultaneous description of the *Christian* Judaizers and the
non-Christian sarkic practitioners in Gal 5:19-21 is easily understood
from Paul's previous identity of the community of the σάρξ in Gal
4:21-31. Especially in 4:23-25 Paul identifies the σάρξ community as
the Jewish community still under the Mosaic or Sinaitic Covenant
(4:25). Again, σάρξ and νόμος are seen by Paul as an inextricable
tandem. Therefore, the identity of those who practice the deeds of the
σάρξ in Gal 5:19-21 is Israel and all those who are attached to her
(i.e., the Judaizing communities). This group is seen by Paul as a
homogeneous whole still being under Torah, and thereby still "in the
flesh." The term σάρξ is appropriate to describe this community
because of both the Judaizers' and Jews' emphasis on σάρξ in kinship
and in circumcision.

Σάρξ is also appropriate as a description of the Jews/Judaizers
within this context because of the contrast of man as σάρξ to God as
πνεῦμα and because of the focus of σάρξ on humanity in its frailty and
transitoriness. Specifically, the Judaizers want to attach the Galatians
to a community that is "in the flesh" and is thereby not indwelt with
God's Spirit. The Jewish (and Judaizer) belief that Torah is God's
gracious gift that will adequately constrain their bodily behavior has
already been indirectly assaulted by Paul in the description of the
σάρξ/πνεῦμα opposition in Gal 5:16-18. Now he directly assaults the

Jews' and Judaizers' fallacious belief about Torah's constraining power by describing the set of behaviors that life ὑπὸ νόμον and σαρκί will manifest in 5:19-21. The tragic irony of these behaviors is that they are not that divergent from the behaviors described in contexts that are mainly Gentile or pagan (e.g., 1 Cor 6:9-11).[19] And this is Paul's ironic emphasis. Joining the Jewish σάρξ community also will place the Galatians within the broader pagan σάρξ community! Only in the Pauline πνεῦμα communities can the Galatians escape the tyranny of the σάρξ!

What Paul is *not* saying in Gal 5:19-21 is that the Christian Judaizers or pious Jews presently do all of the sins that he enumerates in this list of pagan vices. Rather Paul's point is that the list of sins in vv. 19-21 is a litany of the deeds of those who live according to the standards of the σάρξ. Apparently, this was somewhat true of Israel during the Mosaic Law era (e.g., Rom 2:17-24). Israel was "in the flesh" and "under Torah" when she manifested these pagan-like behaviors which are so "evident" (φανερά in 5:19a). Neither Torah nor circumcision prevented the practice of these fleshly deeds (cf. Eph 2:3). Neither will they prevent the Galatians from *continuing to do* these deeds if they attach themselves to Israel (4:21; 5:1-4; 6:12-13). Torah and circumcision did not, do not, and will not compensate for the absence of God's Spirit and the negation of Christ's crucifixion regarding the σάρξ (5:24). Paul's persuasive point in 5:19-21 is to connect the present circumcised community of the σάρξ with the broader pagan community of the σάρξ. In other words, the irony is that circumcision will lead the Galatians *into, not out of* the behavior of paganism! This is because the Judaizers are denying the aeon-changing work of the cross of the Messiah.

Is Paul "Israel bashing"? Not at all![20] Rather, he is *again* showing the inferiority of life under the Mosaic Law (cf. 3:19-4:11) in light of the apocalyptic changes wrought by Christ's death (1:4) and by the giving of the Holy Spirit to those who believe in Jesus (3:1-5). Those Jews who resist life according to the Spirit by not believing in Christ therefore live according to the flesh unaided by God's Spirit and excluded from His kingdom. Hence, Paul's stark point to the Galatians in 5:19-21 is simply:

> Why would you want to attach yourselves to a community which has a very evident history of the deeds of the σάρξ and which is a community that is now devoid of God's Spirit and outside of His kingdom?

Chapter Three sought to underscore the corporate nature of the Galatian conflict and the central issue of group identity to the Galatian Christians (see especially section II and III). We see one very important aspect of this kind of sociological thinking in Gal 5:19-23 in the catalog of vices (5:19-21) and virtues (5:22-23). They are given a concrete embodiment in the Judaizer/Jewish and Pauline communities, respectively. Paul is contrasting in stereotypical terms how members within these two communities would be expected to behave as they sought to walk in the way of that community. This "way" would be that which was modeled and patterned for the Galatians by the leaders of the respective communities. While the community of the σάρξ has a long history in Israel, it is a checkered history, at best, that the Judaizers are representing. By contrast, Paul must have appealed to Jesus and his early followers in his patterning of the community of the πνεῦμα, and he certainly was not reticent about appealing to his own previous behavior while he was in their midst (4:12-20) or elsewhere (e.g., 1:11-2:21; 5:11; 6:14, 17).

Paul linked the list of vices in 5:19-21 to the previous section with δέ and again linked vv. 22-23 to the list of vices with a δέ. Gal 5:24 is also linked to the list of virtues in 5:22-23 with δέ. These linkages give the flow of Gal 5:16-24 a steady, even rhythm and a sense of connection. In spite of this flow, it is probable that the sense of the linkage of the fruit of the Spirit in 5:22-23 to the deeds of the flesh in 5:19-21 is adversative and intended as an obvious contrast. This contrast is heightened by the use of the singular καρπὸς τοῦ πνεύματος in v. 22 versus the plural ἔργα τῆς σαρκός in v. 19. Additionally, the contrast is strengthened by the shortened list of nine virtues versus the longer list of fifteen vices and the sense that "fruit" versus "deeds" engenders. Fung has remarked about Paul's use of καρπὸς τοῦ πνεύματος that

> the phrase directly ascribes the power of the fructification not to the believer himself but to the Spirit, and effectively hints that the qualities enumerated are not the result of strenuous observation of an external legal code, but the natural product ("harvest") of a life controlled and guided by the Spirit (1988, 262).

While the sense of "fruit" does not exclude the believer's active involvement in its cultivation (e.g., 5:16 and 5:25-26), it nevertheless carries with it a tremendous sense of divine enablement for exhibiting such qualities of life:

> The expression "fruit of the Spirit" means that the nine concepts should be taken as "benefits" which were given as or together with

the Spirit. In other words, when the Galatians received the Spirit, they were also given the foundation out of which the "fruit" was supposed to grow (Betz 1979, 286).

Inherent in such a contrast between the behavior of the σάρξ/νόμος way of life versus that of the πνεῦμα way of life is the redemptive historical contrast between life under the Mosaic Covenant versus life under the New Covenant. In fact, the two major Old Testament announcements of the New Covenant are given as gracious contrasts to Israel's failure under the Mosaic Covenant:

"Behold, days are coming," declares the Lord, "when I will make a new covenant with the house of Israel and with the house of Judah, not like the covenant which I made with their fathers in the day I took them out of the land of Egypt, My covenant which they broke although I was a husband to them," declares the Lord. "But this is the covenant which I will make with the house of Israel after those days," declares the Lord, "I will put My law within them, and on their heart will I write it; and I will be their God, and they shall be my people. And they shall not teach again, each man his neighbor and each man his brother, saying, 'Know the Lord,' for they shall all know me, from the least of them to the greatest of them," declares the Lord, "for I will forgive their iniquity, and their sin I will remember no more" (Jer 31:31-34).

"Moreover, I will give you a new heart and put a new spirit within you; and I will remove the heart of stone from your flesh and give you a heart of flesh. And I will put My Spirit within you and cause you to walk in My statutes, and you will be careful to observe My ordinances" (Ezek 36:26-27).

It is also no accident that Paul begins this list of New Covenant or Holy Spirit fruit with ἀγάπη since he had already used this virtue as the contrasting element to Judaizing or Old Covenant distinctions twice in the preceding context:

For in Christ Jesus neither circumcision nor uncircumcision means anything, but faith working through *love* (ἀγάπης) (Gal 5:6).
For you were called to freedom, brethren; only do not turn your freedom into an opportunity for the flesh, but through *love* (διὰ τῆς ἀγάπης) serve one another. For the whole Law is fulfilled in one word, in the statement, "You shall *love* ('Αγαπήσεις) your neighbor as yourself" (Gal 5:13-14).

Life according to the Spirit is to be characterized by ἀγάπη as the first and perhaps foremost virtue of those that should be produced in believers' lives. In a very real sense, ἀγάπη could be called the distinctive of the New Covenant life (Gal 5:6, 13-14; Col 3:12-14; 1 Cor 12:31-13:13; cf. John 13:34-35). However, Paul does not just single out ἀγάπη, but refers to the nine virtues of Gal 5:22-23a (and others like them) as a unit in v. 22b: κατὰ τῶν τοιούτων οὐκ ἔστιν νόμος. What does Paul mean when he says "against such things there is no law"? Two clarifying observations can be made from the immediate context that answer this question. First, this statement is obviously analogous to the parallel summary statement in 5:21b regarding the deeds of the flesh. The repetition of τοιοῦτος (neuter in both cases) from v. 21b to v. 23b signals this analogy and the term functions in a summarizing fashion at the end of both lists. This is not unusual because τοιοῦτος was used to recap vice and virtue lists in Greek ethical writings (examples in BAGD 1979, 821, s.v., 3 a β).

Secondly, both of the τοιοῦτος phrases in Gal 5:21b and 23b summarize the ethical consequences of following the contrasting ways of life of the σάρξ and the πνεῦμα. Those who live σαρκί will practice the deeds of the flesh and will *not* inherit the kingdom of God. Those who live πνεύματι will not be accused of breaking the Mosaic Law because they will possess the relational qualities that fulfill and enhance the neighbor-love core of the Law (Gal 5:13-14). As the New Covenant promised, however, the impetus to fulfill the Law does not come from Torah itself, but from the new Spirit, God's Spirit, that He puts within His people (Ezek 36:26-27). Betz has grasped this Mosaic Law/Spirit contrast:

> In view of the situation which the Galatians have to face, Paul suggests that it is more important to be enabled to act with ethical responsibility than to introduce a code of law which remains a mere demand. In other words, the introduction of Torah into the Galatian churches would not lead to ethical responsibility, so long as the people were not motivated and enabled ethically. If they were motivated and enabled, however, the Torah is superfluous (1979, 289).

Paul's point in commending the way of the Spirit and His fruit in a negative manner regarding the Mosaic Law is a safeguard against the possible Judaizers' criticism about walking πνεύματι. Such criticism is now neutralized in a programmatic manner. The virtues that the Spirit produces in the lives of believers will violate none of Torah's ordinances .

In keeping with his oscillation between the members of the tandem of σάρξ and νόμος, Paul now moves from his discussion of behavior and its constraints in terms of νόμος (5:23b) to a description of behavior in terms of σάρξ in Gal 5:24. Since 5:13, this is the beginning of the fourth movement from σάρξ to νόμος: 1) σάρξ (5:13) to νόμος (5:14); 2) σάρξ (5:16-17) to νόμος (5:18); 3) σάρξ (5:19) to νόμος (5:23b); 4) σάρξ (5:24) to νόμος [τοῦ Χριστοῦ] (6:2). Because this fourth movement is expressed in terms of the victory of walking πνεύματι, the movement is from the death of σάρξ for those identified with Christ Jesus in 5:24 to the fulfillment of the new Law--τὸν νόμον τοῦ Χριστοῦ in 6:2.

However, the power of Paul's description in Gal 5:24 of those attached to Jesus Christ (οἱ τοῦ Χριστοῦ ['Ιησοῦ]) has been largely negated with the traditional understanding of σάρξ. For example, Ebeling is typical of commentators when he writes:

> For Paul, therefore, the ethical realm as such is far from being a realm of triumphs; it is rather a realm of repeated defeats, in which, however, the Spirit cries out "Abba, " making this clear: "Those who belong to Christ Jesus have crucified the flesh with its passions and desires" (v. 24). This execution has been commanded and introduced. But the process lasts as long as life ἐν σαρκί (*en sarki*, in the flesh) endures, not in order to subjugate it by violence or even shorten it arbitrarily, but in order to allow the fruit of the Spirit to gain the upper hand over the works of the flesh. From advocates of death we are to be made witnesses on behalf of life (Ebeling 1985, 255) .

Central to this understanding of the crucifixion of the σάρξ *is* the assumption that it has an ongoing presence in the life of the Christian. Therefore, the death of τὴν σάρκα in 5:24 has supposedly been merely "commanded and introduced," and thereby has set in motion the life long process of flesh-death. The manifold difficulties with such a view of σάρξ have been previously enumerated in discussions of the lexical, theological, contextual, and cultural fallacies inherent in this traditional understanding. At this point, it should suffice to note that Paul is again appealing to the apocalyptical (or redemptive historical) significance of Jesus Christ's crucifixion. His crucifixion has decisively changed the identity of the people of God (cf. Gal 2:15-21).

The definitive contrast between the former identity of the people of God as Israelites and the present identity as those belonging to Christ was most pointedly begun in Gal 5:1-6. The contrast is between those "of Israel" who take up the yoke of Torah and submit to circumcision and those of "Christ Jesus" (ἐν Χριστῷ 'Ιησοῦ in 5:6) who recognize that circumcision and uncircumcision now mean nothing for the identity of the people of God (cf. 6:12-16). Apparently the Judaizers were repeating the traditional Jewish belief that circumcision and

Torah would adequately restrain the bodily behavior of the Galatian Christians (cf. Betz 1979, 6-9). Ironically, they emphasize fleshly marks to restrain fleshly behavior (cf. Col 2:20-23, especially v. 23). Of course, Paul's rejoinder is that walking according to the Spirit and His enablement frees the Christians from this former way of life (5:16-18). This avoids the fleshly deeds that Israelites (and pagans) have made evident (5:19-21) and opens up the Spirit-fruit for those attached to Christ (5:22-23).

In Gal 5:24 Paul asserts his crowning piece of evidence to the superiority of life "in Christ" versus life "in Israel." His evidence is that life ἐν σαρκί has ended for those "of Christ Jesus" because of the aeon-changing effects of Christ's crucifixion. In this context the death of the Christians' σάρξ is the ending of their bodily frailty under the dominion of sin and the στοιχεῖα (4:3) when they were without the indwelling enablement of God's Spirit. For the Jews, the additional dominion of the νόμος over them while they were in the σάρξ led them to wrongly emphasize deliverance through their covenant in the σάρξ with God. Paul's point in Gal 5:24 is that all of this Gentile/Jewish bondage to the σάρξ and all of the Jewish emphasis on the σάρξ is now ended at the cross of Jesus Christ! It is now anachronistic for those belonging to Christ Jesus to talk about life ἐν σαρκί or to be bound to manifest the set of behaviors that accompany life ἐν σαρκί with its passions and lusts. Jesus Christ's death ended the normativeness of the ἔργα τῆς σαρκός (5:19-21) and replaced these with the καρπὸς τοῦ πνεύματιός (5:22-23). Because of the Christian's corporate identity in Christ (οἱ τοῦ Χριστοῦ ['Ιησοῦ]), Paul can say in 5:24 that they crucified their σάρξ (ἐσταύρωσαν is an aorist active). This logically would have occurred at the point of their faith in Christ, through which they were encompassed in him (Gal 3:26).

IV. Conclusion

Therefore, the crucifixion of the σάρξ in Gal 5:24 is a real death that *definitively* ended forever the real life of the σάρξ and its mode of existence for the people of God. The crucifixion of Christ ended the age of bodily frailty for the people of God because it broke sin's power over their bodies (3:19-4:11) and led to the enabling indwelling of God's Spirit (3:1-5). Therefore, it is unthinkable (though obviously not impossible) that the Galatians should want to identify with a community that stubbornly continues in the now-culpable state of being in the σάρξ and continues manifesting the deeds of the σάρξ

(5:19-21). The better alternative of Spirit-enabled life is normative for those who belong to Christ (5:22-23).

This is Paul's point in Gal 5:13-26 as he exhorts the Galatian Christians to choose to walk according to the rule or direction of the Holy Spirit, not according to the rule of the flesh. Should they choose the latter option, however, it would be as Paul earlier stated: Christ would have died needlessly regarding the σάρξ and God's people would continue to live in the frail and enslaved state of the σάρξ (Gal 2:19-21). This is the same choice between the old σάρξ-way of life and the new cross-way of life that Paul will conclude with in Gal 6:12-16. Separating these two great redemptive historical eras and their corresponding ways of life is the aeon-changing event of Jesus Christ's crucifixion that definitively ended the old σάρξ-state for God's people: "Now those who belong to Christ Jesus have crucified the flesh with its passions and desires" (Gal 5:24).

Therefore, rather than functioning as a set of ethical guidelines supposed to reign in the licentious tendencies of the Galatians, Gal 5:13-26 functions far more strategically within the sustained argument of the epistle. If Galatians 5-6 functions as the climax of Paul's argument against the Judaizers, as I have asserted, then Gal 5:13-26 is the very heart of the climax. Paul juxtaposes the conflicting natures of the σάρξ/πνεῦμα antithesis in their starkest polarity in these verses. In this passage we finally see the way of life that flows out of each of these conflicting identities in very vivid portrayal. Certainly Paul is painting with a broad brush and certainly he is dealing with sweeping stereotypes of these two communities. But within a group-oriented culture these are the kind of stereotypical lens through which Mediterranean peoples like Paul and the Galatians view one another. Our exegesis of such stereotypes should be cognizant of such a worldview.

Notes

[1]Matera 1988, 84-88 notes that Gal 5:13-6:10 is itself bracketed by the warnings against circumcision in 5:1-12 and 6:11-17. However, the second warning is really the postscript for the entire epistle, and functions as a summarizing exhortation. Therefore, while this undercuts the bracketing observation, it nevertheless demonstrates the importance of the issue of circumcision by its domination of the postscript.

[2]Paul uses μόνον in Gal 1:23, 2:10, 3:2, 6:12, and 4:18 (with μή) in some type of qualifying sense also (cf. Phil 1:27).

[3]Burton 1921, 292 and BDF 1961, 255 suggest ἔχετε in the appropriate

mood, among other supplied verbs.   Fung 1988, 244 notes no general consensus as to what verb should be supplied.   In such cases where the immediate context does not offer a good choice, the simplest verb and voice seems wisest. Cf. BAGD 1979, 517: III A, 6.

[4]The presence of the article with ἀγάπης in 5:13 may be an anaphoric usage referring back to the anarthrous usage of ἀγάπης in 5:6. However, it is also possible that Paul was wanting to insure that the *hearers* of the epistle clearly heard the contrast between the articular τῇ σαρκί of 5:13b and the τῇ ἀγάπης, of 5:13c.

[5]See Hansen 1989, 152 and Ziesler 1990, 78 for a similar conclusion.

[6]Eldon Epp 1978 has argued that the unifying theme in all of Paul's diverse imageries of what God has done in Christ is that "God has set his people free, has moved them from bondage into freedom...his one paramount point that God, through Christ, has brought freedom to humankind" (100). See also Wright 1994, 233 for a development of this point regarding Gal 4:3, 9.

[7]Supporting the perspective that Christians fulfill, but do not obey the Mosaic Law, see Hong 1992 and Duvall 1994a. Rejecting this distinction are Thielman 1987, 95-100 and Dunn 1993, 290. In particular, see Westerholm (1986-87, 237) who concludes that "the harried apostle appears to have been consistent in at least the following three points:

(i)   Paul never derives appropriate Christian behavior by simply applying relevant precepts from Torah.

(ii)   Paul never claims that Christians "do" (ποιεῖν) the law; they-- and they alone--are said to "fulfill" (πληροῦν) it.

(iii)   Paul never speaks of the law's fulfillment in prescribing Christian conduct, but only while describing its results."

[8]Compare Rom 8:4 and especially 13:8-10 for Paul's connection of πληρόω and the Law in the sense of "fulfill," not "sum up," although this latter sense may be encompassed in the former. The immediate context in Gal 5:13-15 is one of behaving appropriately and thereby fulfilling the Law's basic tenet. See Fung 1988, 245-46. In spite of this sense, however, there seems to be a purposeful ambiguity in Paul's choice of πληρόω which is less exact than "observe" or "do" (Barclay 1988, 143).

[9]The issue of those who qualified as a "neighbor" may have been a part of the issue of social intercourse in Gal 2:11-14, although it cannot be definitively proven at this point.   See Sanders 1990 for an interesting discussion of the possible interpretations of this incident.

[10]I am indebted to Professor Moisés Silva for this crucial insight.

[11]With the aorist subjunctive or future indicative, οὐ μή "is the most definite form of negation regarding the future" (BDF 1961, 184).

[12]I am indebted to Ladd 1974, 470-74 for this basic delineation. Also see Stacey 1956, 162-73 for a survey of the ethical sense of σάρξ.

[13]Additionally, see Porter 1901; Montefiore and Loewe 1974, 295-314; Martyn 1985b, 415-16; and especially Markus 1986.

[14]The validating of Judaistic concerns in Romans 7-8 and Phil 3 is beyond the scope of this paper, but a suggestive survey of these passages in Chapter 7 will recommend that Paul is using σάρξ in exactly the same redemptive historical sense in these passages as he does in Gal 3-6.

[15]See Hoenig 1962-63 for a treatment of this issue from a Jewish perspective. Additionally, see Gen 17:11, 14, 23-25; Ezek 44: 7, 9; Lev 12:3. Compare the additional references to σάρξ added to the circumcision contexts of Gen 34:24 and Jer 9:25 in the LXX. In Jewish literature see Jub. 15:13-33; Jdt 14:10; 4 Ezra 1:31; Sir 44:20 and later in the rabbinic texts of b. Sanh. 99a and b. Shebu. 13a.

[16]See Barclay 1988, 112-17 and Fung 1988, 250-51 for up-to-date interaction with the three main interpretations of the ἵνα clause of Gal 5:17:

1. the σάρξ frustrates the πνεῦμα-inspired desires of the Christian.
2. the two forces of σάρξ and πνεῦμα equally frustrate one another.
3. the πνεῦμα frustrates the desires of the σάρξ.

Additionally, Barclay sets forth a fourth view (112, 115-17):

4. the πνεῦμα will morally limit their freedom and will morally define the moral choices they must make.

While his view is more appealing than the previous three, none of these seems adequate in light of the contextual definition of σάρξ advocated in this book. Therefore, the view represented here actually qualifies as a fifth interpretation.

[17]Epp 1978, 109 raises the interesting possibility that this Pauline imagery may recall Israel's exodus from the bondage of Egypt and cites Rom 7:6, 8:2, 14-15 as other examples where the freedom that the Spirit brings is contrasted to the slavery of being under the Law.

[18]Pequé (1987, 105-24) has noted that *antithesis* is the most appropriate literary genre that explains Gal 5:16-26 and he has suggested the following inner structure for the passage (109):

```
A...πνεύματι     v. 16a
B........σαρκός    v. 16b
C...........νόμον   v. 18
D..............τὰ ἔργα τῆς σαρκός   vv. 19–21a
E................βασιλείαν θεοῦ   v. 21b
D'............'Ο δὲ καρπὸς τοῦ πνεύματός   vv. 22–23a
C'..........νόμος   v. 23b
B'.......σάρκα   v. 24
A'...πνεύματι   v. 25
```

According to Peque's structuring of the passage (112-13), Gal 5:21b is the focal point of Paul's masterful use of antithesis. While I would include Gal 5:13-15 within this structure, its inclusion would not change the focus of Paul's emphasis on the exclusion from the βασιλείαν θεοῦ of those who practice (οἱ πράσσοντες) the deeds of the σάρξ. Compare the similar conclusions of Dahl 1973, 69. Including Gal 5:13-6:2 in a chiasm with Gal 5:21b also at the focal point is Thomson 1995, 116-51.

[19]Charles Cosgrove has also noted that these behaviors are weighted in a certain direction:

> One gets the impression that Paul has loaded a traditional vice list (cf. 1 Cor 6:9-10) with sins of community strife, in order to make the point that *rivalry* is to be taken seriously as the more obvious "sins of the flesh" (1988, 157).

In light of other thorough studies of each of the traits of both the σάρξ and the πνεῦμα (e.g., Barclay 1962), this book will only deal with each list of traits in a holistic fashion. For a helpful fourfold subdivision of the list of the deeds of the σάρξ and the various English translations of these fifteen vices, see Fung 1988, 253-62.

[20]See L. Johnson 1989 for a very insightful treatment of the New Testament's "anti-Jewish slander" in light of the conventions of ancient polemic. One of his four main conclusions is that "by the measure of Hellenistic conventions, and certainly by the measure of contemporary Jewish polemic, the NT's slander against fellow Jews is remarkably mild" (441). Cf. Wortham 1995. See also du Toit 1994b for Paul's use of vilification as a persuasive device.

Chapter 6

The Flesh/Spirit Conflict
in Galatians 6:1-18

This chapter continues the in-depth exegesis of Galatians 5-6 begun in the previous chapter. While the references to σάρξ and πνεῦμα are sparser, the difficult exegetical and theological issues are denser. Therefore, we will have to devote more time to the unraveling of some of these interpretive cruxes in order to understand the context of the references to σάρξ and πνεῦμα.

I. Galatians 6:1-10

This section of the epistle has several significant exegetical issues that must be dealt with in order to understand the one reference to σάρξ and πνεῦμα within these two paragraphs (in 6:8). As these issues are resolved, the meaning of Paul's use of the σάρξ/πνεῦμα antithesis in v. 8 should be clarified.

The argument of *Galatians 6:1-10* can be summarized as follows:

> Some specific manifestations of the deliverance from sin's powers which fulfill the relational goal of the Law within the community of the Spirit are seen in the gracious restoration of sinning members and in the generous financial sharing with appropriate persons within the community.

6:1-5 The reality that even some Christians will be caught in παραπτώματι is to be dealt with by those in the community of the

Spirit (ὑμεῖς οἱ πνευματικοί) in a spirit of gentleness and humility as restoration is sought in mutual concern and burden-bearing, not in arrogant competition.

6:6-10 Also, the community of the Spirit should manifest generous financial sharing, especially with its teachers and other believers, because this is sowing to the Spirit and contrasts with sowing to the flesh, which emphasizes circumcision and Torah-observance and ends in corruption.

Verses 1-10 of Galatians 6 are a specification in two areas of the walk/life that is according to the rule or direction of the Spirit that Paul just summarized in 5:13-15 and 5:25-26 and contrasted with the rule of the flesh in 5:16-24. The specifications are introduced with the vocative ἀδελφοί, which generally introduces a new section in Galatians (e.g., 1:11; 3:15; 4:12; 5:13), although sometimes it is simply used within an argument (e.g., 4:28, 31; 5:11). Some commentators view these ethical specifications as unrelated to the specific problems of the churches in Galatia. Bonnard is typical of this perspective when he writes: "On peut considérer 6.1-10 comme un ensemble indivisible de préceptes moraux courants dans les églises du premier siècle..." (1972, 126). However, there are those commentators who argue the opposite side and advocate that the two areas of specification in Gal 6:1-10 are areas of immediate concern and relevance to the Galatians because one

cannot explain why a supposedly unprovoked exhortation appears in this heated letter in which everything else written seems to be directly called forth by the specific disturbance in Galatia...The point to remember, however, is that the passage *must* be read in the context of the Galatian controversy, for there is no other example in the fiery epistle of general statements unrelated to the specific situation there (Hurtado 1979, 54).

This latter judgment seems to be the correct one and the rhetorical analysis of Chapter 2 was an attempt to underscore the very tight rhetorical structure of all of Galatians, including Gal 5-6. Paul again appears to be addressing specific historical problems in the Galatian churches, not generic nor hypothetical ones. The following analysis should demonstrate that the problems of 6:1-10 are simply specific manifestations spawned by the general nature of the Judaizer threat.

John Barclay has correctly identified the general nature of these specific problems in light of the preceding prohibition of 5:26:

As we have just noted, this verse, together with 5:15 and the emphasis on social sins in "the works of the flesh, " is a clear indication of *the social disharmony threatening the Galatian churches.* It is precisely this vanity, provocation and envy which mark the breakdown of community life in the Galatians churches. Since Paul gives us no precise information, it is precarious to attempt to reconstruct exactly who was provoking and envying whom (1988, 156; emphasis is mine).

Our understanding of Gal 5:13-15 and 5:25-26 makes such a reconstruction less precarious than Barclay imagines due to Paul's contextual association of this fleshly behavior with the Judaizers. *They* are the ones who have apparently argued for and modeled boastful and envious relationships within their communities because of their highly competitive and individualistic core values. Such relationships may have confused the Galatians as to how to relate to lapsed Christians and how to share finances within their churches. It appears highly likely that Paul is addressing each of these issues in turn in Gal 6:1-5 and 6-10 and attempting to correct the unloving influence of the Judaizers on the community life of the Galatian churches.

In *Galatians 6:1-5* there are two key exegetical issues that must be addressed if this paragraph is to be understood. The first is the identities in 6:1 of both the ἄνθρωπος who may be caught or overtaken (προλημφθῇ) in any trespass and also of "you who are spiritual" (ὑμεῖς οἱ πνευματικοί) who are to restore such a one. While some understand the sinner to be any Galatian Christian repenting of his or her involvement in the Judaistic heresy (e.g., Cole 1989, 222-25), this identification seems to read too much into the sketchy data Paul gives.[1] Additionally, this Judaizer identity is built upon the understanding that the attitudes of 5:26 are evidence of Corinthian-type party strife within the Galatian churches that led to one party designating itself as the πνευματικοί (e.g., Cole 1989, 222-23). However, if the negative description of Gal 5:26 is that of the Judaizers' communities (in antithesis to the Pauline communities), then the party strife thesis is greatly weakened. In spite of this weakened thesis, however, the desire to relate 6:1 to 5:26 is admirable. It is probably better achieved when seen as *a contrast* between how the community of the Spirit is to respond to the inevitable lapse of one of its members versus how the community of the flesh responds, given the competitive and destructive attitudes that characterize it (in 5:15 and 5:26). Therefore, the Christian who lapses in 6:1-5 is probably any Christian and this situation may have been a burning issue in the Galatian churches that the Judaizers exploited.[2]

The identity of the πνευματικοί who are to restore (καταρτίζετε) the lapsed Christian may refer to the more mature or more spiritual within the Galatian churches, as many commentators have advocated. Calvin says this of "ye which are spiritual":

> This is not spoken in irony; for however spiritual they might be, they were still not completely filled with the Spirit. It is the duty of such to raise up the fallen. For what is the purpose of their superiority except the welfare of the brethren? The more any man is endowed with grace, the more is he bound to devote himself to the edification of the weaker brethren. But because we are so disordered that even in our best duties we fail, he warns us not to be influenced by the flesh ([1556] 1965, 108).

While these insights are absolutely true, they probably overstate the significance of πνευματικοί in Gal 6:1. The better sense of this term is probably the "lesser sense" of simply "those who belong to the Spirit or have the characteristics of the Spirit" (cf. 1 Cor 2:15; 3:1; 14:37). In other words the πνευματικοί are simply the Christians in Galatia who choose to walk according to the rule or direction of the Spirit. Paul seems to use this designation in a straightforward and non-ironic manner (Betz 1979, 296-97; Barclay 1988, 152, 157). Again, the antithetical argumentation that Paul continues as he contrasts his communities with the Judaizers' communities makes his use of this term easily understandable since he is contrasting the proper behavior for those in the community of the Spirit to the behavior of those in the community of the flesh (the implied σαρκικοί; cf. 1 Cor 3:3). Therefore, the context for determining the referent of οἱ πνευματικοί is a contrasting one with the Judaizers, not a contrasting one within the community of the Spirit. The πνευματικοί are those Christians who choose to walk in obedience to the commands Paul gave in 5:16, 18, and 25, rather than according to the Judaizers' standard of the σάρξ.

The *second* important exegetical issue in Gal 6:1-5 is the meaning of τὸν νόμον τοῦ Χριστοῦ ("the law of Christ") in Gal 6:2. While some scholars like John Calvin do not deem this term to have a lot of theological significance ([1556] 1965, 110), others consider the understanding of this law as one of the most crucial problems in Galatians because it could be construed as a monumental contradiction in Paul's anti-Law polemic in Galatians (e.g., Betz 1979, 299). Several observations about Paul's use can be made as we consider the meaning of τὸν νόμον τοῦ Χριστοῦ. First, the use of this phrase, and probably of the term τὰ βάρη ("burdens"), is likely more of a stylistic device than a theological statement. These terms do have theological (and sociological!) significance to Paul and his audience, but his use of these terms in this context seems primarily stylistic because some words have been used in a striking, extraordinary way, thus causing impact:

> In the letter of Paul to the Galatians a great number of devices has been applied which can all be described as devices of estrangement. This is the dominant feature of the letter from a stylistic point of view. These devices all effectuate a retardation in the reading process and consequently an intensified perception. In general, the devices have been skillfully applied in such a way that the subject-matter (which is in every case, one of the main themes of the letter) is highlighted. In other words, the retardation and consequent intensified perception occur on occasions when the writer really wants his readers to pay attention to what he has to say. A careful balance between estrangement and automatization has been maintained. In addition to all this, most of these devices were regarded as forceful by Hellenistic rhetoricians and are thus most suitable for communicating the subject-matter of this emotional letter (Cronjé 1986, 226).

Cronjé notes that τὸν νόμον τοῦ Χριστοῦ is one of Paul's devices of "defamiliarization" in Galatians because it "must have sounded contradictory to what Paul had to say about the Law, e.g., in 5:4" (1986, 225). Lightfoot seems to concur with this conclusion as his paraphrase of Gal 6:2 indicates: "If you must needs impose *burdens* on yourselves, let them be burdens of mutual sympathy. If you must needs observe a *law*, let it be the law of Christ" ([1890] 1957, 216). Lightfoot goes on to note: "The Apostle seems to have used both βάρη and νόμον (the latter certainly), with a reference to the ritualistic tendencies of the Galatians" ([1890] 1957, 216). While I would prefer to call Paul's use a startling and ironic contrast to the Judaizers' imposing of burdens and Law, nonetheless, Lightfoot was heading in the right direction.

Secondly, in light of Paul's significant stylistic and rhetorical strategy, we can probably safely conclude that τὸν νόμον τοῦ Χριστοῦ is not a technical term for a new messianic Torah (Davies 1980, 142-44; Dodd 1968, 134-48; Longenecker 1964; 183-90) referring to the ethical teachings of Jesus (*verba Christi;* cf. 1 Cor 9:20-21) and setting forth a new type of halakah (Brinsmead 1982, 173-75; Stuhlmacher 1981, 157-61).[3] These understandings are "over interpretations" of the phrase and rhetorically and theologically tangential to the flow of Paul's argument. Additionally, "the law of Christ" is probably not an oblique reference to a very specific dominical command of Jesus to support financially those who preach the gospel (cf. 1 Cor 9:14) (Strelan 1975).[4] This view is counter to the main concern of Gal 6:1-5: the restoration and maintenance of right standing within the community of the Spirit.

Also, because Paul adopts the phrase τὸν νόμον τοῦ Χριστοῦ "in a thoroughly positive and nonpolemical way" (Hays 1987, 274), it is also difficult to conclude "that Paul took over the notion from the opponents" (Betz 1979, 300; cf. Stoike 1971; Brinsmead 1982, 163-85). He may be using βάρη and τὸν νόμον τοῦ Χριστοῦ *in light of the emphases of the Judaizers,* but the risk of misunderstanding would probably be too great in such an inflammable rhetorical situation had Paul "taken the risk of employing a phrase which the Galatians would have heard used in a very unPauline sense" (Barclay 1988, 130).

The three specific views noted above and their respective pitfalls are avoided by those who take νόμος in the more general sense of a guiding principle, norm, or set of precepts: "The conclusion is that the talk of the 'law of Christ' refers simply to the way of life characteristic of the church of Christ" (Räisänen 1986, 82). Räisänen ties this understanding of νόμος to the preceding context:

> It is a question of 'spirit,' of an *attitude*--of showing that love which is the fulfilment of the (Mosaic) law according to 5:14. *Nomos* is being used in a loose sense, almost metaphorically, much as it is used in Rom 3:27 or 8:2. To fulfil the *nomos* of Christ is simply to live the way a life in Christ is to be lived (1986, 79-80) .

While this view has some merit, its weakness is that it greatly understates the parallelism of Gal 5:14 and 6:2. This parallelism establishes the continued specific sense of νόμος and Paul's rhetorical use of this continuity. He is equating the two laws of 5:14 and 6:2, but in a manner that can be greatly specified by observing more of the rhetorical aspects of the immediate context. Richard Hays has supplied some of these in his helpful study of "the Law of Christ":

> In the context of Paul's argument in Galatians, it ought to be apparent that "the law of Christ" functions as an ironic rhetorical formulation addressed to "those who want to be under law" (4:21). In this regard the phrase is closely analogous to the important parallel in 1 Cor 9:21, where Paul counters the (probably rhetorical) inference that he might be *anomos* ("lawless") with the assertion

that he is *ennomos Christou* ("under the law of Christ")...The expression *ennomos Christou* appears to be framed by Paul as a witty (though serious) response to a negative judgment on his apostolic ministry. Likewise, in Rom 3:27 (where the "law of faith" is contrasted to "the law of works") and Rom 8:2 ("the law of the Spirit of life in Christ Jesus has set you free from the law of sin and death"), *Paul seems to have coined an ad hoc "law" formulation as an ironic antithesis to a hypothetical alternative which he wants to reject* (Hays 1987, 275; emphasis is mine).

Hays goes on to assert that

Paul's fondness for this sort of rhetorical antithesis should raise serious doubts against the view that "the law of Christ" must represent the actual platform of Paul's adversaries. *In Galatians, as in Romans, Paul is introducing a wordplay to contrast the shape and quality of the new obedience in Christ to the old obedience under the Mosaic law.* The Galatians want to be under law (4:21); Paul ironically accedes to their desire by exhorting them to live by the "law" of Christ...In view of the absolute opposition between "law" and "Christ" that Paul has deliberately established in the letter (see especially 5:4), the expression "law of Christ" must fall upon his readers' ears as a breathtaking paradox (Hays 1987, 275-76; emphasis is mine).

Therefore, while τὸν νόμον τοῦ Χριστοῦ is another formulation of the law of love in Gal 5:14, it is nevertheless an ad hoc formulation by Paul in light of the highly-charged polemics of the Judaizing controversy, particularly in light of possible antinomian accusations from his opponents. With the use of the phrase "the law of Christ," Paul can both focus on the objective nature of the law of love, and simultaneously upon the intense summation of Torah in Christ: "For Paul the basis of Christian morality was not in a tradition of the words and teaching of Jesus, but in the Person of the Lord whom he served" (Yates 1985, 118).[5] While the relational prominence of love is greatly increased in the New Covenant community of the Spirit (e.g., 5:5-6, 13-14), this does not mean that the standards of the Mosaic Law are now totally discarded. Rather, ὁ πᾶς νόμος is now fulfilled by those who walk according to the rule of the Spirit (5:14) and the resulting fruit of that walk (5: 22-23a) is a yield against which there is no νόμος (5:23b).

This leads to a third and final observation about the law of Christ: its relationship to the Mosaic Law. Paul does not make this relationship explicit within the context of Galatians, so our theologizing is based on observing the implicit affirmations of the text. Within the context of Gal 5:13-6:5, Paul seems to imply that τὸν νόμον τοῦ Χριστοῦ is essentially the Law of Moses. We can conclude this for two reasons:

> 1. Paul is sensitive to the accusation that avoiding the Judaizers' yoke of Torah may lead to antinomianism and *not* fulfilling the Mosaic Law. Therefore, in Gal 5:14 and 5:23b he is explicit about the true and actual fulfillment of the Mosaic Law via walking according to the rule of the Spirit. If there were no ongoing nature of the Law of Moses, then these "fulfillment" aspects would be anachronistic and Paul's rhetoric would be superfluous, and perhaps nonsensical.[6]

> 2. If there is an ongoing validity in fulfilling the Law of Moses (Gal 5:14, 23) and if there is the need to fulfill the law of Christ (6:2), yet Christians are no longer under the tutoring of the Mosaic Law (Gal 3:24-25), then the Law of Christ must be the valid continuation of the Mosaic Law.

This kind of syllogistic conclusion must be tempered with the changes that the Mosaic Law has apparently received in its form as the Law of Christ. First, it most certainly has been *personalized* in the Person of Christ as the term indicates (cf. Rom 10:4). Secondly, it has been "*eschatologized*" in the work of Jesus the Messiah for the fullness of the time (e.g., Gal 4:4-5).[7] And lastly, it has *internationalized* beyond its Israelite boundaries as is now appropriate for the Gentile sons of Abraham (e.g., Gal 3:7-9; 13-14).[8] This means that two things are now simultaneously true of the Mosaic Law:

> 1. As an historical entity expressing God's will for ethnic Israel, the Mosaic Law *has ended* (Gal 3:17-25; 5:18; Rom 6:14; 7:4-6; 2 Cor 3:6-13; cf. Acts 15:1-29 and Heb 7:11-12).

> 2. As a theological entity expressing God's will for His New Covenant people, the "ethical" (versus the "ceremonial") aspects of the Mosaic Law *have continued in the Law of Christ*.

This second point is certainly the more controversial admission due to the unitary nature of the Mosaic Law, as Ladd notes:

> Most of the studies on Paul emphasize the fact that Paul does not explicitly distinguish between the ethical and ceremonial aspects of the law. This is of course true; *but the implicit distinction is unavoidable and should be stressed.* Although circumcision is a

command of God and part of the law, Paul sets circumcision in
contrast to the commandments, and in so doing separates the ethical
from the ceremonial--the permanent from the temporal. Thus he can
commend the ἐντολαὶ θεοῦ to Gentiles, and yet adamantly reject the
ceremonial ἐντολαί, such as circumcision, foods, feasts, and even
Sabbath keeping (Col 2:16), for these are but a shadow of the reality
which has come in Christ (1968, 67; emphasis is mine).

This conclusion seems eminently reasonable due to the eternal
nature of the law of God, yet the redemptive historical nature of the
Law of Moses and the law of Christ (cf. 1 Cor 9:19-21 for all three
laws). Specifically, within the polemical context of Galatians, the
ongoing existence of the eternal law of God in the law of Christ is a
very significant rhetorical device (albeit ad hoc in nature) that further
objectifies the walk according to the rule or direction of the Spirit. It
is a walk that is not just subjective in nature (although one cannot
deny the more "internalized" nature of the New Covenant life, e.g., Jer
31:31-34 and Ezek 36:26-27). It is also a walk that can be described
in terms of "fulfilling" objective standards (πεπλήρωται in 5:14 and
ἀναπληρώσετε[9] in 6:2). Both aspects help Paul deflect any Judaizer
rejoinders about the antinomian nature of his communities.[10]

After this lengthy discussion of the two exegetical issues of the
identities of the ἄνθρωπος and οἱ πνευματικοί of Gal 6:1 and the
meaning of τὸν νόμον τοῦ Χριστοῦ in 6:2, we can now briefly
summarize the significance of Paul's argument in Gal 6:1-5 for the
σάρξ/πνεῦμα antithesis. Essentially, Paul is applying in a specific
(and perhaps common) situation the basic relational distinctive of the
community of the Spirit positively set forth in 5:13b-14, 16, 18, 22-25
in antithetical contrast to the basic relational distinctive of the
Judaistic community of the σάρξ which is described in Gal 5:13a, 15,
17, 19-21, and 26. The basic relational contrast between these two
communities is that the community of the Spirit is fundamentally
committed to serving one another selflessly in love according to the
rule and direction of the Holy Spirit without making fleshly
distinctions, while the community of the flesh is committed to making
distinctions in the flesh (e.g., circumcision) which continue the
boastful, competitive, and envious way of life that now characterizes
being under the Mosaic Law.

The occasion of a fellow believer being overtaken or caught in a
trespass would give opportunity for boasting (elevated status) within
the Judaistic community because of the competitive nature of that
community. Paul knew this personally through his former mastery of
the means of advancement within Judaism (Gal 1:13-14). However,

lapsed believers are treated differently within the community of the Spirit! Paul *continues* to contrast the relational patterns of the opposing communities in Gal 6:1-5 by setting the desired behaviors of the community of the Spirit against the backdrop of the undesirable behaviors of the community of the flesh:

> 6:1 look to yourselves (versus not being aware of your own frailty)
>
> 6:2 bear one another's βάρη (versus placing burdens on others?)
>
> 6:3 don't overestimate your status (versus self-deceptively doing so)
>
> 6:4 examine your own ἔργον (versus seeking status within the community by boasting in regard to another)
>
> 6:5 bear your own load/burden (φορτίον) (versus not being personally accountable)[11]

These contrasts, both explicit and implicit, underscore that lapsed Christians are dealt with by those in the community of the Spirit in a spirit of gentleness and humility as restoration is sought in mutual concern and burden-bearing, not in boastful and challenging competition.

It is as we turn to **Gal 6:6-10** that we encounter one of the more difficult verses in Galatians relating to the σάρξ/πνεῦμα antithesis:

> Gal 6:8 – ὅτι ὁ σπείρων εἰς τὴν σάρκοα ἑαυτοῦ
> ἐκ τῆς σαρκὸς θερίσει φθοράν,
> ὁ δὲ σπείρων εἰς τὸ πνεῦμα
> ἐκ τοῦ πνεύματος θερίσει ζωὴν
> αἰώνιον.

In isolation, this proverbial-type saying seems to be a rather straightforward summary of all that Paul has said about the σάρξ/πνεῦμα antithesis, and some would add, that it sums up the message of the whole letter (e.g., Barclay 1988, 164). The significant difficulty with this interpretation, however, is the immediate context. The paragraph begins with a rather specific discussion of supporting teachers within the churches (6:6) and ends with a similar conclusion in 6:10 (ἄρα οὖν) about "doing good to all persons" (ἐργαζώμεθα τὸ ἀγαθὸν πρὸς πάντας). The effect on 6:6-10 is to bracket the proverbial and eschatological warning of 6:7-9 about sowing and reaping with statements that appear to be financial in their subject matter. Therefore, the general sense of the sowing metaphor in 6:7-9 and the flow of thought in 6:6-10 must be determined first since these are the contextual husks of the σάρξ/πνεῦμα antithesis in 6:8.

It is the view of this book that Gal 6:6-10 is a second specific manifestation of the deliverance from sin's powers within the community of the Spirit (6:1-5 being the first). This second specific application of the general standard of walking according to the rule or direction of the Spirit is also illustrated *within the life of the community of the Spirit*, as was the restoration of a sinning believer in 6:1-5.

Specifically, this second area of community life is not just a general summary of desirable behaviors, but it is an additional, extant problem area in the Galatian churches that Paul is addressing. Again, the rationale can be appealed to that this tightly-argued and highly polemical epistle does not allow for hypothetical or vague prescriptions for Christian living. Rather, the prescriptions of 6:6-10 are very specific and are delivered in Paul's continuing antithetical style of argumentation. The specific problem area of 6:6-10 is that of appropriate financial giving within the community of the Spirit. There are three basic reasons for concluding that this is the context and that the sowing/reaping imagery is a financial one.[12]

First, the δέ that links v. 6 to the preceding paragraph is probably too weak to be adversative (e. g., RSV "but"), and more probably is connective in the sense of "and" (e.g., NASV). The δέ connective gives a sense of continuation to the discussion of 6:1-5, which was about the restoration and maintenance of status within the community of the Spirit. This *topic* is broadly continued with this discussion of financial giving which is directly linked to the maintenance of community life as both a specific example of mutual burden-bearing (6:2) and as an application of bearing your own individual load (6:5). In other words the law of Christ (6:2) is specifically illustrated in 6:6-10 with this discussion of the loving and appropriate use of finances within the community of the Spirit.[13]

Secondly, in addition to the topical linkage to 6:1-5, Paul's use of some of his well-known financial terminology argues even more strongly that 6:6-10 is about financial giving. In 6:6 he encourages the one who is taught the word (ὁ κατηχούμενος τὸν λόγον) to share all good things with the one who teaches (τῷ κατηχοῦντι). This admonition to share (κοινωείτω) is an instruction to "give or contribute a share" (BAGD 1979, 438), i.e., a financial contribution. Paul uses this same κοινωνέω/κοινωνία terminology in referring to the Philippians' frequent financial contributions to him (Phil 1:5, 4:15), to the financial contributions of the Gentile churches to the poor saints of

Judea (e.g., Rom 15:26; 2 Cor 8:4; 9:13), and simply to Christians giving to one another (Rom 12:13).

Additionally, the financial terminology in Gal 6:6-10 is obvious in Paul's use of the sowing/reaping imagery. Elsewhere, he uses this imagery to encourage generous financial giving by the Gentile churches to the Judea poor (2 Cor 9:6-15, esp. vv. 6, 10) and to establish Paul's apostolic right to reap financial support because of his spiritual sowing (1 Cor 9:11).[14] Paul's inclusion of this agricultural imagery in contexts of financial giving introduces the concept of eschatological reward for appropriate giving in the present (e.g., 2 Cor 9:9). This appears to be the function of the sowing/reaping imagery in Gal 6:7-9.

Not quite as obvious is Paul's exhortation in Gal 6:10 to "do good to all persons" (ἐργαζώμεθα τὸ ἀγαθὸν πρὸς πάντας). The financial sense of this summary sentence is mainly determined by the parallelism in ἀγαθόν terminology with 6:6 and 6:9a and by the financial terminology that precedes it in 6:7-9. However, Paul does use ἀγαθόν and ἐργάζομαι/ἔργον together elsewhere in contexts of financial sharing (e.g., 2 Cor 9:8 and Eph 4:28). Therefore, adding up the cumulative evidence, one must conclude that the presence of so much financial terminology in Gal 6:6-10 makes the topic of financial giving the most likely choice as Paul's concern.

Thirdly, and lastly, the careful reconstruction of the possible historical context lends support to understanding Gal 6:6-10 as Paul's corrective of the Judaizers' emphasis on giving within the Galatian churches.[15] Once again the backdrop is the Judaizers' confusion of the Galatians by wrongly attaching them to the community of the flesh, this time through their giving. Again Paul counters with the appropriate model of behavior within the community of the Spirit. Hurtado 1979 makes the case that the financial sharing of Gal 6:6-10 is related to the collection in Gal 2:10. Gal 6:6-10 is postured as Paul's appeal for the Jerusalem collection.[16] A better understanding of the historical background of Paul's remarks is that the Judaizers may have attempted to tie the Galatian churches to Jerusalem *financially* as a part of their general attempt to tie them to the Jerusalem Church (Gal 1:11-2:21).

If the Judaizers were operating under a proselyte model, then they may have advocated that a key part of the Galatians' attachment to Israel as new proselytes was the giving of an offering to the Jerusalem temple or to the Jerusalem Church. This, of course, would endear the Judaizers to their fellow Jews every where, but especially to those in Jerusalem and Judea (cf. the Zealot thesis of Jewett 1971a). While

Paul considered the collection for the Jewish poor very appropriate (Gal 2:10), this kind of proselyte offering wrongly subsumed the Gentile churches under both the Jerusalem Church and ethnic Israel. Therefore, by carefully "mirror-reading" Gal 6:6-10 (Barclay 1987), we can infer three things from Paul' s response to this possible historical setting:

> 1. (6:6) The Galatian Christians should give financially *to those locally who actually teach them the Word*. This giving is what fulfills the mutual burden bearing of the law of Christ (6:2) and the principle of appropriately bearing your own load (6:5). Usually these teachers would be the elders in the local congregations. These teachers should not be bypassed to give to a Temple collection.

> 2. (6:7-9) Giving to the fleshly system of the Judaizers mocks God because the flesh as a mode of existence for Christians has been crucified with Christ (5:24). To give to the flesh is to nullify the Law-free grace of God and to infer that Christ died needlessly (Gal 2:20-21). This fleshly system now operates apart from God's Spirit and should not be given to because it inevitably faces corruption (φθοράν) (6:8a). By contrast, the communities that Paul started are indwelt by God's Spirit and giving to foster their growth yields eternal life to all who are involved (6:8b). Therefore, the Galatians should not be discouraged in the face of Judaistic criticism, or possible persecution, but should continue to give as Paul directed them (6:9).

> 3. (6:10) So then (ἄρα οὖν), the Galatian churches should not be hesitant to give to the needs of all persons (πρὸς πάντας), but their special and particular responsibility (μάλιστα δέ) is not to the Temple or to Israel (who would be in the "all persons" category), but to those who are actually in the household of faith.

In light of the above argumentation about Gal 6:6-10, we can now interpret the σάρξ/πνεῦμα antithesis of 6:8 in light of this context. As a casual hearer/reader of Galatians would expect, Paul has not changed his basic understanding of either of these two terms at this late stage of his argumentation. Rather, he is continuing to draw from the capital he has accrued from Galatians 3 onward in the accounts labeled "σάρξ" and "πνεῦμα." These accounts reveal that the sense of these terms has not changed since they were set in antithesis in Gal 3:3. However, their meanings have been enriched with theological depth as Paul has described the resulting identities and ways of life connected with an emphasis on the σάρξ or an emphasis on the πνεῦμα. The eschatological destiny of these two identities/ways of life is now stated more fully by Paul in Gal 6:8 (cf. 5:21b). While these destinies are stated within the rather narrow context of financial giving, they, nevertheless, function as a general conclusion to the whole σάρξ/πνεῦμα antithesis. This brings to a definitive point the decision that the Galatians face about their community identity and pattern of behavior.

Only one issue needs to be addressed in light of this understanding of Gal 6:8: Why does Paul describe the σάρξ in this context as τὴν σάρκα ἑαυτοῦ? The use of the reflexive pronoun ἑαυτου would seem to support the view that σάρξ is an ongoing part of each Christian so that Paul can speak of "his/her own flesh" (cf. Gal 6:4 and τὸ ἔργον ἑαυτοῦ). This is the generally accepted view (e.g., Bonnard 1972, 126; Mussner 1974, 405-6; Schlier 1971, 277; Bruce 1982, 265). However, such a view is erroneous for several reasons. First, the causal conjunction ὅτι that begins 6:8 gives the further explanation ("because, since, for") for Paul's statement in 6:7 about God not being mocked. The "mockers" were the Judaizers and the entire community of the flesh that denied the change in the fleshly state wrought by Christ's crucifixion (2:20-21) and the death of the σάρξ-state for Christians due to His death (5:24). Granted, the Galatians were in danger of identifying with this community, but the warning to them *is not to be deceived* (6:7a - μὴ πλανᾶσθε) because of the fate that awaits the community of the flesh. This fate has already been expressed in terms of exclusion from the kingdom of God (5:21b). It is repeated in 6:8 in antithesis now to the eschatological destiny of the community of the Spirit. Therefore, the contrast in v. 8 is again between these opposing communities who have very divergent destinies.

Secondly, it is appropriate for Paul to speak of sowing into (the field of) one's own flesh when referring to the Judaizers and the Jewish community (ὁ σπείρων εἰς τὴν σάρκα ἑαυτοῦ) because they were advocating that the Galatians financially invest in a system that *did emphasize* each person's own σάρξ. While the Christian Judaizers technically did not have σάρξ, i.e., a body not indwelt by God's πνεῦμα, they were nevertheless attaching themselves to a community that was "in the σάρξ" (devoid of God's Spirit). By doing this, the Christian Judaizers were personally denying and negating both the benefits of Christ (5:2-4) and His Spirit (5:16-17) in bodily aiding them to live the Christian life. Therefore, they were denying the death of their own σάρξ and were living as if they still were in the σάρξ, and constrained by Torah, i.e., in a frail and transitory body not indwelt by the Spirit. While such an attitude is incredibly anachronistic in terms of the death of Christ (e.g., 1:4; 2:19-21; 3:1-5, 13-14; 4:1-11) and the giving of the Spirit (5:16-18, 25-26), it is still possible to live as if neither of these events occurred! By emphasizing giving to a community that individually emphasized the proper marks on one's own σάρξ and the proper constraint of one's own σάρξ through obedience to Torah, a person in the community of the σάρξ was clearly investing into--sowing into--his/her own σάρξ.[17]

Such an inappropriate *individualistic emphasis* is vividly captured by Paul's terminology ὁ σπείρων εἰς τὴν σάρκα ἑαυτοῦ in Gal 6:8. This is *not* a reference to the ongoing existence of σάρξ in Christians, but rather a description of the on-going existence of σάρξ in the Judaistic/Jewish communities.[18]   Note that the contrast to this individual fleshly investing is investing into τὸ πνεῦμα, or into the Person who *corporately unites them* in both their life and walk (Gal 5:25).

II. Galatians 6:11-18 - The Postscript or Epilogue[19]

This final section of the epistle appears to be an appended personal conclusion written in Paul's own hand (6:11) and concluded with a typical Pauline benediction[20] (6:18).   In between these two verses, as Betz (1979, 23) and others have noted,[21] 6:12-17 is technically the *peroratio* or the brief conclusion.   Within these six verses Paul accomplishes the four ideal parts of a *peroratio* or epilogue as stated by Aristotle (1926, 3. 19. l/p. 467):

1. to dispose the hearer favourably towards oneself and unfavourably towards the adversary;

2. to amplify and depreciate;

3. to excite the emotions of the hearer;

4. to recapitulate.

Rhetorically, these four purposes are marvelously and compactly achieved by Paul as he amplifies and recapitulates the main arguments of the whole epistle in 6:12-17:[22]

> 6:12-13   *the indignatio* (which arouses anger) Paul accuses the Judaizers one final time of primarily being selfish and cowardly regarding persecution for the cross (6:12) and of being dishonorable

in their own observance of the Law, yet desiring to boast arrogantly in the Galatians' observation of it through their circumcision (6:13) (cf. du Toit 1992, 1994a).

6:14-16 *the recapitulatio or enumeratio* (which sums up the main argument, usually in the order in which the speaker discussed them).[23] Paul's honorable actions regarding circumcision (6:14-16) are in antithesis (δέ) to the Judaizers' dishonorable actions (in 6:12-13).

> 6:14 (recapitulating *Gal 1-2*) Paul's status within the people of God (his boast) is only in the cross of the Lord Jesus Christ, which changed the way he related to the fleshly distinctions of the world.[24]

> 6:15 (recapitulating *Gal 3-4*) The reason for Paul's changed relationship with others (γάρ) is because the people of God are now a new creation (καινὴ κτίσις) and the old historical distinctions of circumcision and uncircumcision now do not mean anything.[25]

> 6:16 (recapitulating *Gal 5-6*) And (καί) those who walk (live) according to this rule (κανόνι) of the new creation with no fleshly distinctions will have the peace and mercy which belong to God's true people.[26]

6:17 *the conquestio* (which stimulates pity)[27] Finally, in contrast to the Judaizers' avoidance of persecution through emphasizing circumcision, Paul actually bears on his body the στίγματα τοῦ Ἰησοῦ through his many persecutions of the cross (cf. 5:11) and these "brand marks" are Paul's personal counterpart to circumcision (cf. Bligh 1969, 496-97).[28]

Two points need further development within Paul's pithy and emotionally intense conclusion in 6:11-18. The first involves the further elaboration of the unusual phrase "the Israel of God" in Gal 6:16. The second involves the significance of the epilogue for the σάρξ/πνεῦμα antithesis. The following exegetical insights should help develop the first of these issues, the meaning of τὸν Ἰσραὴλ τοῦ θεοῦ.

First, as S. L. Johnson has noted about Ἰσραήλ, "the term refers to ethnic Israel, a sense that the term *Israel* has in every other of its more than sixty-five uses in the New Testament and in its fifteen uses in Paul" (1986, 182). Peter Richardson additionally makes the point that the Church would not assume this privileged title as long as it held out hope for Israel's repentance and until the break was irrevocable between the two groups (1969, 73). Both of these points seem exegetically sound and reasonable.

Secondly, Paul nevertheless does not use the term *Israel* per se, but creates the wonderful redundancy τὸν Ἰσραὴλ τοῦ θεοῦ. This is a unique term "found only here in the New Testament and never in Judaism" (Betz 1979, 322). The term τὸν Ἰσραὴλ τοῦ θεοῦ is not simply to be understood as the synthetic combination of *Israel* with a genitive modifier, but rather as the rhetorical creation of an entirely different replacement term in the same sense as τὸν νόμον τοῦ Χριστοῦ in 6:2 is a rhetorical creation that replaces νόμος. The lexical entity *Israel* is replaced with the unique lexical entity *the Israel of God*, which may or may not be equal to the former term. Only the context will determine the full sense of the replacement term since it is a *hapax legomenon*. As a result, both *the Israel of God* and *the law of Christ* have not been clearly understood by interpreters, largely because of our failure to stress adequately the ad hoc and rhetorical nature of Paul's use of them. In both cases the rhetorical effect is stunning because the widespread usage of the main term of each phrase (Ἰσραήλ and νόμος) by Paul's opponents is to make exactly the opposite point. Paul's rhetorical commandeering of these terms expertly amplifies the emotions of his audience, as one must do in a good rhetorical conclusion.

Thirdly, Paul rhetorically created the term τὸν Ἰσραὴλ τοῦ θεοῦ to refer to the Galatian Christians--both Jews and Gentiles--who walk according to the rule or κανών that he taught in Gal 6:15 (and thus in Gal 5-6). In other words Paul does view *the Israel of God* as the church in this particular context. However, this is not equivalent to saying that Israel = the Church. We know historically that this equivalency does not really occur in any Christian writing until Justin Martyr's *Dialogue with Trypho. a Jew* in A.D. 160 (Richardson 1969, 83). However, Paul's description of the Galatian Christians as "the Israel of God" seems to be the culmination of his numerous assertions that they are the true "sons of Abraham" in Gal 3:7-14, 29; 4:21-31 and the true "sons of God" in Gal 3:26-28; 4:1-7 (cf. Betz 1979, 322-23).

Especially relevant to understanding "the Israel of God" is Paul's climactic use of the Sarah/Hagar allegory in 4:21-31. In this passage Paul brilliantly reverses the Judaizers' argument and proves that the Galatian Christians are the true "Isaacites" and the Judaizers are actually the "Ishmaelites." In Gal 6:16 Paul is making his final recapitulation of this crucial identity: the true sons of God/sons of

Abraham, i.e., God's beloved Israel, are those who walk according to the rule he gave in 6:15. The term also obviously builds on the implicit contrast to "the Israel that is *not* of God." Within the context of Paul's argument this is clearly the Judaizing Ishmaelites or "Israel born κατὰ σαρκά (4:23, 29).[29] By contrast in Gal 6:16, those who walk according to the κανών of 6:15, i.e., those who walk according to the rule or direction of the Spirit not the flesh (5:16 and 5:25), are the Israel *of God*. The creation of this term does not directly relate to the issue of the Church supplanting ethnic Israel, because Paul allows for ethnic Israel's continued existence as Israel κατὰ σαρκά or Israel not of God, i.e., Israel in a hardened state (Romans 9-11). As the following discussion of the grammar will seek to prove, Paul's straightforward language in Gal 6:16 equates the one who walks according to τῷ κανόνι τούτῳ (according to the rule of the Spirit) with those who should rightly be called "God's Israel." Broadly speaking, Paul seems to be using this term in the sense of "God's new covenant people."[30]

Fourthly, the most natural and straightforward sense of the grammar of Gal 6:16 supports the following translation:[31]

καὶ ὅσοι τῷ κανόνι τούτῳ στοιχήσουσιν, εἰρήνη ἐπ᾽ αὐτοὺς
And as many as shall walk according to this rule, peace (be) upon them,

καὶ ἔλεος καὶ ἐπὶ τὸν Ἰσραὴλ τοῦ θεοῦ.
and mercy also (be) upon the Israel of God.

The grammatical controversies have centered upon the final two καί's and the two ἐπί's. The simplest and most straightforward understanding of the καί's is to see the καί before ἔλεος as continuative (copulative) in linking the "mercy" phrase to the "peace" phrase and the καί after ἔλεος as adjunctive (adverbial) in the sense of "also."[32] This also allows for the simplest reading of the two ἐπί's, i.e., they create an obvious parallelism between the two phrases that contain them. Therefore, the αὐτούς ("them") of the first phrase is the same group as "the Israel of God" in the second phrase. Of course, both of these two terms have their common antecedent in the ὅσοι ("as many as") that begins 6:16.

Fifthly, the interpretation that understands τὸν Ἰσραὴλ τοῦ θεοῦ as referring to Jewish Christians within the Church (e.g., Betz 1979 323; Ellicott [1860] 1978, 154; and Schrenk 1949, 1950) is self-defeating in the sense that Paul's whole argument is that these kinds of distinctions now mean nothing (cf. Dahl 1950). If Paul is actually singling out the Jewish Christians as the special recipients of God's mercy in 6:16, then he is undermining his whole argument (just recapitulated in the previous verse) that circumcision and uncircumcision provide no special spiritual privilege before God! Additionally, this Jewish Christian interpretation understands τὸν Ἰσραὴλ τοῦ θεοῦ without any rhetorical nuances.

Sixthly, while as sound grammatically as the Jewish Christian view, the understanding that Paul uses *the Israel of God* "eschatologically and refers to the Israel that shall turn to the Lord in the future in the events that surround the second advent of our Lord" (Johnson 1986, 186) is equally implausible for contextual reasons. The first objection to this is the common sense one: "How did the end times suddenly intrude into this Judaizers' context?" While there certainly are numerous apocalyptic and eschatological themes in Galatians (Johnson 1986, 194, n. 57), the sudden appearance of one here seems extremely startling and amazingly subtle. Paul is not so much pronouncing a present and future blessing in 6:16 as he is stating the realities that result from making the right choice of communities and patterns of behavior.[33]

In this vein, most harmful to this eschatological interpretation is the fact that 6:16 is the end of Paul's *enumeratio* or *recapitulatio* within his conclusion. Specifically, 6:16 recapitulates Gal 5-6 and the part of the epistle that focuses on the choice of the right κανών of behavior for God's people and on the fruit (of the Spirit) that will follow this choice. Therefore, the expression of a *future* hope for mercy toward that part of Israel which will one day turn to the Lord (under a different and millennial κανών?) seems contextually and theologically misplaced. Richardson's attempt to explain Paul's wish of mercy for these Israelites as "an ironical twist" (1969, 81-82) is equally flawed because of its inordinate dependence upon Paul's alleged cleverness (in the midst of a recapitulation?) and upon his ironic use of "mercy," for which there is no linguistic precedent (Betz 1979, 322).

Seventhly, the very unusual order of ἔλεος following εἰρήνη must have also been startling to the hearers'/readers' ears and surely reflects another of Paul's closing rhetorical efforts. The specific mention of "peace" and the attachment of it to walking according to Paul's κανών is what one would expect from a Jewish Christian like Paul:

> As far as can be verified, Paul never thought of his primary dyadic social location as anything other than Jewish; he talked of himself as a Jew "in Christ." He shared the typically Jewish core

values of interpersonal contentment, the acquiescence in human finitude and human limitation, and the hope of achieving a genuinely human existence. He expected the traditional God of his forefathers to provide help in facilitating the realization of the core value: to become and be what he is as God's creation, a finite and free human being. *The typical Jewish articulation of this core value is "shalom," the Presence of everything necessary for an adequately meaningful human existence realizing the core value.* Paul found this "shalom" or peace "in Christ." For Paul, as a Pharisaic Jew, and for Pharisaic Jews in general, the replication of the core value took the form of studying and practicing Torah (Malina 1986b, 132; emphasis is mine).

Of course, Paul's Jewish Torah gave way to the law of Christ and the walk according to the rule or direction of the Spirit as the focus of his study and practice. It is this new κανών for the καινὴ κτίσις that will still provide God's people with His same εἰρήνη. This is vintage Jewish expression and Paul may be overtly echoing Ps 125:5 and 128:6, where the psalmist pronounces "peace be upon Israel" (Guthrie 1973, 151-52).

However, the placement of "mercy" after "peace" is logically reversed, even within the Pauline corpus (e.g., 1 Tim 1:2; 2 Tim 1:2). How is this to be explained? Additionally, why does Paul promise mercy upon the church when his normal usage of ἐλεόω/ἐλεέω and ἔλεος refers to the leniency in eschatological judgment *that has occurred* when sinners were redeemed (e.g., Rom 9:14-18, 23, 11:30-32, 15:9; 1 Cor 7:25; 2 Cor 4:1; 1 Tim 1:13, 16)?[34] There are no overwhelmingly satisfying answers to these questions, but two points can be made. First, within the corpus of antecedent Jewish literature, there is one well-known example of "peace" preceding "mercy" and that is within the 19th benediction of the *Shemoneh Esreh* (only in the Babylonian Recension).[35] This "Birkat ha-Shalom" ("Blessing of Peace") reads "Bestow *peace*, happiness, and blessing, grace, loving-kindness, and *mercy* upon us and upon all Israel thy People..." (emphasis is mine).

Richardson's thesis is that Paul has given this well-known benediction an ironical twist by following its illogical order of peace/mercy and by asking for mercy for God's people Israel who are presently estranged from his true people, the Church (1969, 81-82). The difficulty of such closing subtlety and irony has already been noted. However, the touch of irony may be valid in the sense that Paul asks for mercy for "the Israel of God," a group which includes both Jews and Gentiles in Christ. *This irony* would be in line with the consistent irony and argumentation that Paul has used throughout Galatians about the Church's identity as the true sons of Abraham, etc. (e.g., 4:21-31). Should Paul be alluding to the *Shemoneh Esreh*, this allusion would indeed be ironic. Additionally, affirming that Gentiles were included within God's mercy upon His people would fly in the face of the Pharisaic theology of the Judaizers that limited God's mercy to a very small and select group and demanded His judgment on all the others (e.g., Pss. Sol. 5:25; 7:10; 9:11; 11:9 13:12; 15:13). Paul's desire to take one last rhetorical swat at such sectarian Jewish sentiments may explain why he awkwardly separated and transposed "mercy" with "peace. "

Secondly, the issue of God's mercy *also* being upon the Gentiles now as the people of God is a well-known theme that Paul sets forth elsewhere in very non-ironic language (e.g., Rom 11:30-32). The Gentiles present reception of God's ἔλεος along with the Jews is Paul's climactic point in Rom 15:7-13 in the lengthy argument about Jewish and Gentile social relations, begun in 14:1. Presently being co-recipients of God's mercy is Paul' s ultimate reason why the Jewish and Gentile Christians should socially accept one another (προσλαμβάνομαι in Rom 14:1, 3 and 15:7).

Therefore, we can reasonably conclude that Paul's unusual reversal of "peace" and "mercy" may be another of his closing rhetorical thrusts underscoring the Torah-free inclusion of the Gentiles within the people of God. The role of Gal 6:16 within the flow of Paul's recapitulating argument in 6:14-16 supports this understanding:

> 6:14 Status within the people of God ("boasting") is properly modeled by Paul as a Jewish Christian because he lives as if the fleshly distinctions of the κόσμος were crucified at the cross of Jesus Christ.

> 6:15 This means that circumcision and uncircumcision are now meaningless distinctions within the new creation of God's people.

> 6:16 Those who walk according to this rule of the new creation, i.e., the rule or direction of the Spirit, will have the *peace* that God always gives to His true people and they will also have the *mercy* that God gives to His true people.[36]

In light of this lengthy discussion of Gal 6:16 and τὸν 'Ισραὴλ τοῦ θεοῦ, one can see that the σάρξ/πνεῦμα antithesis is not directly referred to in this verse. The closest direct references are in 6:12-13, where Paul refers to the Judaizers' desire to make a good showing ἐν σαρκί (v. 12) and to boast in the Galatians' circumcision (ἐν τῇ ὑμετέρᾳ σαρκί in v. 13). This observation leads us to the second and final issue that needs to be addressed in Gal 6:11-18: the significance of the epilogue for the σάρξ/πνεῦμα antithesis. Charles Cousar has not found much significance in Paul's closing paragraph:

> Since "flesh" does appear twice in the conclusion, it is all-the-more surprising that its counterpart "Spirit" is missing. Its absence at least raises a question whether Paul's strategy in the letter is, as Betz says that it is, "to present his defense of the gospel as a defense of the Spirit" (1989, 16),

While agreeing with Cousar's criticism of Betz' purpose of Galatians (see Chapter Two), the absence of πνεῦμα in Paul's epilogue is not as serious as one might assume. First, the two uses of σάρξ in 6:12 and 13 are more specific and "ethical" (better "polemical") than most commentators have admitted. Burton is typical of the majority view of σάρξ, which is too vague and too idealized:

> 6:12 - σάρξ is by metonymy: for the creature side, the corporeally conditioned aspect of life, the external as distinguished from the internal and real, or the secular as distinguished from the strictly religious (1918, 185).
>
> 6:13 - σάρξ is body: the whole material part of a living being (1918, 184).

Alexander Sand corrected this view by categorizing σάρξ in Gal 6:12-13 as "animated body substance as circumcised flesh" which paralleled Paul's use in Phil 3:3-4 (1967, 127, 133-35). Robert Jewett (1971b, 96) added to this specificity when he said:

> The clue is provided in Gal 6:13:...When "flesh" is qualified with the possessive pronoun "your," it is clearly not a power which acts of its own accord. Nor is it a symbol for the material, sensual side of man. Rather it is that flesh which was cut in circumcision!

This assessment of Sand and Jewett seems absolutely correct. The two occurrences of σάρξ in Gal 6:12-13 have too rich a background in Gal 2:14-6:10 to be read in a non-polemical manner at this late stage of the epistle. Within the polemical context of Galatians, Paul has carefully developed the sense of σάρξ as *a body conformed to Judaistic practices and constrained by Torah.* Within Paul's redemptive historical development of this sense, σάρξ now refers to persons *apart from* Christ who still live in the weak and transitory bodily mode of existence that was normative *before* Christ. Therefore, there is an anachronistic side for those who want to "turn back again" (ἐπιστρέφετε πάλιν in 4:9) to the bondage of the στοιχεῖα and the tutelage and guardianship of Torah (3:22-4:11).

All of this theological, historical, ethical and polemical development of σάρξ throughout the epistle now comes to bear in Paul's conclusion in 6:11-18. However, the continuity in understanding his use of σάρξ in Gal 3-6 has been broken with the internal sense of σάρξ that is assumed from 5:13-6:10 in most treatments of Galatians (e.g., Burton 1921, 292 and even Jewett 1971b, 101-9). This creates the unlikely scenario that Paul uses σάρξ in the material, bodily sense in Gal 1-4, in the internal sense of a sinful element in a person's *nature* in 5:13-6:10, and then back to the material, bodily sense in his conclusion to his argument in Gal 6:11-18. Far better is the consistent, yet developing understanding espoused in this book that Paul's "ethical" use of σάρξ from 3:3 onward is perfectly consistent to the end of the epistle. In this sense, the σάρξ/πνεῦμα antithesis is resident in Paul's use of the term σάρξ in Gal 6:12-13. In fact, a significant purpose in his conclusion was to recall his development of this antithesis as he arouses the anger of his audience against the Judaizers in the *indignatio* of 6:12-13. Within this genre, in fact, it would have been inappropriate to mention πνεῦμα. Hence, we just see the σάρξ-side of the antithesis.

One last point about the significance of Gal 6:11-18 for the σάρξ/πνεῦμα antithesis bears repeating. This is Paul's mention in 6:16 of walking according to the rule or pattern of behavior that he has advocated in Gal 5-6 (καὶ ὅσοι τῷ κανόνι τούτῳ στοιχήσουσιν). This phrase is the final part of the *recapitulatio* that does that very thing for his argument in Gal 5-6. The κανών ("rule") is Paul's oft-repeated rule or direction of the πνεῦμα, which opposes the Judaizers' rule of the σάρξ (5:16, 18, 25). The verb στοιχήσουσιν in 6:16 would most certainly reinforce this connection with the rule of the Spirit because of its prior use with πνεῦμα in 5:25 (πνεύματι καὶ στοιχῶμεν). Therefore, while again the specific terms σάρξ and πνεῦμα do not occur in Gal 6:16, Paul's use of the highly associative terms κανών and στοιχέω would most certainly recall the σάρξ/πνεῦμα antithesis to the Galatians' attention.

III. Conclusion

Paul's concern for the Galatian Christians' choice of the correct pattern of behavior or way of life was overtly expressed in the general, antithetical contrast of the community of the σάρξ with the community of the πνεῦμα in Gal 5:13-26. The exegesis of Gal 6:1-10 has revealed that this same concern of Paul's continues in much more specific form in these two paragraphs as he deals with two present problems that have arisen due to the clash of the Judaizers' fleshly values with the standards of life according to the Spirit. In contrast to the Judaizers' pattern, walking according to the rule of the Spirit leads to drastically different actions in the restoration of sinning members of the church (6:1-5) and in the investing and finances and goods in the appropriate members of the community of the Spirit (6:6-10). This exposition of the appropriate actions for those who possess the Spirit (ὑμεῖς οἱ πνευματικοί) must have been very beneficial in helping the Galatians understand the radical difference between the individualistic and competitive pattern of the Judaizers (5:13, 15, 19-21, 26) and the relationally-oriented and cooperative pattern of Paul's communities (5:13-14, 16, 18, 22-25). The areas of dealing with παραπτώματι in the community and distributing money served this purpose quite well.

The exegesis of the epilogue or conclusion in Gal 6:11-18 reinforced the previous analysis that argued for the following rhetorical purpose or main theme of Galatians:

> to persuade the Galatians to reject the Judaizers' non-gospel and to continue in the true gospel which Paul had preached to them because...1) it alone was legitimately confirmed, while the Judaizers' non-gospel was rejected, 2) and it alone placed them in the true people of God through their faith in Christ, 3) and it alone provided them true deliverance from sin's powers through their receiving of the Holy Spirit.

Paul concluded this purpose in 6:11-18 by including his own handwritten verification of the epistle's authenticity (6:11), heightening the indignation against the Judaizers' dishonorable motives and actions (6:12-13), recapitulating the three main points of his argument (6:14-16), and closing with a stimulation for pity toward him due to this bodily marks of apostleship (6:17) and a benediction (6:18). Perfectly consistent to the very end, Paul continues to contrast the antithetical identities and patterns of behavior of the communities of the σάρξ and the πνεῦμα.

Notes

[1]See Lightfoot [1890] 1957, 215.

[2]See Betz 1979, 295-98 for an interesting discussion of Paul's choice of παράπτωμα rather than ἁμαρτία to describe a Christian's lapse and for a defense of the presence of lapsed Christians in the Galatian churches. See Garlington 1991 for a thorough and helpful discussion of Gal 6:1-5.

[3]Räisänen 1986, 78-82 waxes particularly eloquent in refuting this view.

[4]See Young 1977 for a refutation of this viewpoint.

[5]The thrust of Hays' 1987 article is on the paradigmatic value of the whole life of Jesus Christ which establishes the pattern of a free life of service for Christians so that they can recapitulate Jesus' self-giving. As Hays explains,

> Paul modulates the pattern, however, so that Christ's self-giving is treated less as moral ideal for the individual believer than as a paradigm for the community of believers in their relations with one another (289-90).

[6]Additionally, Barclay 1988, 132-33 notes the continuity in Paul's and the early church's use of Lev 19:18 as a summary statement by Jesus of the Mosaic Law: "hence to fulfill the law through love would be to fulfill the law τοῦ Χριστοῦ (as taught by Christ)." See also Thielman 1987, 95-100.

[7]Contra Barclay 1988, 134, Burton 1921, 329 says

> By "the law of the Christ" Paul undoubtedly means the law of God as enunciated by the Christ; just as the law of Moses (Lk 2:23, Acts 13:39) is the law of God as put forth by Moses. By the use of the official term τοῦ Χριστοῦ in preference to 'Ιησοῦ or even Χριστοῦ, the authoritative character of the promulgation is suggested.

See Thielman 1987, 87-167 and 1994, 119-44 for a development of Paul's "eschatologizing" of the Mosaic Law in Galatians. Cf. Hong 1992.

[8]The best verse in the traditional Pauline corpus that illustrates the continued, but internationalized use of the Mosaic Law is Eph 6:2-3. Paul appeals to the fifth commandment of the Decalogue as still being authoritative regarding honoring your father and mother (e.g., Ex 20:12), yet "internationalizes" the promise from long life "in the land (of Canaan)" to long life "on the earth" (ἐπί τῆς γῆς). Calvin's comment is incisive: "But as the same blessing of God is today shed on the whole world, Paul has properly left out the mention of a place, the particular discrimination of which lasted only till the coming of Christ" ([1556] 1965, 213).

[9]This future reading is the harder reading over the better attested aorist ἀναπληρώσατε, which appears more vulnerable to conforming to the preceding imperatives (Metzger 1971, 598).

[10]While agreeing in principle with Calvin's "third use of the Law" (*usus tertius legis*), some of his expressions of this usage in the *Institutes* are problematic because of his view of σάρξ in the life of a Christian:

The third use of the Law (being also the principal use, and more closely connected with its proper end) has respect to believers in whose hearts the Spirit of God already flourishes and reigns...for none has as yet attained to such a degree of wisdom, as that they may not, by the daily instruction of the Law, advance to a purer knowledge of the Divine will. . . In this way must the saints press onward, since, however great the alacrity with which, under the Spirit, they hasten toward righteousness, they are retarded by the sluggishness of the flesh, and make less progress than they ought. The Law acts like a whip to the flesh, urging it on as men do a lazy sluggish ass. Even in the case of a spiritual man, inasmuch as he is still burdened with the weight of the flesh, the Law is a constant stimulus, pricking him forward when he would indulge in sloth (Calvin [1559] 1972, 2.7.12/p. 309).

See Hesselink 1984, 184-91 for a helpful exposition of Calvin's view of the role of the Law in the Christian's life.

[11]See Kuck 1994 for a defense of the "final judgment" sense of Paul's imagery.

[12]See North 1992 for other financial uses of this imagery.

[13]This kind of close connection of 6:6-10 with 6:1-5 is contrary to the conclusions of commentators like Burton 1921, 335, Bonnard 1972, 125, and Mussner 1974, 402 who see no connection to the preceding context.

[14]Linked to the sowing/reaping agricultural imagery is the additional usage of καρπός ("fruit"), which Paul also uses for financial contributions (e.g., Rom 15:28; 1:13). For a solid exegetical defense of καρπός in the sense of financial giving in Rom 1:13 see Kruger 1987.

[15]We will probably never be able to reconstruct the historical context with a full sense of certainty. While the following reconstruction is as speculative as any other that has been proposed, nevertheless it does attempt to do justice to all of the linguistic and historical particulars that we do know. The sense of σάρξ in Gal 6:8 that is advocated in this chapter does not rise or fall totally on this reconstruction.

[16]See the discussion of this thesis in the treatment of Gal 6:6-10 in the rhetorical analysis of Chapter Two. See Snyman 1992 for a contrary analysis of Gal 6:7-10 in which he sees it as the conclusion to Gal 5:13-6:10.

[17]Betz concurs with this interpretation:

"Sowing into the flesh" is done by placing one's hope for salvation upon circumcision and obedience to the Jewish Torah, a move which would result in missing salvation altogether (cf. 5:2-12)...In this sense, "sowing into the flesh" means nothing less than "giving an opportunity to the flesh" (5:13), and the very opposite of "crucifying the flesh" (5:24) (1979, 308).

[18]Bo Reicke 1951, 266 says this of Gal 6:7-9:

> With regard to the situation of the whole letter, these admonitions
> would seem to be directed toward Judaism also; and here when he
> says that he who sows to his own flesh will from the flesh reap
> corruption, he expresses the relationship of the works of the Law to
> the flesh.

If this interpretation is true, and I believe that it is, then Barrett's cry for the consistent translation of σάρξ as "flesh," which places the onus for understanding upon the hearers/readers to interpret the term contextually, is on the mark (1985, 71-72). This would avoid translations of Gal 6:8 like the NIV ("the one who sows to please his sinful nature") and the NEB ("who sows in the field of his lower nature"), which are very confusing.

[19]One of the most helpful works I have read on this final section of Galatians is the presently unpublished paper by Charles B. Cousar (1989), "Galatians 6:11-18: Interpretive Clues to the Letter." My thanks to the author for graciously sending me a copy of his excellent work. See also the fine work by Weima 1993.

[20]Phil 4:23, Phlm 25, and 2 Tim 4:22 are the only other benedictions in the traditional Pauline corpus that include the phrase found in Gal 6:18, μετὰ τοῦ πνεύματος ὑμῶν.

[21]Smit 1989, 21-22 actually calls Gal 6:11-18 the *amplificatio*, but views it in the same manner as Betz.

[22]See *Rhetorica ad Herennium* 2.30.47-50, pp. 145-53 for the following three traditional parts of the *epilogos* or *conclusio* of a deliberative speech.

[23]According to *Rhetorica ad Herennium* 2.30.47, pp. 145-47.

[24]Gal 1-2 is immediately brought to mind in this recapitulating verse with Paul's emphatic use of the first person pronoun ἐμοί, which recalls his intense autobiographical sharing in 1:11-2:21. Contrary to Bligh 1969, 492-93, who sees these remarks as unattractive self-approval on Paul's part, Paul is signaling the "first-person" segment of the epistle. Paul's perspective about boasting (status among the people of God) stands in stark contrast to the basis for the boasting of the Judaizers in 6:12-13. Additionally, the relating of "the cross of our Lord Jesus Christ" to Paul's relationship to the κόσμος brings to mind Gal 2:20-21, which is Paul's climactic conclusion to the lengthy discussion of circumcision begun in 2:1. The "crucified world" to Paul in both Gal 1-2 and 6:14 is not just the existential "enmity to the cross" that Käsemann speaks of (1970, 156), but it is a metaphorical assertion that the typical Jewish Christian distinction about the composition of the κόσμος regarding circumcision and uncircumcision has been killed--crucified (in the perfect tense)--as 6:15 explains (γάρ).

> "World" is that realm where the distinctions of circumcision matter
> a great deal, where people boast in the flesh, where the avoidance of

persecution is a high priority, where the cross of Christ is misunderstood (Cousar 1989, 11).

Gal 6:14 recapitulates the same basic point made earlier about Christ's crucifixion in 1:4; 2:20-21; 3:1-2, 13-14; 5:11, and 5:24 in slightly different terminology. J. Louis Martyn 1985b, 414 has noted this:

> perhaps Paul is telling the Galatians that one knows the old world to have died, because one knows that its fundamental structures are gone, that those fundamental structures of the cosmos *were* certain identifiable pairs of opposites, and that, given the situation among their congregations in Galatia, the pair of opposites whose departure calls for emphasis is that of circumcision and uncircumcision.

See also Minear 1977 and 1979.

[25]As Cousar 1989, 3 has observed, the καινὴ κτίσις of 6:15 stands in antithesis to the κόσμος of 6:14. The Judaizers advocate the continued existence of the κόσμος in 6:12-13 with their compulsion of the Galatians to be circumcised so that the Judaizers may boast in their flesh and avoid persecution from fellow Jews for the cross. In antithesis to this compulsion is Paul's assertion that circumcision and uncircumcision mean nothing, that Jewish Christians like himself should boast only in the cross, and that the στίγματα he bears (6:17) is far more desirable than avoiding persecution. Chilton 1978, 312 notes that the earlier Pharisaic text Jub. 4:26 uses similar language of "new creation" to assert a fresh start in one's dealings with God, and Paul is simply using a theological phrase current in contemporary Judaism to denote freedom from previous strictures (cf. 2 Cor 5:17).

[26]Paul links 6:16 to 6:15 with the double linkage of a καί and a reference to "this rule" (τῷ κανόνι τούτῳ), which refers to the καινὴ κτίσις of no circumcision in v. 15. The use of στοιχήσουσιν specifically recalls 5:25 and 5:16 (see the discussion of στοιχέω in Chapter Four), but it also acts as Paul's key word along with κανόνι to recapitulate all of the pattern of behavior/way of life connected with the community of the Spirit in Gal 5-6. The promise in 6:16b of εἰρήνη ἐπ αὐτοὺς καὶ ἔλεος καὶ ἐπὶ τὸν 'Ισραὴλ τοῦ θεοῦ is, of course, much debated. Peter Richardson's discussion (1969, 74-84) is unsurpassed for thoroughness of treatment and S. Lewis Johnson's article is equally thorough and up-to-date on the literature and exegetical issues. This clause will be dealt with below.

[27]*Rhetorica as Herennium* 2.30.50, pp. 151-53 shows the flexibility of this part of the conclusion and the many facets of one's experience to which one may appeal. Of particular interest is this facet of a *conquestio*: "by showing that we have ever, or for a long time, been in adverse circumstances" (p. 153). Paul appears to be following the rhetorical form of the conclusion and using this specific part to stimulate some degree of pity. However, it also seems that his greater purpose in the *conquestio* of Gal 6:17 is to give an ironic contrast to the Judaizers' body marks with the greater authenticating marks on

his body. Again, Paul uses rhetorical form with great expertise and flexibility to achieve his specific purposes.

[28]As John S. Pobee has noted in his discussion of Gal 6:17,

> If for the Jews circumcision was a mark of their being owned by God, for Paul the permanent marks of the persecutions he underwent branded him as the apostle of Christ. . . [these are] evidence of his devotion to or zeal for the Lord, which is a martyrological motif, as well as a sign or proof of his apostleship (1985, 95 and 96).

Additionally, see the recent discussions in Hanson 1987, 83-86 and Barclay 1995 and the earlier, but thorough article by Borse 1970.

[29]Paul makes this same point in Romans 9:6-13. Cf. Phil 3:3 and 1 Cor 10:18.

[30]This is also essentially the view of Schlier 1971, 283; Cole 1989, 235-37; Guthrie 1973, 152; Calvin [1556] 1965, 118; Lightfoot [1890] 1957, 224-25; and a host of other scholars (see Johnson 1986, 183-84 for a list of seventeen!). For a balanced and nuanced discussion of Paul's terminology here, see Ridderbos 1975, 336-37.

[31]This translation and grammatical understanding is also advocated by Johnson 1986, 186, n. 31.

[32]The continuative (copulative) sense of καί ("and") is clearly the most common and the adverbial or adjunctive sense ("also") is also frequent. The ascensive sense ("even") which blends into the explicative or epexegetical sense ("namely") is much rarer (BDF 1961, 227-29). These facts militate against Paul intending the rarer explicative sense of καί in Gal 6:16. While I agree with the interpretation that understands "the Israel of God" as referring to the church in this context, I do not think that it is grammatically reasonable to argue for the explicative usage to bolster this case. Paul may *never* have used καί in this sense (Ellicott [1860] 1978, 154). See also Ray 1994 and his discussion.

[33]If Gal 6:16 is a "blessing," it certainly does not fit Paul's pattern because of the presence of the conditional voice and the use of a substantival relative clause instead of second person pronouns. In these respects it is unlike all of the other eighteen "blessings" of the Pauline corpus listed by Betz 1979, 321, n. 94, except for Eph 6:23-24. Gal 6:18 actually fits the "blessing" genre far better than 6:16.

[34]There are at least three references within the Pauline corpus where "mercy" is also granted to or requested for Christians: Phil 2:27; 2 Tim 1:16, 18.

[35]The text and translation of the *Shemoneh Esreh* are taken from Richardson 1969, 79.

[36]Guthrie 1973, 152 makes the point also that no doubt Paul introduces this reference to Israel not only because he is echoing it from the Psalm, but also because he wants to assure the Galatians that they will not forfeit the

benefits of being part of the true Israel by refusing circumcision.

Chapter 7

Some Conclusions about the Flesh/Spirit Conflict

We have now arrived at the point in the undergirding of our thesis to attempt to summarize the diverse supporting arguments and to draw some conclusions. The thesis about the meaning of σάρξ and πνεῦμα within Paul's theology in Galatians has been explored from several different perspectives. Galatians has been viewed from these multiple perspectives in order to create a different, more accurate lens for the viewing of these terms. When these various perspectives are then put together, it would be very easy to see them as only a "bundle of unrelated perspectives," rather than as a cohesive and integrated whole. Additionally, seeing only a bundle of data would run the risk of missing the cumulative weight of the various arguments. The first purpose of this conclusion is to attempt to underscore the cohesive nature of the argumentation and to summarize its cumulative weight, and thereby reinforce the viability of the central thesis. The second purpose is to glance beyond Galatians and to discuss briefly those passages that should also be researched to see if the central thesis can be validated in all of the Pauline passages where σάρξ and πνεῦμα occur.

I. A Summary of this Book's Argumentation

Chapter 1 began with the full statement of the central thesis which advocates a polemical and redemptive-historical sense of σάρξ and πνεῦμα in Gal 3-6. Essentially, Paul uses the σάρξ/πνεῦμα antithesis in the epistle not to represent an internal duality within Christians, but to represent an external contrast between the two conflicting eras or modes of existence advocated by the Judaizers and Paul. The term σάρξ was not imported into the crisis by Paul, but rather was used because it was a central term in the Judaizers' identity of the people of God, i.e., God's people are those who are a part of "covenant of the flesh" (the Abrahamic Covenant) via circumcision. Therefore, the "flesh community" is the Judaizer community and it stands in stark contrast to the Pauline community, which is the "Spirit community." Paul makes three basic (and recurring) points about these antithetical communities in Galatians:

1. The σάρξ community is identified and characterized by bodily existence in its frailty and transitoriness (in the O.T. sense of בָּשָׂר) unaided by God's Spirit (e.g., Gal 4:23). By contrast, the πνεῦμα community is identified and characterized by bodily existence aided and enabled by God's Spirit (e.g., Gal 3:2-3) and also bodily liberated from sin's dominion (e.g., Gal 5:22-24).

2. The communities of σάρξ and πνεῦμα represent two successive eras in God's program of redemptive history (Ridderbos 1975, 57-68). The σάρξ community is the community of the νόμος and represents the era of the Mosaic Law (e.g., Gal 3:2-3; 5:13-14, 17-18, 19-21 and 23; 6:12-13). The childish, preparatory, and inferior nature of this redemptive historical era is significantly underscored by Paul in Gal 3:19-4:11 and 5:1-6. Contrasting to this anachronistic and particularistic community identity is the eschatological identity of the community of the πνεῦμα (4:1-7). This identity is appropriate for the era of the universal, non-particularistic proclamation of the Abrahamic blessing of Holy Spirit reception through faith in Christ Jesus (3:8-9, 13-14).

3. The last major point that Paul makes about the σάρξ/πνεῦμα antithesis in Galatians flows out of the first two points. Each of these competing communities is characterized by *an identity* (flesh or Spirit) and a corresponding *pattern of behavior* (walking according to the flesh or according to the Spirit). In Gal 5-6 we see these competing patterns of behavior contrasted side-by-side in terms of general relational patterns ("deeds of the flesh" versus "fruit of the Spirit" in 5:16-24), and then in specific applications to present problems within the Galatian churches (6:1-10). In these contexts when Paul speaks of "walking," it is according to the rule or standard of σάρξ or πνεῦμα, with the former being the Mosaic Law (5:18) and the latter being the law of Christ (6:1-2).

In *Chapter 1* the predominant understanding of σάρξ and πνεῦμα
was seen to be the existential interpretation that views these as internal
entities within the Christian that are in dynamic polarization and
opposition to one another. This view sees "an interior conflict between
flesh and Spirit" (Bruce 1982, 244). Paul is understood to be
exhorting the believer in Christ to choose between these resident
"powers" or capacities in passages like Gal 5:16-18.

Such a widely-held viewpoint has made it very acceptable to extend
the semantic range of σάρξ from the various nuances of its material,
bodily sense to the sense of an immaterial entity called a "nature." In
those Pauline passages deemed "ethical uses," this has led to
translations of σάρξ with amazing theological expressions like "the
sinful nature" (NIV), "the lower nature" (NEB), or "the human nature"
(TEV). These translations and this perspective are built upon the
assumption that Paul is looking at persons vertically or abstractly
(metaphysically) and is delineating these "parts" of persons. While
disagreeing with this understanding, I am not denying that persons
have "parts" or "natures" (capacities for behavior) or that Paul speaks
of them (e.g., Eph 2:3). Rather, I am denying that σάρξ refers to a
"part" of a person and that Paul is speaking in such categories in
Galatians.

The bulk of *Chapter 1* was also spent addressing the historical
issue of the identity of Paul's opponents in Galatia. This was
necessary because their identity and the problems they spawned relate
directly to the predominant understanding of the σάρξ/πνεῦμα conflict
in Gal 5-6. The circular nature of the understanding of these terms
becomes readily apparent when one delves into this issue. Essentially,
the new threat of *libertinism* is supposed to appear quite suddenly in
Gal 5:13 because of the perceived difference in Paul's use of σάρξ from
5:13 onward (e.g., Burton 1921, 292). However, the sifting of internal
and external sources for historical perspective revealed that this is bad
"mirror-reading" (Barclay 1987). Also, it is an unnecessary
complicating of the historical setting due to the alleged internal sense
that σάρξ is supposed to assume so suddenly in Gal 5:13.
Additionally, all of the support verses for the supposed libertinistic
threat were explained quite readily by reference to the Judaistic threat.
In the tightly-argued Epistle of Galatians, Paul was quite simply and
powerfully continuing to do in Gal 5-6 what he had done so
passionately in Gal 1-4: he was addressing the Judaizer threat.

The lengthy rhetorical analysis of Galatians in *Chapter 2* sought to
build upon this insight by accomplishing two goals: 1) by giving a
more accurate rhetorical analysis than that of Betz (1979) and those

who followed him and 2) by validating that Paul's purpose and argument in Galatians is, in fact, a unified polemic against the Judaizers that continues unabated from Gal 1-4 through Gal 5-6. Structurally, this was proven through the demonstration that Galatians has far more rhetorical than epistolary features. Specifically, Gal 5:1-6:10 was shown to be the third and final heading under the proof section of 1:11-6:10. In other words while this section has paraenetic features, it is not a pure paraenesis section in an epistolary sense, but rather continues Paul's polemic. This polemic is summarized in the general proposition of the epistle in 1:11-12: "to persuade the Galatians to reject the Judaizers' non-gospel and to continue in the true gospel which Paul had preached to them."

The first heading (1:11-2:21) sought to prove that the universal nature of Paul's gospel alone was legitimately confirmed, while the Judaizers' particularistic non-gospel was rejected. The second heading in Gal 3:1-4:31 proved through the fulfillment of Scripture that Paul's gospel alone placed the Galatians in the true people of God through their faith in Christ. Ironically, the Galatians were shown to be the true "Isaacites" and the Judaizers the "Ishmaelites" in the climactic application of 4:21-31. Finally, in his third heading in 5:1-6:10, Paul sought to prove that his gospel provided the true deliverance from sin's powers through their receiving of the Holy Spirit, while the Judaizers' non-gospel perpetuated life according to the rule or direction of the σάρξ. For Paul, life according to the σάρξ is another way of saying life ὑπὸ νόμον (Gal 5:18). Paul's approach was a side-by-side comparison of the ways of life of the communities of the σάρξ and πνεῦμα and a powerful demonstration of the superiority of their present deliverance in Christ over the anachronistic deliverance that the Judaizers promised through Torah. The τὰ ἔργα τῆς σαρκός was the resulting pattern of behavior from walking according to the rule of the σάρξ (5:19-21) and the ὁ δὲ καρπὸς τοῦ πνεύματός was the pattern that characterized walking according to the rule or direction of the Spirit (5:22-23).

Unfortunately, the tendency of most interpreters to view Paul's argumentation in Gal 5:13-6:10 "vertically" or abstractly has clouded the power of his "horizontal" or redemptive historical argumentation. However, the battlefield that the Judaizers defined was a theological-historical one: Who really is the true people of God and by what means (by which gospel) is this people formed? Paul's response to this gauntlet is a response *in kind*. His argumentation, even in the realm of the proper pattern of behavior or ethics for God's people in 5:1-6:10, is redemptive historical argumentation. This is appropriate only in response to a theological threat that is rooted in a historically anachronistic view of the people of God (e.g., 4:1-11).

Chapter 3 was an analysis of the social dynamics of the Galatian conflict. The goal of such an analysis was to seek to understand the world view of the first century, Mediterranean person better and to avoid assuming a late-twentieth century, individualistic perspective. The basic perspective that emerged which fundamentally shaped the social dynamics of the crisis is that the Galatians did not have a distinct category for "religion" that was separate from other facets of their culture. Rather, "religion" is imbedded in the other major institutions of "kinship," "politics," and "economics." Therefore, for the Galatians to forsake the gospel Paul preached and to embrace the Judaizers' non-gospel, they would have to be persuaded in *socially significant group terms*, not just in abstract ideological reasoning (by which *we* might be persuaded). Paul's argumentation would have to be from such a perspective also if it has any hope of persuading the Galatians not to forsake his gospel. Without seeing his argumentation in Galatians in this light, we may be guilty of significant lens-distortion.

In light of this basic perspective, five significant facets of Paul's argumentation in socially significant group terms were observed:

1. The Galatians have a *dyadic personality* and engage in *sociological thinking*. They view their identity non-individualistically, i.e., essentially derived from the group in which they are imbedded. Their distinction comes primarily from their group, not from their individual achievement. They engage in group stereotyping of individuals based on the characteristics of the group in which one is embedded. Moral discussions occur primarily at the group level and the most helpful statements of morals are those concretely embodied in a community. The contrasting embodiment of the "ways" of the Judaizer and Pauline communities is what Paul was doing in Gal 5:13-26.

2. Central to Paul's argumentation are the values of *honor and shame* because these values are central to the assessment of one's status within his or her group. The Judaizers promised "acquired honor" for the Galatians within the people of God if they would be circumcised and actively obey Torah. Paul's counter was that the Galatians already had far more honor within God's people because of their "ascribed honor" from being in Christ (3:6-4:7) and to deny the surpassing validity of that honor would be to shame Christ again (3:1-2).

3. Also significant to Paul's argument is his assertion of *God's fatherhood* over them. This involves God's provision and protection of them and the Galatians' response of loyalty to Him. Because of God's omnipotent power, only He can deliver them from the powers of this age (e.g., 1:3-4). However, the Galatians were deserting God (1:6) and risking being severed from the benefits of Christ (5:1-4). They were foolishly considering attaching themselves to a community that would not inherit the kingdom of God (5:21; 6:8).

4. Additionally, *the competing models of kinship* set forth by Paul and the Judaizers show that they did not share the same basic core, as Francis Watson (1986) has asserted. Rather, the Judaizers advocated a core based on "homogeneous ethnic pseudo kinship," while Paul set forth a core based on "pluralistic non-ethnic pseudo-kinship." The difference is in becoming "sons of Abraham." To the Judaizers this involved becoming Jewish through the process of proselytism, which involved circumcision and taking up the yoke of Torah (5:1-11; 6:12-13). To Paul this was accomplished by being "in Christ" through faith in him, not being "in Abraham" through blood kinship (3:7-9, 26-28). Paul's model also afforded full social equality to the Gentiles within the people of God, because circumcision or uncircumcision now means nothing (6:15-16).

5. Lastly, the *contrasting emphases on purity* in Galatia between the Judaizers and Paul reveal radically different means of defilement and foci of concern. In essence the Judaizers defined "purity" in terms of commitment to their group and focused on avoiding contamination from those outside their group. This meant the profane and impure Gentiles had to be purified upon entrance into Israel by finalizing their purification with circumcision (5:2-3; 6:12-13). All who had entered Israel must then avoid defilement and maintain group purity by avoiding intimacy with uncircumcised "outsiders" (2:11-14) and by upholding Torah (3:1-5; 4:8-11, 21; 5:1-6). Paul's rejoinder is that Judaizers' means of purification now mean nothing (6:15-16) and that group reputation is now more important than group commitment (6:1-10). Ironically, the Judaizers' ingrown focus on maintaining purity disregards Torah's central tenet (5:13-15), does not constrain bodily desires (5:16-21), and insures the impurity of corruption (6:8). The community of the Spirit has dealt with the flesh (5:16-18, 24), produces pure behavior (5:22-23), and reaps eternal life (6:8).

The main contribution of *Chapter 3* to the undergirding of the thesis is explaining the reasonableness of viewing the terms σάρξ and πνεῦμα in Gal 5:13-6:18 in a corporate/group sense rather than in an individualistic sense. Given what appears to be the Galatians' view of the world, this corporate perspective seems absolutely essential to understanding both how the Judaizers could confuse the Galatians and how Paul could counter their claims and insure the Galatians' ongoing loyalty to Christ.

Chapter 4 is the fourth and final perspectival study of Galatians: a thematic study that traces the development of the σάρξ/πνεῦμα antithesis in Gal 3-6. This study combines with the historical, rhetorical, and sociological studies of the previous three chapters to form the full-orbed contextual backdrop for the exegesis of Gal 5:13-6:18 in the final two chapters. However, the thematic study of Chapter 4 does more than provide a background for exegesis. It stands on its own as a further block of evidence that Paul was perfectly consistent in his use of σάρξ in a concrete, bodily sense throughout Galatians and does not suddenly shift to the internal, abstract sense of a "nature" in Gal 5:13-6:18. Rather, Paul's consistent enriching of σάρξ in Gal 3-4 with historical and theological depth is what sets the table for his continued use of the term in Gal 5-6.

Gal 3:1-5 establishes the basic antithesis between σάρξ and πνεῦμα but the antithesis is already foreshadowed in 2:15-21. This passage is Paul's rejoinder to those *Jewish Christians* in Antioch who acted as if the Gentile Christians needed to "be Judaized" in order to be fit for inclusion in God's people (2:11-14). Paul makes two points in 2:15-21 that set the stage for the antithesis of σάρξ and πνεῦμα in 3:1-5. The first point is that it is not culpable for these Jewish Christians to live ἐν σαρκί if they are simultaneously living ἐν πίστει in the Son of God as Paul was doing (2:20). In the context of this rebuke to Jewish Christians that is coupled with the proper example of a Jewish Christian (Paul), σάρξ simply refers to the limited, earthly bodies of these Jewish Christians. Living as circumcised believers is *not* culpable if it is lived in the knowledge that God's righteousness is not imparted διὰ νόμου. This is, in fact, Paul's second point, which he makes in 2:21. Living properly as a Jewish Christian as he described in 2:20 (ἐν σαρκί/ἐν πίστει) does not nullify "the grace of God." In the context of Paul's argument, this "grace" is none other than the Judaizing-free offer of the gospel (2:9). Paul also refers to this non-particularistic salvation in 2:5, 14 as τὴν ἀλήθειαν τοῦ εὐαγγελίου. Jewish Christians must not contradict either God's grace (toward the Gentiles) or the truth of the circumcision-free gospel as they continue to live in their circumcised state. Paul clarifies this even further with his reason for not nullifying "the grace of God" in the explanatory statement in 2:21b: εἰ γὰρ διὰ νόμου δικαιοσύνη, ἄρα Χριστὸς δωρεαὰν ἀπέθανεν. Paul's point is a redemptive historical one: the death of Christ changed the role of the Mosaic Law in an age-shattering sense. His death was for the purpose (ὅπως) of delivering his people from the present evil age (1:4). This present age is the age of the Mosaic Law (3:19-4:11). Therefore, to continue to emphasize the importance of σάρξ, i.e., circumcised bodily existence, is to negate the death of Christ and to be anachronistic within God's redemptive plan.[1] The stage is now set for the antithesis of σάρξ and πνεῦμα in 3:1-5.

The placing of σάρξ and πνεῦμα in antithesis in 3:1-5 with ŋo explanation is understandable if the interpretation of Gal 2:15-21 advocated above is accurate. In essence, within Paul's discussion of the general bodily sense of σάρξ he had already subtly pointed to the specific historical manifestation of σάρξ in its circumcised state by the time he mentions it in 3:3. Σάρξ is used in this specified manner for the rest of the epistle, with the exception of the two occurrences in 4:13-14. Historically and theologically, σάρξ also continues to be coupled in a tandem with νόμος, as in 2:20-21 (e.g., 3:2-3; 5:13-14, 17-18, 19-23; 6:12-13). On the other side of the antithesis, πνεῦμα is coupled in tandem with πίστις (in Christ) (e.g., 3:2-3, 13-14; 5:5). Therefore, the antithesis that results is a redemptive historical one that is set, as John Barclay has noted, within an apocalyptic framework:

> But the important distinction in Paul's usage in Galatians is that he employs this dualism within an *apocalyptic* framework. Here Käsemann's insight is of fundamental importance. In the context πνεῦμα is not an anthropological entity nor is it a general term for the spiritual (non-material or divine) realm: it is the eschatological token of the new age, the power that establishes the sovereignty of Christ in the new creation. As its opposite, σάρξ is caught up into the dualism inherent in all apocalyptic thought and is thus associated with "the world" and "the present age" which stand in contrast to the new creation. *It is this apocalyptic dualism which gives to σάρξ its negative "colouring"*: just as the present age is an evil age (1:4), so the flesh is at best inadequate and at worst thoroughly tainted with sin (1988, 204-5; emphasis is his).

The basic antithesis of σάρξ and πνεῦμα in 3:1-5 is developed somewhat unevenly by Paul throughout the rest of Gal 3 and 4. Then, the culmination of the antithesis is reached in the contrasting patterns of behavior associated with σάρξ and πνεῦμα in Gal 5:13-6:10. The clear correspondence of the two ways of life described in this passage with the Judaizer and Pauline communities respectively is made more transparent first, however, with the contrasting of the birth of Ishmael κατὰ σάρκα with the birth of Isaac κατὰ πνεῦμα in 4:23 and 29. Paul creates this application to reverse the apparent Judaizer use of it and to cement the corresponding identities of σάρξ and πνεῦμα with the competing communities in Galatia. This makes the contrasting walks according to the rule of the σάρξ or according to the rule of the πνεῦμα even more effective in Gal 5-6.

If a distilled essence can be drawn from studying the thematic flow of σάρξ and πνεῦμα in Gal 3-6 it is this:

> Paul is doggedly consistent in his use of σάρξ in the polemical and rhetorical sense which he apparently inherited from the Judaizers (as "bodies distinguished by circumcision and constrained by Torah"), and to this readily-understandable sense within the Galatian conflict Paul enriches it with increased redemptive-historical theological significance. Therefore, in Gal 5:13-6:18 we see Paul's use of σάρξ and πνεῦμα in a very developed redemptive-historical manner that flows out of and builds upon the foundation and usage of σάρξ and πνεῦμα in Gal 1-4.

This understanding should be capable of validation in the exegesis of Gal 5-6.

Chapter 5 and *Chapter 6* contain an exegesis of Gal 5:13-26 and 6:1-18, respectively. These two passages are part of the final proof section of the epistle (5:1-6:10) and also contain the epistle's epilogue or conclusion (6:11-18). Rhetorically speaking, we reach the climax of Paul's argumentation in 5:1-6:10. This is immediately obvious in 5:1-12 through the epistle's first overt discussion of circumcision and the warning of the Galatians not to submit to it (5:2-4). In the terms of the immediately preceding application of 4:21-31, the Galatians' submission to circumcision would be living like an Ishmaelite (κατὰ σάρκα) when they were already Isaacites (κατὰ πνεῦμα). Paul's warning about such a change of identities/communities is very severe in Gal 5:1-12. This warning about giving up the freedom that Christ had given them (5:1a) by turning to the implied slavery that comes with circumcision and the Torah-yoke (5:1b-3) sets the stage for Paul's repeated exhortation in 5:13 in parallel terms. However, the exhortation is 5:13 is cast in terms of not using their freedom as those born κατὰ πνεῦμα for an opportunity to live κατὰ σάρκα.

Therefore, Paul's exhortation about the ἀφορμὴν τῇ σαρκί in 5:13 is a second overt warning about choosing to live according to the Judaizers' emphasis on the σάρξ, i.e., on bodies distinguished by circumcision and constrained by Torah. This σάρξ way-of-life is summarized in 5:13-15 and 5:25-26 in contrast to the πνεῦμα way-of-life.[2] These two passages are exhortations cast in the fundamental relational contrast between the σάρξ and πνεῦμα communities. Gal 5:13-15 and 5:25-26 also function as brackets to Paul's picture of the contrasting internal relationships within these communities in 5:16-24. Paul sets forth his basic premise about these antithetical community dynamics in 5:16-18:

> the πνεῦμα way-of-life stands in stark opposition to the σάρξ way-of-life, so that if the Galatians choose to walk according to the rule or direction of the πνεῦμα, they will not be ὑπὸ νόμον and carry out the passion to be circumcised.

The basic admonition and opposition of these two *patterns of behavior* is then embodied by Paul in the concrete interpersonal dynamics and ethics of first, the community of the σάρξ (τὰ ἔργα τῆς σαρκός in Gal 5:19-21), and then in those of the community of the πνεῦμα (ὁ καρπὸς τοῦ πνεύματός in Gal 5:22-23). Gal 5:24 serves as a most fitting redemptive-historical conclusion as to why those in the community of the Spirit do not have to live according to the rule or pattern of the flesh: "Now those who belong to Christ Jesus have crucified the flesh with its passions and desires."

Galatians 6:1-10 contains *two specific applications* of the general patterns of behavior of the communities of the σάρξ and πνεῦμα found in Galatians 5, again in an antithetical manner as the two applications are made. Those in the community of the Spirit (ὑμεῖς οἱ πνευματικοί) are to deal with any Christian overtaken by sin (προλημφθῇ ἄνθρωπος ἔν τινι παραπτώματι) with gentleness and humility as restoration is sought in mutual concern and burden-bearing, not in arrogant competition (as in the community of the σάρξ (6:1-5). Such an attitude fulfills τὸν νόμον τοῦ Χριστοῦ, which is the Mosaic Law in its internalized, "messianized," and universalized New Covenant expression. Additionally, in 6:6-10 Paul corrects what appears to be the Judaizers' teaching on giving to them, and perhaps to Jerusalem. In contrast to this teaching, Paul asserts that the Galatians should give--sow--to their own local teachers of the Word and that they will thereby be sowing eschatologically to the Spirit and not to the flesh-system of the Judaizers, which ends in corruption. This priority in giving does not eliminate giving to all persons (6:10a), but rather establishes the priority (μάλιστα) as those of the household of faith (6:10b).

The postscript or epilogue of Gal 6:11-18 begins with an appended handwritten authentication by Paul (6:11) and ends with a typical Pauline benediction (6:18). In between are six verses that accomplish the four parts of a good rhetorical epilogue, according to Aristotle (1926, 3.19.1/ p. 467). Paul compactly amplifies and recapitulates the epistle's main arguments in these verses (6:12-17):

> *6:12-13* He arouses the Galatians' anger against the Judaizers and their favor toward him by explaining the selfish and cowardly motives of the Judaizers regarding persecution (6:12) and by revealing their arrogant motives in seeking the Galatians' circumcision (6:13).

> *6:14-16* Paul recapitulates the three main points of his argument in order as he contrasts his means of status only through the cross of Christ (6:14) to the Judaizers' means (in 6:12-13), as he explains in 6:15 that circumcision and uncircumcision now mean nothing in the new creation in Christ, and as he promises the peace and mercy that belong to the true people of God in 6:16 when they walk according to the κανών (of the Spirit) which he has taught.

> *6:17* Paul finally closes the loop by appealing to his body marks gained through persecution on behalf of Jesus which contrast to the body marks of the Judaizers (6:12-13) who avoid such persecution.

Again, Paul is perfectly consistent in his antithetical comparison of the Judaizers' identity and pattern of behavior for the people of God with the identity and pattern which he had previously set forth in Galatia. The Judaizers advocated an anachronistic return to the proselyte model which centered on the σάρξ:

> Gentile converts' bodies must be distinguished by circumcision as Jewish bodies are shortly after birth into the commonwealth of Israel and then the Gentiles' bodies must be appropriately constrained by the yoke of Torah.

In Galatians 6 Paul concretely reveals the inadequacy of this previous way of life now that Jesus Christ's death has delivered believers from the present evil age (1:3-4) and now that the Holy Spirit has begun to mediate the rule and direction of life in the fullness of times (4:1-7).

In concluding the summary of this book's argumentation, one more question must be asked: "Is the view set forth in this book totally unique and unsupported by other scholars?" The answer to this question is a qualified "yes." It is qualified because there are scholars like Jewett 1971b who have set forth views that are relatively close to this book's. Even closer, however, is the view espoused by John Barclay in his excellent monograph on Galatians (1988). Barclay undoubtedly is closest of any scholar to my perspective and his view of the σάρξ/πνεῦμα antithesis in Galatians bears close scrutiny:

> The connection with apocalyptic also helps us to see what Paul understood by σάρξ.   Having noted the extremely diverse associations this term can have, it may seem foolish to attempt to give any generalizing definition: it may appear that there is no general notion which could link together all its various uses. Nonetheless, the way Paul employs his πνεῦμα-σάρξ dualism in relation to the apocalyptic themes of the letter suggests that he is using σάρξ to designate *what is merely human*, in contrast to the divine activity displayed on the cross and in the gift of the Spirit (Barclay 1988, 206; emphasis is his).

Barclay goes on to elaborate on this view of σάρξ and concludes his discussion with this summary:

> A much more satisfactory solution emerges if we take σάρξ as 'what is merely human' and see its application to the works of the flesh and the law in social rather than purely individualistic terms. The works of the flesh are merely human patterns of behaviour (especially in social relations) while Jewish observance of the law is a merely human way of life, based on human social realities (kinship, traditions of the fathers and racial exclusiveness). Thus while the flesh can be manifested as human weakness (Gal 4:13-14), or self-centred behaviour (5:15), neither of these is itself the heart of Paul's understanding of the term: the looser definition--'what is merely human'--fits his various uses more comfortably as well as arising quite naturally from his apocalyptic perspective (209).

Barclay speaks also of the ability of this apparent definition of σάρξ to encompass Paul's various uses of it:

> Our observations thus far lead us to conclude that Paul uses σάρξ, as an 'umbrella-term' under which he can gather such disparate entities as libertine behaviour, circumcision, a range of social vices and life under the law. The apocalyptic framework within which he uses the term does give it some general theological content (what is merely human) so that his linkage of these various items is not entirely arbitrary (209-l0).

Overall, Barclay's insights are excellent and essentially in agreement with the views espoused in this monograph.   However, three clarifications need to be made that will clarify the distinctiveness of my perspective:

1.   Σάρξ does have a looser definition in its *overall usage* within the Pauline corpus (see II. below).   However, within those contexts where a Judaizing perspective is addressed, there is a narrower and more specified sense of σάρξ that flows quite logically from the Judaistic polemics themselves.   This is the sense of σάρξ in Galatians and Barclay has unnecessarily broadened it because of his broader understanding of Gal 5:13-6:10 and Paul's argumentation within this section of the epistle.[3]

2.   Barclay's failure to specify σάρξ enough may be due in part to his apparent lack of familiarity with the redemptive-historical perspective, as championed by Ridderbos ([1957] 1982, 1975) and Vos ([1930] 1979, [1912] 1980).   Moisés Silva has legitimately chided Barclay in his review of Barclay's monograph for ignoring these scholars' works (1990, 161).   Recognizing Paul's redemptive-historical perspective and argumentation within Galatians would have enabled Barclay to see that σάρξ is "what is merely human *and* distinctively Jewish" within this context, i.e., σάρξ = bodies distinguished by circumcision and constrained by Torah, rather than distinguished by possession of the Holy Spirit and constrained by His rule and direction.   Σάρξ is always used by Paul in a *general* redemptive-historical sense in those contexts deemed "ethical uses," but this is, of course, the terrain of the further study of σάρξ yet to be done in other Pauline passages (see below).

3.   There are some passages in Galatians where Barclay's looser definition of "what is merely human" is clearly seen to be excessively broad and too vague for the specific context.   The occurrence of σάρξ in Gal 5:16 is one of those examples.   As has been argued above, the parallelism of σάρξ in 5:16 with νόμος in 5:18 demands a specified sense for σάρξ in this verse.   Paul is not resisting "merely human" behavior only, but "merely human and distinctively Jewish" behavior within this context!

Therefore, the unique contribution of this book is really its doggedly consistent reading of the σάρξ/πνεῦμα antithesis within the historical setting of the Galatian conflict.   Such a reading seeks to give adequate weight to the judaizing polemics that Paul faced and answered in his epistle.   Within such a reading of Galatians, the constant principle in interpreting σάρξ has been "less is better."   This means that the interpreter does not need to move beyond the bodily, material sense of σάρξ into the immaterial sense of "a nature" to understand Paul's use of the term.   Neither does the interpreter need to resort to a very loose definition of σάρξ and ignore its very specific setting within Paul's redemptive-historical argumentation.   Rather, the general Old Testament sense of בָּשָׂר and its translation with σάρξ in the LXX is continued in Paul's usage of σάρξ. However, this general usage is enriched with historical and theological insights due to the change wrought by Christ's death and by the giving of the Holy Spirit to God's people. No longer should they live life according to the rule of the σάρξ, but now they are privileged to live life according to the rule or direction of God's πνεῦμα. This is Paul's basic message in Galatians.

II. The Need for Further Study of the SARX/PNEUMA Antithesis in Other Pauline Epistles

The central thesis of this book is that σάρξ and πνεῦμα do not represent an internal duality, but an external contrast between modes of existence and redemptive historical eras. This contrast is viewed on the σάρξ-side as bodily existence in its normal frailty and transitoriness under the dominion of sin, in bondage to the στοιχεῖα τοῦ κόσμου, and not indwelt by God's πνεῦμα. This is universally true of all those before the coming of Jesus Christ, including the Israelites who lived ὑπὸ νόμον. Therefore, within Judaistic contexts which discuss life ὑπὸ νόμον, Paul's use of the σάρξ/πνεῦμα antithesis will *also* have the specification of σάρξ as bodily existence distinguished by circumcision and constrained by Torah. This sense should be capable of being validated in the two Pauline passages where the σάρξ/πνεῦμα antithesis is used against the specific Judaistic perspective. However, the broader sense of σάρξ as human beings in their normal bodily frailty and transitoriness, not indwelt by God's πνεῦμα, should also be capable of being validated in those non-Judaistic passages where the σάρξ/πνεῦμα antithesis is used or where σάρξ is used in this redemptive historical (ethical?) sense. The following brief overview of all of these Pauline passages needing this further investigation is intended to be only suggestive of the conclusion that such a dual validation would indeed occur.

A. The SARX/PNEUMA Antithesis in Non-Judaistic Passages

There are five passages that fit within this category: 1 Corinthians 3:1-3; Romans 13:11-14; Ephesians 2:1-3; Colossians 2:6-23; and a cluster of uses in 2 Corinthians (1:17; 5:16; 10:2-4; 11:18).[4] Both of the terms σάρξ and πνεῦμα appear in some form only in the 1 Corinthian's passage. Nonetheless, all of the uses of σάρξ appear to have some "ethical" dimension (better "redemptive historical") and need some further study.

Paul rebukes the Corinthian Christians for being σαρκίνοις rather than πνευματικοῖς in *1 Cor 3:1-3*. To be πνευματικοῖς would be to live in a manner of appraising all things (ἀνακρίνει [τὰ] πάντα in 2:15) according to the νοῦν Χριστοῦ (2:16). However, the Corinthians were living as babies in Christ (νηπίοις ἐν Χριστῷ in 3:1). They are still milk-drinkers, not solid food eaters in their spiritual diet after the several years they have known Christ. They are, therefore, still σαρκικοί (3:2-3a). Paul validates this fleshliness in 3:3b (γάρ) with the continued existence of jealousy and strife (ζῆλος καὶ ἔρις) among them (cf. Gal 5:20; Rom 13:13; and Jas 3:14, 16).

Particularly significant to validating this book's view of the meaning of σάρξ in these kinds of passages is the final part of Paul's validation in 3:3c: οὐχὶ σαρκικοί ἐστε καὶ κατὰ ἄνθρωπον περιπατεῖτε; To be "fleshly" is to be walking (living) only "according to man." In other words this is to live as if you are on your own as a human being and unaffected and unaided by God. This is, of course, to be living like a non-Christian (e.g., 1 Cor 2:14). Therefore, to be "fleshly" is to be "non-Christianly." It is to be living as if your only standards and resources were κατὰ ἄνθρωπον. It is to live as if you were bodily on your own and unaided by God's Spirit. Such a life stands in stark contrast to the Christian who is πνευματικός (1 Cor 2:15) and whose pattern of behavior should reflect such an identity. That is why the Corinthian's non-Christian pattern of behavior regarding jealousy and strife was unthinkable to Paul and contrary to the Spirit-like pattern of behavior that they should have been manifesting. They were reverting back to the behavior of their previous identity and mode of existence as non-Christians, i.e., as σαρκικοί. This passage clearly seems to fit the basic sense of σάρξ that we have advocated.[5]

The same understanding of σάρξ as applying to the Christians' previous lives as non-Christians is also found in *Rom 13:11-14*. This passage is within the paraenetic portion of Romans (12:1-15:13) and is a straightforward exhortation to the Romans not to return to their former immoral pattern of behavior. Paul's conclusion to this exhortation is in v. 14: ἀλλὰ ἐνδύσασθε τὸν κύριον Ἰησοῦν Χριστὸν καὶ τῆς σαρκὸς πρόνοιαν μὴ ποιεῖσθε εἰς ἐπιθυμίας. The key point to note in this passage is that the focus in on *the lust* of the σάρξ, not on the σάρξ itself. Paul uses εἰς with ἐπιθυμίας in the sense of "with reference or respect to" (BAGD 230, #5) as he exhorts about making provisions in regard to these passions. Rather than clarifying that Christians have a part of themselves that is termed σάρξ, Paul is instead warning that the Christians should avoid creating opportunities for the ἐπιθυμίας associated with the σάρξ that are still a part of their experience. This is the defensive side of the offensive action that Paul has already exhorted the Roman Christians to take against these resident ἐπιθυμίας in their bodies in Rom 6:12-14 and 8:12-14. *This fits Paul's general pattern of exhorting Christians to deal with the ongoing manifestations of the σάρξ, rather than battling against the σάρξ itself.* But this observation anticipates the conclusion of the following analysis.

Ephesians 2:1-3 is one of Paul's descriptions of the depth of human sinfulness that precedes one of his descriptions of the depth of God's mercy and grace (2:4-10). In particular in 2:1-2 he speaks in the second person plural of "you" (the Gentiles) being morally dead in "your" sins and walking according to the satanic rule of this world. Some anti-Judaistic sentiment comes to bear in a left-handed way in Eph 2:3 when Paul switches to the first person plural and includes himself and the Jewish people in this universal sinfulness (καὶ ἡμεῖς πάντες = "we too all"): "Among them we too all formerly walked in the lusts of our flesh, indulging the desires of the flesh and of the mind, and were by nature children of wrath, even as the rest." Long ago Calvin noted this inclusion:

> Lest he should seem to slander the former character of the Ephesians, or as a Jew to despise the Gentiles, he associates himself and his race with them. This is not said in hypocrisy, but in a sincere confession of glory to God. Yet it may seem strange that he should admit that he had walked in the lusts of the flesh, when on other occasions he claims that his life had been throughout irreproachable. I reply, this applies to all who have not yet been regenerated by the Spirit of Christ. However praiseworthy in appearance the life of some may be because their lusts do not break out in the sight of men, there is nothing pure or incorrupt save from the fountain of all purity (Calvin [1556] 1965, 141).

This specific reference of σάρξ to the Jewish people parallels the interpretation advocated in this monograph that Gal 5:19-21 is a description of life within the community of Israel. Paul's stark description in Eph 2:3 would make this understanding of Gal 5:19-21 quite reasonable. However, given the very subtle confrontation with Judaistic sentiments that Eph 2:3 represents and the non-Judaistic context of Ephesians in general, the two references to σάρξ in this verse should probably be understood in the more general sense of human frailty and transitoriness without the additional sense of the

bodily distinction of circumcision and the constraint of Torah. This
would follow the pattern that has been emerging in Paul's use of σάρξ
in non-Judaistic contexts. It simply refers to the former mode of
existence of Christians (ποτε), whether they were Gentiles or Jews (ώς
καὶ οἱ λοιποί in Eph 2:3c). Paul goes on to say in Eph 2:11-22 that
the fleshly distinction between Gentiles and Jews due to circumcision
(2:11-12) has been abolished in Christ Jesus' σάρξ (2:13-17). This has
given access ἐν ἑνὶ πνεύματι through Him (2:18) and has included
Gentiles ("you") in the habitation of God ἐν πνεύματι (2:22). While
his use is more subtle than in Galatians, it is clear, nevertheless, that
Paul uses σάρξ and πνεῦμα in a redemptive historical sense in Eph 2.[6]

Another non-Judaistic passage is *Colossians 2:6-23*. However, like
Eph 2:3, this passage also has Jewish elements within it. This is due
to the generally accepted view that the threat of a proto-gnosticism
with some syncretized Jewish practices was being addressed in
Colossians. Since this was not a specific Judaistic threat that
emphasized "the covenant in the flesh," the four occurrences of σάρξ
in 2:11, 13, 18 and 23 should be understood in the more general sense
of bodies that are frail and transitory and that are not indwelt by God's
Spirit. Again also, σάρξ is used solo apart from being in antithesis
with πνεῦμα. These four uses conform to the usage of σάρξ in the
previous three passages in referring to the bodily state of non-
Christians before coming to know Christ:

Col 2:11 emphasizes the true circumcision of τοῦ σώματος τῆς
σαρκός, which is without hands in Christ.

Col 2:13 contrasts the former state of death in παραπτώμασιν and
in the uncircumcision τῆς σαρκὸς with the present state of life with
Christ.

Col 2:18 warns that those deceiving the Colossians are ones who
are vainly puffed up by the alleged authority of the working of their
νοὸς σαρκός rather than by submitting to Christ.

Col 2:23 ironically concludes that all of the anachronistic, overly-
harsh ascetic practices which are the work of men (2:22) never
adequately restrained the sinful satisfaction of τῆς σαρκός, which
only being in Christ can do (3:1-11).

The combined effect of these four uses of σάρξ is one that
emphasizes the helplessness (2:11, 13) and wrong-headedness (2:18,
23) of human life apart from the redeeming work of Christ. If the

former state is not adequately acknowledged, then the latter state is greatly heightened.

In light of this general effect, one more specific point can be made. In Col 2:11 Paul uses the seemingly redundant expression "in the putting of τοῦ σώματος τῆς σαρκός" in parallelism to "in the circumcision of Christ." Following many commentators (e.g., Calvin [1556] 1965, 332), translations like the NIV translate the first phrase as "in the putting off of the sinful nature." However many problems such a translation has, the most obvious one is that it ignores the presence of τοῦ σώματος in the translation, i.e., unless one wants to admit that "the sinful nature" has a body!

A far better contextual solution seems to be the recognition that Paul is using a play on words with σάρξ and its role in circumcision. Apparently the troublers in Colossae were advocating the use of circumcision to provide some kind of cleansing from the alleged innate bodily defilement. This obviously involved the putting off or removal of part of the σάρξ--the frail and temporary human body. Paul ironically overwhelms such a theology with the truth that, in Christ, the entire σῶμα of the σάρξ has been put off in the spiritual circumcision of Christ. The aorist participle συνταφέντες that begins the next verse (2:12) explains that this removal of *the entire body of human frailty* is what was buried with Christ in baptism so that the new body of resurrection life might replace it (e.g., 2:12b-15; cf. Rom 6:1-11). Therefore, Paul can speak of the death of the members of their earthly bodies to various sins in Col 3:5-11 because the former bodily condition of frailty and sin-dominance has ended (2:20) and their lives are now raised up to newness with Christ (3:1-4). It seems that Paul has simply used the rhetoric and terminology of the threatening group (again!) and has turned it on its head to refute it. However, this suggestion demands significant further study.

The fifth and final set of non-Judaistic uses is in *2 Corinthians 1:17, 5:16, 10:2-4, and 11:18*. In these passages Paul appears to use σάρξ and its derivations (e.g., σαρκικά in 10:4) in the general sense of "what is merely human" (i.e., bodily weak, frail, transitory, and only human, not God-like). Additionally, there is a redemptive historical sense to the first three passages, as this brief survey reveals:[7]

> *2 Cor 1:17*   Paul rhetorically asks if he purposes "according to the flesh" (ἢ ἃ βουλεύομαι κατὰ σάρκα βουλεύομαι) with the vacillations that go with such frail choices. In 1:21-22 he contrasts this weak human purposing with the establishing and authorizing he and his companions actually have in Christ through the authoritative anointing of the Holy Spirit. Therefore, this σάρξ/πνεῦμα contrast

in this opening use of σάρξ creates a redemptive historical backdrop for understanding Paul's further use of σάρξ in the epistle.

2 Cor 5:16 The pivotal event that ends knowing persons according to the flesh (ἀπὸ τοῦ νῦν οὐδένα οἴδαμεν κατὰ σάρκα) is the death and resurrection of Christ in vv. 14-15. Additionally, Christ Himself cannot be known κατὰ σάρκα any longer (v. 16b) because of the age-changing significance of His death and resurrection for His identity. The redemptive historical significance of the ending of the κατὰ σάρκα-perspective also applies to any person who is ἐν Χριστῷ in v. 17, because he or she is a new creation and now also shares in the universal ministry of reconciling the world to God (vv. 18-21). Clearly σάρξ has a strong redemptive historical dimension in this passage (cf. Ridderbos 1975, 64-68).

2 Cor 10:2-4 The redemptive historical significance of the ending of the κατὰ σάρκα-way-of-life for those in Christ is applied to the realm of spiritual warfare in this passage. Paul uses a word-play with σάρξ in this passage to make this point against some who regard Paul and his companions ὡς κατὰ σάρκα περιπατοῦντας (v.2). He clarifies via the word-play in v. 3 that although he and his companions *do walk* ἐν σαρκί, they *do not war* κατὰ σάρκα (v. 3b) with weapons that are σαρκικά (v. 4a). Rather, their weapons are "divinely powerful" (v. 4b, δυνατὰ τῷ θεῷ = an intensive dative) so that they can destroy the spiritual strategies against the knowledge of God (vv. 5-6). All of this is necessary for Paul to fulfill his apostolic calling of preaching the gospel to the unreached regions (vv. 7-18).

2 Cor 11:18 This passage does not have the level of significance of the previous three because it appears to be a more casual use of σάρξ. Here Paul speaks of boasting κατὰ σάρκα like many of those who have done so to the Corinthian Church. He goes on to detail his Jewish pedigree (v. 22) and his suffering for Christ (vv. 23-29). The emphasis in both explanations is on Paul's *bodily condition*, and this points to more of a bodily sense for σάρξ in v. 18.

Summary: The five non-Judaistic Pauline passages where σάρξ has ethical or moral significance reveal that such significance appears to be rooted in a redemptive historical perspective that the σάρξ/πνεῦμα antithesis represents or that σάρξ alone can signify. The sense of σάρξ within this perspective is that it is *what is merely human* because it is before or apart from the aeon-shattering work of Jesus Christ's death and resurrection and the giving of the Holy Spirit to God's people that followed. This previous way of life is ἐν σαρκί because it is lived in frail, transitory bodies that are under the dominion of sin, even for the

Jews (Eph 2:3). However, this frail condition ended for those in Christ when this bodily condition was put off by the circumcision in Christ (Col 2:11-13) and the Holy Spirit was given (1 Cor 2:15-3:3). Therefore, a whole new pattern of life has opened up to those who are in Christ and they should walk in it (Rom 13:11-14; 2 Cor 5:16; 10:2-4; 1 Cor 3:1-3).

B. The SARX/PNEUMA Antithesis in Judaistic Passages

Only two passages cleanly fit within this category: Philippians 3:3-4 and Romans 7-8. Both can be dealt with only suggestively because of the constraints of this survey.

Philippians 3:3-4 is clearly a discussion of a Judaistic threat of some sort in Philippi. Σάρξ occurs once in v. 3 and twice in v. 4 within this specified context. Paul had used σάρξ previously in Phil 1:22 and 1:24 as a synonym for his σῶμα (1:20). However, his ironic and alliterated tripartite warning against the Judaizers in Phil 3:2 signals a very specific and different setting than that of the previous uses: βλέπετε τοὺς κύνας ("dogs"), βλέπετε τοὺς κακοὺς ἐργάτας ("evil workers"), βλέπετε τὴν κατατομήν ("mutilation"). Again, Paul appropriates the emphases of his opponents, in this case circumcision, and shows how this concern or need has been superabundantly met in Christ: (3:3) ἡμεῖς γὰρ ἐσμεν ἡ περιτομή, οἱ πνεύματι θεοῦ λατρεύοντες καὶ καυχώμενοι ἐν Χριστῷ Ἰησοῦ καὶ οὐκ ἐν σαρκὶ πεποιθότες.

Here we again encounter the classic σάρξ/πνεῦμα antithesis and the more specified sense of σάρξ as "what is merely human *and* distinctively Jewish." This is clear contextually because of Paul's explanation in vv. 4-6 of the last phrase in v. 3, καὶ οὐκ ἐν σαρκὶ πεποίθησιν. The connective καίπερ ("although") and the repetition of πεποίθησιν and πεποιθέναι in v. 4 explain that "putting confidence in the flesh" is putting confidence in *circumcised flesh* and in the yoke of Torah (vv. 5-6). Therefore, the contrast in v. 3 between "worshipping in the Spirit of God and boasting in Christ" and "having had no confidence εην σαρκί" is a redemptive historical contrast between two historically successive means of forming the people of God. The Judaizers' appeal to the σάρξ is an anachronistic and inadequate appeal in light of Jesus Christ's death and resurrection (vv. 7-11).

This follows the same apocalyptic pattern of reasoning that we encountered in Galatians, only not in as overt, nor developed a form, as is befitting the lesser threat level in Philippi. Additionally, the Galatian pattern of the discussion of the *true identity* of the people of

God followed by the discussion of their *correct pattern of behavior* seems to be followed in Phil 3:1-11 and 3:12-21, respectively.[8] Therefore, the specified view of σάρξ within Judaistic contexts seems to be validated by Paul's use in Phil 3:3-4.

The second passage where Paul uses σάρξ in a Judaistic context is *Romans 7-8.*[9] The Judaistic nature of this context is determined by three major indicators at the beginning of the passage:

> 1.) The vocative address of ἀδελφοί in Rom 7:1 is specified with the explanatory phrase γινώσκουσιν γὰρ νόμον λαλῶ. These "brothers" are described partitively from the rest of the Roman Church by their knowledge of Torah. They are the *Jewish Christians* within the Roman Church.
> 2.) The topic is *Torah*, not Roman Law or law in general, because the specific example of vv. 2-3 was a debated point of Torah We know this because the Jewish Law had this immediate death provision and Roman Law did not, and because almost all of the previous forty uses of νόμος in Romans refer to Torah, not the law principle.
> 3.) The newness/oldness and Spirit/letter contrasts of Rom 7:6 clarify the intent of the marriage illustration of 7:1-5 because these contrasts are clear Pauline references to the New Covenant and Mosaic Covenants, respectively (cf. 2 Cor 3:1-11). Therefore, the contrast that is introduced in Rom 7:1-6 is the redemptive historical movement from the Mosaic Covenant to the New Covenant and the ramifications of this movement for the role of Torah in the lives of these Jewish Christians (e.g., 7:4).

Rom 8:1-17 continues this same contrast between the Law and the Spirit, only expanding the νόμος-side of the contrast with its familiar tandem member σάρξ, which had already been added in 7:5. Therefore, Rom 7:1-6 and 8:1-17 are both passages that speak of the progression from the flesh/Law era to the Spirit/Christ era, with special reference to the ramifications of this redemptive historical progression to the present role of Torah. This bracketing effect with 7:1-6 and 8:1-17 leads to an important structural observation about Rom 7:7-25 and the discussion about Torah and flesh contained in it: this discussion must be read within a redemptive historical light and the redemptive historical significance with which Paul enriches σάρξ in these types of Judaistic contexts must be heavily weighted.

Additionally, Paul's clear and overt temporal statements in these bracketing passages about the *former era* of σάρξ must be adequately weighted:

7:5a   ὅτε γὰρ ἦμεν ἐν τῇ σαρκί,.....("For when we *were* in the
                                              flesh")[10]
7:6a   νυνὶ δὲ κατηργήθημεν ἀπὸ τοῦ νόμου ἀποθανόντες ἐν ᾧ
       κατειχόμεθα,.....("But *now* we were released from the Law
                                    because we died [to that] by which we
                                    were being confined")

To be ἐν τῇ σαρκί in 7:5a is the same as being ὑπὸ νόμον in 7:6a.
Again, we encounter Paul's familiar tandem of σάρξ and νόμος as a
twofold reference to the past redemptive historical era of the Mosaic
Law. This era for God's people has been historically succeeded by the
era of the πνεῦμα, as Paul baldly declares in Rom 8: 9:

ὑμεῖς δὲ οὐκ ἐστὲ ἐν σαρκὶ ἀλλὰ ἐν πνεύματι, εἴπερ πνεῦμα
θεοῦ οἰκεῖ ἐν ὑμῖν. Εἰ δέ τις πνεῦμα Χριστοῦ οὐκ ἔχει,
οὗτος οὐκ ἔστιν αὐτοῦ.
("But you are *not in the flesh*, but *in the Spirit*, since the Spirit of
God dwells in you. And if anyone does not have the Spirit of
Christ, this person does not belong to Him.")

Therefore, the two references to σάρξ in Rom 7:18 and 7:25 and
the one reference to σάρκινός in 7:14 must be viewed within this very
clear and overt redemptive historical argumentation that Paul initiates
in 7:1. Within this type of antithetical argumentation, the absence of
any mention of πνεῦμα until Rom 8:2 is also significant. This is
Paul's first use of πνεῦμα since 7:6. The occurrence in 8:2 is
significant because it follows the logical and temporal contrast of 8:1:
Οὐδὲν ἄρα νῦν κατάκριμα τοῖς ἐν Χριστῷ. ("There is therefore *now*
no condemnation for those in Christ Jesus.") This absence of
condemnation "in Christ Jesus" is then explained by Paul in 8:2-17 in
contrast to being "under the Law" (8:2-4) and "in the flesh" (8:3-9, 12-
13). The clear thrust of Paul's argument is that the redemptive
historical era of νόμος/σάρξ has been superseded by the redemptive
historical era of Χριστός/πνεῦμα. The sense of condemnation that is
described in Rom 7:15-24 is therefore that which *previously occurred
during the era of the Mosaic Law*. In other words there was in the
past a sense of the condemnation of sin for those *in Moses* that is in
the present now absent for those *in Christ*.

Moreover, when Paul begins his discussion of the possible
sinfulness of the Mosaic Law with the rhetorical question of 7:7 ("Is
the Law sin?"), he is initiating a very sensitive and lengthy
explanation (7:7-25) of life under the "oldness of the letter" in 7:6c.
Such a discussion might reinforce the already negative conclusion that
the Jewish Christians in Rome might have reached about his view of
Torah. This is in light of his previous argumentation about God's
people no longer being ὑπὸ νόμον (e.g., 6:14), coupled with a

slanderous report that had preceded his epistle (Rom 3:8). Therefore, in Rom 7:7-25 Paul argues that the Law is holy, righteous, and good (7:12). However, he also argues that Torah is *inadequate* as a means of totally constraining bodily behavior because of the pervasive dominion of sin over its subjects. This very fervent exposition of the Mosaic Law's *inadequacy* in 7:7-25 comes on the heels of Paul's point about the *inappropriateness* of living as if the deceased husband of Torah is still alive in 7:1-6. Both of these points are directed toward "those who know Torah" within the Roman Church (7:1). All of this is to say that Romans 7 is Paul's rejection of the Mosaic Law as the means of constraint for Christians because it is both *inappropriate* in the era of the Spirit, since it was a former mate, and it is *inadequate* as such a constraint, since God did not design Torah to conquer σάρξ.

Therefore, Paul's first person narrative of the coming of the Law to Israel at Mt. Sinai in 7:7-13[11] is followed by his first person narrative of the diagnostic and condemning function of the Law throughout Israel's post-Sinai history in 7:14-25. The rhetorical or literary use of the first person has long since been recognized since Kümmel's monograph in 1929 and is most appropriate within such an inflammatory context for several reasons.[12] However, the redemptive historical argumentation of Romans 7 has been recognized only sporadically.[13] This may be due in part to the main hermeneutical question used to address Romans 7: "Is Paul describing a Christian or a non-Christian?" Such a question has tended to frame the discussion of this passage in a manner that is not particularly conducive to a redemptive historical understanding.

However, if Paul's argumentation is viewed apart from this main hermeneutical question and through a redemptive historical lens (which appears to be more appropriate in this context), then he is probably describing neither a Christian or non-Christian. Rather, he is describing *the pious Israelite during the Mosaic Law era* who struggled with the diagnostic and condemning work of Torah because he or she was still ἐν σαρκί, i.e., in a body distinguished by circumcision and constrained by Torah, yet still under sin's dominion and not indwelt by God's πνεῦμα (7:14). This condition led to a unique state of wretchedness for the believing Israelite (7:24) that is now removed only in Christ Jesus (8:1) through His death, burial, and resurrection (6:3-11; 8:2-11).[14]

Therefore, the Jewish Christians in Rome should learn from their shared Israelite history with Paul about the proper and limited function of Torah during the era of the σάρξ. This was a past era that they were in and Torah was a necessary corollary of that era (7:5).

However, they must not try to impose Torah upon the Gentile Christians in Rome as a proper constraint for their behavior in the new era of the Spirit (7:6). Within this specific historical and polemical Judaistic context, σάρξ takes on the more specified sense of "what is mere human *and* distinctively Jewish." Such an insight adds great significance to Paul's statements about being σάρκινός in 7:14, about nothing good dwelling ἐν τῇ σαρκὶ μου in 7:18, and about serving the law of sin τῇ σαρκί in 7:25. Rather than being general anthropological statements, these are more likely polemical statements against the efficacy of circumcision and Torah-keeping in constraining bodily behavior. This is why Paul clearly explains the *appropriate* and *adequate* means of constraining bodily behavior through the person of the Spirit. He explains the New Covenant ministry of the Spirit in terms of fulfilling Torah and in contrast to attempting to do so in a Judaistic manner in 8:2-4. In an echo of Gal 5:13-14, Paul culminates his explanation in Rom 8:4: ἵνα τὸ δικαίωμα τοῦ νόμου πληρωθῇ ἐν ἡμῖν τοῖς μὴ κατὰ σάρκα περιπατοῦσιν ἀλλὰ κατὰ πνεῦμα.

The contrast between those who walk κατὰ σάρκα and those who walk κατὰ πνεῦμα is then expanded in 8:5-8 in language reminiscent of Gal 5:16-25. This contrast is not simply a contrast between non-Christians and Christians. Rather, the issue is what one would suspect within a Judaistic context: "How do you please God, keep His law, and have life and peace?" Paul's answer to each aspect is to walk κατὰ πνεῦμα not κατὰ σάρκα. He then clarifies in various ways in 8:9-17 the distinctions of life κατὰ πνεῦμα. Particularly noteworthy is his clarification of the Roman Christians' life within the πνεῦμα, not within the σάρξ, in 8:9 and his definition of υἱοὶ θεοῦ in 8:14: "For all who are being led by the Spirit of God, these are sons of God." Such a clarification has meaning only within a context where the definition of "sons of God" is being debated. Paul elaborates this clarification of 8:14 in 8:15-17 with reasoning that parallels his argumentation in Gal 3:1-14 where the possession of the Spirit confirms the Christians' true sonship as children of God.

Summary: After this cursory and suggestive treatment of Philippians 3 and Romans 7-8, there appears to be enough evidence to validate the more specific sense of σάρξ as "what is merely human and what is distinctively Jewish." This appears to be the enriched sense of σάρξ which flowed out of the polemical interaction with Judaistic or Pharisaic Christians within passages such as these and Galatians 3-6. Of course, this can be definitively confirmed only after much more exhaustive exegetical study of these corollary passages. Such study lies beyond the parameters of this study. However, the brief glimpse of these passages that was taken seems to point to the existence of ample evidence to validate the central thesis of this book. This thesis is that σάρξ has a redemptive historical sense in passages historically considered "ethical uses" of σάρξ and Paul's conception of the σάρξ/πνεῦμα antithesis is one of external historical eras rather than one of internal anthropological natures. A reading of all of these passages, both non-Judaistic and Judaistic, that is more doggedly consistent with Paul's world view and with the specific concerns of each historical setting should surely validate this understanding.

Notes

[1]The brief discussion of Gal 2:15-21 by Erich Stauffer in *TDNT* 2:257-58 in his article on ἐγώ is remarkable and incisive. He concludes his remarks on this passage with this statement:

> At this point Paul has to use I rather than We because he sees more plainly and acts more consistently than Peter. He thus draws the conclusion in an I sentence: οὐκ ἀθετῶ τὴν χάριν τοῦ θεοῦ. Nevertheless, this is not because we have here his own private concern or personal way. It is rather that he takes seriously the situation of salvation history which must be expressed in his life, and has taken a way which Peter and the rest must also tread. He has made the break and taken the step as a τύπος who summons to μίμησις. The sketch of salvation history in Galatians is further developed by Paul in Romans (357-58).

See also Fee 1994b for the same perspective. Cf. Lambrecht 1977-78.

[2]The πνεῦμα side of the antithesis is implied in 5:13-15.

[3]There is an obvious circularity here between a term and its context that cannot be avoided in anyone's interpretation, but that can only be validated in the careful exegesis of the passage.

[4]In some of the lists of the "ethical or moral uses" of σάρξ, more passages are listed within this category (e.g., Ladd 1974, 469; Davies 1957, 163; Burton 1918, 186; Robinson 1926, 113-18; Stacey 1956, 158-64; and Robinson 1952, 22-26). In particular, there are two additional passages that occur in some of the lists: 1 Cor 5:5 and 2 Cor 7:1. In both of these passages, σάρξ simply seems to be used synonymously for σῶμα, and are not therefore pertinent to the present discussion. However, this identification is debated in 1 Cor 5:5 (e.g., NIV translates σάρξ with "the sinful nature"; cf. Thiselton 1973 and Campbell 1993).

[5]Also arguing this perspective is Fee 1994b, 820.

[6]When translations like the NIV translate σάρξ in Eph 2:3 with "sinful nature," they destroy any hope of grasping Paul's redemptive historical point in Eph 2 about the ending of the era of the σάρξ and the beginning of the era of the πνεῦμα for God's people.

[7]See Fee 1994b, 820-1 for the same understanding.

[8]Silva 1988, 207-12 for a defense of the view taken in this paper that Judaizers may still be in view in Phil 3:17-19.

[9]For a fuller discussion of Romans 7, see Russell 1994.

[10]This translation and emphasis and the following ones are mine.

[11]Of those holding this view, see Moo 1986 and Wright 1991, 196-200.

[12]For example, Stowers 1995 identifies Paul's rhetorical and literary technique in Rom 7:7-25 as a "speech-in-character" that represents not himself, but another person or type of character. In this passage, Stowers suggests the character represented is that of a Gentile God-fearer.

[13]See Moo 1986, 130, note 4 for a list of nine advocates. Cf. Karlberg 1986. For a recent defense, see Seifrid 1992.

[14]See Wright 1991, 196-200 for a similar conclusion.

Works Cited

Abrahams, I. 1967. *Studies in Pharisaism and the Gospels. First and Second Series.* Cambridge: Cambridge University Press, 1917, 1924; reprint, New York: KTAV Publishing House (page references are to reprint edition).

Achtemeier, Paul J. 1990. *Omne Verbum Sonat*: The New Testament and the Oral Environment of Late Western Antiquity. *JBL* 109:3-27.

Aland, K, ed. 1980. *Vollstandige Konkordanz zum griechischen Neuen Testament.* Berlin & New York: Walter de Gruyter.

Aletti, Jean-Noël. 1992. La *Dispositio* Rhétorique dans les Épîtres Pauliniennes. Proposition de Méthod. *NTS* 38:385-401.

Allison, Dale C., Jr. 1992. Peter and Cephas: One and the Same. *JBL* 111:489-95.

Allo, Ernest Bernard. 1934. Le défaut d' éloquence et de 'style oral' de Saint Paul. *RSPT* 23:29-39.

Arichea, Daniel C., and Eugene A. Nida. 1976. *A Translators Handbook on Paul's Letter to the Galatians.* Helps for Translators Series. New York: United Bible Societies.

Aristotle. 1926. *The "Art" of Rhetoric.* Translated by John Henry Freese. Loeb Classical Library, Aristotle vol. 22, no. 193. Cambridge: Harvard University Press.

Arnold, Clinton E. 1996. Returning to the Domain of the Powers: *Stoicheia* as Evil Spirits in Galatians 4:3, 9. *NovT* 38:55-76.

Arzt, Peter. 1994. The"Epistolary Introductory Thanksgiving" in the Papyri and in Paul. *NovT* 36:29-46.

Aune, David E. 1984. Review of *Galatians--Dialogical Response to Opponents. CBQ* 46:145-47.

Aus, R. D. 1979. Three Pillars and Three Patriarchs: A Proposal concerning Gal 2:9. *ZNW* 70:252-61.

Baarda, T. 1992. TI ETI ΔIΩKOMAI in Gal. 5:11. *Apodosis* or *Parenthesis*? *NovT* 34:250-6.

Baasland, Ernst. 1984. Persecution: A Neglected Feature in the Letter to the Galatians. *ST* 38:135-50.

Bachmann, H. and W. A. Slaby, eds. 1985. *Computer-Konkordanz zum Novum Testamentum Graece.* 2nd ed. Berlin & New York: Walter de Gruyter.

Bamberger, Bernard J. 1968. *Proselytism in the Talmudic Period.* Cincinnati: Hebrew Union College Press, 1939; reprint, New York: Ktav Publishing House (page references are to reprint edition).

Barclay, John M. G. 1987. Mirror-Reading a Polemical Letter: Galatians as a Test Case. *JSNT* 31:73-93.

_____. 1988. *Obeying the Truth: A Study of Paul's Ethics in Galatians.* Studies of the New Testament and Its World, ed. John Riches. Edinburgh: T & T Clark.

_____. 1995. Paul among Diaspora Jews: Anomaly or Apostate? *JSNT* 60:89-120.

Barclay, William. 1962. *Flesh and Spirit: An Examination of Galatians 5:19-23.* London: SCM Press, Ltd.

Barrett, C. K. 1953. Paul and the "Pillar" Apostles. In *Studia Paulina. In Honorem Johannis de Zwaan Septuagenarii.* Haarlem: De Erven F. Bohn N. V.

_____. 1980. Galatians as an "Apologetic Letter." *Int* 34:414-17.

_____. 1982. The Allegory of Abraham, Sarah, and Hagar in the Argument of Galatians. Chap. in *Essays on Paul.* Philadelphia: Westminster Press.

_____. 1985. *Freedom and Obligation: A Study of the Epistle to the Galatians*. Philadelphia: Westminster Press.

_____. 1986. Boasting (καυχᾶσθαι, ktl.) in the Pauline Epistles. In *L'Apotre Paul*, ed. A. Vanhoye, 363-68. Bibliotheca Ephemeridum Theologicarum Lovaniensium 73. Leuven: Peeters/Leuven University Press.

Barth, Markus. 1968. Jews and Gentiles: The Social Character of Justification in Paul. *JES* 5:241-67.

Bauckham, Richard. 1979. Barnabas in Galatians. *JSNT* 2:61-70.

Bauer, Walter. 1979. *A Greek-English Lexicon of the New Testament and Other Early Christian Literature*. Translated and adapted by William F. Arndt and F. Wilbur Gingrich. 2nd ed. edited by Frederick Danker. Chicago: The University of Chicago Press.

Baur, Ferdinand C. 1875a. *Paul, His Life and Works*. 2 vols. Translated by E. Zeller. London: Williams and Norgate.

_____. 1875b. *The Church History of the First Three Centuries*, Vol. 1. Translated by Allan Menzies. London: Willliams and Norgate.

_____. 1963. *Auswewahlte Werke in Einzelausgaben*. Vol. 1. Edited by K. Scholder. Stuttgart: Frommann.

Beker, J. Christiaan. 1980. *Paul the Apostle. The Triumph of God in Life and Thought*. Philadelphia: Fortress Press.

_____. 1988. Paul's Theology: Consistent or Inconsistent? *NTS* 34:364-77.

_____. 1989. Paul the Theologian. Major Motifs in Pauline Theology. *Int* 43:352-65.

Bellah, Robert N., Richard Madsen, William M. Sullivan, Ann Swidler, and Steven M. Tipton. 1985. *Habits of the Heart. Individualism and Commitment in American Life*. New York: Harper & Row.

Berger, Klaus. 1980. Die impliziten Gegner. Zur Methode des Erschliessens von "Gegnern" in neutestamentlichen Texten. In *Kirche. Festschrift für Günther Bornkamm zum 75. Geburtstag*, Hrsg. D. Lührmann und G. Strecker, 373-400. Tübingen: J. C. B. Mohr.

Best, Thomas F. 1983. The Sociological Study of the New Testament: Promise and Peril of a New Discipline. *SJT* 36:181-94.

Betz, Hans Dieter. 1973. 2 Cor 6:14-7:1: An Anti-Pauline Fragment? *JBL* 92:88-108.

_____. 1974. Spirit, Freedom, and Law: Paul's Message to the Galatian Churches. *SEÅ* 39:145-60.

_____. 1975. The Literary Composition and Function of Paul's Letter to the Galatians. *NTS* 21:353-79.

_____. 1976. In Defense of the Spirit: Paul's Letter to the Galatians as a Document of Early Christian Apologetics. In *Aspects of Religious Propaganda in Judaism and Early Christianity*, ed. Elisabeth Schussler-Fiorenza, 99-114. University of Notre Dame Center for the Study of Judaism and Christianity in Antiquity 2. Notre Dame: University of Notre Dame Press.

_____. 1979. *Galatians: A Commentary on Paul's Letter to the Churches in Galatia*. Hermeneia--A Critical and Historical Commentary on the Bible. Philadelphia: Fortress Press.

_____. 1986. The Problem of Rhetoric and Theology According to the Apostle Paul. In *L'Apotre Paul*, ed. A. Vanhoye, 16-48. Bibliotheca Ephemeridum Theologicarum Lovaniensium 73. Leuven: Peeters/Leuven University Press.

_____. 1987. *Der Galaterbrief, Ein Kommentar zum Brief des Apostels Paulus an die Gemeinden in Galatien*. München: Kaiser.

Bitzer, Lloyd. 1968. The Rhetorical Situation. *Philosophy and Rhetoric* 1:1-14.

Blackman, Philip, ed. and trans. 1977. *Mishnavoth*. 7 vols. 2d ed. New York: Judaica Press.

Blass, F. and A. Debrunner. 1961. *A Greek Grammar of the New Testament and Other Early Christian Literature*. Revised by A. Debrunner. Translated and edited by Robert W. Funk. Chicago: The University of Chicago Press.

Bligh, John. 1966. *Galatians in Greek: A Structural Analysis of St. Paul's Epistle to the Galatians with Notes on the Greek*. Detroit: University of Detroit Press.

_____. 1969. *Galatians: A Discussion of St. Paul's Epistle*. Householder Commentaries 1. London: St. Paul Press.

Boers, Hendrikus. 1994. *The Justification of the Gentiles. Paul's Letters to the Galatians and Romans*. Peabody, MA: Hendrickson Publishers.

Bonnard, Pierre. 1972. *L'Epitre de Saint Paul aux Galates*. 2nd ed. Commentaire du Nouveau Testament 9. Neuchatel and Paris: Delachaux & Niestle.

Borchert, Gerald L. 1994. A Key to Pauline Thinking--Galatians 3:23-29: Faith and New Humanity. *RevExp* 91:145-51.

Borgen, Peder. 1988. Catalogues of Vices, The Apostolic Decree, and the Jerusalem Meeting. In *The Social World of Formative Christianity and Judaism*, eds. Jacob Neusner, Peder Borgen, Ernest S. Frerichs, and Richard Horsley, 126-41. Philadelphia: Fortress Press.

Borse, Udo. 1970. Die Wundmale und der Todesbescheid. *BZ* 14:88-111.

Botha, Pieter. J. J. 1992. Greco-Roman Literacy as Setting for New Testament Writings. *Neot* 26:195-215.

_____. 1993. The Verbal Art of the Pauline Letters: Rhetoric, Performance and Presence. In *Rhetoric and the New Testament. Essays from the 1992 Heidelberg Conference*. JSNTSup 90. ed.

Stanley E. Porter and Thomas H. Olbricht, 409-28. Sheffield: Sheffield Academic Press.

Böttger, Paul G. 1991. Paulus und Petrus in Antiochien. Zum Verständnis von Galater 2.11-21. *NTS* 37:77-100.

Bouwman, Gijs. 1987. Die Hagar-und-Sara-Perikope (Gal 4,21-31)-- Exemplarische Interpretation zum Schriftbeweis bei Paulus. In *ANRW*, Teil 2: Principat, Band 25, 4. Teilband, ed.Wolfgang Haase, 3135-55.

Bowers, Paul. 1980. Paul and the Religious Propaganda in the First Century. *NovT* 22:316-23.

_____. 1991. Church and Mission in Paul. *JSNT* 44:89-111.

Brandenburger, Egon. 1968. *Fleisch und Geist: Paulus und die dualistische Weisheit.* Wissenschaftliche Mongraphien zum Alten und Neuen Testament 29. Neukirchen-Vluyn: Neukirchener Verlag.

Braswell, Joseph P. 1991. "The Blessing of Abraham" versus "the Curse of the Law": Another Look at Gal 3:10-13. *WTJ* 53:73-91.

Braude, William G. 1940. *Jewish Proselyting In the First Five Centuries of the Common Era--The Age of the Tannaim and Amoraim.* Providence: Brown University.

Brehm, H. Alan. 1994. Paul's Relationship with the Jerusalem Apostles in Galatians 1 and 2. *SWJT* 37:11-16.

Bring, Ragnar. 1961. *Commentary on Galatians.* Translated by Eric Wahlstrom. Philadelphia: Muhlenberg Press.

Brinsmead, Bernard H. 1982. *Galatians--Dialogical Response to Opponents.* SBLDS 65. Missoula: Scholars Press.

Brown, John. 1981. *An Exposition of the Epistle of Paul the Apostle to the Galatians.* Edinburgh: T & T Clark, 1853; reprint, Minneapolis: Klock & Klock Christian Publishers, Inc. (page references are to reprint edition).

Brown, Schuyler. 1989. Philology. In *The New Testament and Its Modern Interpreters*, eds. Eldon Jay Epp and George W. MacRae, 127-47. Philadelphia: Fortress Press and Atlanta: Scholars Press.

Bruce, F. F. 1975. Further Thoughts on Paul's Autobiography. In *Jesus und Paulus. Festschrift für Werner Georg Kümmel zum 70.Geburtstag*, Hrsg. E. Earle Ellis und Erich Grässer, 21-29. Göttingen: Vandenhoeck & Ruprecht.

_____. 1982. *The Epistle to the Galatians--A Commentary on the Greek Text*. The New International Greek Testament Commentary, eds. 1. Howard Marshall and W. Ward Gasque. Grand Rapids: William B. Eerdmans Publishing Company.

_____. 1984. "Called to Freedom": A Study in Galatians. In *The New Testament Age: Essays in Honor of Bo Reicke*, ed. William C. Weinrich, 1:61-71. Mercer: Mercer University Press.

_____. 1985a. The Spirit in the Letter to the Galatians. In *Essays on Apostolic Themes: Studies in Honor of Howard M. Ervin*, ed. Paul Elbert, 36-48. Peabody, MA: Hendrickson Publishers.

_____. 1985b. The Church of Jerusalem in the Acts of the Apostles. *BJRL* 67:641-61.

Bullinger, E. W. 1968. *Figures of Speech Used in the Bible Explained and Illustrated*. London: Messrs. Eyre and Spottiswoode, 1898; reprint, Grand Rapids: Baker Book House (page references are to reprint edition).

Bultmann, Rudolf. 1951. *Theology of the New Testament. Volume 1*. Translated by Kendrick Grobel. New York: Charles Scribner's Sons.

_____. 1955. *Theology of the New Testament, Volume 2*. Translated by Kendrick Grobel. New York: Charles Scribner's Sons.

Bundrick, David R. 1991. *TA STOICHEIA TOU KOSMOU* (Gal 4:3). *JETS* 34:353-64.

Burke, Trevor J. 1995. The Characteristics of Paul's Adoptive-Sonship (Huiothesia) Motif. *IBS* 17:62-74.

Burton, Ernest DeWitt. 1918. *Spirit, Soul. and Flesh: The Usages of Πνεῦμα, Ψυχή, and Σάρξ in Greek Writings and Translated Works from the Earliest Period to 180 A.D.; and of their Equivalents* רוּחַ נֶפֶשׁ, *and* בָּשָׂר *in the Hebrew Old Testament.* Historical and Linguistic Studies, Second Series, Vol. 3. Chicago: University of Chicago Press.

_____. 1921. *A Critical and Exegetical Commentary on the Epistle to the Galatians.* The International Critical Commentary. Edinburgh: T & T Clark.

Bynum, W. F., E. J. Browne, Roy Porter, eds. 1981. *Dictionary of the History of Science.* Princeton: Princeton University Press.

Byrne, Brendan. 1979. *"Sons of God"--"Seed of Abraham": A Study of the Sonship of God of All Christians in Paul against the Jewish Background.* Analecta Biblica 83. Rome: Biblical Institute Press.

Calvin, John. [1556] 1965. *The Epistles of Paul The Apostle to the Galatians, Ephesians. Philippians and Colossians.* Translated by T. H. L. Parker. Calvin's New Testament Commentaries 11, eds. David W. Torrance and Thomas F. Torrance. Grand Rapids: William B. Eerdmans Publishing Company.

_____. [1559] 1972. *Institutes of the Christian Religion.* Translated by Henry Beveridge. Edinburgh: Calvin Translation Society, 1845; reprint, Grand Rapids: William B. Eerdmans Publishing Company (page references are to reprint edition).

Campbell, Barth. 1993. Flesh and Spirit in 1 Cor 5:5: An Exercise in Rhetorical Criticism of the NT. *JETS* 36:331-42.

Campbell, D. A. 1992. The Meaning of ΠΙΣΤΙΣ and NOMOΣ in Paul: A Linguistic and Structural Perspective. *JBL* 111:91-103.

Caneday, Ardel. 1989. "Redeemed from the Curse of the Law" The Use of Deut 21:22-23 in Gal 3:13. *TrinJ* NS 10:185-209.

Catchpole, David R. 1976-77. Paul, James and the Apostolic Decree. *NTS* 23:428-44.

Cathcart, Robert. 1981. *Post Communication: Rhetorical Analysis and Evaluation.* 2nd ed. The Bobbs-Merrill Series in Speech Communication. Indianapolis: Bobbs-Merrill Educational Publishing.

Chilton, B. D. 1978. Galatians 6:15: A Call to Freedom before God. *ExpTim* 89:311-13.

Classen, von Carl Joachim. 1991. Paulus und die antike Rhetorik. *ZNTW* 82:1-33.

_____. 1993. St. Paul's Epistles and Ancient Greek and Roman Rhetoric. In *Rhetoric and the New Testament. Essays from the 1992 Heidelberg Conference.* JSNTSup 90. ed. Stanley E. Porter and Thomas H. Olbricht, 265-91. Sheffield: Sheffield Academic Press.

_____. 1995. Zur rhetorischen Analyse der Paulusbriefe. *ZNW* 86:120-1.

Cohen, Shaye J. D. 1983. Conversion to Judaism in Historical Perspective: From Biblical History to Postbiblical Judaism. *Conservative Judaism* 36:31-45.

Cohn-Sherbok, Daniel. 1982. Paul and Rabbinic Exegesis. *SJT* 35:117-32.

_____. 1983. Some Reflections on James Dunn's 'The Incident at Antioch (Gal. 2.11-18).' *JSNT* 18:68-74.

Cohon, Samuel S. 1987. Proselytism. Chap. in *Essays in Jewish Theology.* Cincinnati: Hebrew Union College Press.

Cole, R. Alan. 1989. *The Letter of Paul to the Galatians.* 2nd ed. Tyndale New Testament Commentaries 9. Grand Rapids: William B. Eerdmans Publishing Company.

Cook, David. 1992. The Prescript as Programme in Galatians. *JTS* 43:511-9.

Corbett, Edward P. J., ed. 1969. *Rhetorical Analyses of Literary Works*. New York: Oxford University Press.

_____. 1971. *Classical Rhetoric for the Modern Student*. 2nd ed. New York: Oxford University Press.

Cornelius, E. M. 1994. The Relevance of Ancient Rhetoric to Rhetorical Criticism. *Neot* 28:457-67.

Cosgrove, Charles H. 1987. The Law has given Sarah No Children (Gal. 4:21-30). *NovT* 29:219-35.

_____. 1988. *The Cross and the Spirit: A Study in the Argument and Theology of Galatians*. Mercer: Mercer Unniversity Press/Peeters.

Cousar, Charles B. 1989. Galatians 6:11-18: Interpretive Clues to the Letter. Unpublished SBL Pauline Seminar Paper.

Craffert, Pieter F. 1991. Towards an Interdisciplinary Definition of the Social-Scientific Interpretation of the New Testament. *Neot* 25:123- 44.

_____. 1992. More on Models and Muddles in the Social-Scientific Interpretation of the New Testament: The *Sociological Fallacy* Reconsidered. *Neot* 26:217-39.

_____. 1993. The Pauline Movement and First-Century Judaism: A Framework for Transforming the Issues. *Neot* 27:233-62.

_____. 1996. Relationships between Social-Scientific, Literary, and Rhetorical Interpretation of Texts. *BTB* 26:45-55.

Cranford, Lorin L. 1994. A Rhetorical Reading of Galatians. *SWJT* 37:4-10.

Cranford, Michael. 1994. The Possibility of Perfect Obedience: Paul and an Implied Premise in Galatians 3:10 and 5:3. *NovT* 36:242-58.

Cronjé, J. Van W. 1986. Defamiliarization in the Letter to the Galatians. In *A South African Perspective on the New Testament*, ed. J. H. Petzer and P. J. Hartin, 214-27. Leiden: E. J. Brill.

_____. 1992. The Stratagem of the Rhetorical Question in Galatians 4:9-10 as a Means towards Persuasion. *Neot* 26:417-24.

Crownfield, Frederick R. 1945. The Singular Problem of the Dual Galatians. *JBL* 64:491-500.

Dahl, Nils A. 1950. Der Name Israel: 1. Zur Auslegung von Gal. 6,16. *Judaica* 6:161-70.

_____. 1973. Paul's Letter to the Galatians: Epistolary Genre, Content, and Structure. Unpublished paper for the SBL Paul Seminar.

_____. 1977. Promise and Fulfillment. Chap. in *Studies in Paul: Theology for the Early Christian Mission*. Minneapolis: Augsburg Publishing House.

Daube, David. 1949. Rabbinic Methods of Interpretation and Hellenistic Rhetoric. *HUCA* 22:239-64.

_____. 1956. The Interpretation of a Generic Singular. Chap. in *The New Testament and Rabbinic Judaism*. London: The Athlone Press.

Davies, W. D. 1957. Paul and the Dead Sea Scrolls: Flesh and Spirit. In *The Scrolls and the New Testament*, ed. Krister Stendahl, 157-82. New York: Harper & Row.

_____. 1974. *The Gospel and the Land. Early Christianity and Jewish Territorial Doctrine*. Berkeley: University of California Press.

_____. 1980. *Paul and Rabbinic Judaism*. 4th ed. Philadelphia: Fortress Press.

_____. 1984. *Jewish and Pauline Studies*. Philadelphia: Fortress Press.

Dewey, Joanna. 1995. Textuality in An Oral Culture: A Survey of the Pauline Traditions. *Semeia* 65:37-65.

Dickson, William P. 1883. *St. Paul's Use of the Terms Flesh and Spirit*. Glasgow: James Maclehose & Sons.

Dodd, Charles H. 1953. The Mind of Paul: 1. Chap. in *New Testament Studies*. Manchester: Manchester University Press.

_____. 1968. Ἔννομδ Χριστοῦ. Chap. in *More New Testament Studies*. Manchester: Manchester University Press. Previously published in *Studia Paulina. In Honorem Johannis de Zwaan Septugenarii*. Haarlem: De Erven F. Bohn N. V., 1953.

Domeris, W. R. 1993. Honour and Shame in the New Testament. *Neot* 27:283-97.

Donaldson, Terence L. 1994. 'The Gospel That I Proclaim among the Gentiles' (Gal. 2.2): Universalistic or Israel-Centred? In *Gospel in Paul. Studies on Corinthians, Galatians and Romans for Richard N. Longenecker*. JSNTSup 108. eds. L. Ann Jervis and Peter Richardson, 166-93. Sheffield: Sheffield Academic Press.

Douglas, Mary. 1966. *Purity and Danger. An Analysis of Concepts of Pollution and Taboo*. New York: Frederick A. Praeger, Publishers.

_____. 1973. *Natural Symbols: Explorations in Cosmology*. New York: Pantheon Books, 1970; reprint, New York: Vintage Books (page references are to reprint edition).

Drane, John W. 1975. *Paul: Libertine or Legalist?* London: SPCK.

Duncan, George S. 1934. *The Epistle of Paul to the Galatians*. The Moffatt New Testament Commentary. London: Hodder Stoughton.

Dunn, James D. G. 1982. The Relationship between Paul and Jerusalem according to Galatians 1 and 2. *NTS* 28:461-78. See additional note in the reprint by the author in *Jesus, Paul and the Law. Studies in Mark and Galatians*, 126-8. Louisville, KY: Westminster/John Knox Press, 1990.

_____. 1983a. The Incident at Antioch (Gal. 2:11-18). *JSNT* 18:3-57. See additional note in the reprint by the author in *Jesus, Paul and the Law. Studies in Mark and Galatians*, 174-82. Louisville, KY: Westminster/John Knox Press, 1990.

_____. 1983b. The New Perspective on Paul. *BJRL* 65:95-122. See additional note in the reprint by the author in *Jesus, Paul and the Law. Studies in Mark and Galatians*, 206-14. Louisville, KY: Westminster/John Knox Press, 1990.

_____. 1990. The Theology of Galatians. Chap in *Jesus, Paul and the Law. Studies in Mark and Galatians*, 242-64. Louisville, KY: Westminster/John Knox Press, 1990.

_____. 1992. The Justice of God. A Renewed Perspective on Justification by Faith. *JTS* 43:1-22.

_____. 1993a. Echoes of Intra-Jewish Polemic in Paul's Letter to the Galatians. *JBL* 112:459-77.

_____. 1993b. *The Epistle to the Galatians*. Black's New Testament Commentaries IX. Peabody, MA: Hendrickson Publishers.

_____. 1993c. *The Theology of Paul's Letter to the Galatians*. New Testament Theology Series. Cambridge, UK: University Press, Cambridge.

Du Toit, A. B. 1992. Alienation and Re-identification as Pragmatic Strategiesin Galatians. *Neot* 26:279-95.

_____. 1994a. Galatians 6:13: A Possible Solution to an Old Exegetical Problem. *Neot* 28:157-61.

_____. 1994b. Vilification as a Pragmatic Device in Early Christian Epistolography. *Bib* 75:403-12.

Duvall, J. Scott. 1994a. "Identity-Performance-Result": Tracing Paul's Argument in Galatians 5 and 6. *SWJT* 37:30-38.

_____. 1994b. Pauline Lexical Choice Revisited: A Paradigmatic Analysis of Selected Terms of Exhortation in Galatians 5 and 6. *FilNeot* 7:17-32.

Eadie, John. 1977. *Commentary on the Epistle of Paul to the Galatians*. Edinburgh: T & T Clark, 1884; reprint, Minneapolis: James and Klock Christian Publishing Co. (page references are to reprint edition).

Easley, Kendell H. 1984. The Pauline Usage of *PNEUMATI* as a Reference to the Spirit of God. *JETS* 27:299-313.

Ebeling, Gerhard. 1985. *The Truth of the Gospel--An Eposition of Galatians*. Translated by David Green. Philadelphia: Fortress Press.

Ehrman, Bart D. 1990. Cephas and Peter. *JBL* 109:463-74.

Ellicott, Charles J. 1978. *A Critical and Grammatical Commentary on St. Paul's Epistle to the Galatians*. Boston: Draper and Halliday, 1860, 2nd ed; reprint, Minneapolis: James Family Publishing Co. Gaston, Lloyd. 1987. *Paul and the Torah*. Vancouver: University of British Columbia Press.

Ellis, E. Earle. 1968. "Those of the Circumcision" and the Early Christian Mission. *SE* 4:390-99.

_____. 1978. Paul and his Opponents. Chap. In *Prophecy and Hermeneutic in Early Christianity*. Grand Rapids, MI: William B. Eerdmans Publishing Company.

_____. 1981. *Paul's Use of the Old Testament*. Edinburgh: Oliver & Boyd and Grand Rapids, MI: William B. Eerdmans Publishing Company, 1957; reprint, Grand Rapids, MI: Baker Book House (page references are to reprint edition).

Epp, Eldon Jay. 1966. *The Theological Tendency of Codex Bezae Cantabrigiensis in Acts*. SNTSMS 3. Cambridge: At the University Press.

_____. 1978. Paul's Diverse Imageries of the Human Situation and His Unifying Theme of Freedom. In *Unity and Diversity in New*

Testament Theology, ed. Robert A. Guelich, 100-116. Grand Rapids, MI: William B. Eerdmans Publishing Company.

Esler, Philip F. 1995. Making and Breaking an Agreement Mediterranean Style: A New Reading of Galatians 2:1-14. *BibInt* 3:285-314.

Espy, John M. 1985. Paul's 'Robust Conscience' Re-examined. *NTS* 31:161-88.

Fairweather, Janet. 1994a. The Epistle to the Galatians and Classical Rhetoric: Parts 1 & 2. *TynBul* 45:1-38.

_____. 1994b. The Epistle to the Galatians and Classical Rhetoric: Part 3. *TynBul* 45:213-43.

Fee, Gordon. 1994a. Freedom and the Life of Obedience (Galatians 5:1-6:18). *RevExp* 91:201-17.

_____. 1994b. *God's Empowering Presence. The Holy Spirit in the Letters of Paul*. Peabody, MA: Hendrickson Publishers.

Feuillet, André. 1982. Structure de la section doctrinale de l'Épitre aux Galates (III,1-VI,10). *RevThom* 82:5-39.

Fletcher, Douglas K. 1982. The Singular Argument of Paul's Letter to the Galatians. Ph.D. diss., Princeton Theological Seminary.

Forbes, C. 1986. Comparison, Self-Praise and Irony: Paul's Boasting and the Conventions of Hellenistic Rhetoric. *NTS* 32:1-30.

Fredriksen, Paula. 1991. Judaism, the Circumcision of Gentiles, and Apocalyptic Hope: Another Look at Galatians 1 and 2. *JTS* 42:532-64.

Friedrich, Gerhard, ed. 1967-1974. *Theological Dictionary of the New Testament*. Vols. 5-9. Translated and edited by Geoffrey W. Bromiley. Grand Rapids, MI: William B. Eerdmans Publishing Company. S.v. "μετατίθημι, μετάθεσις," by Christian Maurer, "σάρξ, σαρκικός, σάρκινος," by Eduard Schweizer and "στοιχέω, στοιχεῖον," by Gerhard Delling.

Fung, Ronald Y. K. 1980. Justification by Faith in 1 & 2 Corinthians. In *Pauline Studies. Essays presented to Professor F. F. Bruce on his 70ᵗʰ Birthday*, eds. Donald A. Hagner and Murray J. Harris, 246-61. Grand Rapids, MI: William B. Eerdmans Publishing Company.

_____. 1982. A Note on Galatians 2:3-8. *JETS* 25:49-52.

_____. 1988. *The Epistle to the Galatians*. The New International Commentary on the New Testament, ed. F. F. Bruce. Grand Rapids, MI: William B. Eerdmans Publishing Company.

Funk, Robert W. 1966. *Language, Hermeneutic and the Word of God*. New York: Harper and Row.

Garland, David E. 1994. Paul's Defense of the Truth of the Gospel Regarding Gentiles (Galatians 2:15-3:22). *RevExp* 91:165-81.

Garlington, D. B. 1991. Burden-bearing and the Recovery of Offending Christians (Galatians 6:1-5). *TrinJ* NS 12:151-83.

Gaston, Lloyd. 1987. *Paul and the Torah*. Vancouver: University of British Columbia Press.

Gaventa, B. R. 1986. Galatians 1 and 2: Autobiography as Paradigm. *NovT* 28:309-26.

_____. 1990. The Maternity of Paul: An Exegetical Study of Galatians 4:19. In *The Conversation Continues: Studies in Paul & John in Honor of J. Louis Martyn*, eds. Robert T. Fortna and Beverly R. Gaventa, 189-201. Nashville: Abingdon Press.

_____. 1991. The Singularity of the Gospel. A Reading of Galatians. In *Pauline Theology. Volume I: Thessalonians, Philippians, Galatians, Philemon*. ed. Jouette M. Bassler, 147-59. Minneapolis: Augsburg Fortress Press.

Geertz, Clifford. 1976. "From the Native's Point of View": On the Nature of Anthropological Understanding. In *Meaning in Anthropology*, eds. Keith H. Basso and Henry A. Selby, 221-37. Albuquerque: University of New Mexico Press.

George, Timothy. 1994. *Galatians.* The New American Commentary 30. Nashville, TN: Broadman & Holman Publishers.

Georgi, Dieter. 1965. *Die Geschichte der Kollekte des Paulus fur Jerusalem.* Theologische Forschung, vol. 38. Hamburg: Evangelischer Verlag.

Goddard, A, J. and S. A. Cummins. 1993. Ill or Ill-Treated? Conflict and Persecution as the Context of Paul's Original Ministry in Galatia (Galatians 4:12-20). *JSNT* 52:93-126.

Goldenberg, Robert. 1988. The Place of Other Religions in Ancient Jewish Thought, with Particular Reference to Early Rabbinic Judaism. In *Pushing the Faith: Proselytism and Civility in a Pluralistic World,* eds. Martin E. Marty and Frederick E. Greenspahn, 27-40. New York: The Crossroad Publishing Company.

Gordon, T. David. 1987. The Problem at Galatia. *Int* 41:32-43.

Gräbe, P. J. 1992. Paul's Assertion of Obedience as a Function of Persuasion. *Neot* 26:351-8.

Greenwood, David. 1970. Rhetorical Criticism and *Formgeschichte*: Some Methodological Considerations. *JBL* 89:418-26.

Gundry, Robert H. 1976. *SOMA in Biblical Theology with Emphasis on Pauline Anthropology.* SNTSMS 29. Cambridge: Cambridge University Press.

Guthrie, Donald. 1973. *Galatians.* The New Century Bible Commentary. Grand Rapids: William B. Eerdmans Publishing Company.

Hahn, Ferdinand. 1965. *Mission in the New Testament.* SBT 47. Translated by Frank Clarke. Naperville, Illinois: Alec R. Allenson.

Hall, Robert G. 1987. The Rhetorical Outline for Galatians--A Reconsideration. *JBL* 106:277-87.

_____. 1991. Historical Inference and Rhetorical Effect: Another Look at Galatians 1 and 2. In *Persuasive Artistry. Studies in New*

244   *The Flesh/Spirit Conflict in Galatians*

Testament in Honor of George A. Kennedy. JSNTSup 50. ed. Duane F. Watson, 308-20. Sheffield: Sheffield Academic Press.

_____. 1996. Arguing Like an Apocalypse: Galatians and an Ancient *Topos* Outside the Greco-Roman Rhetorical Tradition. *NTS* 42:434-53.

Hamilton, Neill Q. 1957. *The Holy Spirit and Eschatology in Paul.* Scottish Journal of Theology Occasional Papers 6. Edinburgh and London: Oliver and Boyd.

Hansen, G. Walter. 1989. *Abraham in Galatians--Epistolary and Rhetorical Contexts.* JSNTSup 29, ed. David Hill. Sheffield: Sheffield Academic Press.

_____. 1994a. *Galatians.* The IVP New Testament Commentary Series 9. Downers Grove, IL: InterVarsity Press.

_____. 1994b. Galatia. In *The Book of Acts in Its First Century Setting. Volume 2, The Book of Acts in Its Graeco-Roman Setting.* eds. David W. J. Gill and Conrad Gempf, 377-95. Grand Rapids, MI: William B. Eerdmans Publishing Company.

_____. 1994c. A Paradigm of the Apocalypse: The Gospel in the Light of Epistolary Analysis. In *Gospel in Paul. Studies on Corinthians, Galatians and Romans for Richard N. Longenecker.* JSNTSup 108. eds. L. Ann Jervis and Peter Richardson, 194-209. Sheffield: Sheffield Academic Press.

Hanson, Anthony T. 1974. *Studies in Paul's Technique and Theology._ Grand Rapids: William B. Eerdmans Publishing Company.

_____. 1987. *The Paradox of the Cross.* JSNTSup 17, ed. David Hill. Sheffield: Sheffield Academic Press.

Harnisch, W. 1987. Einubung des neuen Seins. Paulinishche Paranese am Beispiel des Galaterbriefs. *ZTK* 84:279-96.

Harris, William V. 1989. *Ancient Literacy.* Cambridge: Harvard University Press.

Hartman, Lars. 1986. On Reading Others' Letters. In *Christians Among Jews and Gentiles*, eds. George W. Nickelsburg and George W. MacRae, 137-46. Philadelphia: Fortress Press.

Harvey, A. E. 1968. The Opposition to Paul. *SE* 4:319-32.

Hawkins, John Gale. 1971. The Opponents of Paul in Galatia. Ph. D. diss., Yale University.

Hay, David M. 1969. Paul's Indifference to Authority. *JBL* 88:36-44.

Hays, Richard B. 1983. *The Faith of Jesus Christ: An Investigation of the Narrative Substructure of Galatians 3:1-4:11.* SBLDS 56. Chico, CA: Scholars Press.

_____. 1987. Christology and Ethics in Galatians: The Law of Christ. *CBQ* 49:268-90.

Hengel, Martin. 1974. *Judaism and Hellenism. Studies in the Encounter in Palestine during the Early Hellenistic Period.* 2 Vols. Translated by John Bowden. Philadelphia: Fortress Press.

Herford, R. Travers, ed. 1962. *The Ethics of the Talmud: Sayings of the Fathers.* 3d ed. Cincinnati: Jewish Institute of Religion, 1945; reprint, New York: Schocken Books (page references are to the reprint edition).

Hesselink, I. John. 1984. Christ, the Law, and the Christian. An Unexplored Aspect of the Third Use of the Law in Calvin's Theology. In *Readings in Calvin's Theology,* ed. Donald K. McKim, 179-91. Grand Rapids: Baker Book House.

Hester, James D. 1984. The Rhetorical Structure of Galatians 1:11-2:14. *JBL* 103:223-33.

_____. 1986. The Use and Influence of Rhetoric in Galatians 2:1-14. *TZ* 42:386-408.

_____. 1991. Placing the Blame: The Presence of Epideictic in Galatians 1 and 2. In *Persuasive Artistry. Studies in New Testament in Honor of George A. Kennedy.* JSNTSup 50.

ed. Duane F. Watson, 281-307. Sheffield: Sheffield Academic Press.

Hill, Archibald A. 1970. Laymen, Lexicographers, and Linguistics. *Lg* 46:245-58.

Hirsch, E. D., Jr. 1967. *Validity in Interpretation*. New Haven and London: Yale University Press.

Hoehner, Harold W. 1989. A Chronological Table of the Apostolic Age. 2d revised ed. From Chronology of the Apostolic Age. Th.D. diss., Dallas Theological Seminary, 1965.

Hoenig, Sidney B. 1962-63. Circumcision: The Covenant of Abraham. *JQR* n. s. 53:322-34.

_____. 1965. Conversion during the Talmudic Period. In *Conversion to Judaism: A History and Analysis*, ed. David Max Eichhorn, 33-66. Hoboken, NJ: KTAV Publishing House.

Hong, In-Gyu. 1992. The Law and Christian Ethics in Galatians 5-6. *Neot* 26:113-30.

_____. 1994. Does Paul Misrepresent the Jewish Law? Law and Covenant in Gal. 3:1-14. *NovT* 36:164-82.

Houlden, J. L. 1983. A Response to James D. G. Dunn. *JSNT* 18:58-67.

Howard, George. 1979. *Paul: Crisis in Galatia*. SNTSMS 35. Cambridge: Cambridge University Press.

Howell, Don N., Jr. 1993a. Pauline Eschatological Dualism and Its Resulting Tensions. *TrinJ* NS 14:3-24.

_____. 1993b. Pauline Thought in the History of Interpetation. *BibS* 150:303-26.

_____. 1994. The Center of Pauline Theology. *BibS* 151:50-70.

Hübner, Hans. 1984. Der Galaterbrief und das Verhaltnis von antiker Rhetorik und Epistolographie. *TLZ* 109:241-50.

Hughes, Frank W. 1994. The Gospel and Its Rhetoric in Galatians. In *Gospel in Paul. Studies on Corinthians, Galatians and Romans for Richard N. Longenecker*. JSNTSup 108. eds. L. Ann Jervis and Peter Richardson, 210-21. Sheffield: Sheffield Academic Press.

Hurtado, Larry W. 1979. The Jerusalem Collection and the Book of Galatians. *JSNT* 5:46-62.

Isenberg, Sheldon R. 1975. Power through Temple and Torah in Greco-Roman Palestine. In *Christianity, Judaism and Other Greco-Roman Cults*, ed. Jacob Neusner, 2:24-52. Vol. 12 in 2 Parts, *Studies in Judaism in Late Antiquity*, ed. Jacob Neusner. Leiden: E. J. Brill.

Jaquette, James L. 1994. Paul, Epictetus, and Others on Indifference to Status. *CBQ* 56:68-80.

Jegher-Bucher, Vreni. 1990. Formgeschichtliche Betrachtung zu Galater 2,11-16. Antwort an James D. Hester. *TZ* 46:305-21.

Jeremias, Joachim. 1969. *Jerusalem in the Time of Jesus*. 3rd ed. Translated by F. H. and C. H. Cave. Philadelphia: Fortress Press.

Jewett, Robert. 1971a. Agitators and the Galatian Congregation. *NTS* 17:198-212.

_____. 1971b. *Paul's Anthropological Terms: A Study of Their Use in Conflict Settings*. Arbeiten zur Geschichte des antiken Judentums und des Urchristentums 10. Leiden: E. J. Brill.

_____. 1979. *A Chronology of Paul's Life*. Philadelphia: Fortress Press.

_____. 1994. Gospel and Commensality: Social and Theological Implications of Galatians 2:14. In *Gospel in Paul. Studies on Corinthians, Galatians and Romans for Richard N. Longenecker*. JSNTSup 108. eds. L. Ann Jervis and Peter Richardson, 240-52. Sheffield: Sheffield Academic Press.

Jobes, Karen H. 1993. Jerusalem, Our Mother: Metalepsis and Intertextuality in Galatians 4:21-31. *WTJ* 55:299-320.

Johnson, H. Wayne. 1988. The "Analogy of Faith" and Exegetical Methodology: A Preliminary Discussion on Relationships. *JETS* 31:69-80.

Johnson, Luke T. 1989. The New Testament's Anti-Jewish Slander and the Conventions of Ancient Polemic. *JBL* 108:419-41.

Johnson, S. Lewis. 1986. Paul and "The Israel of God": An Exegetical and Eschatological Case-Study. In *Essays in Honor of J. Dwight Pentecost*. ed. Stanley D. Toussaint and Charles H. Dyer, 181-96. Chicago: Moody Press.

Joos, Martin. 1972. Semantic Axiom Number One. *Lg* 48:257-65.

Judge, E. A. 1972. St Paul and Classical Society. *JAC* 15:19-36.

Karlberg, Mark W. 1986. Israel's History Personified: Romans 7:7-13 in Relation to Paul's Teaching on the "Old Man." *TrinJ* NS 7:65-74.

Käsemann, Ernst. 1970. The Pauline Theology of the Cross. *Int* 24:151-77.

_____. 1971. *Perspectives on Paul*. Translated by Margaret Kohl. Philadelphia: Fortress Press.

Kennedy, George A. 1984. *New Testament Interpretation through Rhetorical Criticism*. Chapel Hill: The University of North Carolina Press.

Kern, Philip H. 1994. Rhetoric, Scholarship and Galatians: Assessing an Approach to Paul's Epistles. Ph. D. diss., University of Sheffield.

Kertelge, K. 1992. The Assertion of Revealed Truth as Compelling Argument in Galatians 1:10-2:21. *Neot* 26:339-50.

King, Daniel H. 1983. Paul and the Tannaim: A Study in Galatians. *WTJ* 45:340-70.

Kittel, Gerhard, ed. 1964-1967. *Theological Dictionary of the New Testament*. Vols. 1-4. Translated by Geoffrey W. Bromiley. Grand Rapids: William B. Eerdmans Publishing Company. S.v. "ἐγώ" by Erich Stauffer; "καυχάομαι, καύχημα, καύχησῖ," by Rudolf Bultmann.

Knox, John. 1987. *Chapters in a Life of Paul*. Rev. ed. Edited with introduction by Douglas R. A. Hare. Macon, GA: Mercer University Press.

Koester, Helmut. 1982. *Introduction to the New Testament. Volume Two: History and Literature of Early Christianity* Berlin and New York: De Gruyter and Philadelphia: Fortress Press.

Koptak, Paul E. 1990. Rhetorical Identification in Paul's Autobiographical Narrative (Galatians 1.13-2.14). *JSNT* 40:97-115.

Kraft, Charles H. 1979. *Christianity in Culture. A Study in Dynamic Biblical Theologizing in Cross-Cultural Perspective*. Maryknoll, NY: Orbis Books.

Kraftchick, Steven J. 1985. Ethos and Pathos Appeals in Galatians Five and Six: A Rhetorical Analysis. Ph.D. diss., Emory University.

Kruger, M. A. 1987. TINA KARPON, "Some Fruit" in Romans 1:13. *WTJ* 49:167-73.

_____. 1992. Law and Promise in Galatians. *Neot* 26:311-27.

Kuck, David W. 1994. 'Each will bear his own burden.' Paul's Creative Use of an Apocalyptic Motif. *NTS* 40:289-97.

Kuhn, Karl Georg. 1957. New Light on Temptation, Sin, and Flesh in the New Testament. In *The Scrolls and the New Testament*, ed. Krister Stendahl, 94-113. New York: Harper & Brothers Publishers.

Kümmel, Werner Georg. 1929. *Romer 7 und die Bekehrung des Paulus*. Untersuchungen zum Neuen Testament, Heft 17, hrsg. H. Windisch. Leipzig: J. C. Hinrichs' Sche Buchhandlung.

_____. 1973. "Individualgeschichte" und "Weltgeschichte" in Gal. 2:15-21. In *Christ and Spirit in the New Testament*, eds. Barnabas Lindars and Stephen S. Smalley, 157-73. Cambridge: Cambridge University Press.

_____. 1975. *Introduction to the New Testament.* Revised English ed. Translated by Howard Clark Kee. Nashville: Abingdon Press.

Ladd, George E. 1968. Paul and the Law. In *Soli Deo Gloria*, ed. J. McDowell Richards, 50-67. Richmond: John Knox Press.

_____. 1974. *A Theology of the New Testament.* Grand Rapids: William B. Eerdmans Publishing Company.

_____. 1975. The Holy Spirit in Galatians. In *Current Issues in Biblical and Patristic Interpretation*, ed. Gerald F. Hawthorne, 211-16. Grand Rapids: William B. Eerdmans Publishing Company.

Lake, Kirsopp. 1979. Paul's Controversies. Chap. in *The Beginnings of Christianity*, ed. F. J. Foakes Jackson and Kirsopp Lake, 5:212-23. London: Macmillan, 1920-1933; reprint, Grand Rapids: Baker Book House (page references are to reprint edition).

Lambrecht, Jan. 1977-78. The Line of Thought in Gal 2: 14b-21. *NTS* 24:484-95.

_____. 1991. Transgressor by Nullifying God's Grace. A Study of Gal 2,18-21. *Bib* 72:217-36.

Lategan, Bernard. 1988. Is Paul Defending His Apostleship in Galatians? *NTS* 34:411-30.

_____. 1989. Levels of Reader Instructions in the Text of Galatians. *Semeia* 48:171-84.

_____. 1991. Formulas in the Language of Paul. *Neot* 25:75-87.

_____. 1992. The Argumentative Situation of Galatians. *Neot* 26:257-77.

_____. 1993. Textual Space as Rhetorical Device. In *Rhetoric and the New Testament. Essays from the 1992 Heidelberg Conference.* JSNTSup 90. ed. Stanley E. Porter and Thomas H. Olbricht, 397-408. Sheffield: Sheffield Academic Press.

Lea, Thomas D. 1994. Unscrambling the Judaizers: Who Were Paul's Opponents? *SWJT* 37:23-29.

Leary, T. J. 1993. Of Paul and Pork and Proselytes. *NovT* 35:292-3.

Lemmer, H. R. 1992. Mnemonic Reference to the Spirit as a Persuasive Tool (Galatians 3:1-6 within the argument of 3:1-4:11). *Neot* 26:359-88.

Lerner, M. B. 1987. The Tractate Avot. In *The Literature of the Sages*. Compendia Rerum Iudaicarum ad Novum Testamentum, Section Two, Part One, ed. Shmuel Safrai, 263-81. Assen/Maastricht: Van Gorcum and Philadelphia: Fortress Press.

Liddell, Henry George, and Robert Scott. 1968. *A Greek-English Lexicon*. Revised and augmented by Henry Stuart Jones with Roderick McKenzie and with a supplement by E. A. Barber. 9th ed. Oxford: At the Clarendon Press.

Lightfoot, J. B. 1953. *St. Paul's Epistle to the Philippians*. London: Macmillan, 1913; reprint, Grand Rapids: Zondervan Publishing House (page references are to the reprint edition).

_____. 1957. *The Epistle of St. Paul to the Galatians*, 10th. ed. London: Macmillan, 1890; reprint, Grand Rapids: Zondervan Publishing House (page references are to reprint edition).

Longenecker, Richard N. 1964. *Paul, Apostle of Liberty*. New York: Harper & Row.

_____. 1990. *Galatians*. Word Biblical Commentary, Vol. 41. Dallas: Word Books, Publisher.

_____. 1994. Graphic Illustrations of a Believer's New Life in Christ: Galatians 4:21-31. *RevExp* 91:183-99.

Loubser, J. A. 1994. The Contrast Slavery/Freedom as Persuasive Device in Galatians. *Neot* 28:163-73.

_____. 1995. Orality and Literarcy in the Pauline Epistles. Some New Hermeneutical Implications. *Neot* 29:61-74.

Louw, Johannes P., and Eugene A. Nida, eds. 1988. *Greek-English Lexicon of the New Testament Based on Semantic Domains*. 2 vols. New York: United Bible Societies.

Luedemann, Gerd. 1984. *Paul, Apostle to the Gentiles. Studies in Chronology*. Translated by F. Stanley Jones. Philadelphia: Fortress Press.

_____. 1989. *Opposition to Paul in Jewish Christianity*. Translated by M. Eugene Boring. Philadelphia: Fortress Press.

Lull, David John. 1980. *The Spirit in Galatia: Paul's Interpretation of PNEUMA as Divine Power*. SBLDS 49. Chico, CA: Scholars Press.

Lütgert, Wilhelm. 1919. *Gesetz und Geist: Eine Untersuchung zur Vorgeschichte des Galaterbriefes*. Beiträge zur Förderung christlicher Theologie, vol. 22, book 6. Gütersloh: Bertelsmann.

Luther, Martin. 1963. *Luther's Works*. Edited by Jaroslav Pelikan and Walter A. Hansen. Vol. 26, *Lectures on Galatians 1535, Chapters 1-4*. Translated by Jaroslav Pelikan. St. Louis: Concordia Publishing House.

_____. 1964. *Luther's Works*. Edited by Jaroslav Pelikan and Walter A. Hansen. Vol. 27, *Lectures on Galatians 1535, Chapters 5-6*. Translated by Jaroslav Pelikan. St. Louis: Concordia Publishing House.

_____. 1979. *Commentary on Galatians*. Translated by Erasmus Middleton. Ed. John P. Fallowes. London: Harrison Trust, 1850; reprint, Grand Rapids: Kregel Publications (page references are to reprint edition) .

Lyons, Campbell N. D. 1994. From Persuasion to Subversion: A Review of Past and Current Trends in Defining Rhetoric. *Neot* 28:429-56.

Lyons, George. 1985. *Pauline Autobiography: Toward a New Understanding.* SBLDS 73. Atlanta: Scholars Press.

MacDonald, Margaret Y. 1988. *The Pauline Churches: A Socio-historical Study of Institutionalization in the Pauline and Deutero-Pauline Writings.* SNTSMS 60. Cambridge: Cambridge University Press.

Mack, Burton L. 1990. *Rhetoric and the New Testament.* Minneapolis: Augsburg Fortress Press.

Malan, F. S. 1992. The Strategy of Two Opposing Covenants. Galatians 4:21-5:1. *Neot* 26:425-40.

Malherbe, Abraham J. 1986. *Moral Exhortation, A Greco-Roman Sourcebook.* Library of Early Christianity 4, ed. Wayne A. Meeks. Philadelphia: The Westminster Press.

_____. 1988. *Ancient Epistolary Theorists.* SBLSBS 19, ed. Bernard Brandon Scott. Atlanta: Scholars Press.

Malina, Bruce J. 1979. The Individual and the Community-- Personality in the Social World of Early Christianity. *BTB* 9:126-38.

_____. 1986a. "Religion" in the World of Paul. *BTB* 16:92-101.

_____. 1986b. *Christian Origins and Cultural Anthropology. Practical Models for Biblical Interpretation.* Atlanta: John Knox Press.

_____. 1993. *The New Testament World. Insights from Cultural Anthropology.* rev. ed. Atlanta: John Knox Press.

Markus, Joel. 1986. The Evil Inclination in the Letters of Paul. *IBS* 8:8-20.

Martin, Troy. 1995. Apostasy to Paganism: The Rhetorical Stasis of the Galatian Controversy. *JBL* 114:437-61.

Martyn, J. Louis. 1985a. A Law-Observant Mission to Gentiles: The Background of Galatians. *SJT* 38:307-24.

_____. 1985b. Apocalyptic Antinomies in Paul's Letter to the Galatians. *NTS* 31:410-24.

_____. 1991. Events in Galatia. In *Pauline Theology. Volume I: Thessalonians, Philippians, Galatians, Philemon.* ed. Jouette M. Bassler, 160-79. Minneapolis: Augsburg Fortress Press.

Marxsen, Willi. 1968. *Introduction to the New Testament.* Translated by G. Buswell. Philadelphia: Fortress Press.

_____. 1978. *Einleitung in das Neue Testament.* 4th ed. Gütersloh: Gerd Mohn.

Matera, Frank J. 1988. The Culmination of Paul's Argument to the Galatians: Gal. 5.1-6.17. *JSNT* 32:79-91.

_____. 1992. *Galatians.* Sacra Pagina Series 9. Collegeville, MN: The Liturgical Press.

Matlock, R. Barry. 1996. *Unveiling the Apocalyptic Paul. Paul's Interpreters and the Rhetoric of Criticism.* JSNTSup 127. Sheffield: Sheffield Academic Press.

McEleney, N. J. 1974. Conversion, Circumcision and the Law. *NTS* 20:319-41.

McLean, Bradley H. 1991. Galatians 2.7-9 and the Recognition of Paul's Apostolic Status at the Jerusalem Conference: A Critique of G. Luedemann's Solution. *NTS* 37:67-76.

Meeks, Wayne A., ed. 1972. *The Writings of St. Paul.* A Norton Critical Edition. New York: W. W. Norton & Company Inc.

_____. 1982. The Social Context of Pauline Theology. *Int* 36:266-77.

_____. 1983. *The First Urban Christians. The Social World of the Apostle Paul*. New Haven: Yale University Press.

Merk, Otto. 1969. Der Beginn der Paranese im Galaterbrief. *ZNW* 60:83-104.

Metzger, Bruce M. 1971. *A Textual Commentary on the Greek New Testament*. New York: United Bible Societies.

Minear, Paul S. 1977. The Crucifixion of the World. Galatians 6:14-15. Chap. in *To Die and to Live. Christ's Resurrection and Christian Vocation*. New York: The Seabury Press.

_____. 1979. The Crucified World: The Enigma of Galatians 6,14. In *Theologia Crucis--Signum Crucis*, hrsg. Carl Andresen und Gunter Klein, 395-407. Tübingen: J. C. B. Mohr (Paul Siebeck).

Montefiore, C. G., and H. Loewe. 1974. *A Rabbinic Anthology*. New York: Schocken Books.

Moo, Douglas J. 1986. Israel and Paul in Romans 7:7-12. *NTS* 32:122-35.

Moore, George Foot. 1971. *Judaism in the First Centuries of the Christian Era*. 2 vols. Cambridge: Harvard University Press, 1927, 1930; paperback edition, New York: Schocken Books (page references are to paperback edition).

Morgado, Joe, Jr. 1994. Paul in Jerusalem: A Comparison of His Visits in Acts and Galatians. *JETS* 37:55-68.

Moulton, James H., and George Milligan. 1930. *The Vocabulary of the Greek Testament. Illustrated from the Papyri and Other Non-Literary Sources*. Grand Rapids: William B. Eerdmans Publishing Company.

Moxnes, Halvor. 1980. *Theology in Conflict. Studies in Paul's Understanding of God in Romans*. NovTSup 53. Leiden: E. J. Brill.

_____. 1988a. Honour and Righteousness in Romans. *JSNT* 32:61-77.

_____. 1988b. Honor, Shame, and the Outside World in Paul's Letter to the Romans. In *The Social World of Formative Christianity and Judaism*, eds. Jacob Neusner, Peder Borgen, Ernest S. Frerichs, and Richard Horsley, 207-18. Philadelphia: Fortress Press.

_____. 1989. Social Integration and the Problem of Gender in St. Paul's Letters. *ST* 43:99-113.

Munck, Johannes. 1959. *Paul and the Salvation of Mankind*. Richmond: John Knox Press.

Murphy-O'Connor, Jerome. 1993. Paul in Arabia. *CBQ* 55:732-7.

Mussner, Franz. 1974. *Der Galaterbrief*. Herders theologischer Kommentar zum Neuen Testament 9. Freiburg: Herder.

Neusner, Jacob. 1971. *The Rabbinic Traditions about the Pharisees before 70*. 3 vols. Leiden: E. J. Brill.

_____. 1973. *The Idea of Purity in Ancient Judaism*. Leiden: E. J. Brill.

_____. 1978. The Use of the Later Rabbinic Evidence for the Study of First-Century Pharisaism. In *Approaches to Ancient Judaism: Theory and Practice*, ed. Willliam Scott Green, 215-25. Missoula, Montana: Scholars Press.

_____. 1979. *From Politics to Piety. The Emergence of Pharisaic Judaism*. 2nd ed. New York: KTAV Publishing House, Inc.

_____, ed. and trans. 1987. *Scriptures of the Oral Torah*. San Francisco: Harper & Row, Publishers.

Newton, Michael. 1985. *The Concept of Purity at Qumran and in the Letters of Paul*. SNTSMS 53. Cambridge: Cambridge University Press.

Neyrey, J. H. 1988. Bewitched in Galatia: Paul and Cultural Anthropology. *CBQ* 50:72-100.

_____. 1990. Reading Paul in Social Science Perspective. Chap. in *Paul in Other Words. A Cultural Reading of His Letters,* 11-20. Louisville, KY: Westminster/John Knox Press.

Nickelsburg, G. W. E. 1993. Jews and Christians in the First Century. The Struggle over Identity. *Neot* 27:365-90.

Nida, Eugene A., and Charles R. Taber. 1969. *The Theory and Practice of Translation.* Helps for Translators, vol. 8. Leiden: E. J. Brill.

North, J. L. 1992. Sowing and Reaping (Galatians 6:7b): More Examples of a Classical Maxim. *JTS* 43:523-7.

O'Brien, P. T. 1993, 1995. *Gospel and Mission in the Writings of Paul. An Exegetical and Theological Analysis.* Grand Rapids, MI: Baker Books.

O'Neill, J. C. 1972. *The Recovery of Paul's Letter to the Galatians.* London: SPCK.

Ong, Walter. 1982. *Orality and Literacy.* New York: Methuen & Co., Ltd.

Paget, James Carleton. 1996. Jewish Proselytism at the Time of Christian Origins: Chimera or Reality? *JSNT* 62:65-103.

Panier, L. 1986a. Parcours: Pour lire l'epitre aux Galates. lere serie. *Semiotique et bible* 42:40-46.

_____. 1986b. Parcours pour lire l'epitre aux Galates. *Semiotique et bible* 43:23-29.

Parunak, H. Van Dyke. 1992. Dimensions of Discourse Structure: A Multidimensional Analysis of the Components and Transitions of Paul's Epistle to the Galatians. In *Linguistics and New Testament Interpretation. Essays on Discourse Analysis.* ed. David Alan Black with Katharine Barnwell and Stephen Levinsohn, 207-39. Nashville, TN: Broadman Press.

Patte, Daniel. 1983. *Paul's Faith and the Power of the Gospel. A Structural Introduction to the Pauline Letters*. Philadelphia: Fortress Press.

Pelser, G. M. M. 1992. The Opposition of Faith and Works as Persuasive Device in Galatians (3:6-14). *Neot* 26:389-405.

Pelser, G. M. M., A. B. du Toit, M. A. Kruger, H. R. Lemmer and J. H. Roberts. 1992. Discourse Analysis of Galatians. Addendum to *Neotestamentica* 26 (2):1-41

Peque, M. Martinez. 1987. Unidad de forma y contenido en Gal 5,16-26. *EstBib* 45:105-24.

Perelman, Ch., and L. Olbrechts-Tyteca. 1969. *The New Rhetoric: A Treatise on Argumentation*. Translated by John Wilkinson and Purcell Weaver. Notre Dame: University of Notre Dame Press.

Peristiany, J. G. 1966. Introduction. In *Honour and Shame. The Values of Mediterranean Society*, ed. J. G. Peristiany, 9-18. Chicago: The University of Chicago Press.

Perriman, Andrew C. 1993. The Rhetorical Strategy of Galatians 4:21-5:1. *EQ* 65:27-42.

Pesch, Rudolf. 1979. Peter in the Mirror of Paul's Letters. In *Paul de Tarse: Apotre du Notre Temps*. Série monographique de "Benedictina" Section paulinienne 1. Rome: Abbaye de S. Paul h.l.m.

Pfleiderer, Otto. 1891. *Paulinism: A Contribution to the History Of Primitive Christian Theology*, 2nd ed., Vol. 1. Exposition of Paul's Doctrine. Translated by Edward Peters. London and Edinburgh: Williams and Norgate.

Pitta, A. 1992. *Disposizione e messaggio della lettera ai Galati: Analisi rectorico-letteraria*. Analecta Biblica 131. Rome: Pontificio Istituto Biblico.

Pitt-Rivers, Julian. 1966. Honour and Social Status. In *Honour and Shame. The Values of Mediterranean Society*, ed. J. G. Peristiany, 19-75. Chicago: The University of Chicago Press.

Pobee, John S. 1985. *Persecution and Martyrdom in the Theology of Paul.* JSNTSup 6. Sheffield: Sheffield Academic Press.

Porter, Frank Chamberlin. 1901. The Yecer Hara: A Study in the Jewish Doctrine of Sin. In *Biblical and Semitic Studies.* New York: Charles Scribner's Sons.

Porter, Stanley E. 1993. The Theoretical Justification for Application of Rhetorical Categories to Pauline Epistolary Literature. In *Rhetoric and the New Testament. Essays from the 1992 Heidelberg Conference.* JSNTSup 90. ed. Stanley E. Porter and Thomas H. Olbricht, 100-22. Sheffield: Sheffield Academic Press.

Potter, Jack M., May N. Diaz, and George M. Foster, eds. 1967. *Peasant Society. A Reader.* Boston: Little, Brown and Company.

Poythress, Vern S. 1984. Adequacy of Language and Accomodation. In *Hermeneutics, Inerrancv, & the Bible,* eds. Earl D. Radmacher and Robert D. Preus, 349-76. Grand Rapids: Zondervan Publishing House.

Pretorius, E. A. C. 1992. The Opposition ΠΝΕΥΜΑ and ΣΑΡΞ as Persuasive Summons (Galatians 5:13-6:10). *Neot* 26:441-60.

Pyne, Robert A. 1995. The "Seed," the Spirit, and the Blessing of Abraham. *BibS* 152:211-22.

Quintilian. 1920-1922. *The Institutio Oratoria of Quintilian.* 4 vols. Translated by H. E. Butler. Loeb Classical Library, nos. 124-127. Cambridge: Harvard University Press.

Räisanen, Heikki. 1986. *Paul and the Law.* Philadelphia: Fortress Press.

Ray, Charles A., Jr. 1994. The Identity of the "Israel of God." *Theological Educator* 50:105-14.

Reed, Jeffrey T. 1993. Using Ancient Rhetorical Categories to Interpret Paul's Letters: A Question of Category. In *Rhetoric and the New Testament. Essays from the 1992 Heidelberg Conference.*

JSNTSup 90. ed. Stanley E. Porter and Thomas H. Olbricht, 292-324. Sheffield: Sheffield Academic Press.

_____. 1996. Are Paul's Thanksgivings 'Epistolary'? *JSNT* 61:87-99.

Reicke, Bo. 1951. The Law and this World according to Paul. Some Thoughts concerning Gal 4:1-11. *JBL* 70:259-76.

[Cicero] *Rhetorica ad Herennium*. 1954. Translated by Harry Caplan. Loeb Classical Library, [Cicero] vol. 1, no. 403. Cambridge: Harvard University Press.

Richardson, Peter. 1969. *Israel in the Apostolic Church*. SNTSMS 10. Cambridge: Cambridge University Press.

Richter, Philip J. 1984. Recent Sociological Approaches to the Study of the New Testament. *Religion* 14:77-90.

Ridderbos, Herman. 1953. *The Epistle of Paul to the Churches of Galatia*. Translated by Henry Zylstra. The New International Commentary on the New Testament. Grand Rapids: William B. Eerdmans Publishing Company.

_____. 1975. *Paul: An Outline of His Theology*. Translated by John Richard DeWitt. Grand Rapids: William B. Eerdmans Publishing Company.

_____. 1982. *When the Time Had Fully Come*. Grand Rapids: William B. Eerdmans Publishing Company, 1957; reprint, Jordan Station, Ontario: Paideia Press (page references are to reprint edition).

Riesner, Rainer. 1994. *Die Frühzeit des Apostels Paulus*. Tübingen: J.C.B. Mohr (Paul Siebeck).

Robbins, Vernon K. 1995. Oral, Rhetorical, and Literary Cultures: A Response. *Semeia* 65:75-91.

Robbins, Vernon K., and John H. Patton. 1980. Rhetoric and Biblical Criticism. *The Quarterly Journal of Speech* 66:327-50.

Roberts, J. H. 1986a. Pauline Transitions to the Letter Body. In *L'Apotre Paul*, ed. A. Vanhoye, 93-99. Bibliotheca Ephemeridum Theologicarum Lovaniensium 73. Leuven: Peeters/Leuven University Press.

_____. 1986b. Transitional Techniques to the Letter Body in the *Corpus Paulinum*. In *A South African Perspective on the New Testament*, eds. J. H. Petzer and P. J. Hartin, 187-201. Leiden: E. J. Brill.

_____. 1991. ΘΑΥΜΑΖΩ: An Expression of Perplexity in some Examples from Papyri Letters. *Neot* 25:109-22.

_____. 1992. Paul's Expression of Perplexity in Galatians 1:6: The Force of Emotive Argumentation. *Neot* 26:329-38.

Robinson, H. Wheeler. 1926. *The Christian Doctrine of Man*. 3rd ed. Edinburgh: T & T Clark.

Robinson, J. Armitage. 1979. *Commentary on Ephesians*. London: Macmillan, 1903; 1904 (2nd ed.); reprint of 2nd ed., Grand Rapids: Kregel Publications (page references are to reprint edition).

Robinson, John A. T. 1952. *The Body: A Study in Pauline Theology*. SBT 5. London: SCM Press.

Rogers, Elinor MacDonald. 1989. *A Semantic Structure Analysis of Galatians*. Semantic Structure Analyses Series, ed. John Callow. Dallas: Summer Institute of Linguistics, Inc.

Ropes, J. H. 1929. *The Singular Problem of the Epistle to the Galatians*. HTS 14. Cambridge: Harvard University Press.

Rosenbloom, Joseph R. 1978. *Conversion to Judaism: From the Biblical Period to the Present*. Cincinnati: Hebrew Union College Press.

Rusam, von Dietrich. 1992. Neue Belege zu den στοιχεῖα τοῦ κόσμου (Gal 4,3.9; Kol 2,8.20). *ZNTW* 83:119-25.

Russell, E. A. 1984. Convincing or Merely Curious? A Look at Some Recent Writing on Galatians. *IBS* 6:156-76.

Russell, Walter B. 1988. An Alternative Suggestion for the Purpose of Romans. *BSac* 145:174-84.

————. 1994. Insights from Postmodernism's Emphasis on Interpretive Communities in the Interpretation of Romans 7. *JETS* 37:511-27.

Sampley, J. Paul. 1976-77. "Before God, I do not lie" (Gal. 1:20) Paul's Self-Defence in the Light of Roman Legal Praxis. *NTS* 23:477-82.

————. 1977. Societas Christi: Roman Law and Paul's Conception of Christian Community. In *God's Christ and His People. Studies in Honour of Nils Alstrup Dahl*, eds. Jacob Jervell and Wayne A. Meeks, 158-74. Oslo: Universitetsforlaget.

Sand, Alexander. 1967. *Der Begriff "Fleisch" in den Paulinischen Hauptbriefen*. Biblische Untersuchungen 6. Regensburg: Verlag Friedrich Pustet.

Sanders, E. P. 1973. Patterns of Religion in Paul and Rabbinic Judaism: A Holistic Method of Comparison. *HTR* 66:455-78.

————. 1977. *Paul and Palestinian Judaism: A Comparison of Patterns of Religion*. Philadelphia: Fortress Press.

————. 1983. *Paul. the Law. and the Jewish People*. Philadelphia: Fortress Press.

————. 1990. Jewish Association with Gentiles and Galatians 2:11-14. In *The Conversation Continues: Studies in Paul and John in Honor of J. Louis Martyn*, eds. Robert T. Fortna and Beverly R. Gaventa, 170-88. Nashville: Abingdon Press.

Schmidt, A. 1992. Das Missionsdekret in Galater 2.7-8 als Vereinbarung vom ersten Besuch Pauli in Jerusalem. *NTS* 38:149-52.

Schiffman, Lawrence H. 1985. *Who Was a Jew? Rabbinic and Halakhic Perspectives on the Jewish-Christian Schism*. Hoboken, NJ: KTAV Publishing House.

Schlier, Heinrich. 1971. *Der Brief an die Galater*. 5th ed. Kritisch exegetischer Kommentar über das Neue Testament 7. Göttingen: Vandenhoeck & Ruprecht.

Schmithals, Walter. 1965. *Paul and James*. Translated by Dorothea M. Barton. SBT 46. Naperville, IL: Alec R. Allenson, Inc.

_____. 1972. *Paul & the Gnostics*. Translated by John E. Steely. Nashville: Abingdon Press.

_____. 1983. Judaisten in Galatien? *ZNW* 74:27-58.

Schrenk, Gottlob. 1949. Was bedeutet "Israel Gottes?" *Judaica* 5:81-95.

_____. 1950. Der Segenwunsch nach der Kampfepistel. *Judaica* 6:170-90 .

Schurer, Emil. 1973-1987. *The History of the Jewish People in the Age of Jesus Christ (175 B.C.-A.D. 135)*. 3 vols. Revised and edited in English by Geza Vermes, Fergus Millar, Matthew Black, and Martin Goodman. Edinburgh: T & T Clark.

Scott, James M. 1992. *Adoption as Sons of God. An Exegetical Investigation into the Background of ΥΙΟΘΕΣΙΑ in the Pauline Corpus*. WUNT 2. Reihe 48. Tübingen: J. C. B. Mohr (Paul Siebeck).

Scroggs, Robin. 1975. The Earliest Christian Communities as Sectarian Movement. In *Christianity, Judaism and Other Greco-Roman Cults*, ed. Jacob Neusner, 2:1-23. Vol. 12, *Studies in Judaism in Late Antiquity*, ed. Jacob Neusner. Leiden: E. J. Brill.

_____. 1980. The Sociological Interpretation of the New Testament: The Present State of Research. *NTS* 26:164-79.

Seifrid, Mark A. 1992. The Subject of Rom 7:14-25. *NovT* 34:313-33.

Seltzer, Robert M. 1988. Joining the Jewish People from Biblical to Modern Times. In *Pushing the Faith: Proselytism and Civility in a Pluralistic World*, eds. Martin E. Marty and Frederick E.

Greenspahn, 41-63. New York: The Crossroad Publishing Company.

Sherry, Patrick. 1984. *Spirit, Saints. and Immortality.* Albany: State University of New York Press.

Sills, David L., ed. 1968. *International Encyclopedia of the Social Sciences.* New York: The Macmillan Company and The Free Press. S.v. "Honor," by Julian Pitt-Rivers and "Pollution," by Mary Douglas.

Silva, Moisés. 1983. *Biblical Words & their Meaning: An Introduction to Lexical Semantics.* Grand Rapids: Zondervan Publishing House.

_____. 1988. *Philippians.* The Wycliffe Exegetical Commentary, gen. ed. Kenneth Barker. Chicago: Moody Press.

_____. 1990a. Review of *Obeying the Truth: A Study of Paul's Ethics in Galatians. WTJ* 52:160-62.

_____. 1990b. Text and Language in the Pauline Corpus. *Neot* 24:273-81

Sjoberg, Gideon. 1960. *The Preindustrial City. Past and Present.* New York: The Free Press.

Smit, Joop. 1984. Naar een nieuwe benadering van Paulus' brieven. De historische bewijsvoering in Gal 3,1-4,11. *Ti jdschrift voor Theologie* 24:207-34.

_____. 1985a. Paulus, de galaten en het judaisme. Een narratieve analyse van Galaten 1-2. *Ti jdschrift voor Theologie* 25:337-62.

_____. 1985b. "Hoe kun je de heidenen verplichten als joden te leven?" Paulus en de torah in Galatan 2,11-21. *Bijdragen* 46:118-40.

_____. 1986. Redactie in de brief aan de galaten. Retorische analyse van Gal. 4,12-6,18. *Tijdschrift voor Theologie* 26:113-44.

_____. 1989. The Letter of Paul to the Galatians: A Deliberative Speech. *NTS* 35:1-26.

Smith, Christopher C. 1996. Ἐκκλεῖσαι in Galatians 4:17: The Motif of the Excluded Lover as a Metaphor of Manipulation. *CBQ* 58:480-99.

Smith, Morton. 1960. The Dead Sea Sect in Relation to Ancient Judaism. *NTS* 7:347-60.

Snyman, A. H. 1992. Modes of Persuasion in Galatians 6:7-10. *Neot* 26:475-84.

Stacey, W. David. 1956. *The Pauline View of Man*. London: Macmillan & Co. Ltd.

Stamps, Dennis L. 1993. Rethinking the Rhetorical Situation: The Entextualization of the Situation in New Testament Epistles. In *Rhetoric and the New Testament. Essays from the 1992 Heidelberg Conference.* JSNTSup 90. ed. Stanley E. Porter and Thomas H. Olbricht, 193-210.. Sheffield: Sheffield Academic Press.

Standaert, B. 1985. La rhetorique et l'epitre aux Galates. *Foe et Vie* 84:33-40.

_____. 1986. La rhetorique ancienne dans Saint Paul. In *L'Apotre Paul*, ed. A. Vanhoye, 78-92. Leuven: Peeters/Leuven University Press.

Stanley, Christopher D. 1990. 'Under a Curse': A Fresh Reading of Galatians 3.10-14. *NTS* 36:481-511.

Steinhauser, Michael G. 1989. Gal 4,25a: Evidence of Targumic Tradition in Gal 4,21-31? *Bib* 70:234-40.

Stendahl, Krister. 1976. *Paul Among Jews and Gentiles*. Philadelphia: Fortress Press.

Stevens, George B. 1897. *The Pauline Theology*. Revised ed. New York: Charles Scribner's Sons.

Stoike, Donald Allen. 1971. "The Law of Christ": A Study of Paul's Use of the Expression in Galatians 6:2. Th.D. diss., Claremont University.

Stowers, Stanley K. 1986. *Letter Writing in Greco-Roman Antiquity.* Library of Early Christianity 5, ed. Wayne A. Meeks. Philadelphia: The Westminster Press.

_____. 1995. Romans 7.7-25 as a Speech-in-Character (προσωποποιία). In *Paul in His Hellenistic Context.* ed. Troels Engberg-Pedersen, 180-202. Minneapolis: Augsburg Fortress Press.

Strelen, John G. 1975. Burden-bearing and the Law of Christ: A Reexamination of Galatians 6:2. *JBL* 94:266-76.

Stuhlmacher, Peter. 1981. *Versohnung, Gesetz und Gerechtigkeit. Auf satze zur biblischen Theologie.* Gottingen: Vandenhoeck und Ruprecht.

Suhl, Alfred. 1987. Der Galater--Situation und Argumentation. In *ANRW* Teil 2: Principat, Band 25, 4. Teilband, ed. Wolfgang Haase, 3067-3134. Berlin/New York: Walter de Gruyter.

Taylor, Nicholas. 1992. *Paul, Antioch and Jerusalem. A Study in Relationships and Authority in Earliest Christianity.* JSNTSup 66. Sheffield: Sheffield Academic Press.

Thielman, Frank S. 1987. From Plight to Solution: A Framework for Understanding Paul's View of the Law in Romans and Galatians against a Jewish Background. Ph.D. diss., Duke University.

_____. 1994. The Law of Moses & the Law of Christ in Galatians. Chap. in *Paul & the Law: A Contextual Approach*, 119-44. Downers Grove, IL: InterVarsity Press.

Thiselton, Anthony C. 1973. The Meaning of Σάρξ in 1 Corinthians 5:5: A Fresh Approach in the Light of Logical and Semantic Factors. *SJT* 26:204-28.

_____. 1980. *The Two Horizons. New Testament Hermeneutics and Philosophical Description with Special Reference to*

Heidegger. Bultmann Gadamer. and Wittgenstein. Grand Rapids: William B. Eerdmans Pubhlishing Company.

Thomson, Ian H. 1995. Galatians 5.13-6.2: Warning or Appeal? Chap. 4 in *Chiasmus in the Pauline Letters.* JSNTSup 111. Sheffield: Sheffield Academic Press.

Tolmie, D. F. 1992. 'Ο ΝΟΜΟΣ ΠΑΙΔΑΓΩΓΟΣ 'ΗΜΩΝ ΓΕΓΟΝΕΝ ΕΙΣ ΞΡΙΣΤΟΝ: The Persuasive Force of a Pauline Metaphor (Gl 3:23-26). *Neot* 26:407-16.

Turner, Nigel. 1963. *A Grammar of New Testament Greek, Vol. 3--Syntax.* Edinburgh: T & T Clark.

_____. 1976. *A Grammar of New Testament Greek, Vol. 4--Style.* Edinburgh: T & T Clark.

Tyson, Joseph B. 1968. Paul's Opponents in Galatia. *NovT* 10:241-54.

_____. 1973. "Works of Law" in Galatians. *JBL* 92:423-31.

Ulrichs, von Karl Friedrich. 1990. Grave verbum, ut de re magna Nochmals Gal 1,18: ἱστορῆσαι Κηφᾶν. *ZNTW* 84:262-9.

Verseput, D. J. 1993. Paul's Gentile Mission and the Jewish Christian Community. *NTS* 39:36-58.

Vorster, J. N. 1990. Toward an Interactional Model for the Analysis of Letters. *Neot* 24:107-30.

_____. 1992. Dissociation in the Letter to the Galatians. *Neot* 26:297-310.

_____. 1995. Why opt for a rhetorical approach? *Neot* 29:393-418.

Vos, Geerhardus. [1912] 1980. The Eschatological Aspect of the Pauline Conception of the Spirit. In *Redemptive History and Biblical Interpretation. The Shorter Writings of Geerhardus Vos,* ed. Richard B. Gaffin, Jr, 91-125. Phillipsburg, NJ: Presbyterian and Reformed Publishing Co.

_____. 1979. *The Pauline Eschatology*. Princeton: Princeton University Press, 1930; reprint, Grand Rapids: Baker Book House (page references are to reprint edition).

Vos, Johan S. 1992. Die hermeneutische Antinomie bei Paulus (Galater 3.11-12; Römer 10.5-10). *NTS* 38:254-70.

_____. 1994. Paul's Argumentation in Galatians 1-2. *HTR* 87:1-16.

Vouga, Francois. 1988. Zur rhetorischen Gattung des Galaterbriefes. *ZNW* 79:291-92.

Walker, William O., Jr. 1992. Why Paul Went to Jerusalem: The Interpretation of Galatians 2:1-5. *CBQ* 54:503-10.

Wallace, Daniel B. 1990. Galatians 3:19-20: A *Crux Interpretum* for Paul's View of the Law. *WTJ* 52:225-45.

Walter, Nikolaus. 1986. Paulus und die Gegner des Christusevangeliums in Galatien. In *L'Apotre Paul*, ed. A. Vanhoye, 351-56. Bibliotheca Ephemeridum Theologicarum Lovaniensium 73. Leuven: Peeters/Leuven University Press.

Walton, Steve. 1996. Rhetorical Criticism: An Introduction. *Themelios* 21:4-9.

Wanamaker, C. A. 1983. A Case against Justification by Faith. *Journal of Theology for Southern Africa* 42:37-49.

Watson, Duane F. 1988a. The New Testament and Greco-Roman Rhetoric: A Bibliography. *JETS* 31:465-72.

_____. 1988b. A Rhetorical Analysis of Philippians and its Implications for the Unity Question. *NovT* 30:57-88.

Watson, Francis. 1986. *Paul, Judaism, and the Gentiles: A Sociological Approach*. SNTSMS 56. Cambridge: Cambridge University Press.

Wax, Murray L. 1984. "Religion" as Universal: Tribulations of an Anthropological Enterprise. *Zygon* 19:5-20.

Wead, David W. 1978. The Centripetal Philosophy of Mission. In *Scripture, Tradition, and Interpretation*, eds. W. Ward Gasque and William S. Lasor, 176-86. Grand Rapids: William B. Eerdmans Publishing Company.

Wedderburn, A. J. M. 1993. The 'Apostolic Decree': Tradition and Redaction. *NovT* 35:362-89.

Wegenast, Klaus. 1962. *Das Verstandnis der Tradition bei Paulus und in den Deuteropaulinen*. Wissenschaftliche Monographien zum Alten und Neuen Testament, no.8. Neukirchen: Neukirchener Verlag.

Weima, Jeffrey A. D. 1993. Gal. 6:11-18: A Hermeneutic Key to the Galatian Letter. *CTJ* 28:90-107.

_____. 1994. *Neglected Endings. The Significance of the Pauline Letter Closings*. JSNTSup 101. Sheffield: Sheffield Academic Press.

_____. 1995. The Pauline Letter Closings: Analysis and Hermeneutical Significance. *Bulletin for Biblical Research* 5:177-98.

Wenham, David. 1993. Acts and the Pauline Corpus. II. The Evidence of Parallels. In *The Book of Acts in Its First Century Setting. Volume 1, The Book of Acts in Its Ancient Literary Setting*. eds. Bruce W. Winter and Andrew D. Clarke, 215-58. Grand Rapids, MI: William B. Eerdmans Publishing Company.

_____. 1996. Piecing Together Paul's Life: A Review Article. *EQ* 68:47-58.

Wessels, G. F. 1992. The Call to Responsible Freedom in Paul's Persuasive Strategy. Galatians 5:13-6:10. *Neot* 26:461-74.

Westerholm, Stephen. 1986-87. On Fulfilling the Whole Law (Gal. 5:14). *SEÅ* 51-52:229-37.

_____. 1988. *Israel's Law and the Church's Faith--Paul and His Recent Interpreters*. Grand Rapi ls: William B. Eerdmans Publishing Company.

White, John L. 1972. *The Form and Function of the Body of the Greek Letter: A Study of the Letter Body in the Non-Literary Papyri and in Paul the Apostle*. SBLDS 2. Missoula, Montana: Scholars Press.

_____. 1984. New Testament Epistolary Literature in the Framework of Ancient Epistolography. In *ANRW* Teil 2: Principat, Band 25, 2. Teilband, ed. Wolfgang Haase, 1730-56. Berlin/New York: Walter de Gruyter.

_____. 1986. *Light from Ancient Letters*. Foundations & Facets: New Testament. Philadelphia: Fortress Press.

Whiteley, D. E. H. 1966. *The Theology of St. Paul*. Philadelphia: Fortress Press.

_____. 1973. Galatians: Then and Now. *SE* 6:619-27.

Williams, Sam K. 1987. Justification and the Spirit in Galatians. *JSNT* 29:91-100.

_____. 1988. *Promise* in Galatians: A Reading of Paul's Reading of Scripture. *JBL* 107:709-20.

Wilson, R. McL. 1968. Gnostics--in Galatia? *SE* 4:358-67.

Wilson, Stephen G. 1992. Gentile Judaizers. *NTS* 38:605-16.

Winger, Michael. 1994. Tradition, Revelation and Gospel: A Study in Galatians. *JSNT* 53:65-86.

Winninge, Mikael. 1995. *Sinners and the Righteous. A Comparative Study of the Psalms of Solomon and Paul's Letters*. Coniectaneea Biblica New Testament Series 26. Stockholm: Almqvist & Wiksell International.

Wolf, Eric R. 1966. *Peasants*. Englewood Cliffs, NJ: Prentice-Hall.

Wortham, Robert A. 1995. The Problem of Anti-Judaism in 1 Thess 2:14-16 and Related Pauline Texts. *BTB* 25:37-44.

Wright, N. T. 1991. *The Climax of the Covenant. Christ and the Law in Pauline Theology.* Minneapolis: Fortress Press.

_____. 1994. Gospel and Theology in Galatians. In *Gospel in Paul. Studies on Corinthians, Galatians and Romans for Richard N. Longenecker.* JSNTSup 108. eds. L. Ann Jervis and Peter Richardson, 222-39. Sheffield: Sheffield Academic Press.

_____. 1996. Paul, Arabia, and Elijah (Galatians 1:17). *JBL* 115:683-92.

Wuellner, Wilhelm. 1977. Paul's Rhetoric of Argumentation in Romans: An Alternative to the Donfried--Karris Debate over Romans. In *The Romans Debate*, ed. Karl P. Donfried, 152-74. Minneapolis: Augsburg Publishing House.

_____. 1979. Greek Rhetoric and Pauline Argumentation. In *Early Christian Literature and the Classical Intellectual Tradition*, eds. W. R. Schoedel and R. L. Wilken, 177-88. Theologie Historique 53. Paris: Beauchesne.

_____. 1987. Where Is Rhetorical Criticism Taking Us? *CBQ* 49:448-63.

Yates, Roy. 1985. Saint Paul and the Law in Galatians. *ITQ* 51:105-24.

Young, E. M. 1977. "Fulfil the Law of Christ." An Examination of Galatians 6:2. *Studia Biblica et Theologica* 7:31-42.

Ziesler, John A. 1990. *Pauline Christianity.* rev. ed. Oxford Bible Series. Oxford/New York: Oxford University Press.

_____. 1991. Justification By Faith in the Light of the 'New Perspective' on Paul. *Theology* 94:188-94.

Index of Scripture References

New Testament

3:17, 151
3:19-4:11, 25, 137, 157, 161,
  166, 202, 208
3:19-4:7, 95
3:19-4:3, 153
3:19-25, 58
3:21, 110
3:22-4:11, 193
3:22-25, 3
3:22-23, 23
3:22, 25
3:23, 25, 137, 154
3:24-25, 178
3:25-29, 95, 96
3:26-4:11, 78
3:26-4:8, 98
3:26-29, 3, 58
3:26-28, 102, 187, 206
3:26, 103, 104, 166
3:27-29, 100
3:28, 103, 104, 108
3:29, 102, 103, 133, 187
4, 8, 27, 30, 66, 136, 137, 208
4:1-11, 23, 59, 64, 125, 185,
  205
4:1-10, 33
4:1-7, 22, 59, 82, 83, 96, 110,
  128, 131, 133, 156, 187,
  202, 211
4:1-5, 3
4:1-3, 25, 159
4:1, 151
4:3, 25, 82, 83, 99, 106, 128,
  137, 153, 166, 168
4:4-6, 153
4:4-5, 3, 8, 82, 95, 178
4:4, 3, 141, 154
4:5, 102, 154
4:5-7, 82
4:7, 103, 153

4:8-16, 28
4:8-11, 3, 25, 47, 50, 59, 83,
  95, 99, 106, 128, 131, 137,
  159, 206
4:8-10, 3, 6, 25, 82
4:9-10, 78
4:9, 17, 82, 168, 193
4:10, 13
4:11, 83
4:12-6:10, 50, 51, 52, 78
4:12-20, 50, 59, 64, 71, 78, 79,
  100, 162
4:12, 50, 59, 78, 81, 84, 172
4:13-19, 51
4:13-16, 59
4:13-14, 2, 8, 140-1, 212
4:13, 131
4:14, 131
4:15-20, 73
4:15, 78
4:17-20, 59
4:17-18, 95
4:17, 12, 28, 79, 107, 149
4:18, 167
4:20, 51, 65
4:21-6:10, 86
4:21-31, 3, 13, 23, 51, 59-60,
  64, 68, 79, 80, 98, 132, 134,
  146, 153, 160, 187, 191,
  204, 209
4:21-30, 51
4:21-23, 59
4:21, 24, 26, 81, 100, 106,
  132, 134, 147, 154, 161,
  176, 177, 206
4:22-5:1, 110
4:23-25, 160
4:23, 6, 8, 11, 131, 132, 133,
  147, 157, 188, 202, 209
4:24-27, 59-60, 101

Index of Authors